Sandow the Magnificent

Sport and Society

Series Editors

Benjamin G. Rader
Randy Roberts

*A list of books in the series
appears at the end of this book.*

Sandow the Magnificent

EUGEN SANDOW
AND THE BEGINNINGS
OF BODYBUILDING

DAVID L. CHAPMAN

UNIVERSITY OF ILLINOIS PRESS   URBANA AND CHICAGO

First paperback edition, 2006
© 2006, 1994 by the Board of Trustees of the University of Illinois

∞ *This book is printed on acid-free paper.*

Library of Congress Cataloging-in-Publication Data
Chapman, David L., 1948–
Sandow the Magnificent : Eugen Sandow and the beginnings of
bodybuilding / David L. Chapman.
p.   cm.
Includes bibliographical references (p.   ) and index.
ISBN 0-252-02033-2
1. Sandow, Eugen, 1867–1925. 2. Bodybuilders—United States—
Biography. 3. Bodybuilding—United States—History. I. Title.
GV545.S26C43   1994
646.7'5'092—dc20
[B]   93-15736
CIP

PAPERBACK ISBN-10   0-252-07306-1
PAPERBACK ISBN-13   978-0-252-07306-9

To D. Berryman

Contents

Preface

Strong as a Sandow! Not very long ago that phrase had a potent meaning to millions of people all over the globe. Under Eugen Sandow's influence, countless men and boys proudly inflated their chests and flexed their biceps in front of bathroom mirrors, infused with the desire to become as mighty as the great strongman himself.

Our fathers and grandfathers considered Sandow the epitome of masculine beauty—regally handsome and supremely strong. He seemed to be a Greek statue come to life, and they had never seen anything quite like him. He burst upon the athletic scene at the century's turn like a Krupp cannon shell, revolutionizing the concept of what a really strong man looked and acted like. In his wake, he left a new sport —bodybuilding—and a growing interest in health and fitness.

Surprisingly, little reliable information is available about his life, but that is not to say that there is a shortage of biography, for Sandow left many books, articles, and interviews. These, however, are riddled with contradictory stories and spurious facts. Like a medieval palimpsest that has been written on over and over, the confusing layers of Sandow's story are enough to bewilder even the most persistent historical detective.

In addition to possessing one of the finest physiques of his age, Sandow was also an accomplished liar when it came to autobiographical exploits. According to his own, generally fanciful, account, Sandow had a romantic life, rich with incident. He obviously took great pleasure in telling how he arose from weakness and obscurity to become one of the strongest and most renowned men of his age. What a pity so little of the tale is true.

Just as he invented himself, Sandow was also the creator of

something much more durable: he invented the business of body-building. Sandow was the first athlete to make a comfortable living by displaying his muscular physique. He did this by devising a vaudeville act which showed that he had a theatrical sense as well developed as his musculature. Since he was such a magnificent showman, Sandow was eager to present an interesting biography to the public. Whether it was accurate or not was not his concern. He was a very popular and charismatic person, and many people who should have known better fell under his spell.

Sandow was a man of action, not of letters. Despite the many books that were published under his name, it is highly unlikely that with his limited command of English he wrote them all, especially not the early ones. With all of those ghost writers levitating through the pages, it is no wonder that the story of his life became muddled very quickly. Certain areas of Sandow's life story must always remain obscure. All we can do at this distance is to speculate. Those who search for some defining element in his life that might explain his motivations will look in vain. As with most people, there is no "Rosebud" in Sandow's biography. So it is left to those who come after to try to sift through all the contradictory tales to arrive at what might be the real story.

There are a few reliable sources for information, and I have attempted to use these when sorting out the details of Sandow's life. There are biographies of people who knew him, there are contemporary accounts of his performances, there are Sandow's own works, and there are even a few letters and manuscripts that have survived the ravages of time and neglect.

A contemporary humorist has advised, "When there are two conflicting versions of a story, the wise course is to believe the one in which people appear at their worst."[1] I have not followed this adage to the letter, but experience has convinced me of its general truth, and I have applied it to Sandow where I thought appropriate. In the end, like every student of the past, I have had to use my own best judgment when choosing which version of a story to believe and which to reject.

In spite of all these difficulties, I have made every effort to give the reader a true picture of Sandow and his era. In this I have been generously assisted by many people. David P. Webster of Irvine, Scotland, graciously opened up his historical collection to me. Leo H. Gaudreau of Middleton, Massachusetts, and Charles Smith of Austin, Texas (two colleagues who are now sadly deceased), together gave unstinting assistance and advice. Robert Stull provided rare photographs and important information on Sandow's early days. William Hinbern aided with the loan of several valuable books. Joe Weider supported my work and published my articles. Joe Roark of St. Joseph, Illinois, provided much assistance in locating obscure magazine articles. Robert L. Peters of the University of California, Irvine, and Paul Trachtenberg did much legwork in England for me. Chris Davies of Sheffield, Sandow's great-grandson, responded often and enthusiastically to my numerous inquiries. Terry and Jan Todd, directors of the Todd-McClean Collection at the University of Texas, provided every possible assistance in allowing me to use their fine collection of strongman materials.

Thanks also to the following people and institutions: Suzanne Foisy of the Sport Information Resource Centre, Ottawa; Rudy V. Busto of the Peabody Museum at Harvard University; John C. Grimek, formerly of *Muscular Development;* Angelo Iuspa; Gladys Hansen, San Francisco Public Library; Douglas Haller, California Historical Society; Danny Friedman, Victoria and Albert Museum; Wendy Warnken, Museum of the City of New York; Dorothy Swerdlove, New York Public Library; Thelma Harrison, expert on British physical education; Herb Juliano, University of Notre Dame Library; the staff of the British Library; Chicago Historical Society; Phillip Clayton-Gore of the Public Record Office, Kew; Russ Kingman, the noted authority on Jack London; and Jack Berryman of the University of Washington. Finally, I wish to acknowledge the gracious assistance of the late John Parke Custis McMurran, the better craftsman.

1

The Early Years
1867–89

Hidden away in a lonely corner of Putney Vale Cemetery near London lies the grave of one of the most important figures in the history of sport. The crumbling Victorian headstones on the surrounding tombs lie toppled and scattered. The weeds grow thick and lush around the marble angels, the stone crosses, and the granite urns. But curiously, no stone marks the last resting place of Eugen Sandow. His plot, unlike those around him, is unmarked and unknown—save but to the few. The man who began the sport of bodybuilding, who popularized fitness and health spas, sleeps for all eternity unmourned and nearly forgotten.

The story of Sandow's life is one of Dickensian richness. He struggled up from anonymity and, by a combination of luck and talent, molded a business and sporting network that stretched to the far corners of the British empire—and yet in death he is cheated out of all recognition and remembrance. History has cruelly played him false.

His name is neither recorded in history books nor discussed in university lectures, yet he dramatically changed the way we view ourselves and our bodies. His contribution, however unfamiliar, was as cataclysmic in its particular way as many louder social explosions. In Sandow's own day his name was instantly recognizable. A blond, blue-eyed, Teutonic Adonis, he was the very picture of robust good health and manly strength. But Sandow's mark on the male self-image has not been totally erased. That transformation is still discernible to a careful observer. To understand fully Sandow's impact on the modern psyche, however, it is necessary to look back at what preceded him in the realms of male beauty.

The full-chested, muscular ideal that we accept today as being the height of masculine good looks was not always the case. Early in the nineteenth century, a slender, wispy physique was considered the ne plus ultra of manly attractiveness. The hardworking middle-class clerks and businessmen had no time for sport or exercise; they were too busy pursuing the almighty dollar to take time out for healthy recreation. A romantic, consumptive helplesness was in vogue, and tanned muscularity was generally considered the exclusive attribute of lowly navvies and field hands.

One observer confirms this situation by giving this startling picture of masculine perfection in 1839: "An American exquisite must not measure more than twenty-four inches round the chest; his face must be pale, thin, and long; and he must be spindle-shanked. . . . There is nothing our women dislike so much as corpulency; weak and refined are synonymous."[1]

Even the British had noticed America's physical decline. "Americans grow thinner, lighter, and shorter lived," confirmed one British journalist. The writer was convinced that the regular defeats suffered by Yankee athletes were "purely on account of want of staying power."[2]

A thin physique, pale complexion, and languid air constituted male perfection for several decades, but with the growing prosperity of the post–Civil War era, a new but equally unhealthy paragon began to appear. "A fat bank account tends to make a fat man," wrote George Beard in 1879. "Wealth," he continued, "if it be abundant and permanent, supplies all the external conditions possible to humanity that are friendly to those qualites of the physique—plumpness, roundness, size—that are rightly believed to indicate well-balanced health."[3] A large bay window on a gentleman was thus considered as much a sign of robust good health as it was of sturdy prosperity. A double chin, a big cigar, and a tightly stretched watch chain across an ample field of vest was an ideal devoutly to be pursued. It appeared that in some quarters at any rate, fit was out and fat was in. But somewhere between the thin and the portly concept of manliness, another body type was making itself known. This was the muscular ideal.

When most of the world's population was engaged in labor on the land, there was little time or energy left for developing one's body. By the early nineteenth century, increasing numbers of Europeans and Americans were leaving their farms and coming to cities to find work and recreation. In a desire to improve health and forge their bodies into more shapely vessels of the soul, many men began to look for ways to mold their muscles. In response to this desire several entrepreneurs opened gymnasiums dedicated to building the body beautiful.

The Europeans led the way with these early "Temples of Hygeia." There had long been a tradition of muscle building that stretched back to Aristotle, Galen, Celsus, and other classical writers, but it was not until the nineteenth century that these ideas were put into palpable and accessible form. The German physical education instructor Friedrich Jahn began his athletic and nationalistic movement called the *Turnverein* in 1812. The huge Gymnase Triat opened in Paris in 1847, and Archibald MacLaren began his operation at Oxford eleven years later. By the early 1860s Americans had followed the European lead by establishing gymnasiums in many of the larger eastern cities.[4]

There were many reasons for this upsurge of interest in the body and in fitness. With the increase in urban employments, many men used exercise as a tonic against the effects of sedentary brain work. There was also growing interest in sport, which naturally called for more emphasis on the workings of the healthy body. In English-speaking countries, athletes were given the added incentive of a religious motive in their exercises.

The movement known as "muscular Christianity" had taken hold with surprising tenacity. The main tenent of muscular Christianity was that the best Christians were the strongest and fittest. They could unite their moral strength with their physical strength in order to promote good works and spread sanctity wherever they went.

Exercise had a further moral benefit, as Victorian and Edwardian schoolmasters had long believed. It helped one avoid the allures of vice. According to the conventional wisdom of the day, games and muscular activity tired one out, therefore one was too fatigued to explore forbidden pleasures. "Sensualism," confirmed a critic in 1858, "both at school and in the world, is found to lie among the quieter natures." Victorian readers were well aware that by "sensualism" the author meant the twin boogers of public school education: masturbation and homosexuality. Clement Dukes, physician to Rugby School, went so far as to counsel expulsion of non-athletes. "The boy who does not join in games, but swaggers and lounges about should, after failing to *make* him take part in them, be weeded out and got rid of, before he has the opportunity of corrupting others through his idleness and the evil it engenders."[5] Thus Puritanism and athleticism were joined in a happy but chaste marriage.

Perhaps the greatest dividend of this interest in exercise was that increasing numbers of men had adopted the sinewy paragon of masculinity as their own. These early pioneers of muscle were in the ascendent, but it took time before their ideals were adopted by the general public.

In the latter part of the nineteenth century, there was clearly an upsurge of interest in health and building the body. It remained the occupation of a small minority, however, languishing on the edges of popularity. All that was needed was an impetus to thrust the movement closer to center stage. That motivating impulse arrived in the shape of Sandow, for under his inspiration thousands of ordinary people sought to improve their bodies.

The thin, consumptive look of the early century and the portly model of the later eventually gave way to a muscular ideal that has remained more or less steady to our own time. Eugen Sandow was the crowning realization of that ideal form, and thanks to him nearly every young man who could tried to reproduce the strongman's physique. This feeling became so pervasive that one arbiter of fin de siècle taste announced that the most complimentary thing a girl could whisper in the ear of an impressionable undergraduate was "You college boys are so Sandow-like." This blandishment, he assures us, is "as sweet as attar of roses, a monthly allowance check, or maple sugar."[6]

So Sandow changed attitudes, left his mark, and deserves to be remembered. And yet this athletic pacesetter lies neglected in an unmarked grave, a prisoner of his own oblivion.

The odyssey that would lead to that unmarked grave in Putney Vale began fifty-eight years before in the ancient Hanseatic port of Königsberg on the cold shores of the Baltic. There on April 2, 1867, Sandow was born. At that time Königsberg was a lonely outpost of German culture surrounded by Slavs. In the popular imagination East Prussia had always been a land of rich, fat farmlands and even richer and fatter Junkers. It was equally the home of prosperous merchants and of charging Uhlans.

"As a child, I was exceedingly delicate. More than once, indeed, my life was despaired of. Until my tenth year I scarcely knew what strength was."[7] Sandow wrote that in 1897, and to back up this story there is a picture of the sickly and delicate lad at the age of ten on the preceding page. All this is very ironic considering the powerful man of muscle Sandow later became. Some years before, however, in an earlier book, Sandow wrote that as a child he was healthy and well-formed but there was nothing of the prodigy about him, physically or mentally. The earlier version is undoubtedly closer to the truth, although Sandow continually claimed later in life that he had been frail and weak as a child. It is easy to understand why, since he was attempting to show that anyone could attain superior strength—even one whose life was "despaired of"—provided of course he followed Sandow's system of physical training.

Sandow's father was made out to be a prosperous jeweler and dealer in precious stones and metals, but according to a well-informed associate, Papa was nothing more than a greengrocer who had a small stand in the marketplace.[8] We know even less of his mother except that she was either Russian or of Russian descent. According to his own account, by 1894 both his parents were dead. Sandow also admitted to having a half-brother and claimed that he was a professor at the University of Göttingen.[9]

In Sandow's version of the story, about the year 1877 his father took the young boy on a holiday to Italy. There the lad was struck by the beauty of the ancient statues of the gods and heroes. He remembered asking his father if people were as well developed in these modern times. Papa ruefully replied that luxury had robbed contemporary man of his health and strength: "The heroes of old, my little Eugen, never lolled at ease in a carriage or a railway train. . . . They were ever active, ever exercising their bodies."[10] The boy was obviously impressed with the antique statuary. "The memory of these muscular figures was ever present, and when we returned to my home in Königsberg I wanted to become strong like them."[11] Thus the seed of greatness was planted in little Eugen's head—at least in *his* version of the story.

It will perhaps never be known whether this trip to Italy ever actually occurred—though it sounds extremely suspicious. The statues and sunny weather of the south had to remain a distant dream, for Sandow was fated to languish in East Prussia for several more years. "Until I was eighteen I remained delicate. At that age I began to study anatomy."[12] In one version of the story Sandow's father sent the young man to the University of Göttingen to make a physician of him; in another he mentions simply studying anatomy. In later years many people were impressed by his knowledge of musculature, so it is not so farfetched to believe that he somehow learned as much of physiology as would later stand him in good stead.[13]

There are other incidents which smack of the truth. In his first official biography, the author, Graeme Mercer Adam, reports that the young Sandow was continually running off to visit the circus or the wrestling arena, "but these were forbidden indulgences."[14] So great was his ambition to become strong "that we find him repeatedly running away from home, and as repeatedly and ignominiously being brought back." Sandow's rocky relationship with his parents was always on the edge of breaking into open discord. Some sort of a breach obviously developed. Adam hints at the quarrel by reporting that Sandow's parents at first wanted their son to become a Lutheran minister, but later relented when it became obvious that he had no inclinations in that field. He also had little predilection for education in general. The evidence indicates that his schooling was spotty at best. In a letter he wrote in German when in his twenties, this suspicion is borne out, for Sandow makes several simple errors in grammar—errors a well-educated scholar would be able to avoid.[15]

Typically, Sandow's early youth remains an enigma. This element of mystery and cover-up is nowhere more obvious than in Eugen Sandow's own name, for he was born Friedrich Wilhelm Müller. There has been a great deal of controversy over why he changed his name, who did it, and when it was done. According to several authorities, it was Sandow's teacher, Attila, who caused the name change. Some have theorized that the name came from the Berlin suburb of Spandau, but this explanation is not very satisfactory. Several writers have guessed that the similarity between the names *Sandow* and *Samson* might explain the dilemma—though not very well. Finally, in 1949 the English magazine *Health & Strength* published the answer to this problem. They were successful in locating Sandow's widow and his two daughters, and one of the questions they placed to them was just this one of Sandow's change of name. The answer was maddeningly simple: he had merely taken his Russian mother's maiden name, Sandov, and Germanized it to Sandow.[16]

The young man remained in East Prussia until 1885, increasing his athletic prowess and emulating his acrobatic idols whenever possible. One of the places where Sandow could pursue his bodybuilding exercises was at the local *Turnhalle,* or gymnasium. Thanks largely to an energetic and farsighted countryman, Friedrich Ludwig Jahn, Germany had long been in the vanguard of physical education. Jahn had begun the *Turnvereine* [German gymnastic movement] largely in response to the humiliating defeats suffered by the Prussians at the hands of the Napoleonic invaders in 1812. Part German nationalist, part athletic, the *Turnvereine* grew rapidly and was soon an accepted part of every major German city. It has been estimated that by 1870, there were 1,500 societies in Germany alone, and many others besides in the areas the Germans colonized in the New World. Before World War II put an effective end to them, German gymnastic societies numbered in the millions around the world. The local *Turnhalle,* therefore, offered youths a place where they could forge their bodies and a love for the Fatherland at the same time. It was here that Sandow made his first attempts to build his physique according to the teachings of the Turners.[17]

Despite the decrees of his father, Sandow had decided on a

performing career, and he would let nothing stand in his way, not even the demands of the Prussian military. By the time he had reached the age of eighteen, he was eligible to do his national service in the Prussian army, but since this did not at all accord with his plans, young Müller left his homeland in order to avoid the irksome duty.[18] Later on, after many of his early successes, he was invited to perform in the theaters of the Fatherland but was forced to turn these offers down since even then he was a fugitive from the law. It was not until he had gained the respect and the fortune of a seasoned performer that he dared return to Germany.

Despite Sandow's many visits to the gymnasium, his progress was discouragingly slow. The impatient young man was at last forced to admit that after a long time of working out, his progress had been only slight. Ironically, Sandow achieved none of the goals so fervently espoused by Jahn. All those visits to the *Turnhalle* neither filled young Sandow with an overwhelming patriotism nor did they significantly improve his physique. He needed a quicker method for achieving physical perfection. Besides, Pan-Germanism and the theories of others did not set well with his independent spirit. Sandow had set his sights on other targets, and he was destined to aim beyond the borders of his quiet German backwater. East Prussia had little more to offer him. It was time to move on.

According to Professor Edmond Desbonnet, author of a seminal history of physical culture, *Les Rois de la Force,* Sandow joined a traveling circus and left Königsburg by that means. He was reported to have performed in the Russian capital, St. Petersburg, where he did a jockey act.[19] From there he traveled all over Europe with the circus for two years, eventually becoming one of the leading acrobats. He would have probably remained in that capacity for some time longer had it not been for one difficulty: the circus went bankrupt. Thus Sandow found himself in Brussels, alone and out of pocket.

The circus where Sandow performed must have been a very humble operation. According to Desbonnet, the establishment did not even have a proper name. The single word "Circus" without the name of the proprietor appeared on the front of a run-down building near the Place Royale in Brussels. When the circus went broke, the nineteen-year-old Sandow had to scramble for work in order to feed himself. Unfortunately, the young man had neither costume nor props, so it was virtually impossible for him to find employment as a performer, and he was soon in dire financial straits.[20]

This account of the story differs greatly from Sandow's own official version. His biographer, Adam, claims that when his father sent him to

Belgium to study anatomy, he could not keep his mind on his lessons because of his obsession with bodybuilding. This neglect of his education eventually led to a rift between Sandow and his father, culminating in Papa's total suspension of his son's allowance.[21] Whatever the reason, the results were the same: Sandow was alone in a foreign city in an extreme situation of financial embarrassment.

At this melancholy point in Sandow's career, one of the most important figures in his life enters: Professor Attila. Attila, who was born Louis Durlacher in 1844 in Karlsruhe, Germany, was a helpful éminence grise lurking behind the scenes in Sandow's life. His name is remembered today not for any feats of his own (though he was a competent performer in his own right) but rather for his protégés and pupils. His most famous pupil was the young Friedrich Müller, whom the world would soon know as Sandow.[22]

Attila began his career as a music hall entertainer in song and dance routines. While working in this role, he met a professional strongman performing in one of these theaters, Felice Napoli. As his name implies, the muscleman was born in Naples in 1820 and was reputed to have been one of the best performers in his field. Attila also wanted to become a strongman, so he apprenticed himself to Napoli, learning all the tricks of the trade.[23]

Gradually, by luck, charm, and skill, Attila was able to gain the attention of some of the most influential men in Europe. There is a story Attila liked to tell about his early years. He was a young, seventeen-year-old army recruit who was assigned to guard detail on the estate of the duke of Baden. One day while he was on duty, he spied a perambulator rapidly rolling downhill toward a private lake. Inside was the duke's infant son. Just as it hit the water, Attila jumped into the lake, rescued the child, and gained the undying friendship of the duke. What became of the neglectful nanny is anyone's guess.[24] True story or not, the fact remains that throughout his long life Attila seemed never to lack royal patronage. When he later began his own school of physical culture, Attila numbered among his students Alexander III, czar of Russia, King George of Greece, and even the corpulent bon vivant Edward VII of England.

Attila spoke five languages and was a suave, cultured man—he was even reputed to have been an accomplished pianist. But he also had a proud, unbending side. Many years later, when his little daughter asked him what his first name was, he replied sternly, "Professor!"[25] It is his role as teacher for which he is most remembered. In 1887 he was running a school of physical culture in Brussels. In June of that year Attila was chosen to perform before Queen Victoria at her Golden

Jubilee, so he must have met Sandow in the autumn or winter of the same year.

After being unceremoniously sacked in Brussels, Sandow found himself at loose ends. According to Desbonnet, Sandow roamed the streets in despair, alone and ignored. "Lingering along a river one morning, he noticed a crowd by the wharf. It was a group of amateurs who had come there to see Attila's weights and lifting equipment." Sandow mixed in with the group of novice athletes and handled the weights so easily that Attila, in need of an assistant, hired him on the spot.[26]

According to Siegmund Klein, who later married one of Attila's daughters, some art students who were also pupils of Attila mentioned to the strongman that they had a model who had the finest physique that they had ever seen. Attila asked them to bring the young man to him. After seeing Sandow stripped down, Attila decided to take him on as a prize pupil at once.[27]

Whatever the details of their meeting, the partnership was to be a valuable though often stormy one for both parties. Under Attila's tutelage, Sandow began to develop his body on a more regular and scientific basis. But Attila was doing much more than just improving his young pupil's already muscular frame. From the very first, it must have been obvious that he had stumbled onto an extraordinary athlete—one who had the makings of a fine showman. He consequently worked on Sandow's grace, suavity, and stage presence as much as his physique. Knowingly, Attila launched Sandow's career.

What exactly did Attila do for Sandow? Before his meeting with the elder strongman, Sandow had developed his physique as an acrobat and gymnast. The early photographs of him tend to bear this out: Sandow's physique is lean and sinewy but without the bulk that he later acquired. After his contact with Attila, however, Sandow began to put on more mass and to acquire the body of a bona fide muscleman. This transformation can largely be attributed to the older man's credence in the use of heavy weights.

In the early years of weight training there was a great deal of opposition to systems that created purely cosmetic muscles without corresponding strength. A thick and muscular physique was all very well, but the true test of a strongman was what he could lift. With his mentor's help, Sandow eventually freed himself from the restrictive bonds of this belief.

Professor Attila's greatest contribution to Sandow and to weight training in general was his insistence on using heavy weights. This in itself was flying in the face of popular wisdom. It was commonly believed that lifting weights heavier than five or ten pounds would eventually lead the athlete to a condition called muscle binding, in which the unfortunate victim became so muscular that he could not move his limbs.

Attila was one of the few teachers who realized that this was all a lot of nonsense. He knew that gradually increasing the amount of weight the athlete trains with, known as *progressive weight training,* was the only path to muscularity and strength. Thus, thanks to this technique and Attila's expertise Sandow was transformed from a wiry acrobat to a heavily muscled athlete.[28]

The professor was also very innovative when it came to creating new techniques and equipment. It is said that he was the first to devise shot-loading globe barbells and to have had a hand in coming up with the more efficient plate-loading bells. He originated the Roman column feat, the Roman chair, and the human bridge trick.[29] (For a description of these and other lifts, see the "Glossary of Weightlifting Terms.") Whether he actually did invent all of these things is a moot point. The important fact is that he made them all popular and accessible to other athletes like Sandow. It was this spirit of experimentation that is Attila's greatest legacy to physical culture.

In addition to his careful guidance, Attila also introduced the young athlete to others who might help him. Professor Edmond Desbonnet met Sandow at this time and kept up with the young Prussian's movements for the rest of his life. It is thanks to him that much of our reliable biographical data is now preserved. Another man prominent in the world of strength also became acquainted with Sandow in 1887: Charles Éstienne, better known as "Batta." He was only a year older than Sandow, but he had already established himself as a strongman in northern France and the Low Countries.

Sandow's introduction to Batta was not a particularly auspicious one. Batta was working at the Alcazar, a small cafe, earning seventy francs a night as a performing strongman. One day Sandow walked into the cafe seeking employment. While the manager finished his meal, Sandow started to perform impromptu feats of grip strength with the chairs and other materials at hand. When the German remarked impetuously that no one had ever duplicated his feats of hand strength, Batta, who had been seated in the back, jumped up and repeated everything that the young man had done. When he finished, he firmly but politely informed Sandow that the Alcazar already had a performing strongman, namely himself, and that it was useless for him to show off his strength in the hopes of getting a job. Not one to feel insecure or to hold a grudge, Batta was reported to have seen Sandow later in

Attila's establishment and predicted that he would someday have a brilliant athletic career.

Batta was an interesting figure in the history of bodybuilding. He was tall, elegant, and handsome. He was known as the "Gentleman Athlete" because of his good manners and his reputation as a dapper dresser. It seems reasonable to suppose that these characteristics made an impression on Sandow, for he too gained a reputation for dressing elegantly.

Batta also had a flair for showmanship which was not lost on Sandow. In an old poster, he is touted as "Le Damoclès Fin de Siècle" (the turn-of-the-century Damocles) because of his penchant for performing feats of strength under—or over, as the case may be—several very sharp knives. He was also famous for supporting great weights while in the "Tomb of Hercules" position, that is, abdomen stretched up, arms back, legs front. Sandow also used this idea in his own performances later on.[30]

Another early dividend of Sandow's apprenticeship to Attila was that he began to work as a model. In the period between 1887 and 1889 Sandow posed for many artists and sculptors. Although most of these works were highly forgettable, he continued to use modeling as a good supplement to his income as a performer. One of the earliest pieces for which he posed was *St. Michael Vanquishing Satan* by the Belgian sculptor Charles Van der Stappen. Sandow appears in this work not as the armored figure of St. Michael but rather as the nude, writhing image of Satan. It is a very ungainly piece, but the remarkable physique of the athlete is clearly discernible.[31]

One of the finest sculptures for which he modeled at this time was *Le Dénicheur d'Aigles* (The Robber of the Eagles' Nest) by the Flemish artist Joseph Maria Thomas Lambeaux, known as Jef Lambeaux. The sculptor was famous in his day for the use of indecipherable symbols in his work. Indecipherable or not, Sandow's superb body is shown to great effect in this creation. His finely muscled legs are tensed as he attempts to fight off the attack of an enraged eagle. If this piece even comes close to representing Sandow as he really appeared at this juncture in his life, then his body was already strong and hard.[32]

Desbonnet reports that when he met Sandow in Brussels, he was so impressed that he presented him to Lambeaux and Van der Stappen personally. "Between his posing session," he wrote, "Müller [Sandow] trained under the direction of Attila for music hall engagements; at the same time, he perfected himself in physical culture under the direction of Batta."[33] So it is clear that he was receiving assistance from many quarters.

Young Sandow was also making a name for himself in the athletic community in Brussels. One witness remembered seeing him when he visited the Free Gymnastic Society in the Place de la Chapelle. Sandow impressed the members as being shy and taciturn, but also admirably muscled and with a superb sense of balance. This last quality was demonstrated in a unique and entertaining way. Sandow placed a handkerchief on the floor—it was a large red and white one such as were carried by country folk. "He placed his feet together upon it, and taking a weight of 25 kilos [about 55 pounds] in each hand, turned a somersault and came back with his feet together on the handkerchief. It was magnificent!"[34] Clearly, Sandow was acquiring the instincts of a skilled performer.

Satisfied that his pupil was ready to be put to the test, Attila brought Sandow on professional visits to Rotterdam, Antwerp, and other towns close by, working in a strongman act. They eventually returned to Brussels with their modest gains. They also found some students at the University of Leyden who were willing to pay for lessons in physical culture.

After this brief tour of the cities around northern Belgium, Sandow parted company with Attila and went off on his own to Amsterdam. Whether this departure was friendly is not known. We do know however that the relationship between the two was often a tempestuous one. It is equally mysterious why Sandow chose Amsterdam as his next stop. He mentions specifically that there was very little interest in strength displays, wrestling, or gymnastics in the Dutch capital. Perhaps he felt that he would be an innovative performer in a place where he would have virtually no competition. He states that he knew no one in the city at this time, though he had an easy manner and made friends quickly. "He had, moreover, youth and hope on his side, and by this time, had acquired remarkable strength, with a varied though miscellaneous experience of circuses, theaters, and shows."[35]

After a few days of seeking employment, he found that no one was interested in strongman acts and the theater managers refused to pay his asking price of ten guilders a night. Alone and depressed, in a strange city, his hotel bill rapidly going in arrears, and most of his valuables in hock, Sandow found himself in a very despondent situation. But then he came up with one of those ideas born only to a great showman. He realized that he needed publicity—he needed a gimmick —something to call attention to himself. His solution was an ingenious one.

Outside cafes and in other places where people congregated were weightlifting machines which stalwart Dutchmen could test their strength with. They resembled slot machines with a large lever designed to measure the force one expended when it was pulled down. Sandow found a willing cabman to take him around to these various machines in the dead of night. With his last few guilders, he put a coin in each of these machines and pulled the handle down, then past the maximum until the mechanism was broken—a feat only very strong man could accomplish.

In the morning when it became obvious that every weightlifting machine in the city had been wrecked, people shook their heads ruefully and wondered at the audacity of the deed. It was speculated that a gang of ruffians had committed the crime, since it was thought that no one person could have had the strength to do it. There was even a reward of one thousand guilders offered to anyone who could give information leading to the arrest of the guilty parties.

The vandalism caused an immediate stir, and there were many theories advanced as to how and why the feat was carried out. As usual in such cases, the event faded quickly from the public's mind and was forgotten. The staid Dutch burghers read of other happenings over their strong morning coffee. But when the machines were then damaged for a second time, and after an interval even a third occasion, it was clear that something had to be done.

"After the second of the wrecking exploits," Adam reported, "it was of course not easy to guard against surprisal, for by this time the police were officiously on the *qui vive,* while every porter and nightwatchman was but too anxious to obtain the civic reward. The cabman, with Sandow, had almost completed the third night's round when the latter was espied by a porter at one of the cafes just as he was giving the wrench to a machine which threw it out of gear and broke the springs. The porter, realizing the apparent strength of the nightly depredator, kept at a respectful distance from the strongman, but having the reward of the authorities before his eyes was not willing to lose the chance of bagging his game."[36]

But this time, however, Sandow contrived to be arrested. He had already gained the needed publicity and was ready to reap his own peculiar reward. So when the officer shortly arrived with his posse of deputies, Sandow was content to be calmly escorted to the police station. Once there, he was questioned repeatedly about his exploits and about the rest of the gang who had helped him. Sandow protested persistently that he alone had destroyed the machines; besides, he was really free from guilt in the matter as he had honestly paid the fee, and he had merely been exercising his arm strength. There were a lot of puzzled looks and head scratching for a while until Sandow offered a proof of his strength. He heaved the largest constable several feet into the air, held him there for a moment, and then gently placed him down again at his side. This was the first time he recorded using this ploy, although certainly not the last, which undeniably got the attention of its dismayed victim. It also seemed to convince the police that the young man was as strong as he said he was.

Still, Sandow might have languished in jail for a while had it not been for his friend and associate, Attila. Sandow had sent for him earlier, and he arrived just in time to bail his protégé out of the Dutch prison.[37] But by now Sandow had achieved the notoriety he had set out to find, and almost at once he began to harvest the heady benefits of celebrity. First, he was granted free room and board at his hotel. But more important, the theater which had formerly refused his act at ten guilders a week now hired him on for twelve hundred.

His unexpected prosperity allowed both Attila and him the luxury of traveling around the vicinity, giving strongman shows as they went. That summer Attila was lucky enough to secure a booking for them at the Crystal Palace at Sydenham, south of London. They accordingly left the Continent and headed for England. Shortly after they began the run, however, Attila met with a disaster. While he was swinging two conical 56-pound weights overhead with his right hand, one slipped out of his grasp and broke one of the bones in his forearm. It was only a relatively minor injury, but it was enough to force them to cancel the rest of their engagement. Once more Sandow was out of work.[38]

After the accident, Attila elected to remain in England to recuperate, and Sandow drifted back across the channel to France, where he eventually landed in Paris. Here his luck left him once more. After arriving in the French capital, he ran out of money very quickly since he could find work neither as a performer nor as a model. He learned from a waiter friend the names and addresses of the leading sculptors, and then memorized the French for "Do you want a model?" and proceeded on his way. After a day of nothing but mortifying rebuffs, he came to the last name on his list. He knocked at the entrance of the atelier and was surprised when the sculptor himself answered. "Do you want a model?" Sandow inquired in his best French. The man's "Non" was cold and conclusive. Dejected, the strongman descended the stairs. He had peered through the door, so briefly opened. Sandow had seen that the artist was working on the statue of a Greek god: just his line. Desperate for employment, he decided to try again.

"It was more than flesh and blood and an empty stomach could stand," he wrote later. "The courtyard was deserted, the staircase silent and none too light. That decided me. I stripped off my upper garments and wasted no time in mounting to the studio. I thundered at the door.

It flew open, and I prepared to follow in, but it stopped on a chain! The sculptor was evidently determined that callers should not worry him. He came to the door, yelling, apparently in anger. As I could not get my body in, I thrust in my arm. It stopped him; for a moment he was struck dumb.

"The next instant he had removed the chain and pulled me into the studio, where I stood with his gaze fixed upon me in profound admiration of my muscular development, which held him speechless. Then, his eyes agleam with excitement, he launched himself upon me, and as is the way of foreigners, embraced me in his wild enthusiasm, kissing me on both cheeks, while I thanked heaven that my persistency had met with its reward."

The artist not only hired Sandow on the spot but also fed him a sumptuous dinner, uncorking a bottle of his best champagne, which he used to celebrate what he called his "find."[39]

The affectionate sculptor whom Sandow described was Gustave Crauck. He had a studio near the École des Beaux Arts and was a teacher at that institution for some time. He was also one of the most popular portrait sculptors of the Second Empire, having done busts of such celebrities as Maréchales MacMahon and Niel and even the beautiful Empress Eugénie.[40] Sandow's obituary in the *Times* of London noted that "When he was in his prime, he served as the model for the figure of the Lapith in the 'Combat du Centaure' by Gustave Crauck, the French sculptor." Undoubtedly, that was the work which he was hired for.

After a while Sandow either had difficulty finding work or simply grew tired of modeling. He took up with a strolling circus performer named François with whom he made an agreement to play in a show which they would exhibit all over France and Italy. The tour was a moderate success; at least it kept body and soul together for the moment. The principal part of the attraction was a pantomime titled *L'Afficheur* (The Poster Hanger). In the play Sandow and François appeared under the stage name of "Les Frères Rijos." François played Harlequin in this wild farce. "He was dressed as a huge doll which Sandow juggled and tossed about the stage, threw over walls, and pitched in at windows, with a freedom which disguised from the audience the fact that it was a living man, and not a stage property that was being shuttlecocked about."[41] Though their performance was a comedy, and a particularly active one at that, it was clear that Sandow possessed amazing strength and balance.

When the two players progressed as far as Rome, Sandow abruptly parted company with his partner and struck out on his own as a wrestler and performer of strength feats. Hired by a local theater, he was directed by another athlete, Protto, who also helped him find additional work as an artist's model. King Humberto and other members of his court in residence formed a Sandow cult of the moment. The royals cheered him at performances in the Eternal City and also came to him for lessons in wrestling and physical culture. Their patrician patronage was helping Sandow to achieve an enviable reputation in his field.[42]

While in Italy, Sandow received his first important challenge from a well-known wrestler named Bartoletti. The Italian offered a stake of five thousand francs. While it was no surprise to Sandow, the Romans were astonished when the visitor won the match. Savoring his victory, the young Prussian began a series of peregrinations around Italy which lasted for a year, wrestling, exhibiting, modeling, and living as best he could.[43] There are some early photographs of him at this period which show a finely developed, though still immature, athlete swinging an Indian club and striking heroic poses. They bear witness to his growing athletic proficiency.

It was also at this time that he encountered one of the most pathetic and unlikely figures in the nineteenth century: Crown Prince Frederick of Prussia. Frederick had heard of the young German's prowess as an athlete and sent word to Sandow, who was staying at that time in Venice, that his presence was required at the prince's villa at San Remo on the Italian Riviera. Naturally, he rushed to comply with the wishes of one who would very shortly become the emperor of his Fatherland. Sandow thus had the honor of performing before the future kaiser and his royal consort, Princess Victoria, daughter of the queen of England. The crown prince was stricken with throat cancer and was attempting to recuperate, but he was still a man of much fortitude. "With old-time pride in his own powers, Frederick took a complete pack of playing cards and with a strong, quick turn of the wrists, tore them in two. It might have been courtly etiquette to leave the Emperor to the enjoyment of the pride he felt in the work of his hands; but someone informed His Majesty that Sandow could beat him at his own trick, and it was with pleased surprise, and no admixture of envy, that he witnessed *two* packs torn apart by the renowned athlete." The future emperor was so impressed by what he saw Sandow do that he took a fine ring from his finger and presented it to the young athlete. Then the prince sadly allowed that he would gladly exchange his royal position with Sandow merely to have his robust good health—this, at least, is the story Sandow told.

It seems fairly certain that Sandow and Frederick met in some situation, but it is highly unlikely that it occurred as Sandow says it did.

Frederick William, the unhappy crown prince of Prussia, arrived at San Remo in November of 1887 and installed himself at a lovely villa on the shores of the Mediterranean in the midst of an exotic garden. Almost immediately the prince's health deteriorated. He was often depressed and was severely admonished by his physicians not to speak and not to get cold. He spent most of that winter in bed. It was clear to all around him that his terrible condition was worsening every day. On February 9, 1888, the situation came to a head, for after a frightening seizure, a long-delayed tracheotomy was performed on him. After this he seemed to be improving, but with one exception: he would never be able to speak again. By the end of February the prince was well enough to consider leaving the Riviera, and by March 9 this decision was made for him—his father, the emperor, was on his deathbed and Frederick and Victoria were urgently summoned back to Berlin.[44]

If Sandow did visit him, it must have been after the prince's operation in February of 1888 and before he left on March 9. That they did actually meet seems likely, for Sandow was very fond of displaying the ring which was given to him by the kaiser; he even published a photo of it in *The Strand* magazine. The ring consisted of a beautiful French enamel, encircled with brilliants, with the initial *F*, and a crown over it made of diamonds.[45] Nevertheless, Sandow's account of the particulars of their meeting is obviously thrown into doubt since Frederick was still weak and was unable to speak.

After his meeting with Crown Prince Frederick, Sandow returned to Venice and continued his wrestling career. He was later reticent about his fighting since he considered it beneath his dignity. He once remarked, "You can't engage in a prize-fight and be a gentleman."[46] And the same went for wrestling. But one match that must have been as memorable as it was disastrous was with a man who ironically had the name of Müller. This Müller was a rather rough customer with a well-deserved reputation for brutality. One of his favorite ploys was to grab his opponent's hand and break his fingers in order to win the match. Sandow must have been somewhat wary of his adversary when they both finally came to the ring, for the bout started out slowly, with much circling and preliminary sparring. At last, though, Müller grabbed Sandow's wrist and tried to snap it back, at the same time forcing his fingers deep into his flesh, crushing the veins till they burst. Even though this tactic caused him intense pain, Sandow managed to break free. He maneuvered himself behind the wrestler and squeezed him in a savage bear hug until Müller's faced blackened and blood gushed from his mouth, and he fell upon the floor as if he were dead.

But Müller was not dead. He ended up with four broken ribs.

Sandow, on the other hand, was worse off than he had expected. He was bleeding internally in his arm and received lacerated nerve fibers. It took him four months to recover fully from this Pyrrhic victory.[47] After this unpleasant experience Sandow undoubtedly took greater care in picking his wrestling partners.

For the rest of 1888 Sandow traveled around, giving exhibitions of strength and accepting a few wrestling challenges, but, understandably, he seemed to have lost his zest for the sport. Sometime in this period he met Aubrey Hunt, an American artist who was then living in Italy. According to everything published by Sandow himself, Hunt was the pivotal figure who really started him on the road to success.

Sandow describes the meeting thus:

> In 1889 I made the acquaintance of Aubrey Hunt, the artist, who was then at Venice. One of the most charming views in the neighbourhood was to be gained from the grounds of my villa near Lido. Naturally, Mr. Hunt wished to paint it, and it was a pleasure to be able to afford him the facility. One result of our acquaintance was that Mr. Hunt painted me in the character of a gladiator in the Coliseum at Rome. I am told that it is a very striking likeness.
>
> It was from Mr. Hunt that I learned that Sampson was offering, at the Royal Aquarium in London £100 to the person who could perform the feats of his pupil, Cyclops, and £1,000 to anyone who could beat his own. Mr. Hunt suggested that I should accept the challenge, and it was my original intention to come to London with him. It was ultimately decided, however, that I should start without delay, and the journey to England was made on the same day that I first heard of the challenge.[48]

Probably the only element of truth in the section quoted above is that Hunt did indeed paint Sandow as a Roman gladiator; the rest appears to have been nothing more than the flimsiest of fabrications.

E. Aubrey Hunt was born February 17, 1855, in Weymouth, Massachusetts. He came to England in 1873 but left shortly after that for Paris where he studied for five years with the master of the *académie* style, Gérôme. In 1878 Hunt returned to London, where he opened a studio. In 1881 he was accepted into the prestigious Royal Academy. Much of his time was spent abroad: in the late 1880s he was in Italy; in 1896–97 he was in North Africa. After wandering for a while, Hunt settled down in the south of England where he had a home in Surrey. He continued to exhibit his works regularly, with showings in 1896 and 1898 at the Paris Salon. He died at Hastings on November 22, 1922.[49]

It seems most probable that Sandow met Hunt in early 1889 while both men were in Italy. Hunt did paint a portrait of Sandow as a gladiator in that year. The painting shows Sandow in a leopard-skin costume, with one heavily muscled arm slightly bent in front, and the other partially out of sight. In the background there is only the vaguest suggestion of a crowded arena. One wonders what would have happened had the unfortunate strongman been forced to face an opponent, for he carries no sword or other weapon—he merely stands there heroically, his handsome blond head gazing pensively to one side. The painting bears a striking resemblance to a contemporary photograph of the athlete, and the artist obviously took advantage of this existing image. The photograph and the painting are remarkably identical: both show Sandow clothed in a leopard skin, and both show him in a pose that varies only slightly from one another.

Many years later Sandow described their meeting in a scenario reminiscent of *Death in Venice.* He explained that he was taking the sea baths on the Lido. "I had quitted the water and was making my way up the beach when I noticed that I had become the particular attraction for a gentleman sauntering by. As I apologized in passing him, he stopped to compliment me upon what he was pleased to term my 'perfect physique and beauty of form.' "[50]

Sandow had the good sense to cultivate his liaison with the painter, for it probably provided him with the entrée into polite society that he had previously lacked. He knew how to use his charm and his fine physique to advance himself in the set of urbane, civilized expatriates then living in Venice. He had been forced to live by his wits for several years and he knew the value of a good introduction and how far it might carry him. Perhaps this is what one of Sandow's biographers meant when he said rather cryptically, "Over in his studio Aubrey Hunt discovered he had engaged a model who could do much more with his muscles than a painter might suppose."[51]

Artists have long been suspected of fooling around with their models. Was this the case with Sandow and Hunt? The answer, of course, must be that we shall never know for sure. But from the unusually convincing hints in the surviving accounts, there was at least a strong suspicion that Sandow was receiving more than a modest glance or two from the easel.

Artist's models of both sexes were certainly viewed with unease and even distaste by the Victorian public. A leading historian of the period, Peter Gay, has written about middle-class Victorian attitudes toward sex and the troublesome subject of models. Gay cites a friend of John Ruskin, an eminent Victorian art critic and writer, who once declared to Ruskin that "the woman who was made an Academy model could not be a virtuous woman." Artist William Mulready likewise warned that modeling is a "dangerous profession" for which "poor innocent creatures" must be carefully prepared.[52] So at least the perception existed that some dalliance occasionally took place between the artist and his subject. Whatever happened, Hunt at least left a fine painting to commemorate their meeting.

When Hunt finally finished the portrait, it was either purchased by or presented to the sitter, for the likeness hung in Sandow's London home for a while, and then later in his Institute of Physical Culture in St. James's Street. It remained a favorite of Sandow's, for he admitted that "my eyes never rest upon that picture but it recalls the many happy days we spent together."[53] He and Hunt kept up their friendship for quite some time, for there exists a photograph of the strongman which is inscribed by Sandow to the artist and given to him in 1902, thirteen years after their first meeting.[54]

While Sandow insisted many times over that Hunt was the one who started him on the road to the top, the facts point in another direction. Desbonnet, who was in a position to know, says that Sandow learned of the Sampson challenge not from Hunt but rather from his old mentor, Attila.[55] This version is much more believable, so it is probable that Sandow was summoned by Attila, who was then living in London. According to Siegmund Klein, Attila had long wanted to match his young protégé with Sampson and Cyclops, and in 1889 he felt that time was ripe for their dethroning. Whatever the case, it is certainly clear that Sandow's official version does not match up with the facts of the case. Why? Perhaps he thought it would be more genteel to have been discovered by an artist. Most likely he simply wanted to discount the importance of his old teacher, Attila. It was well known that teacher and pupil later on quarreled bitterly, so perhaps he felt that by modifying the facts he could get back at Attila and honor Hunt in one fell swoop.

Sandow certainly stayed in Italy until at least May of 1889, for a silver medal has survived which was presented to him by "Il Circolo Atlètico Romano" clearly dated "Maggio 1889."[56] It seems most probable that he left around that time, and headed at a leisurely pace first to Paris and then on to London. There he would rendezvous with his teacher, Attila.

When Sandow arrived in Paris, he found the city alive with excitement, for the great Exposition Universelle de Paris had just opened. One of the visitors to the city was a wealthy young French aristocrat, the count de Furnimbac. The count was fond of travel, art, sports, and absinthe. It was his interest in these last two that brought him into contact with Sandow.

De Furnimbac was in the habit of touring the sights at the Exposition during the day and then retiring with some cronies to a cafe in Montmartre where he could play at the billiard tables. One evening he went with a friend of his, Mazin, a popular wrestler, to a favorite cafe where the count began drinking absinthe. Like so many others, he had found himself addicted to the greenish liquor some years before, and despite his interest in weight training and health, nothing seemed able to wean him away from his favorite beverage.

On the evening in question, the count, after downing several glasses of absinthe, discovered that the table which he always used for his game was occupied by two young, German-speaking men. Awaiting his turn, the count had a few more drinks, all the while growing more and more impatient. One of the billiard players was a young man with blond, curly hair and piercing blue eyes. De Furnimbac grew madder and madder as he listened to the two young men chat amiably in German. It was more than a patriotic French aristocrat could endure. Filled with alcoholic rage, he scolded the men in a staccato outburst of rapid French. They were not within their rights speaking a foreign language in his presence—especially not German. Unfortunately, neither man seemed to understand the count's drunken ravings. The blond German fastened his steely gaze on the angry Frenchman in a stare designed to dampen the count's Gallic bravado. Its effect, however, was only momentary, for after the two had resumed their play, their adversary rudely interrupted the game. Astonished, the blue-eyed stranger attempted to make his play over, but before he could do so, the count took up one of the nearby pool cues and savagely beat the German in the face. Stunned, angered, and with a bleeding nose, the young man stalked menacingly toward the count. He grabbed the aggressor by the coat collar and by his belt, lifted him with the greatest of ease, and banged him down on the billiard table with a resounding thump.

The flustered count, obviously not expecting such a display of pure strength, was reported to have sobered instantly. He suddenly became embarrassed at his savage behavior. The strangers, however, remained calm and paid their bill. But before leaving the place, the young man with the icy blue eyes offered a little German advice that even the count could understand: "Absinthe, es ist nicht gut für Sie."

Despite the later efforts of both Mazin and de Furnimbac to identify the young German, they were unsuccessful. Eventually, the count left Paris and the Exposition, supposedly cured of his dependence on drink. Some years later, Mazin, the wrestler, mentioned to his friend a wonderful athlete whom he had just seen in London. His name was Sandow—a name he felt would become famous someday. De Furnimbac went to London shortly thereafter and made it a point to see Sandow's act. In the course of this performance, it suddenly dawned on the count that this was the extremely strong young German who had slammed him down on the billiard table several years earlier. Overcome with shame, the count determined to apologize to the young athlete for his earlier bad behavior.

Immediately following the end of Sandow's performance, he left his box and went to the athlete's dressing room. De Furnimbac was profuse in his apologies. "Monsieur Sandow, I beg your forgiveness. I am the one who under the influence of alcohol struck you in a Paris billiard parlor in 1889 and whom you did not chastise as I deserved." After piously warning him of the indulgence in distilled spirits, Sandow graciously forgave the Frenchman.

The next day a valet delivered a small box to Sandow's home. When he opened the package, he found a note again begging his pardon and asking him to accept the gift which accompanied the letter. This was a gold chronometer made by the clockmaker Bennett, "with a combination of ingenious mechanical adaptations, for striking the hours, minutes and seconds, a perpetual calendar, and other curious and elaborate contrivances." According to Desbonnet, who took an interest in the tale and recorded it faithfully, the penitent count followed Sandow's career, and in 1925 made a special trip to London in order to pay his last respects to "one that he had so brutally and regretfully struck."[57]

Exciting and varied though his life had been up to his point, it was nothing compared to what lay in store for the young German. Eighteen eighty-nine was to be an *annus miribilis* for Sandow, for it marked an important juncture in his career. His fortunes were to take a turn for the better. His wandering apprentice days were drawing to a close.

2

The First Triumph
1889

Appearing at the music hall attached to the Royal Aquarium in Westminster were two outrageous athletic charlatans: Sampson and Cyclops. They had put together a popular act involving feats of strength and trickery. To make their performance seem more credible, Sampson, the brains of the partnership, loudly announced each night that he would pay anyone foolish enough to try it one hundred pounds sterling if he could duplicate the feats of his "pupil" Cyclops, and five hundred pounds if anyone could duplicate his own feats. To Attila, who had by this time started his own physical culture studio in Bloomsbury, Sampson's offer was too good to pass up. He sent for Sandow, who was then in Italy, encouraging him to come to London and take up the challenge.

As Attila well knew, it was a common tactic for vaudeville strongmen to issue dares from the stage for anyone to come up and attempt to duplicate his feats. This was a fairly safe offer, for most strongmen had devised tricks that were nearly impossible for uninitiated amateurs (and professionals too, for that matter) to perform. These feats often included tricks of dexterity, strength, and acrobatics that would foil even the mightiest athlete if he were unused to the materials or lacked a carefully tuned sense of balance.[1]

Their opponent in this case, Charles A. Sampson, was a man who was even more slippery than the average professional Hercules. He was born on April 16, 1859, in the French city of Metz in Lorraine. Eventually, he emigrated to America, where he took up residence in Detroit, Michigan. The strongman was well formed and muscular, but obviously

not so powerful as he tried to make his credulous fans believe. Sampson
once reported that his great strength came about as a very literal bolt
from the blue. At the tender age of fourteen he was struck by a
tremendous flash of lightning. The boy languished on his sickbed for
six months, and when he eventually recovered Sampson found that he
had acquired an almost superhuman strength.[2]

His appearance at the Royal Aquarium, however, was not his first
venture upon the boards of the British music hall. Prior to this he had
appeared at the Canterbury Theatre of Varieties, where he claimed to
lift overhead a barbell boldly marked *2,240 Pounds*—one imperial ton!
The bell rested on two large barrels. As a gesture of his honesty,
Sampson invited several members of the audience to come up and try
to lift the enormous weight—all unsuccessfully. After this, Sampson's
manager gave a long, flowery speech explaining the great degree of
difficulty involved in this trick. Then following a long drumroll and
suitable grimaces and false starts, the strongman slowly and painfully
raised the bell higher and higher until he held it at arm's length above
his head.

When he returned the weight to the barrels, he was always greeted
with a thunderous ovation. He might have gotten away with this ruse,
except that one night someone tried to lift the barbell *after* Sampson
had finished, not before when they were invited to. It seems that while
the manager was giving his long introductory speech, two secret holes
were opened in the weight and the heavy sand inside was drained into
the barrels on which it rested.[3]

Despite this brush with exposure, Sampson did not retreat from
the theatrical scene; he merely regrouped his efforts and came up with
new "feats of strength." Throughout his career, he had gained a reputation for harness lifting, and one of his first efforts at this involved lifting
an elephant. The ponderous creature was put on a large wooden
platform over which a sturdy scaffolding had been constructed. The
strongman then dramatically mounted the scaffold and placed a leather
harness over his head connected by chains to the platform below. After
much grunting and theatrics, the platform was slowly raised six or seven
inches above the floor. Sampson would then collapse, letting the platform and pachyderm drop the few inches to the stage as attendants
rushed to give the strongman a few whiffs of sal volatile. One night
though, Sampson collapsed, but the platform mysteriously remained
suspended in midair. The management thought it best to ring down the
curtain unceremoniously.

In 1891, two years after his fateful match with Sandow, Sampson
had apparently improved his harness apparatus, for he succeeded in

convincing some important people who should have known better that he lifted two large bay horses and two accompanying hostlers whose combined weight added up to 3,809 pounds. Several weeks later he claimed to have lifted an astonishing 4,008 pounds. Despite the best efforts of many people (Sandow included), no one could say for sure how the wily Sampson engineered these feats of legerdemain—for they certainly had nothing to do with real strength.[4]

Several years earlier, Sampson had met and hired a strapping young Polish wrestler who called himself "Cyclops." His real name was Franz Bienkowski, and he looked every inch the oldtime vaudeville strongman. He was heavyset with a thick, bull neck. He shaved his head and had gracefully curling mustaches. His greatest claim to fame was the supposed ability to tear coins in two. There are many who believe this was another sleight of hand and that no one could mangle coins the way Cyclops claimed he could.[5] Whatever the case, he was a perfect foil for the clever and volatile Sampson: he was strong looking and not too bright. So with these colorful and unusual characters poised to attack, it is little wonder that the ensuing battle attracted unusual attention both in the close circle of performing strongmen and in the public at large.

As soon as he had made the channel crossing, Sandow contacted his old master, Attila, who immediately started preparing him for the upcoming contest. One of the first stops he had in London was at the prestigious National Sporting Club. Attila knew that since his young charge was virtually unknown in England, it would be necessary to obtain a few credentials before scoring his future victories. That way he would have a little moral and political backing should the need arise.

By the time Sandow and Attila attempted to gain allies there, the venerable NSC had been in existence as an informal body for many years. The club came into being when prize fighting was one of London's most popular sports. The prince regent was a member of a rowdy NSC coterie called "the fancy" which often came afoul of the law, but the prince's attendance at their boisterous assemblies prevented the magistrates from having them all imprisoned.

Despite the antics of the royal reprobate, the society's more reputable members gradually attempted to turn boxing into a respectable sport. Thus, the organization was officially founded in 1891 with this purpose in view. It enforced the rules of its most famous member, the marquis of Queensberry, stamped out fixed fights, and by the turn of the century awarded the Lonsdale Belts to fighters of merit. Perhaps appropriately, the club's headquarters are still on the boulevard named after their erstwhile protector, Regent Street.[6]

With Attila acting as his interpreter, Sandow arrived at the National Sporting Club and asked to present his case before the director, Mr. John Fleming. The members of the club greeted the two courteously but without enthusiasm. No one could quite believe that Sandow had the strength to defeat such well-known strongmen as Sampson and Cyclops. Fortunately, Sandow was able to perform one of his most convincing (and most frequently used) acts of strength: he spied one of the members who displayed the greatest girth and then lifted him bodily from the floor and gently placed him on a nearby table. Fleming was pleased with the display, but became even more fervent when the young East Prussian stripped off his clothing and his magnificent physique became apparent to all.[7]

After attending several of Sampson's performances, Attila and Sandow were ready to make their move. On the evening of October 29, 1889, Fleming and other members of the National Sporting Club took a box at the Aquarium and waited until the Frenchman made his nightly challenge. Apparently, Sampson was no less amazed than the audience when Attila arose and announced that he had a challenger who was ready to take on Sampson immediately. No doubt seeing little bank notes rapidly flying away, Sampson attempted to squirm out of his predicament. He did not know who this young man was, and how dare he take on "The Strongest Man on Earth"? Sandow would have to beat Cyclops first, only then would he submit to a contest. But just to show that his heart was in the right place, Sampson handed over £100 to the manager of the theater, Captain Molesworth, for safe keeping. This was not at all satisfactory to Sandow, Attila announced. He had come all the way from Italy for the £500, and for nothing less. Sampson proclaimed that he was in the right and refused to budge from his position. There the situation might have remained had it not been for a hastily arranged compromise between Fleming and Molesworth. Sandow would compete against Cyclops first, then if he was victorious he would go against his master at a later date. Reluctantly, Sandow and Attila agreed.

With the stipulations finally settled, Attila, Fleming, and the entire NSC group trooped onto the stage along with their man, Sandow. The audience by now was getting impatient with all these claims and counterclaims. It cannot be said that Sandow had the sympathy of the galleries; this was soon to change, however. Sandow came on the stage dressed in a fine suit of evening clothes specially prepared to be ripped off at once. Underneath he wore an athletic costume complete with tights and Roman sandals. To make his appearance seem even more debonair, he also donned a stylish monocle. Keeping this bothersome item in its proper position is said to have caused him more trouble than he was to experience in his contest with Cyclops.

As he came on stage, thanks to the monocle, Sandow tripped over some of the weights and other properties on stage causing a great deal of derisive laughter to come from the hall. The mood of the audience quickly changed, however, when he finally got rid of the pesky eyepiece, ripped off his foppish evening dress, and revealed a beautiful, well-formed, athletic physique. Sampson and Cyclops were also visibly moved by this revelation.

Finally the contest began in earnest. Cyclops picked up one 150-pound dumbbell and then another weighing 100 pounds and pressed them both above his head. Sandow responded by lifting the 150 pounds once and the 100 pounds twice over his head. The challenger had thus won round one almost effortlessly.

Test two was presented again by Cyclops, who jerked a 220-pound barbell overhead using both hands. Much to the delight of the audience, by now switching their allegiance to the young underdog, Sandow was able to press the same weight as his rival using only one hand.

The third test was a "press on back." Cyclops got down on the stage floor on his back and slowly lifted a barbell weighing 250 pounds into the air. Sandow was able to duplicate this feat easily. Since the last test had been successfully completed and since Sampson and his pupil did not seem able to think up any new stunts, Fleming and the other NSC members concluded that the contest was over and that Sampson must pay his debt. Not so, complained the fiery-tempered showman. Sampson explained loudly that before a true test of strength was complete it had to include a measure of endurance. Therefore, all the stunts had to be performed over and over again until only one man remained. The audience, however, had different ideas; they had no desire to sit in their seats and be bored to death waiting for one of the men to collapse. It seemed obvious to them that Sandow was certainly the equal, and probably the superior, of Cyclops.[8]

"Cries and counter-cries were heard," reported a witness, "and a soldier made himself conspicuous in the gallery by the animated manner in which he took the part of the newcomer, and by taunting Sampson with having lost his money."[9] While all the commotion was going on, Sandow quietly sat down to rest.

The turmoil was finally calmed by Molesworth, who announced that since he was the stakeholder, he would make sure that justice was done. Could Sampson name some final test that would decide the issue once and for all? Sampson agreed reluctantly. Cyclops stepped forward and picked up a dumbbell marked 150 pounds in his right hand and a kettle bell weighing 100 pounds in his left. He slowly lifted the dumbbell overhead twice, then let it crash dramatically to the floor of the platform.

Shouts of "Don't do it; don't try it; you have already won your money!" greeted the young athlete as he came forward and felt the weight of the ponderous dumbbell.[10] He smiled suavely in response to the warnings as he poised the heavy bell in his right hand and grasped the other in his left. Then, almost effortlessly, Sandow raised and lowered the bell not twice but seven times amid thunders of applause.

Once more Sampson flew into a paroxysm of indignation and chagrin, but to no avail. The £100 prize money was handed over to the young German with the promise of another meeting to determine whether Sandow was superior to Sampson or not. Sandow had been victorious in the first battle, but the war was far from won.

After their triumph over Cyclops, Sandow and Attila retired home in order to plot their next moves. Because they had seen several of Sampson's performances, they knew that one of his favorite tricks was the breaking of chains which he would wrap around his arm and then burst by muscle contraction. In order for this feat to be accomplished well, it was necessary to have trick chains that fit perfectly. So after nosing around for a while, they found the maker of Sampson's chains in a little street off Leicester Square. Not only were they able to get chains that were perfectly molded to Sandow's arm, but they also arranged for the maker to be present in the audience at the Aquarium on the night of the contest in order to verify that these chains were exactly the same kind and quality as the ones Sampson used in his act.[11]

By all accounts the scene at the Aquarium on the night of Saturday, November 2, was something akin to a madhouse. The news had spread throughout the sporting world of London that something big was in the making. Large groups of people crowded around, trying to get in to see the contest between Sampson, the self-proclaimed "Strongest Man on Earth," and the young, virtually unknown German lad. It was reported later that tickets were being sold from £1 to £5—one source even put the top price at 50 guineas.[12] "The beauty of the turnstile system was well illustrated," remarked the reporter from the *Daily News*, "for without these revolving barriers of iron the eager multitude would probably have carried the place by storm."[13]

Finally, the curtain rose. Sampson came to the footlights, dapper, radiant in medals, tights, and dainty boots, and smiling with confidence. He made a little speech, the first of an unforgivable series delivered or attempted before the evening ended. He wanted fair play; he offered £500 to anyone who would come on the stage and perform the feats he performed. Never mind where such a man came from; let him appear.

But to Sampson's relief and the audience's amazement, no one came forward. Where was Sandow? Sampson paced nervously back and forth across the stage waiting for his adversary, but no one appeared. Sampson again made a short speech stating that he did not want the challenge money, that he would donate it to charity, and besides he was cold, there was a draft in the hall. Again he paced back and forth.[14] Finally, he swung his cape around with a flourish and was about to skulk offstage when a great commotion arose caused by a group of men vaulting over the side-box onto the stage. It was the National Sporting Club group again, led by Fleming. They had been trying to gain entrance into the theater all the while, but because of the huge throng outside and a doorman who stubbornly refused to open the stage door for anyone, they had been delayed. If it had not been for Sandow who broke down the door, they might still be waiting outside.[15]

At last Sandow entered. There was general cheering at seeing the young German. The two judges for the evening were both peers of the realm: the marquis of Queensberry, the originator of the rules of boxing and the nemesis of Oscar Wilde, and Lord de Clifford, an avid sportsman of the day. It can only be imagined what sort of mental state Sandow was in—he had just barely missed the entire action. Yet he never gave the impression of being perturbed in the slightest. "Phlegmatic" was how he was described.[16]

"A beginning might never have been made," remarked a reporter, "but for the judges, who decided that Sampson must do the feats of strength he was in the habit of doing every night." As a result of this move to get things rolling, some wag in the front stalls shouted out, "Ah, I always said the House of Lords was a useful institution."

Sampson began the exhibition with iron pipe bending. He used his chest, leg, and arms to bend the pipe and then straighten it back again by blows. He did the work gracefully and swiftly. Sandow labored more, was clumsy, and took more time, but eventually he performed the task. Upon completion of this first feat, Sampson made a few loud and disparaging remarks about his opponent's apparent difficulty in performing the job. But the audience remained firmly on the side of the challenger—besides, as Molesworth announced, Sandow had never done the trick before in his life.

Then came the feat of breaking a wire rope fastened around the chest. Sampson performed it with the ease of one accustomed to the trick of twisting the ends of the wire strands together. Sandow was obviously unacquainted with the knack, and it was only after the audience shouted a few instructions and several fruitless tries that he succeeded. "It was a splendid effort of strength. The man seemed like to burst in his effort to obtain the requisite expansion of chest." When at last he was able to break the iron rope, most of the audience leaped to its feet and cheered raucously.[17]

Perhaps a little overconfident, Sampson next proceeded to his forte: chain breaking. He put one on his own forearm and coolly offered another to Sandow. It was obviously too small for the German, and he rejected it with a gesture of contempt. To everyone's surprise, Sandow brought out a chain of his own from his pocket and, true to his word, the chain maker was in the audience and was happy to verify that the chains were exactly the same as those used by Sampson. In order to verify the strength of his chains even further, Sandow passed them to members of the audience, taking them back at last from a pretty woman who sat conveniently near the stage.[18] The spectators may have been satisfied, but not the explosive Frenchman: "The unfortunate Sampson protested, gesticulated, argued, trod the deck, and generally cavorted around." But all this was to no avail, for Sandow was able to break his chain as easily as Sampson.

Sampson was clearly outraged that his rival had so easily beaten him at his own game. He ranted and raved to the audience until they shouted him down. Then he turned his attentions to the judges, but with equal success. Finally, amid much hubbub, the judges said that they would declare Sandow the winner of the contest if the German would perform some further proofs of strength on his own. Accordingly, he first lifted a stiffened and upright man from the ground and then did some crowd-pleasing feats with an improbably large dumbbell weighing 150 pounds.

All this time Sampson was throwing one of his frequent connip-tion fits. Someone shouted from the stalls offering Sampson £50 if he could duplicate any of Sandow's feats. But by this time he had had enough. Sampson grabbed his cape and stalked off the stage in a frightful huff. Finally, the only one left was Sandow. The judges duly named him the winner. He said a few words of thanks in German, and the eventful evening was over.

Unfortunately for the vanquished strongman, there was a clause in Sampson's contract which stated that if he were ever defeated after one of his nightly challenges, then his contract with the theater would become null and void.[19] It is no wonder, then, that Sampson carried his protests of unfairness off the stage and into the press.

As it turned out, however, there were other reasons for Sampson's vociferous outbursts, but they were not destined to be revealed for another five years. For now he had to be content with writing to every newspaper he could think of pleading for another chance, another match with the upstart German. However, the theatergoing public was beginning to wonder if Sampson really was "The Strongest Man on Earth."

Sampson had another reason for acting the role of the slighted hero: there was still the matter of the £500 prize. This had never been paid to Sandow, despite the ruling of the judges. For a man who often resorted to lawsuits on the flimsiest pretexts, Sandow strangely declined to press the matter in the courts. He meekly settled for an award of £350 paid to him by the Aquarium management. But all thought of litigation was put aside in the excitement of the moment. Sandow was victorious. That was all that mattered.

Shortly after this, Sampson quietly left town. With the cheek of the professional charlatan, he took up his strongman act in various cities in the United States and Europe. In 1893 he turned up in Michigan, where among other things, he claimed to have lifted the heavy cannon in front of the Detroit City Hall.[20] In 1895 he published a self-serving book called *Strength* in which he made many extravagant claims of Herculean power.

During the year 1898 he surfaced again in the Russian capital, St. Petersburg, still proclaiming himself "The Strongest Man on Earth." True to form, he continued to use a number of fancy tricks, trying to convince the gullible public that he was as strong as he said he was. One person who was not convinced was the great wrestler and strongman George Hackenschmidt, "The Russian Lion." Hackenschmidt showed up at one of Sampson's performances and easily exposed his tricks. After the show Sampson tried to talk the Russian into returning with him to London and there challenging Sandow to another match—this time with a much more formidable partner. But Hackenschmidt refused, and there the matter rested.

The Russian again encountered Sampson in 1904. By this time Hackenschmidt was residing in London, making a living as a wrestler. Sampson called at his home and Hackenschmidt immediately saw that Sampson was suffering severe financial hardship. The older man asked the Russian Lion for a loan of £10. He was willing to put up his weights and other paraphernalia as collateral for the loan. Hackenschmidt agreed and handed him the note, and Sampson duly deposited all of his equipment in the basement of the house. That was the last the Russian ever saw of him, for sometime after that Sampson managed to get into the house, take back the equipment, and leave town for good. He disappeared from sight, finally fading mercifully into the murk of history.[21]

Meanwhile the youthful, twenty-two-year-old victor was reaping the benefits of instant celebrity. "When we left the Aquarium after the contest," Sandow wrote, "the great crowd followed us cheering, and the four-wheeled cab into which we got, was lifted up by these enthusiasts. The crowd cheered us all the way to my rooms."[22] Newspapermen clamored to interview him, everyone wanting to know more of this remarkable young man. Sandow—probably on the advice of Attila— maintained for a moment the fiction that he was not interested in the slightest in a music hall career, but this was just a ploy to raise the stakes with the theater managers. By the time he went to bed that night, Sandow had a contract to appear at the Alhambra Music Hall for the very generous sum of £150 per week. Attila was paid the less magnificent sum of £30 per week and agreed to act as mentor-cum-manager to the burgeoning star. Sandow had taken another step on the long road to greater glory. He must have found it very difficult to sleep that night.

3

A Growing Reputation
1890–93

Sandow's star rose quickly and shone brightly. His performances at the Alhambra played to sold-out houses every night. It seemed that his name was being mentioned in nearly every quarter of the kingdom. His praises were being sung by a great many people quite literally. Alec Hurley, a well-known music hall coster singer and sometime husband of the great Marie Lloyd, featured a popular song about Sandow. The chorus, which was sung to a lively march tune, proclaimed lustily:

> Up jumped Sandow like a Hercules,
> Lifting up the iron bars
> And breaking them with ease.
> Sampson looked astonished and said it wasn't fair.
> But everyone knows Sandow was the winner there.[1]

Edward, Prince of Wales, was another of Sandow's early admirers. He came to see the strongman and after the performance visited backstage. He asked to have Sandow's photograph—a request that the athlete was happy to obey.[2]

Throughout his career Sandow was acutely aware of the value of having good photographs of himself. He always sought out the best lensmen all over the world. Probably the first really famous photographer to take Sandow's picture was Henry Van der Weyde. He turned out a beautiful set of poses showing the young strongman clad only in a fig leaf. Van der Weyde's fashionable Regent Street studios were patronized by many famous society and show people. He had made photographic history in 1872 when, using a gas-driven dynamo and a four-foot reflector, he was the first to set up an electrically lit studio. He advertised a 24-hour portrait service. It is said that the ubiquitous Prince of Wales dropped in late one night for a portrait after an evening of ogling the chorus girls at the opera.[3]

In the nineteenth century visual images were much less common than they are today. Illustrations in newspapers were rare and often crudely executed engravings, and personal snapshots were still many years off. The dominant form of image was the cabinet photo, a card-backed portrait measuring about 4 by 6½ inches. Celebrities like Sandow would often have their pictures taken, and then prints would be sold by the photographer to the public. In this way Sandow's likeness became well known to many people who might never have seen him in the regular course of things. Young ladies could therefore admire his countenance in privacy, young men could take inspiration from his bulging muscles, and theatergoers could procure lasting souvenirs of Sandow's electrical performances. But the photographs were being exchanged in other groups, too.

Sir Edmund Gosse was an eminent scholar, critic, and poet of the time. He was also a discreet homosexual. It was thanks to Gosse that Sandow's photographs were disseminated far and wide among the members of his coterie. One of the recipients of these pictures was another British literary man living in tubercular exile in Switzerland, John Addington Symonds. "The Sandow photographs arrived," Symonds gleefully wrote to Gosse in 1889. "They are very interesting, and the full length studies quite confirm my anticipations with regard to his wrists, ankles, hands, and feet. The profile and half-trunk is a splendid study. I am very much obliged to you for getting them for me."[4] These comments almost certainly refer to the Van der Weyde series that had appeared earlier that year and which must have been passed around excitedly almost as soon as they appeared in the photo shops.

Gosse's predilection for collecting photographs was well known among the chosen few. In 1889 the great British poet Robert Browning died. Gosse was expected to attend the tedious memorial ceremonies that were held in Westminster Abbey, so in order to relieve the boredom he brought along a few of his favorite photos and sneaked surreptitious peeks at them throughout the service.[5] Since this was the same year the Van der Weyde series appeared, the photos he took along were almost certainly of Sandow.

If Gosse attended one of Sandow's live performances, his reactions to it have not survived, but luckily a record of the act does exist. The reporter from *Sporting Life* was at the Alhambra in November of 1889, and he gave a lively description of the show. Attila was the first to appear on the stage. He began by lifting a few 56-pound weights as if they were toys and by raising 112 pounds with one arm. Then he hefted a bar of steel weighing 90 pounds and finished by balancing the bar on his chin. "After wielding a dumbbell of 150 pounds, he bent backward over a chair, and returning, brought the 150 pound dumbbell with him—a very creditable feat of strength which the audience applauded."

Then Sandow stepped out on the stage wearing his pink tights and blue vest, his mighty chest sparkling with medals. He was cheered heartily by the audience. "He commenced his entertainment by posing and then putting both hands at the back of his head, and moved his biceps in a marvelous manner." He then picked up the 150-pound barbell, moved with it slowly and gracefully, and then turned a somer-sault while still holding the heavy weight. He next picked up a male attendant who weighed about 140 pounds and held him easily above his head with one hand.

Other feats of weightlifting followed, but the performance culmi-nated in one of his most spectacular tricks. Sandow assumed the "Tomb of Hercules" position and a special board was placed on his knees and shoulders. The audience gaped in amazement as every available weight was heaped on the board, and finally when it was thought that he could take no more, Professor Attila himself leapt upon the board brandishing a heavy club. The audience cheered and shouted its approval as the two performers bowed to the admiring throng. Incredibly, his erstwhile adversary, Sampson, was spied in the Alhambra that night grimly watching the triumphant athlete win plaudit after plaudit. And even Sampson would have to agree with the columnist who said of the young Sandow, "He came, was seen, and conquered."[6]

One of the things that amazed audiences the most was Sandow's physical appearance. People had been conditioned to thickset, music hall strongmen—huge mountains of flesh and sinew. When they real-ized that Sandow was just as strong, despite his noble, well-proportioned look, they were doubly surprised and impressed. "He is positively handsome in form, feature, face, and limb," one journalist proclaimed. "The only proportion appearing somewhat out of balance being the enormous muscular development from shoulder to wrist, his arms seeming to have been hewn out of marble. He is the beau-idéal of athletic elegance."[7] Clearly, here was a new and original talent ready to take the theatrical and athletic world by storm.

Sandow remained in London until February of 1890, then he launched a tour of the major provincial cities of Britain. For three months Sandow and Attila visited a surprising number of towns: Bristol, Birmingham, Manchester, Liverpool, Newcastle, and others. These were primarily one-night or one-week stands—an extremely trying tour even for a strongman.[8] It must have come as a great relief when he was able to get away during the summer for a brief holiday on the Continent. Consequently, he parted from his old friend, Attila, and crossed the Channel.

One morning while in Germany he took his daily ride near the ancient city of Aachen. As he trotted down a quiet country road, Sandow's horse suddenly shied. In front of them stood what appeared to be a huge giant of a man. He stood six feet two inches in height and weighed nearly four hundred pounds. "His head was as huge and grotesque as any pantomime mask, with a nose the size of an ordinary fist. As for his fist, it would have made more than three of mine, and when a five shilling piece was placed beneath the ball of his finger, believe me, it was impossible to see it." This was, as he later discovered, a worker in a local quarry by the name of Karl Westphal. Sandow immediately saw brilliant possibilities for the man if he could be persuaded to come back with him to London and become part of his music hall act. After a short conversation with the man, Sandow agreed to pay him 140 marks a week, many times his original salary of 5 marks at the quarry.

As soon as the two arrived in London, Sandow hailed a "growler," a sturdy, four-wheeled cab, so called because of the din they made when traversing the London cobblestones. Somehow, Westphal got one foot in, then drew in his body, resting against the far side of the cab wall. But when he attempted to bring his other foot in, the floor gave way, crashing the first foot to the street. After soothing the cabby, they finally made it home in a large pantechnicon van.

Because of his freakish appearance, Sandow made sure that the giant stayed indoors most of the time. All the while Sandow tried to train the man to take part in his performances. Unfortunately, this proved to be a difficult task. The massive Westphal, whom Sandow decided to rename "Goliath," was not a very apt student. After seven or eight weeks of fruitless work, Sandow decided to settle for a few feats of cannon carrying and wrestling and not much else.

At last an act was arranged for the Royal Music Hall. In this Goliath was to surprise Sandow, lumber after him, and try to catch him. They would wrestle for a while and Goliath would appear to be the victor. "Then, in order to finish me," Sandow wrote, "he took a cannon weighing 400 pounds, and placing it on his broad shoulders, prepared to fire. In a moment or so I returned with some clubs. It was now the turn of the giant to show alarm and gradually to retire with the cannon still on his back into a frame of refuge. I at once climbed to the top, and getting into a position above my antagonist I lifted him, refuge, and cannon with one finger, a few inches off the ground. During this part of the performance we fired the cannon, and the whole display was brought to a conclusion by placing my arm through a leather belt which girt his waist, and carrying him off above my head."[9]

Not surprisingly, this partnership did not last for long. Goliath left his employer, married his landlady, and the two started a show of their own. Used to working with partners, Sandow next teamed up with "Loris," a somewhat less extraordinary performer. Unfortunately, this duo lasted even more briefly, and they parted sometime after the Christmas season of 1890–91.[10]

But throughout all Sandow's moves and changes, one nagging question remains: where was Attila? Somewhere along the line he had been dismissed and Sandow had taken on a new manager. A reason for this rift is found in a fragment of a letter sent to Attila at this time. "You would have had as much as I," Sandow wrote in a flowing German Gothic hand. In all probability this refers to Attila's salary. Earlier Sandow had paid his former master the relatively modest sum of £30 per week to work as his assistant, so perhaps Attila rebelled against this. "You know that I was always honest with you and that you had my whole confidence. I would have left all things up to you as before had you supported me in good and in bad." Obviously, Sandow's finances were not as secure as he led readers to believe in his later books.

"Now, Attila," he continues, "please see things from my point of view and think about it *honestly*. You have to agree that you would have done exactly the same as I did." Perhaps he was forced to let Attila go because the audiences were beginning to abate, or perhaps he was simply ready to strike out on his own. He concludes by saying, "I would like to see you before you leave London so I will know where you will be going." And he signs the letter, "Your *constant*, true friend, Sandow."[11] But despite the conciliatory words, Attila must have felt that his former pupil was being ungrateful for all the guidance and help he had given him since the two had first met about four years earlier in Brussels. It was a blow to his pride that he could not forgive.

The departure from London that Sandow mentions in his letter probably refers to Attila's trip to Paris about this time. Smarting from his dismissal, Attila decided to get revenge. He would go to the Continent and find another strongman—one whom he could forge into an even greater talent than Sandow.

Once he arrived in the French capital, he did not have far to look. Amidst the scantily clad girls of the Folies-Bergère there was a young Italian strongman by the name of Luigi Borra. Physically he was not massive, but he bore an uncanny resemblance to Sandow. He had curly hair, a mustache, and a well-muscled, thick-waisted body similar to the young German's. By a strange twist of fate the Italian had been a wrestler in his native country at the same time Sandow had fought there. Borra had actually been victorious over Sandow on several occasions. Here, thought Attila, was the perfect rival for his cocky former pupil.

Borra came to London, changed his name to Milo, and started performing. Almost at once he issued a challenge to Sandow for a test of strength. But Sandow did what Attila least expected: he simply ignored it. Again and again the gauntlet was thrown down by Milo and Attila, but to no avail. Sandow's popularity did not seem to be affected in the slightest; in fact, he seemed to have more engagements than ever. So after a while, the whole thing just simmered down. Borra continued to perform strength acts on the English music hall stage, and when the Boer War broke out, he was quick to take advantage of all the interest in the military. He changed his stage name once more to "Brinn, the Cannon Ball King" and starred in a review called "Pastimes on a Battleship." On a set bristling with cannons, Borra came out dressed as a naval officer. He juggled shells and projectiles, hand-balanced on the ends of rifle butts, and even perched a heavy cannon on his chin. He continued performing for quite a while and was still in fine shape until his death in 1955.[12] But Sandow had not heard the last from Attila.

As if Borra and Attila were not enough, Sandow had also to contend with another rather odd problem at this time. Bringing down the house has always been the goal of most popular entertainers, but in this case it was almost literal. Sandow lived on the upper floor of a lodging house run by one Mrs. Brackenbury. Here the athlete was in the habit of working out with his weights on a regular basis. One day, however, he must have been particularly zealous, for he ended up doing major damage to the ceilings, walls, and furniture. A frightful scene ensued with Mrs. Brackenbury. She was not put off by his great strength, and eventually she brought him before a magistrate, who ordered the athlete to pay all damages.[13]

It was punishment of a different sort that Sandow had to face later that same year. One of the drawbacks of Attila's departure was the loss of his good counsel. This became all too apparent in an unfortunate match that threatened to destroy the good reputation that Sandow had built up in the sporting community. On December 10, 1890, the Royal Music Hall in Holborn was reserved for a momentous contest of weightlifting between Hercules McCann and Sandow. "Hercules," who was born just plain Henry McCann, had devised a strongman act with his brother "Samson" (né Louis). They had long been suspicious of

Sandow's claim that he could bent press 250 pounds, so they decided to challenge him to a verification of this lift. As if it were an afterthought, they also included an overall weightlifting contest. This match was to become an important one in the history of the sport, for an elaborate system of scales was used; it is therefore one of the first contests where we can be absolutely sure of the weights.

The redoubtable marquis of Queensberry along with weightlifting pundit Professor John Atkinson and Mr. Shirley B. Jevons were to be the judges for this contest. The competition was to consist of six feats of strength, three selected by Hercules McCann, three by Sandow. The stakes were to be £150 a side, but Sandow had agreed to pay the brothers £50 win or lose, and the brothers had promised to pay £50 if Sandow could lift the 250-pound weight. There was apparently a great deal of interest in the proceedings, for several newspapers ran descriptions of the event. The account in the *Morning Post* of December 11 is generally regarded as a good one. The reporter wrote that the match started at three o'clock in the afternoon, and after a careful weighing in of the material, the contest was ready to begin. "Sandow proceeded to take up the challenge to lift the 250 pound weight for £50. The young German performed the feat—perhaps the most difficult in the programme —with complete success, and was loudly applauded." The regular contest then began, Hercules setting the first task, which was to raise with the left hand from the ground at arm's length above the head a weight of 170 pounds. Sandow followed him, and finally accomplished the feat after three attempts, the limit allowed for each trial. Then, amidst renewed applause, Sandow raised a dumbbell weighing 226 pounds with his right hand above the head. But when it came Hercules' turn, he would have none of this and refused to attempt the feat. His decision provoked many cat calls and a good deal of hissing. He then proceeded to his own test, which was to raise a 150-pound weight with the left hand above the head. Both men were able to perform his lift successfully.

Sandow next lifted 198 pounds with his left hand and dared Hercules to duplicate it. He could not. But now it was Hercules' turn—his last test was to lift simultaneously two dumbbells, one weighing 120 pounds and the other 112 pounds. The *Morning Post*'s account describes the results:

> This feat the challenger performed with apparent ease at the first attempt. Somewhat to the surprise of his supporters, Sandow was unequal to the task in which his opponent's superior weight was obviously an advantage. The last of the six trials was initiated by Sandow. It consisted in raising at

arm's length above the head 210 pounds with the right hand and 49 pounds with the left. This very trying feat was accomplished after two unsuccessful attempts, and called forth a general burst of cheering. There were loud and prolonged cries for McCann, but as before, Hercules refused the challenge, heedless of the ironical remarks showered upon him.

Thus the contest came to an end. To those in the audience it seemed obvious who the winner was. Sandow had performed coolly, only failing in one lift, whereas McCann had refused twice to take up the weights Sandow had presented. The judges retired for about fifteen minutes to discuss the verdict. At last the marquis of Queensberry solemnly announced that Hercules, not Sandow, had won the competition, but the latter had won the special prize of £50. This decision came as a complete surprise to the audience, and outbursts of outrage and dissent were heard throughout the hall. For a while it seemed as if complete pandemonium had broken out.

Then, shouting louder than the rest, persistently pushing his way through the crowd from the back of the hall, who should appear on stage but Sandow's ever-present rival, Sampson. He declared loudly and excitedly that Sandow was the winner despite what the judges ruled. This was more to the liking of the gentlemen in the theater, for they began cheering. Surely, if Sampson, the man whom Sandow had beaten so soundly almost a year before, could see that the young German was the winner, why couldn't the judges? To say the least, it was a very confused and generally disgruntled crowd that left the Royal Music Hall that afternoon.[14]

Despite the unsatisfactory results of the contest between Sandow and Hercules McCann, the match was significant for several reasons. Probably the most important was that it was the first major contest to be closely monitored and judged by men who knew what they were doing. The officials were either knowledgeable in weightlifting or were lifters themselves. All of the weights were scrupulously weighed and the style of lifting was closely watched. The contest thus laid the foundations for all subsequent lifting matches.

Even so, the public was clearly confused. Perhaps one of the explanations for the ruling was that the judges knew that Sandow's favorite form of lift, the bent press, was easier to accomplish than the clean and jerk style of McCann. This style of lifting was supposedly invented by Attila, and certainly he made sure that his pupil used it from the earliest stages of his career. The bent press (or "screw press" as it is sometimes called because of the twisting movement of the weight) was a favored exercise of strength athletes everywhere for a time, and it was popular with vaudeville athletes because it was relatively easy to perform but looked spectacular. Today it is considered something of a dinosaur among modern weightlifters. Many serious athletes deride the press as more a balancing trick than a legitimate lift. Thus, despite the efforts of Siegmund Klein and others in the 1930s to revive interest in it, the bent press was washed up as a competitive lift by the mid–1940s.[15]

Sandow, on the other hand, had always used the lift with great success, and his perplexity must have made one thing clear to him: he could have used some help from his old friend Attila. After all, at twenty-three years of age, Sandow simply did not have the experience to deal with all the demands of professional weightlifting.

"Had Sandow's friends exercised a little judgement in drawing up articles of agreement," confirmed a contemporary newspaper account, "Hercules would never have won the contest at the Royal in Holborn yesterday. Technicalities defeated Sandow whose work was better and cleaner than that of Hercules."[16] The whole episode must have left a sour taste in the strongman's mouth, and it was not until about a year later that he was able to savor the sweetness of retaliation.

Throughout that year Sandow continued to perform in strength shows and to build his abilities to continually higher levels. By the beginning of 1891 he had honed his strength and his skill at lifting to a degree that was surprising even to himself. He was ready for the next test, and he did not have long to wait.

Professor Atkinson of the London Athletic Institute offered a grand competition for a gold championship belt. This was to be awarded to the man who would make the best English record in weightlifting. The competition was to take place at the International Hall of the Cafe Monaco in Piccadilly Circus on the night of January 29, 1891. Sandow wanted to make a name for himself in the athletic world, so he was understandably anxious to break all the records set by his former opponent, Hercules McCann.

As usual, the hall was crowded on the evening of the contest. Sandow got down to business by lifting a dumbbell weighing 179 pounds with his right hand. Hercules had previously set the record for this lift at 170 pounds, so the first record of the evening had been shattered with apparent ease. "Next in order," wrote the gentleman from *Sporting Life,*

came a two-handed feat. This time Sandow lifted a bell weighing 126 pounds with his right hand and 119 pounds with his left hand. It will be remembered that when Hercules put up his two bells of 120 pounds and

112 pounds, he used a mighty jerk, and Sandow failed to get the bells up at all. There was no doubt about last night's attempt. Sandow got the two bells to his shoulder in very neat style. Then he started to press them up, but hesitated momentarily. The pause looked ominous, but slowly and surely the arms began to straighten and in a few seconds the two masses of iron were held aloft, Sandow not only wiping Hercules' record off the slate, but making the new one in magnificent style.

One of the judges expressed some concern that Sandow's arm had not been perfectly straight, but Professor Atkinson, who was acting as referee, convinced him that with such enormous biceps "it was simply impossible to get the arm like a ram-rod."

The next test of strength was a lift of 160 pounds with the left hand. Fortunately, Sandow encountered little difficulty with this feat. "He first curled the weight up to the shoulder," it was reported, "and then slowly pressed it until it was well over his head."

At this point Sandow had done what he had set out to do: he had broken every record that had previously been set by Hercules McCann. He had won the championship belt and had demonstrated to all concerned that he was the best lifter in the kingdom. But this was not enough for him—Sandow wanted to set a few records of his own.

First, a barbell weighing 250 pounds was stood on end in front of him. But before he attempted to lift the weight, Sandow asked Professor Atkinson if the stage was all right. "Over 400 pounds in one spot is a big weight," the strongman observed. This figure referred to the bell and his own weight. The Professor assured him that the stage was safe. So, pausing to get a good grip, Sandow brought the bell to his chest and then slowly pushed the enormous weight up until he had it at arm's length. "Dropping the bell shoulder high, he again pushed it up, and tried the performance again, but the bell turned in his hand when it was half-way up, and he dropped it to the floor with a crash that made everyone's teeth jar." But he was successful on the second attempt, thereby becoming the first man in history to raise so great a weight.

His next task was to lift a 177-pound barbell and to press it overhead. This he did with very little difficulty. "The work was so cleanly done that the spectators gave the performer round after round of applause." A 161-pound plate bell was the next weight to be lifted, this time using his left hand only. Slowly Sandow curled the bell to his shoulder, and then he began to press the weight overhead. "As the iron rose in the air a faint 'Oh!' was heard, and Sandow looked daggers at the place from which the sound emanated. It seemed to unnerve him for a moment, but getting a good grip of the bell, he held it aloft as though it were a walking stick."

The judges were so impressed by Sandow's obvious power and finesse that they requested him to perform some special feats of strength. This he consented to do. He stood beside the scales, supervising the weighing process, and when the officials omitted to weigh the two nuts that were used as fastenings on the bells, he called their attention to the oversight, observing, "I want credit for all I do." Since the nuts weighed more than a pound each, this was not as petty as it sounded.

At last Sandow was ready to lift the 70.5-pound plate bell. "Sandow raised it to his shoulder. Then gradually dropping the weight until his arm was at right angles with his body, accomplished one of the greatest feats of genuine strength ever known in this or any other country."

For his final feat Sandow again took up a 70.5-pound bell in his right hand and a 56-pound ring weight in his left. He raised them to his shoulders, and then gradually muscled the weights out to a horizontal position. The ring of the 56-pound kettle bell was down so that no assistance could be had from the wrist. "The ease and coolness of the performance electrified everyone, and for some minutes no one seemed to realize the magnitude of the achievements. When one individual did start the applause, it soon swelled in volume, and for some minutes the noise was deafening."

After a while Professor Atkinson motioned for the crowd to quiet down. "You have not only eclipsed all Hercules' performances," he said as he handed Sandow the richly decorated championship belt, "but you have set a lot of tasks that will remain on record for a long time. In addition to this, you have given us an exhibition of pure strength that seems phenomenal. I have great pleasure in presenting to you the championship belt, which I hope you will find pleasant to look at in after life, and I also hope that you may live many years to enjoy it." Sandow looked as if he wanted to reply to this gracious speech as he accepted the trophy, but his inability to express himself clearly in English seemed to stop him. Instead, his eyes expressed his gratitude eloquently enough.

Sandow was indeed proud of his fine belt. It was made of blue satin, richly studded with gold decorations. In the center an elaborate scroll-work shield was engraved with the particulars of the contest. It was a fitting prize for the record-breaking evening.

Capitalizing on his added fame after the competition, Sandow arranged for a tour of a few provincial cities. Starting in the spring of 1891, the athlete began extended theatrical runs in both Liverpool and Birmingham.[17] It was in the latter city that Sandow had his portrait done by the respected photographer H. Roland White. He was shown posing proudly in his new championship belt. Later he made White's picture the frontispiece to his first book.

By the spring of the next year he was ready for another holiday on the Continent. This time he decided to travel to Italy and the south of France, with an extended stay in Monte Carlo in order to try his luck at the gaming tables. On his way back to England, he had a brief stop in Nice. There he arranged for a trunk-load of valuables with about £2,000 worth of jewelry, prize medals, and other souvenirs to be sent ahead to London. Sandow took the trunk with its precious cargo to the railway station himself, but before he could speak to the porter, two men came forward and offered themselves as interpreters, but as he spoke French well enough, Sandow brushed them off quickly. He then proceeded to make the proper arrangements for the shipment of the trunk, and boarded the train for Paris. After he had arrived at his destination, he discovered that the trunk had also arrived, but all the valuables were missing. In their place the enraged strongman found about fifty red bricks.

Not losing a beat, Sandow turned around and took the next train back to Nice. As soon as he got there, he found the porter he had originally spoken to. The startled man said that the two "interpreters" who had spoken to Sandow previously had convinced him that they were friends of the strongman and that he had asked them to send the trunk to London via other channels. Accordingly, they took the trunk with them and substituted another in its place. Sandow grabbed the red cap, and the two roamed the streets until they sighted the thieves. Sandow roughly collared the men from behind and while he banged their heads together like cymbals, the porter ran off to find the nearest gendarme. When the two men regained consciousness, they produced the pawn tickets for Sandow's goods and thus he was able to recover most of his stolen property. The two miscreants learned "how ugly a customer Sandow may be found should occasion call for the exercise by him of his strength."[18]

Back in England, Sandow began his usual round of activities and promotions. One of the judges for the earlier weightlifting competition had been Lieutenant-Colonel G. Malcolm Fox, the inspector of gymnasia for the British army and director of physical training for the famous British military school at Aldershot. Fox had become very interested in Sandow and his performances and in the possible value of incorporating some of the young strongman's techniques in the army's regimen of training for its recruits. There was no conscription in Britain at this time. It was an all-volunteer army that fought Queen Victoria's many little wars. But a great percentage of the young men who chose to enlist had to be rejected because of their poor physical condition. In 1866, for example, the army had rejected recruits at the rate of 380 per 1,000 on physical grounds, while the figures for the years between 1864 and 1867 were even higher, 408 per 1,000.[19] Finding men who were fit enough to go on active service was a continual problem for the military. The vast majority of those who wanted the queen's shilling in their pockets were city slum dwellers whose physical condition was generally weedy, anemic, and frail, and whose only reason for joining was simply to avoid starvation. The only short-term solution to the corresponding dearth of new recruits was to lower the physical criteria by which soldiers were selected for service. Even these lax standards did not significantly help, for in 1900 half the volunteers had to be rejected because they were underdeveloped. At one point the artillery was permitted to accept men of shorter stature, but only if they were exceptionally broad in the shoulders and chest. This ruling caused one veteran recruiting sergeant to complain to his officer, "Beg yer pardon, sir, but the Almighty don't make men in the shape you order 'em."[20] The only apparent solution was to encourage young people to exercise and keep fit. It was therefore in this direction that physical education traveled.

Despite its problems, the British army was slowly emerging from the Dark Ages in its attitudes toward the physical development of young cadets. At Sandhurst, the prestigious officer's training school, all sport had been strictly forbidden for the first fifty years of the school's existence. It was argued that gymnastics would cause the students to become "too active and nimble and not stiff enough for the ranks."[21] The great general Lord Garnet Wolseley remarked in exasperation about the rival academy, Aldershot, "I can conscientiously assert that I never learnt anything there, nor heard of any regimental officer who did. There was no one there who was capable of teaching us."[22] Unfortunately, the great general had long since departed by the time Sandow and Fox arrived, otherwise he might have had quite a different opinion of the school.

In order to raise interest in physical culture for the military, Fox arranged for a number of special exhibitions in which prominent army physicians would lecture to the men on physical education, using Sandow as a model. One of these took place on December 12, 1892, and was reported in *The Lancet,* then as now one of the most respected medical journals. The lecturer for this occasion was Surgeon-Major Deane of the medical staff.

He began his talk by pointing out that exercise and sport were all very good for health, but they only developed certain parts of the body. Sandow, he noted, had succeeded in improving nearly every muscle in his body by the use of scientific exercises. Deane then asked Sandow to perform a few tricks for the edification of the gentlemen in the packed lecture hall. Consequently, he stripped and demonstrated his amazing muscle control. "Clasping his hands behind his head, he was able to make his biceps rise and fall in time to music." One after another he demonstrated the various muscles that he had cultivated so carefully. He then "applied the hands of some of the bystanders to the skin over the chest walls and other parts of the trunk of his body, with the result that a young fellow described the sensation as being like that of 'moving your hand over corrugated iron.'" Sandow next showed his fine chest expansion by inflating and deflating his lungs. Biceps, triceps, flexors, extensors, pectorals, he displayed them all with the grace of a finely tuned performer. The soldiers gaped in near disbelief as he took a large, India-rubber chest expander and stretched it across his back. "The action of the muscles of the back caused them to look like snakes coiling and uncoiling themselves under his skin." It was clear that they had never seen anything like the young German athlete before.

To top off the demonstration, Sandow ripped two decks of cards in half with his bare hands and then turned a neat and precise somersault at the end of his performance. "It is scarcely necessary to add," *The Lancet* reported, "that with cadets for an audience, Sandow did not lack applause." It was later reported that there was a great run on every available dumbbell and piece of weightlifting equipment at the Royal Military Academy.[23]

Lieutenant-Colonel Fox continued to be a great fan and admirer of Sandow, and when Sandow published his first book in 1894, he dedicated it to Fox. This testimonial read in part, "In grateful remembrance of many acts of friendly courtesy, and as a tribute of admiration for a gallant soldier and a zealous advocate of physical training alike for military man and the civilian."

Fox's zeal for physical education did not go unnoticed among civilians either, for shortly after his demonstration with Sandow, he was appointed Inspector of Physical Training for all public elementary schools. His principal task was to introduce a system of exercises by teaching the children various military drills. The lieutenant-colonel and his visiting instructors persisted in their endeavors well into the 1920s, by which time thousands of youngsters had marched in formation ceaselessly up and down school playgrounds.[24] Fox, his peripatetic teachers, and especially the children no doubt wished Sandow would come back for a repeat performance. The young athlete, however, was destined for other glories.

Aldershot marked one more triumph in a growing list. Like a

young Alexander, it must have seemed to Sandow that he had no more worlds to conquer. But that was soon to change dramatically, and the winds of that change blew from the west, across the Atlantic.

4

New York and Chicago
1893–94

By 1893 Sandow was twenty-six years old, and his fame had increased considerably. He had already toured England, Scotland, and Ireland; there could not have been anyone in the realm of the variety theater who was not familiar with his name. But the huge financial success that he saw others acquiring had continued to elude him. He was reasonably well known, yet he had hardly risen to the rank of a superstar in the music hall firmament, and his salary was correspondingly nonstellar. This was soon to change, though, and the unwitting agent of that change was Henry S. Abbey of the firm Abbey, Scheffel and Grau, vaudeville impresarios of New York City.[1]

Abbey's representatives in Europe contacted the young German strongman early in 1893 and arranged for him to come to America, where they hoped he would be as big a hit as he had been in England. Accordingly, Sandow and a young Dutch friend, Martinus Sieveking, booked passage on the liner *Elba* and arrived in New York in June, ready to begin what the athlete hoped would be a long run.[2]

Then as now, summer in New York was not the best time to debut a new act, and from the beginning it was obvious that Sandow was being poorly managed. Used to being the principal act on the bill, the strongman was surprised to learn that Abbey had other ideas for him. The Casino Theater in New York was a large, showy building which specialized in musical and variety acts. It was built in the Moorish style with exotic minarets and domes and with an airy rooftop garden for smaller acts. It was managed by a very shrewd man, Rudolph Aronson.

He had been responsible for bringing such talented artists to New York as composers Johann Strauss and Camille Saint-Saëns and the famous skirt dancer, La Loie Fuller. The Casino was running the musical farce *Adonis* at the time, so when Abbey approached Aronson concerning Sandow he was not exactly anxious to take on a new act. Abbey must have been getting desperate, however, for Aronson reported in his memoirs that the impresario came to him and made the manager of the Casino an offer. "Aronson," Abbey said, "I will let you have Sandow for what he costs me, $600 a week. You place him between two of the acts or at the finish of your operetta at the Casino, and I'm sure he will fill the house." Aronson reflected for a while, and then replied, "Although this attraction is somewhat out of my line . . . I will give you fifty percent of our receipts after we have cleared the average weekly receipts." Abbey jumped at the chance, eager to have Sandow off his hands.[3]

Unfortunately for Abbey, Aronson, and especially Sandow, the city was suffering through one of its intense July heat waves. The ticket-buying public showed no inclination to coop themselves up in a hot, stuffy theater during the terrible spell. High temperatures automatically produced low attendance. Of course the most prominent critics and theatrical personages had fled the concrete griddle for the breezy beaches and green hills, not to return until New York cooled down. Sandow's run at the Casino was obviously doomed from the start.

Those patrons stalwart enough to brave the heat would see Sandow's performance beginning at 10:30. At the end of *Adonis,* Henry Dixey, the principal actor, climbed atop a classical pedestal and posed as a statue. The curtain was thus brought down for him, but when it was raised again, the delicate and wispy Dixey had been replaced by Sandow in the exact same pose. The reporter from the *New York World* could hardly believe his eyes. "When New York has seen Sandow after Dixey, New York will realize what a wretched, scrawny creature the usual well-built young gentleman is compared with a perfect man. Sandow, posing in various statuesque attitudes, is not only inspiring because of his enormous strength, but absolutely beautiful as a work of art as well." The New World had obviously never seen the likes of Sandow before. "One look at him is enough to make the average young man thoroughly disgusted with himself, and to make him give up his nightly habit of standing in front of his glass in his pajamas and swelling his chest with pride."[4]

The *New York Herald* was hardly less enthusiastic: "Such knots and bunches and layers of muscle they had never before seen other than on the statue of an Achilles, a Discobolus, or the Fighting Gladiator." Furthermore, the reporter seemed surprised at Sandow's youth: "The face was that of little more than a boy—smooth, with rosy cheeks and a little blond moustache. The chin, however, was square and heavy. The neck was massive, and the shoulders seemed a yard apart. The arms looked as though hickory-nuts and walnuts had somehow been forced under the skin, causing it to bulge out in abrupt lumps."[5]

Most people who saw Sandow for the first time were amazed at his appearance. "It was hard for the spectators when a calcium light was turned on the figure standing on a pedestal in the back of the darkened stage to believe that it was indeed flesh and blood that they beheld." The general public was not the only group to be surprised by the strongman's physique. As the correspondent from the *Herald* noted, even the medical men were startled. "See how his ribs show!" remarked a physician who sat near the reporter. "I thought they were ribs, too," confided the newsman, "until I felt of them in Sandow's dressing room after his performance last Tuesday night. The ridges that stood out so plainly were of muscle, and not of bone."[6]

After assuming several poses in the glare of the spotlight, Sandow began with the performance he had been using in Britain: work with two 56-pound dumbbells including acrobatics and somersaults, the living weights—in which he lifted a large barbell into the air and then brought it down again and two grown men were released from inside the oversized bells. The finale was part of Sandow's spectacular trademark. Three trained horses were driven across a platform while the athlete was in the Tomb of Hercules position.

It was a good show, but not good enough to draw the huge crowds envisaged by Abbey. Still, it could not be denied that he had gotten extremely good notices from the press. Even staid *Harper's Weekly* took note of the Teutonic muscleman and characteristically drew a moral lesson. Although they observed that being able to support horses and lift hundreds of pounds of living and dead weight might not serve any artistic or utilitarian purpose, yet, "We perhaps would be greater intellectually than even we are, were we to devote a little more care and attention in that direction with possible salutary and sanitary results."[7]

Like others before them, many of the reporters were amazed to see a man as well formed and muscular as Sandow. One paper was quick to point out that the bodybuilder's waist was not much larger than svelte Lily Langtry's and that his chest was much bigger around than that belonging to portly Grover Cleveland. At least among the press corps, "this German bunch of muscle" had made an impression.[8]

Sandow himself must have been disappointed by the attendance at these nightly performances, but if this was the case he did not let on. He was determined to enjoy all that America had to offer. The only fault that he confessed to finding in New Yorkers was their fondness for drink. "They like to give you a bath of cock-tails," he complained facetiously, "and if a bath should not suffice, they would think nothing of making a river for you." He had to admit however, that he found the Manhattan, Martini, and Oyster very tasty indeed.[9] But America's fancy drinks were not the only things Sandow was enjoying.

Speculation about the private lives of public figures is a risky but tantalizing business, especially at a century's distance. When the person is the enigma that was Sandow, yesterday's gossip and today's conjectures are all the more equivocal. Certain things, however, are undeniable. The truth is that Sandow was definitely a womanizer. The truth is also that his tastes ran in other directions too.

Crossing the Atlantic with him was Martinus Sieveking, described as Sandow's "great and inseparable friend." Sieveking was a Dutch pianist and composer who had known Sandow from his years in Belgium and Holland. The two men had been living together for some time, and when they arrived in New York, they again set up housekeeping on West Thirty-eighth Street. The reporter from the *World* painted a touching picture of the two men at home. Sieveking, who was described as "an unusually brilliant artist," and Sandow were "bosom friends," he reported. Sieveking, he added:

> thinks that Sandow is a truly original Hercules, and that no one has ever lived to be compared to him. Sandow thinks that Mr. Sieveking is the greatest pianist in the world and that he is going to be greater. It is pleasant to see them together. Mr. Sieveking, who is a very earnest musician, practices from seven to eight hours a day on a big three-legged piano. He is decidedly in earnest. He practices in very hot weather stripped to the waist. While he plays, Sandow sits beside him on a chair listening to the music and working his muscles. He is fond of the music, and Sieveking likes to see Sandow's muscles work. Both enjoy themselves and neither loses any time.[10]

This scene of happy domesticity is corroborated by a most unlikely source, the famous courtesan—or "grande horizontale," as she was called in that more genteel time—La Belle Otéro. Caroline Otéro was one of the most scandalous and colorful figures of the Belle Époque. Her lovers included many of the rich, famous, and titled men of her era. King Leopold of Belgium, Prince Albert of Monaco, the future Kaiser Wilhelm of Germany, Prince (later King) Edward of England, and many others had been willing to pay dearly to enjoy her company and her bed. Though nominally a dancer, she was much more famous (and reputedly talented) as a jewel-bedecked hetaera. The waspish critic of a New York newspaper had once written sarcastically of her performance, "We have seen Otéro sing, we have heard her dance." She may not have impressed the critics with her terpsichorean skills, but she was unexcelled at playing the quintessential femme fatale.[11]

In 1891 La Belle Otéro was in London playing at the Empire Music Hall the same months Sandow was performing at the Alhambra Music Hall. Thinking of herself as the ideal sensual woman, the exotic dancer resolved to see her counterpart of masculine beauty in the flesh—the whole flesh. "I had heard about Sandow for a long time and was anxious to meet him," wrote Otéro many years after the event. "I sent him a note, but he never answered, even though he certainly knew who I was." When she did not hear from him, she assumed he was one of those rare animals, a man who refused to philander. "I made up my mind that if Sandow wouldn't come to me, I'd go to him." Accordingly, she cut short her performance at the Empire one night and rushed to Sandow's theater where she was able to catch part of his act. Seeing him appears to have been something of a revelation to her. "What a physique!" she exclaimed. "What muscles! My God! I never saw anything like it before in my life.

"I ran back to his dressing room and got there while he was taking his bows. When he entered the room he recognized me, of course, and I know he was flattered that I'd come. But, as I found out, there were scores of other women waiting for him outside the stage door that night, and every night, I'm sure.

"I told him I thought his act was marvelous and that I'd like him to join me and a few of my friends at a small supper party I was giving that evening in my hotel. He said he was happy to accept and would be along just as soon as he was dressed. I nearly told him he needn't bother."

But unknown to the strongman, Otéro had other more devious designs. She had never planned any dinner party at all. She had one goal, and that was to get Sandow into her rooms . . . alone. "I'd made myself as glamorous as I could, and I felt that even if Herr Sandow was a faithful husband he might, for once, forget his wife wherever she was."

She concludes her story sadly, revealing the real reason for their failed tryst. "It was all over very soon. I should have taken the cue when Herr Sandow refused to drink my fine champagne and asked for milk. Faugh! But hindsight is so superior to foresight. Poor fellow! He must have had a bad hour or two with me before I sent him back to the young man he was living with."

Was this merely the pique of a woman scorned? It is a well-documented fact that Otéro did not scruple to tell lies when she thought it would benefit her. Was this little anecdote a figment of the

Spanish dancer's imagination? But if so, why tell it at all? After all, it is not very flattering to the lady—at least it does not show her in the most favorable light. As usual, there remain only questions, seldom answers.

Ironically, Otéro was not the only femme fatale who was spurned by Sandow. In 1892, while traveling through Paris, Sandow caught the eye of another "grande horizontale," Émilienne des Lançons, who invited the strongman to her house for an intimate tête-à-tête. But the evening did not end as she had hoped, and her guest left a short time later with the courtesan's somewhat bedraggled virtue unbesmirched by Sandow. Émilienne, however, felt insulted, so she devised a mischievous and mortifying revenge.

Several days later Sandow was rehearsing some of his stunts at a local music hall when Émilienne swept in, recognized the object of her unrequited lust, and immediately beamed upon him a derisive smile. She then held up the little finger of her right hand and wiggled it while shouting sarcastically, "Bonjour, Sandow!" Sandow at once bowed politely and doffed his hat. Holding the headpiece in both hands, and imitating the gesture and teasing intonation of the spurned woman, he directed the vast opening of his hat toward her upraised little finger and replied smilingly, "Bonjour, Émilienne!"[12]

Despite his close escape from the clutches of Otéro and Émilienne, Sandow was destined to get into more serious trouble over women during his stay in America. On July 1, close to the end of his run, "There was," as a newspaper luridly reported, "a scene at the Casino stage door which the patrons did not see, and which, if they had known of it, would have proved enough of an incentive for them to have purchased a reserved place on the spot." An agitated young lady stepped up to Sandow and said roughly, "I want to speak to you." Sandow brushed her aside brusquely, but before the man could get away, the woman took out a rawhide whip and lashed the strongman viciously three times across the face. A policeman, who had been conveniently near, promptly arrested the infuriated woman. The next day Sandow decided to prosecute his assailant and have her charged with assault and battery as well as a more serious crime: blackmail.[13]

The lady in question was Sarah E. Swift, internationally known for her performances as "Lurline, the Water Queen," the naughty toast of two continents. Lurline had made a vaudeville career for herself out of the unlikely talent of holding her breath under water in a large aquarium. The real secret of her popularity, however was her shapely body which was revealed in all its costume-clinging splendor as soon as she was immersed. No one seemed to care that she could stay under water for a full two and a half minutes.

The reasons behind her attack reveal a particularly sordid side to Sandow's character. According to the Water Queen, Sandow owed her £11 16 shillings. When the strongman was working in a Belgian circus, he asked the woman for a loan in order to purchase a suit of fashionable clothing. After receiving the money, Sandow absconded with his erstwhile partner, François. The two men left for Italy without bothering to repay Sandow's benefactor.

It was during this stay in Italy that Attila sent for him, and then later engineered Sandow's victory over Sampson and Cyclops. The two men eventually talked the pretty but gullible Water Queen into loaning Sandow even more money, for she asserted to the New York newspapers that it was she who put up stakes of £500 for the contest between the men in London.

The most damning aspect of her accusations came when the angry and bitter woman revealed Sandow's duplicity in his supposedly great victory over Sampson. "We paid a man named Schlag £20 to make chains and coins of brittle material," she claimed. When the night of the Sampson/Sandow trial came, Lurline positioned herself carefully in the audience. When a set of true and sturdy chains was passed around for spectators to test, Lurline was on hand and deftly substituted the specially prepared chains for the real ones.

No wonder Sampson was so surprised when his challenger managed to snap the chains. His fury was the anger of the trickster tricked. Lurline claimed that Sandow "had such a guilty conscience that he has never attempted to collect the £500 from Sampson." So Sandow had good reason for wanting Lurline kept quiet for as long as possible. A long stay in jail must have seemed the answer to his prayers. Thus, Sandow had the woman prosecuted for blackmail, claiming that the money she demanded was to keep her from revealing his professional secrets.

When the day of the trial arrived, it proved to be bitter and brief. First, Sandow denied all the charges vehemently. But then, the Water Queen's lawyers sprang an unpleasant surprise. They told the judge they had contacted Attila, who was then performing in Paris, and he had agreed to come to New York to testify against his former protégé. Vindictive in the extreme, Attila was prepared to swear that Lurline's testimony was completely correct. He was also going to tell the court and, more importantly, the press "many things about Sandow's career equally unpalatable to the strong man."[14]

The judge granted the Water Queen a continuance until mid-September to allow enough time for Attila to cross the Atlantic. In return, she agreed to admit to assaulting Sandow and was expected to pay a fine.

When Attila finally arrived in America, he was still furious over the way things had turned out. The excessively litigious Sandow reacted to this crisis in a way that had always served him well. He had his former master hauled before a judge and jury. The courtroom journalists were quick to pick up on the venomous animosity between the two men. "If looks could kill, if scowls were clubs," one newsman wrote of the trial, "Sandow and Attila would today be corpses, dead with a thousand stabs or battered beyond recognition."

Still reeling from Attila's speedy trip to New York, the desperate Sandow had Attila arrested for sending a rude, threatening letter. In the malicious missive, Attila reportedly called Sandow a "blackguard," a "clog of quicksilver," and other choice epithets that promised to burn a hole through the letter paper. In reply to the charge, the older man claimed that Sandow had him arrested simply because he wanted to avoid an embarrassing weightlifting match with "Romulus," Attila's latest strength discovery.[15]

After all the high emotions that were stirred up by the various trials, the results were somewhat anticlimactic. Sandow quietly settled with both Lurline and Attila. Somehow harmony was restored, and all the participants in this sordid exercise were satisfied. In time, the bad feelings which had festered between the two former partners cleared up and the wounds slowly healed. Years later the two men would become friends again. As fate would have it, Attila found that he liked New York so much that he decided to make the city his home. He opened a gymnasium and was proud to admit that he was the "Tutor and Trainer of the Invincible Sandow" to anyone who would care to listen.

As exciting as all of this was, perhaps there were other reasons for Attila's hasty trip to New York. According to a later article in the *Police Gazette*, "Attila would never have come to America but for the timely advice of Richard K. Fox, editor of the *Gazette*, who met the strongman abroad and advised him to come over here. He [Attila] says it was the best advice he ever received, and that by heeding it, he laid the foundation of his fortune." So perhaps much of the subsequent theatrics at the trial might have been produced less from motives of pure choler and more for the entertainment of the public and the publicity it would provide the main characters.[16]

Whatever his reasons for coming to America, Attila continued to train strongmen. In May of 1896, at the age of fifty-four, he married Rosa Sanders, a young lady he was coaching to become a professional strongwoman. Their daughter Grace later married muscleman Siegmund Klein, thus beginning a lineage of strength.[17] Attila's ideas on training and weightlifting were subsequently published around the world and became the basis for the sport we know today. So perhaps if it had not been for Lurline and her little horsewhip, the history of bodybuilding might have gone off in a completely different direction.

Attila thus had his gym and small revenge and Lurline had her money; but ironically, while these two antagonists were sorting out their problems, Sandow's destiny was being shaped in Chicago, halfway across the continent, by men he never met. The strongman was soon to find other triumphs and other opportunities, but his greatest stroke of luck was to find an agent-manager fresh from the Midwest who understood how to package him as a show business superstar.

Despite its urban veneer, nineteenth-century Chicago still retained the brash, raw feel of a boomtown. After Mrs. O'Leary's cow had done its work, much of burned-out Chicago had been rebuilt. Mixed in with the pungent aroma from the stockyards was the smell of new mortar and fresh brick. It was nevertheless a thrilling perfume in the nostrils of the city's business leaders; it smelled of progress, success, and money. In order to garner even further glory, a group of railroad, wheat, and beef barons had banded together early in the decade in a bold, energetic consortium that was determined to change forever the way the world viewed America and the city on the lake.

These midwestern moguls had captured a signal honor for the metropolis: out of all the communities in the United States, Chicago was chosen to be the site of the biggest celebration the world had yet seen. It was to be the "World's Columbian Exposition," a commemoration on a truly grand scale of the four hundredth anniversary of the discovery of America, and Eugen Sandow was fated to play an integral role in this exhibition.

When the plans for the fair were laid before one of the financiers of the event for the first time, he exclaimed, "Oh gentlemen, this is a dream!"[18] And that pretty fairly remained the reaction of those who saw the real thing. There were over six hundred acres of sparkling white palaces, canals, lagoons, parks, and fountains. From the top of the gigantic Ferris wheel—the first one ever constructed—the visitor saw the noble and breathtaking vista of the "Great White City": there was the Court of Honor, the long colonnades of the Manufactures Building, the Palace of Fine Arts with its stately dome, the Electrical Building filled with the mysteries of the new power source, and all the pavilions of the foreign powers—even the emperor of Japan and the sultan of Turkey had arranged for buildings.

Everywhere the carnival spirit and an overall feeling of wonder permeated the atmosphere. Little Egypt wiggled and hoochy-kooched nightly on the Midway Plaisance, the amusement section of the fair. Even the states got into a sort of friendly rivalry. Montana contributed a monumental statue modeled by the buxom actress Ada Rehan, made of pure silver. Not to be outdone, California countered with a huge knight in full armor made entirely of prunes.[19]

"They say," wrote curmudgeonly old Henry James, "one should sell all one has and mortgage one's soul to go there, it is esteemed such a revelation of beauty. People burst into tears, cast away all sin and baseness, and grow religious under its influence."[20] Less sarcastic and more representative of the feelings of the twenty-seven million people who visited the fair were the comments of British writer Sir Walter Besant. Overwhelmed by its grandeur, he admitted, "Nowhere, at any time, has there been presented to the world any group of buildings so entirely beautiful in themselves and in their arrangement, as this group at Chicago, which they call the World's Fair."[21]

The great influx of people drawn by the fair not only needed bed and board, they also required a little post-fair diversion. The job of providing a pleasant evening's entertainment fell upon the ample shoulders of one of Chicago's most prominent arbiters of musical tastes: Florenz Ziegfeld, Sr. Though overshadowed today by his more famous offspring, the older Ziegfeld was something of a local celebrity in his own day. Shortly after he arrived from Germany, Ziegfeld awarded himself the august title of Doctor and then founded a musical college. Over the years this institution gained many pupils and a good reputation among Chicago's artistic cognoscenti.[22] It was no surprise, therefore, that Dr. Ziegfeld was appointed director of musical events for the exposition. He had great and elaborate plans for the amusement of the visitors: he would have nothing but the best—the best hall and the best European performers. But this was not to be. Just as his preparations were being completed for his theater, it caught fire and burned to the ground. Thus, Dr. Ziegfeld had to start all over again. This time he chose to refit the old National Guard Armory Building in Lake Park. He would turn the huge, barnlike building into a great theater. He called the new hall "The Trocadero."[23]

Unfortunately, since he was overburdened with the job of turning the armory into a proper theater, Dr. Ziegfeld did not have the time to go off in search of talent to fill it. He decided to send his twenty-six-year-old son, Florenz Jr., to go in his place. That would prove to be a fateful decision for all concerned.

Ziegfeld Sr. had long tried to interest his son in the classics of the concert hall. Among other indignities, young Flo had been forced to take a job in his father's dreary musical college. The doctor attempted to immerse his son in a sea of whining violins and mournful oboes. He even made Florenz the institute's treasurer. Young Ziegfeld's heart was with the glittery variety acts of the popular theater, however, and not with classical music.

The young man had already tried his hand at several crude forms of show business. At the age of twenty-two, he staged an extravaganza at a local park which he called "The Dancing Ducks of Denmark." Though he claimed the birds were imported, they actually came from a local poultry farm. Visitors handed over fifteen cents to witness the ducks dance. While a sprightly tune was played, the creatures quickly lifted their feet in time to the music while quacking loudly. Investigation by two skeptical spectators uncovered the reason for their herky-jerky movements: Ziegfeld had placed the hapless birds on an iron grid which was lit from underneath by gas jets which warmed the platform giving the ducks no alternative but to dance. When informed, the authorities closed the show.

Ziegfeld later exhibited a large, beautifully lit fish tank which was absolutely empty except for the water that filled it. Those who had paid to get in were promised a look at "The Invisible Brazilian Fish." This show was also speedily shut down.[24]

Dr. Ziegfeld must have experienced more than a few misgivings when he nervously bade his son farewell in the winter of 1892. Florenz was departing for Europe with big plans for his father's Trocadero Theater. He had received strict instructions on the type of acts he was to seek out, but instead of hiring the classical musicians his father wanted, Flo quickly engaged every likely variety act he could find in the music halls of London, Paris, and Berlin. Papa had particularly asked that his son bring back the great German conductor Hans von Bülow, but in his place Flo hired something called the "Bülow Military Band" of Hamburg, a decidedly inferior group. Among others, he engaged "The Great Zanzic," who was reputed to produce "startling and unaccountable phenomena by invisible agencies." The Three Marvelles, billed as "grotesque eccentrics," were chosen to bounce across the Trocadero stage, and the Mühlemann Swiss Mountaineer Trio from Interlaken were to yodel and clog dance nightly.

When young Flo returned to Chicago, Papa Ziegfeld was alarmed to find that instead of Europe's finest musicians, he had a lot of music hall turns ready to disgrace him if they ever set foot on a stage. Ziegfeld Sr. shot out a furious barrage of telegrams to every musical agent he could think of, ordering a second group of musicians more to his liking to come to Chicago at once. But a drawback to his assemblage was immediately apparent when their performances began: the players were definitely second-rate. Because of this the audiences stayed away. Papa soon found himself some $30,000 in the hole. It did not take much of this to persuade Sr. that Jr. might have had the right idea after all, so soon Flo's variety acts started leaking into the program. Happily, business picked up somewhat, but both men realized that what they needed was a headliner, a major attraction in order to perk up the bill.[25]

Once again a worried Ziegfeld Sr. saw his son off. Florenz was headed for New York, looking for the Trocadero's main attraction, but this time he was determined not to disappoint his father. Thus it was that the youthful agent found himself sitting in the Casino Theater on an impossibly hot evening checking out the thin talent he encountered in *Adonis*. He must have felt quite discouraged as the curtain dropped on the uninspired, listlessly acted play. But when the curtain went up again with Sandow on a pedestal, adrenalin coursed through the fledgling manager's body. The youthful entrepreneur was out of his seat and on his way backstage almost before Sandow had lowered the first barbell. Ziegfeld had found his headliner. His luck had presented him with a perfect subject to glorify.

As Ziegfeld raced down the aisle, he was surely aware of the stir Sandow had caused among the feminine members of the sparse audience. He must have noticed how the ladies stopped their chattering and stared at the stage in admiration and amazement when Sandow revealed his eye-catching muscles. Though they were few in numbers, the women responded enthusiastically to the strongman. His thrilling persona produced a sensation even on a languid and sultry night. Ziegfeld surely heard the unmistakable sounds of feminine pleasure throughout the hall, and he shrewdly assessed the value of those fluttering female hearts. Despite his relative inexperience, Ziegfeld recognized a hot theatrical property when he saw one. To him, Sandow represented money in the bank.[26]

It is not known exactly what Ziegfeld said to Sandow backstage, but it must not have taken much convincing to make the performer realize that he could be managed better by the energetic agent than he had been by Abbey. The next morning Ziegfeld showed up at the theater and announced to Abbey and Aronson that he would take Sandow off their hands. It was an offer gratefully and quickly accepted. As for Sandow, he settled with Ziegfeld for 10 percent of the box office receipts. None of the participants, except Ziegfeld, ever dreamed that through the new agent's skillful management Sandow would earn far in excess of the $600 per week Abbey had been paying him.[27] Sandow had a few remaining engagements to complete, but as soon as these had been satisfied he set off for Chicago and immortality.

While awaiting Sandow's arrival, Ziegfeld was hard at work preparing the way. The tireless impresario papered the town with posters of the scantily clad muscleman and placed rather lurid advertisements in local theater programs to tantalize the public. He also made up highly romanticized and largely fictitious biographies of Sandow to catch the media's eye. "Our city is entitled to the best," crowed one of these notices, "more especially in the year of Columbian celebration. We have a large variety of appreciable entertainments, and it is but fitting and just to crown our most sanguine expectations with exhibitions by this powerful giant, whose hobby it seems is to toy with a thousand pound ball, and lift a double team of draft horses 'merely to keep his hand in.' "[28] Ziegfeld's statements about Sandow became ever more extravagant as the strongman's arrival approached. "Sandow," one notice screamed, "stands out against the background of history like some great Olympian giant—a veritable Colossus of Rhodes."[29] In an era of overblown rhetoric and fantastic claims, Ziegfeld stopped at nothing to publicize his greatest bankable attraction.

The Trocadero Theater was packed to the ceiling on the night of August 1, 1893, when Sandow was slated to appear in the inaugural performances of his Chicago run—a testament to Ziegfeld's skill and persistence. There was even a contingent of the Windy City's upper crust—and the blue-blooded society matrons waited just as impatiently for a glimpse of Sandow as the plebeians in the balconies.

Promptly at eight o'clock the curtain went up on a series of minor acts. Acrobats, dancers, and singers all came on stage and performed, then went off. At last, Sandow's great friend Martinus Sieveking mounted the podium and the orchestra struck up a lively march composed especially for the occasion. The curtain was raised and Sandow began his turn with a flourish of muscles. Posing, weightlifting, the human barbell stunt, and a spectacular harness lift rounded out his act. It was clear that Sandow had enthralled the entire audience, even the stuffy, nouveau riche patricians, for at the end of the performance Ziegfeld Jr. walked in front of the footlights and made a daring proposal. Any woman willing to donate $300 to charity would be allowed to come to the strongman's private dressing room and feel his muscles. Mrs. Potter Palmer and Mrs. George Pullman immediately stood up and made their way backstage. The next day when they reported to their many prominent friends about this pleasant experience, it was obvious that Sandow's reputation was assured. The public flocked to see the handsome strongman in ever increasing numbers.[30]

Quick to cash in on a good thing, a neighboring theater, The

Grotto, imported its own man of iron, Sebastian Miller, but no one could really compete with the magnificent Sandow. Even Miller's bombast, horseshoe twisting, and a $1,000 challenge to all comers to duplicate his feats on stage came to naught, and he was forced to give up and leave town.[31] In his wake came another rival, none other than Sandow's old opponent, Charles Sampson. Blown in by an ill wind from who knows where, Sampson made some loud noises about a possible rematch between himself and the man who beat him at the London Aquarium, but thankfully—at least for Sampson—nothing came of it. Sampson could do little more than to hurl a few invective comments at Sandow. He called him "a Philistine," but that was tantamount to firing a pistol at a battleship. Sampson soon gave up and left the Grotto Theater too.[32]

Thanks to Ziegfeld's Machiavellian public relations, Sandow found himself courted, written about, and fawned over. Hardly a day went by without at least some notice of him appearing in the papers. The drama critic for the *Chicago Daily News,* Amy Leslie, took a stroll with him through a wooded dell on the fairgrounds. She was surprised to find that the strongman was actually a gentle, happy fellow, fond of nature's beauty. On their walk, Sandow paused to pick part of a snapdragon blossom, explaining to Miss Leslie, "Now, when we were little in Germany, we took these blossoms and pressed them so, and if the mouth of the flower opened, that meant our mothers were calling us to come home." But at that moment an irate guard came up and destroyed their sylvan idyll. He explained that Sandow had broken the park rules by plucking a flower. Foolishly, the guard roughly grabbed Sandow's elbow. The German athlete reacted by picking up the startled man and holding him at arm's length, examining him as if he were some curious specimen of Chicago fauna. At Miss Leslie's pleadings, he finally put the guard down. Ziegfeld made much of this little incident, quickly pointing out that however ferocious he might act on stage, Sandow was really a gentle giant, equally comfortable with a bouquet of flowers or a heavy barbell in his hand.[33]

As he proved again and again, Ziegfeld was the consummate master at milking every available situation for as much publicity as possible. One of his greatest triumphs involved the famous rolling chairs of the fair. These were elaborate wheelchairs that were available to invalids and weaklings so that they could enjoy the exposition in comfort. Ziegfeld talked Sandow into seeing the sights in one of these. When the athlete remonstrated, saying that it would never do for a strongman to be seen in one of the contraptions, Ziegfeld did his best to soothe him. "Oh, they don't know you yet," he assured him. "You get in and try it."

But the clever manager had arranged for two things previously, both concealed from the strongman: first, the person chosen to push the chair was a scrawny hunchback; and second, newspaper reporters were strategically stationed along their route. The next day the papers ran the story complete with ludicrous illustrations under the headline "The Strong Man Too Strong to Walk."[34]

Ziegfeld's canny manipulation was also apparent in Sandow's name being connected with the famous turn-of-the-century sex symbol Lillian Russell. The sultry musical star had come to Chicago for the same reason Sandow had: to perform at the exposition. Although the singer and the strongman were seen together often enough for the newspapers to mention the pair and even to link them romantically, there was never anything really serious between them. But thanks to the athlete's manager, their friendship was soon the talk of both Chicago and New York. There was even a Ziegfeld-inspired rumor that the noted beauty and the handsome strongman were soon to wed. Colonel William d'Alton Mann, author of a New York gossip column, continued the speculation by remarking that Sandow "has given audiences to a number of beautiful Chicago girls within the last week or so, and as he has managed to quite capture most of their hearts, why not the airy and erstwhile fairy Lillian's? I have no comment to make on the match should it come, so to speak, but protest in all seriousness that the couple would look simply magnificent marching up the aisle of the church together."[35]

The percentage of truth Ziegfeld injected into this propaganda is hard to gauge, but one small clue is found in the inscription the American beauty wrote on a photographic portrait that she gave to Sandow in 1893. It reads, "With Mr. Sandow's permission, I am yours cordially, Lillian Russell."[36] This is obviously not the language of lovers. But that was not what the public wanted to hear, so rumor and hearsay continued to connect the two whenever possible.

Another of Ziegfeld's successful innovations was a change in Sandow's stage costume. Prior to this, he had appeared before the public clad in a blue top and discreet pink tights that covered him from neck to toe. It was his manager's idea to discard the tights and to have him appear on stage wearing nothing but his brief jersey.[37] We may be sure that the ladies were definitely pleased with this shocking and novel change.

Fortunately for posterity, there was one person who not only got to see Sandow in the flesh but got to work with him too. This was Al Treloar. Later he became a well-known vaudeville strongman in his own right, but at this point in his life he was lucky to have any sort of job at all. Nineteen-year-old Treloar had been part of an acrobatic duet that was successful enough to have been booked into the Chicago fair, but just before he was to open his act, his partner ran out on him. Somehow Treloar met Sandow and was invited to stay with the show. He was with Sandow's act for two seasons and was thus afforded a wonderful opportunity to scrutinize both Sandow and Ziegfeld at close range. "Sandow was tops when it came to posing," wrote Treloar some fifty years after the event, "and that's why his reputation has not diminished with the passing years."[38]

Treloar was also impressed by Sandow's keen mind. He noted that when Sandow came to America he could hardly speak English, but in a short time his vocabulary and pronunciation were considerably improved, though they were far from perfect. Sandow's charm, intelligence, and panache clearly had registered on a great many people by this time.

Treloar once made the mistake of trying to impress the Great Sandow with his own lifting ability. He was backstage before one of the strongman's performances and was feeling particularly frisky. He decided to show Sandow what he was capable of. The young man made sure his employer was watching, and then he lifted a 240-pound bell that was used in the show. After he had replaced the heavy barbell, he was met by an agitated Sandow. "Vell," he remarked sarcastically, "I now hope you iss satisfaction."[39] He never forgave Treloar's upstaging audacity.

Despite his early association with Sandow, Treloar's big break as a performer took place in 1904 when he won a physique contest in Madison Square Garden. He then traveled around the country performing under the name "Albert, the Perfect Man" with his wife, Edna Tempest.

Al Treloar is one of the most important of the early physique stars primarily because he took the techniques of scientific bodybuilding to America's West Coast. In 1894, after his stint with Sandow, Treloar attended Harvard University where he took a degree in physical education. Eventually, he applied for the job of director of physical education at the prestigious Los Angeles Athletic Club in 1907. He remained at this post for forty-two years.

An intelligent and careful observer, Treloar had a good understanding of Sandow's performances. Because he witnessed Sandow's shows at close hand, Treloar was able to make some keen judgments about them. He noticed, for example, that Sandow's stage demeanor was influenced by Prussian military formality. "When Sandow stepped forth as a full-fledged 'strong-man,'" Treloar wrote, "he naturally fell into the [Prussian] way, partially at least, of the short stepping, foot stamping and exaggeratedly erect standing of the military style."[40]

Another thing that stood out in the memories of people who saw him at this time was Sandow's beautiful, glowing skin. One spectator who saw Sandow in Chicago recalled that his skin "was velvety and most extraordinary. I do not think it had ever been well tanned in the sun—but at all events it was a transparent white without blemish. He shaved the hair, and the skin reflected the light with a glow."[41]

Perhaps it was partly because of his glowing, silky skin that Sandow was so energetically pursued by the ladies. His photos sold extremely well no matter where he performed, and it is quite obvious that many of these pictures were especially posed for what used to be termed "the palpitant pulse trade." The muscleman's popularity was not just confined to matinee girls either. A French visitor to America, Paul Bourget, noted with surprise that even the wealthy society ladies of Newport displayed Sandow's nude portrait in their opulent sitting rooms. Whatever the reason, almost all the accounts of Sandow's theatrical appearances contain descriptions of the crowds of anxious beauties who crowded around the stage door, attempting to catch the eye of the handsome strongman.[42]

Sandow's obvious sexual appeal and nude display are all the more surprising when one considers the moral climate of the nation at the time. The United States had bred an amazing number of cranks and bluenoses who were quite adamant about concealing the naked human form. When the ubiquitous Mrs. Trollope visited an exhibition at the Pennsylvania Academy of Fine Arts a generation earlier, she found a screen in front of the room containing nude antique statuary. A female attendant told her that she could enter, as all ladies could, "when there be no gentlemen watching them." The acerbic English visitor found this restriction to be patently absurd.

Even at the turn of the century, the self-appointed arbiter of purity Anthony Comstock had declared that "nude paintings and statues are the decoration of infamous resorts, and the law-abiding American will never admit them to the sacred confines of the home." It was clear that many Yankees would agree with him.[43]

The situation was, if anything, more prudish in Britain. At a Liverpool track meet in the latter half of the century, a contestant whose dress was considered too revealing was forced to wear a coat in the walking race. Though the athlete was fully covered, the *Athletic Review* still sniffed indignantly, "It is by no means an edifying sight to see competitors come to the scratch in tights or fleshings and scanty drawers."[44]

The appearance of Sandow's nude portrait in wealthy society girls' bedrooms thus seems all the more surprising. Those pictures clearly represented cracks in the Victorian wall of prudery. Still, there are a couple of possible explanations for the presence of Sandow's image in the rooms. First, the middle-class morality expressed so eloquently by Comstock did not really apply to the American aristocracy. These were the children of the worldly, cultured elite who had been exposed to the freer attitudes of Europe. Although carefully chaperoned through their adolescent years, most girls were very familiar with the statuary and artwork that was so abhorred by Comstock and his confederates.

Second, girls had long been in the habit of collecting pictures of their favorite male idols, and Sandow was simply one of a long list of theatrical personalities who occupied the daydreams of American girls. Additionally, since Sandow was posed as a classical statue, his nudity was considered faintly educational—a chaste tableau vivant recalling the glory that was Greece. Besides, Sandow sported an adequate fig leaf that covered all the offending regions of his physique. Thus tutors and guardians were inclined to look with a kindlier eye on that which might shock a later parent.

It comes as some surprise to learn that images of naked men in nineteenth-century publications were probably not quite so rare as many moderns might think. The historian Roberta J. Park has noted the profusion of nude images in the American press. "By the 1890s," she writes, "it was not at all unusual to find photographs of seminude athletes and illustrations of fig-leaf adorned males in a host of books and periodicals."[45] Even so, the author detects a double standard. Pictures of men in skimpy attire might have gotten past the censors, but corresponding pictures of half-clad females would have been unthinkable.

Few of Sandow's sporting and theatrical contemporaries chose to pose in the nude, but they had tried plenty of other equally shocking antics. After all, the Victorian public half expected athletes to carry on outrageously. Drinking, gaming, and philandering were accepted patterns of behavior for wrestlers, prizefighters, and other members of "fast" society. Sandow almost certainly fell into this mind-set with particular eagerness, especially during his years with Ziegfeld. Like other sporting gentlemen, Sandow was expected to dress in absurdly elegant suits and to affect the manners and breeding of a slumming aristocrat. It was not long before stories of Sandow's amorous adventures were making the rounds. With Ziegfeld's help he had become a symbol of power and exaggerated sexual potency.

Perhaps the most prominent of the Victorian sportsmen who shocked the public with their antics was the boxer John L. Sullivan. *Police Gazette* editor Richard K. Fox reported his excesses with particular relish. According to the pink-paged magazine, Sullivan was a depraved, oversexed, Irish bully who went on drunken benders that lasted several weeks and left the champion trembling with the D.T.'s. Sullivan was commonly dosed with a mixture of tea and whiskey during his marathon fights, and when during the forty-fifth round of one combat he began to spew up the contents of his battered stomach, one smart aleck noted that the champion "rejected the tea but held the whiskey."

Sullivan's successor as champion, significantly nicknamed "Gentleman" Jim Corbett, made a name for himself as an elegant man about town. Even more scandalous was the talented but unfortunate black champion, Jack Johnson, who delighted in shocking Caucasian sensibilities by dressing nattily, escorting flamboyant white prostitutes, and driving expensive automobiles.[46]

Although Sandow could drink and cat around with the randiest of his sporting rivals, he never really fit into the traditional role of an athlete. This confusion of identity conceals a more problematic question. If an athlete is one who pits his muscles and skill against others, then the professional Hercules does not fall into that category. Sandow and the other strongmen of the stage had all developed their bodies beyond the normal muscularity of their fellows. This they accomplished by a regimen of exercise and progressive weight training. They made their livings, however, by demonstrating feats of lifting and balance rather than by formalized competitions with each other. While there were occasional theatrical contests among rival strongmen, these were aimed more at increasing box office revenues than any measurement of pure strength.

On the other hand, bodybuilding and physique development have always been by their very nature different from other sports. Physique competitions are of course more subjective than other sporting endeavors. In a bodybuilding contest there is no goal line to cross, no projectile to throw, no clear-cut game to win. There are, however, as many forms of competition as there are competitors. Physique athletes flex in comparison with their fellow contestants, but most of all they work alone in a solitary quest to perfect their musculature, laboring constantly to correct what they perceive as their physiological defects. Their greatest challengers, therefore, are not the ones standing next to them on the posing dais; rather, their most persistent rivals are the ones they see in the mirror.

In 1951 W. Arthur Long, a former employee of Sandow, considered the question of whether his boss was really an athlete or not. His answer is as probably as close as anyone can come to the truth. Long theorized that it all depends on one's definition of the word *athlete*. If it means someone who trains for some special event, then Sandow was certainly not an athlete. "But if by athlete we mean what we knew

Sandow to be—immensely strong, capable of lifting great weights, and performing other very out-of-the-ordinary things, then he WAS an athlete and a great one."[47]

So Sandow and his music hall rivals were thus neither fish nor fowl since they could not be thought of as athletes or theatrical performers. They were clearly both. Sandow obviously enjoyed both the glamor of the stage and the solitary work of the gymnasium. So perhaps it is best to consider the vaudeville strongmen as Sandow did himself: as "theatrical athletes."

Regardless of whether he was an athletic or a theatrical star, some aspects of Sandow's life were blown out of proportion by enthusiastic journalists, and the strongman's philandering was apparently one of these traits. One contemporary witness questions whether Sandow's womanizing had been exaggerated or not. Hunter McLean wrote, "I did not see anything at all which would have led me to suspect he played around with the ladies." Still, McLean wisely admits that he might have been mistaken. He concluded, "I know Mr. Ziegfeld told me that they did run after him. But Mr. Ziegfeld himself knew something about both men and women and also was himself an artist."[48]

Another person who knew something of men, women, and artists was the well-known actor Otis Skinner. He relates an amusing incident which occurred during the exposition. Like so many others, Skinner had been drawn to Chicago by the clarion call of ready work. He was engaged to play Orlando in Shakespeare's *As You Like It* in an outdoor theater called "The Sylvan Dell." In one of the scenes of the play, Orlando has a wrestling match with a character known as "Charles, the Wrestler." The producers of this spectacle thought it would be a novel idea to invite Sandow to play the part of the muscular pugilist. "When the proposition was put to him," Skinner reports, "he warmed immediately to the idea":

> "Me? I act; I play anyt'ing in de worl'."
>
> Then rather suspiciously: "Who I wrestle?" He was informed that his opponent was an actor named Skinner, a person of no great physical prowess.
>
> "He's strong man?"
>
> "Well, not exactly. You see, in this play you and he have this bout, and he throws you, and—"
>
> "He what!!"
>
> "He throws you—it's in the play."
>
> "Look 'ere! See dose people?" and Sandow pointed to a long queue at the Trocadero box-office. "Who dey come to see? Me, Sandow, stronges' man in de worl'. Nobody can t'row me."

"But that's the way it's in this play."
"Dat's all right. You change de play—I wrestle."

And that is how Sandow missed his chance to become an actor in a Shakespearean play. His name was taken off the programs and the billboards, and the entire production was postponed until another Charles could be located. Perhaps it was just as well that Sandow bowed out, since the play received only lukewarm notices when it actually went on a couple of weeks later.[49]

But Sandow was becoming a unique presence in his own right by this time. This was partly due to his ability to make himself the center of attention no matter where he went or how crowded the room. One of his methods was particularly effective in taverns. Feeling successful and secure in Chicago, Sandow decided to acquire Sultan, a 200-pound German boarhound. When Sandow entered a barroom, he would sometimes take the beast with him. It had been trained to stand on its hind legs and rest its forepaws upon the bar, and in doing so became as tall as a good-sized man. Sultan must have startled more than a few tipsy patrons when he was spied gleefully lapping up a large, frothy glass of lager.[50]

Sandow also loved to display his strength and often created amicable havoc with his destructive escapades. When he was particularly delighted with his high-spirited shenanigans, the strongman would emit an uncharacteristic falsetto giggle—a sure sign that some boyish prank had just been perpetrated.[51] Perhaps he had just broken the porcelain butter dish into many pieces, or more spectacularly, bent an ordinary teaspoon with one hand, rolling the handle inward until it filled the bowl of the spoon. Sandow would then give these out as souvenirs. The athlete would often delight in squeezing the backs of chairs until they broke into splinters, or if he was feeling particularly rambunctious, he would punch his fist through the bottom of a cane chair. To any self-respecting maitre d', that soprano laughter must have been about as welcome as the measles.[52]

Of course, all of this was just more grist for Ziegfeld's publicity mill. Anything that kept his man in the public eye was money in the bank. Thanks in part to all the favorable press, Sandow was pulling in magnificent box office receipts on a nightly basis. After six weeks, the Ziegfelds were able to divide the handsome sum of $30,000, and by the time Sandow's run had ended, Papa Ziegfeld literally wept with joy when he contemplated all the greenbacks that had accumulated.[53]

It was wealth of a different sort that became the ultimate legacy of the Columbian Exposition. The fair exposed vast numbers of Americans to European and world culture, it brought together in one place many of the varied aspects of our own uniquely American culture, and it pointed the way to the future by displaying the new, progressive technologies that were destined to revolutionize the way Americans lived.

It was no accident that Sandow appeared in Chicago at the same time that philosopher and historian Henry Adams was wandering amazedly among the pounding dynamos of the fair. The young scholar would soon see in the gleaming and powerful machinery a new symbol of the modern world, just as Sandow would come to represent a new Adam to populate it. The force of steel and steam were joined for the first time to the force of sinew and will in a bold symbolic union there on the shores of Lake Michigan. Thus, both dynamo and muscleman had played their respective roles.[54] To perceptive minds, the lesson had been proffered.

By November of 1893 most of the fair's plays and performances had closed down. With the first chill of autumn, the gondolas and rolling chairs and exhibits had all been taken away. The grand palaces and tree-covered walkways, the foreign pavilions and midway attractions, these all stood mute and empty. The Great White City had served its function. It had thrilled and amazed its visitors, and now it only waited for the wrecker's ball. Only one building, the Palace of Fine Arts was deemed by public vote to be the sole structure which would survive. It can be seen today, still standing where it was erected nearly one hundred years ago.

The Trocadero was the same as the other buildings and attractions. The theater too closed its doors for the last time on November 4. Shortly after that a grateful Florenz Ziegfeld, Jr., presented Sandow with a fine gold medal bearing an inscription testifying to the strongman's record-breaking run.[55] But rather than an ending, the closing of the Trocadero signified a beginning. It was to be the start of a business relationship bigger and better than either man could have possibly imagined at the time.

5

The Tour of America
1894–96

Four days after the closing of his Chicago engagement, Sandow was in the office of C. B. Cline, business manager of Koster & Bial's Music Hall in New York. Modeled on its English counterparts, Koster & Bial's was one of the best and most prestigious variety theaters in America. Every major act touring the United States eventually spent some time at the famous music hall. Mr. Cline signed Sandow to an engagement to begin the next winter. Mr. Bial, obviously glad to have Sandow on the forthcoming season's bill, announced, "When Sandow appeared at the Casino last summer, almost everybody was out of town. His appearance at our house, therefore, will be practically his debut here."[1]

After his visit with the Koster & Bial people, Sandow sailed back to England the very next day. He had been in America for only a few months, and he was returning to Europe a wealthy man. Sandow departed on November 9, but he had to be back in New York by December 16, when he was scheduled to open his new run. While in England, he was able to find someone to put together his first book.

Graeme Mercer Adam was an English writer of no very great pretensions, but he was the one chosen to edit *Sandow's System of Physical Training*, which was published in New York the following year. The book is a gorgeous, baroque volume with hundreds of photographs, drawings, and special features, and it must have been many months in preparation. The work was sold at Sandow's performances and was even advertised in Ziegfeld's stationery. No expense was spared on the volume, and it thus has the undeniable honor of being the most beautiful publication ever produced on the subject of bodybuilding.

While on holiday, Sandow had the leisure to visit with old friends and to make new ones. Before he returned to America, he made a discreet stop in Manchester, where he visited Blanche Brookes, the daughter of a well-known local photographer who had turned out a fine series of pictures of the athlete several years earlier. He and Blanche had met four years previously when Sandow was touring the provincial cities of Britain. Their long-distance friendship was destined to continue secretly and to intensify even after the strongman returned to the New World.[2]

But affairs of the heart could not stop Sandow's rise at this point, and his run at Koster & Bial's began on schedule that winter. Originally he had been booked to perform there for only eight weeks, but because of his very great reception Sandow remained until March 10, nearly twice his original run.

Koster & Bial's, like other American variety theaters, had evolved along lines similar to the British music hall. Originally, both were barroom entertainments, but they gradually grew more refined. Koster & Bial's originally served drinks to customers seated at tables exactly like its English counterparts. As time passed, the vaudeville houses in America grew more and more theaterlike, eventually doing away with the drinking and seating the audience in rows like a legitimate playhouse. Sandow undoubtedly felt at home by now in places like this.[3]

As a headliner, Sandow would have been carefully positioned on the bill. In big-time theaters there were anywhere from seven to nine acts on a program, with five acts for the small-time houses. The usual place for a spectacular "dumb act" (that is, without speaking) like Sandow's would be either just before the first intermission or in the very final spot. Since Sandow was the main attraction of his own company, he appeared at the end, forming a grand finale to the evening's entertainment. Ziegfeld could further affect the star's prestige by making sure that the people who performed on the same bill with him were of excellent quality, but not so stellar that they outshone the real luminary.[4]

While he was performing at Koster & Bial's, Sandow posed for his most famous and finest set of photographs at the noted Sarony studios. The photographer, Napoleon Sarony, was quite an eccentric. His flair for odd costumes, along with his flowing beard and mustache, made him an object of great wonder and attention, especially among artists and bohemians of all stripes. He often delighted in strolling down Broadway in an astrakhan cap, a calfskin vest with the hairy side out, and trousers tucked into highly polished cavalry boots. "No wonder," wrote one historian, "that he was the swell photographer of his day." But it was not his odd appearance nor the real Egyptian mummy that stood guard by the door to his studio that made him such a sought-after artist; it was his skillful and artistic posing that made him society's favorite. Sarony was particularly good at shooting theater people. He had an ability to pose his subjects in a way to bring out their best qualities. It is said that during his career he produced forty thousand photographs of members of the dramatic profession alone—and that is probably the best testimony to his powers as a photographer.[5] This is all the more remarkable when we remember that it was no mean feat to record a satisfactory expression and posture when the usual patron of the gallery had to remain totally immobile for the twenty to thirty seconds required for a good exposure.

Despite all the discomforts, Sandow presented himself to the photographer, eager to have himself immortalized on a cabinet card. He was posed in a variety of different attitudes, both clothed and, save for a fig leaf, nude. He was photographed demonstrating his exercises, flexing his muscles, and in fine and heroic poses. It is probably this last category that shows both Sandow and Sarony to best effect. Sandow swinging his war club, Sandow as the dying gladiator, Sandow as the Farnese Hercules: all these have become classics of early physique photography. Theatrical photographs had become a very profitable business in the nineteenth century, and Sarony was one of the most prosperous of dramatic photographers. Although he sold some pictures at his Union Square studios, most of Sarony's business probably came from middlemen who bought pictures from him at wholesale prices and then resold them in theaters, hotels, or by mail. In 1893 when Sandow originally sat for his portrait, cabinet cards sold to the public for thirty-five cents each and larger formats for as much as five dollars apiece.

Since the market was potentially so great, the photographer would often expose a great number of plates during a session with a big star like Sandow. When Lillie Langtry posed for him, Sarony shot forty poses of her during the first hour of their session and fifty more of her a few days later—all this because he had a contract to supply a Parisian dealer with five hundred photographs of the Jersey Lily. Since the strongman was equal in popularity to many of his female rivals, Sandow's portraits must have been taken with a similar frequency.

The great photographer was, in fact, so taken with Sandow that he included him in a deluxe collection known as *Sarony's Living Pictures*.

These were carefully hand-colored tableaux vivants that were put together into a single opulent volume. Sandow figures prominently in the book posed as Hercules, Samson, and other personifications of strength. These colorful fantasies represented Sarony's desire to combine the art of painting with that of photography in one magnificent creation. Unfortunately, *Living Pictures* is not quite painting and no longer photography, so the collection merely reveals the photographer's confusion over the fundamentals of his medium.[6]

"Photographs of Sandow by Sarony for sale at the Cigar Stand" read the notice in the Koster & Bial's program. The management of the theater was quick to take advantage of the new and exciting photos of the strongman. Also in the program was a careful rundown of every aspect of Sandow's act at the music hall, thereby preserving for us a complete picture of his performance. Once again, Ziegfeld's clever and historically inaccurate rhetoric is discernible in these descriptions:

> History does not record of the great gladiators of ancient Rome such wonderful muscular development as Mr. Sandow possesses. His four hundred phenomenally developed muscles exhibited in the cabinet in the following manner:
>
> 1. Muscular Repose, all of the muscles relaxed.
> 2. Muscular Tension, all the muscles firm as steel.
> 3. Abdominal Muscles, when tense, producing the wonderful checkerboard arrangement of fibres, the existence of which modern anatomists deny, plainly visible at a distance of three hundred feet.
> 4. The Biceps (muscles of the upper arm), the Triceps (muscles of the back of the arm), the Trapezius (muscles which raise the shoulder).
> 5. The Serratus Magnus (muscles covering the ribs under the arm); the magnificent development of this muscle is without parallel, even in the ideal Greek statues.
> 6. The Muscles of the Back, showing plainly all three layers.
> 7. The Action and Uses of the different Muscles.
> 8. The Chest Expansion. Sandow's normal chest measurement is forty-seven inches, expanded it is sixty-one inches—an expansion of fourteen inches. The greatest expansion ever known at the Olympic Games in Rome was six inches. The chest measurement of the average man is thirty-four inches, and his expansion is two inches.

After the poses, Sandow exhibited his muscle control by making his muscles dance. But as one newspaper reporter remarked of the act to this point, "All these displays simply raised the expectancy of the audience." They wanted to see him *lift* something, and Sandow was happy to comply. He turned somersaults holding two 56-pound dumbbells, then did the same stunt with his legs tied together, showing "that his muscles were not only a trick, but a reality." He bent pressed 300 pounds, then he lifted pianist Martinus Sieveking above his head, "handling him as though he were a bag of shavings." He next climbed atop his "Roman Column," a metal pole with leg supports enabling him to bend backwards and lift improbably heavy weights. Finally, he assumed the "Tomb of Hercules" position, had a platform put across his upraised abdomen, and bore the weight of two horses and a pony. At the end of his act, the applause was reported to have been deafening.[7]

As thrilling as his performances were on stage, they were eclipsed by the private exhibitions which he gave after the regular show. People of the twentieth century like to think that they invented sex and that the Victorian era was a dark terra incognita of sexual repression and stifled libidos; this simply was not the case. Ziegfeld and Sandow knew how to tap the inner urgings of the people who witnessed their performances and to turn it to profit—and they did not hesitate to use some daring tactics to do so. Sandow had earlier established the feature of post-performance green room receptions, and they quickly became a regular part of his routine, but it was not until he got to New York that they really began to attract attention. Although they were directed at a very different audience, the receptions were every bit as carefully choreographed as his regular performances.

As soon as Sandow took his last bow and walked off the stage, he went to his dressing room, where he stripped and then plunged himself into a bathtub filled with ice water. Emerging, he donned a pair of scanty briefs and proceeded to a nearby annex of the music hall. "It is tastefully covered, walls and ceiling, with purple and black materials, and illuminated by incandescent electric lights," wrote a witness.[8] Sandow positioned himself beneath a spotlight at one end of the room, and he always made sure there were never more than fifteen people present at any of these intimate levees. Sandow then proceeded to lecture on the different muscles of his body.

After he described each muscle, the strongman circulated among the group. At one of these cozy gatherings, a reporter from the *Police Gazette* was there to record all the salacious details. "I want you to feel how hard these muscle are," Sandow announced. "As I step before you, I want each of you to pass the palm of your hand across my chest."

When the men in the small audience were given the opportunity to caress the handsome athlete's muscles, "expressions of astonishment and admiration swept over their faces." Then it was the turn of the ladies.

As he approached the first of his female admirers, she drew back timidly.

"Oh, please," she squeaked demurely, "Never mind."

"Ah, but you must," Sandow insisted. "These muscles, madam, are hard as iron itself, I want you to convince yourself of the fact."

Tenderly, Sandow took the woman's gloved hand in his own and ran it slowly across the muscle in question. Apparently, this was too much excitement for the delicate creature, for she suddenly paled and staggered back. She was only able to gasp, "It's unbelievable!" before emotion got the better of her.

A uniformed attendant rushed forward and caught the swooning woman, uncorked a vial of smelling salts, and waved it beneath her nose.[9]

Apparently, the rest of the audience was not as sensitive as this timorous fan. One thing seems certain, however: while his admirers were fondling Sandow's muscles, they were satisfying feelings other than mere curiosity.

Sandow's daring backstage receptions go a long way toward proving that the Victorian era was not quite the repressive age that moderns like to imagine. This is confirmed by the strongman's impact on his audiences. Part of the reason for the athlete's extraordinary theatrical success was his popularity with young women. Wherever he appeared, Sandow was certain to be pursued by crowds of matinee girls who would send him flowers, sweet-scented letters, and other tokens of affection. There is also evidence to suggest that Sandow was not immune to these attentions.[10]

Although Sandow was the first physically attractive strongman to become popular, there were others who followed his lead. A contemporary physique star, Bobby Pandour (1876–1914), was an athlete in several senses of the term. A fellow strongman remembered visiting Pandour one morning at his friend's Parisian hotel room. There he found the strongman lounging in his pajamas and surrounded by a large, animated crowd of ladies clad only in their diaphanous negligees. The strongman was apparently none the worse for wear despite a performance that must have been every bit as exhausting as the one he did on stage.[11]

Sandow and Pandour, of course, were not alone in their sexual antics. It was no accident that Sandow's abandonment of the tights and capacious leopard skins coincided with his elevation as a male sex symbol. The sight of all those naked muscles apparently had a liberating effect on some members of his audience. In his own way, therefore, Sandow was helping to knock down a few walls of Victorian repression.

Later, when Sandow began marketing his exercise equipment and methods, a more or less secret subtext of his many books and courses was that working out could increase or revive flagging sexual potency. One of Sandow's claims was that his method of physical culture could restore "lack of vigour," an Edwardian euphemism for impotence.

Rival strongmen were blunter in their connection between performance on the exercise mat and in the marital bed. "It is a wise law of Nature that woman shall ever be drawn to the strong and vital man," announced Lionel Strongfort (pseudonym of Max Unger) in his booklet with the suggestive title *Do It with Muscle!*

Playing on male insecurities, Strongfort explains away possible failure in the boudoir in witheringly simple terms. "Yes, faint-hearted lover, you very likely have her if your body is fit or when you make it so. If she seems cold to your advances a full length mirror will probably disclose the reason why. If you're not up to snuff physically, then make yourself so."[12]

Sandow certainly had no need to worry about such things. He was concerned about advancing his career, and one opportunity to do so came up on March 6, at the end of his Koster & Bial's run. On that date he went along with Mr. Koster and Mr. Cline to visit Thomas Alva Edison's primitive motion picture studio in West Orange, New Jersey.[13] There he performed for the Kinetoscope. This was an unwieldy peepshow device which worked by running a continuous loop of film past the viewers' eyes. Thanks to a new celluloid film developed by George Eastman, Edison had been freed from using cumbersome glass plate negatives; this meant that motion could finally be captured by the camera. The Wizard of West Orange had tinkered with the idea of movies quite early, but it was not until 1894 that he was ready for the first commercial showing of his new invention.[14]

On March 10, 1894, the *Orange [New Jersey] Chronicle* gave an account of Sandow's visit to Edison's headquarters. "Sandow," it reported, "had previously stated that he would charge $250 for coming out to give the exhibition, but would gladly come for nothing for the privilege of shaking the hand of Edison, the greatest man of the age . . . special pictures of various poses were taken. . . . [One was] of Mr. Edison feeling Sandow's muscles with a curious expression on his face." The strongman then indulged in some good-natured horseplay by picking up Mr. Cline and sending him "sailing through the air and out of the door."[15]

Viewers who wanted to see the Sandow motion picture had to crowd into dark, narrow "Kinetoscopic Parlors" where the various box-like machines were lined up, each with a different show. The spectator who peered into the narrow peephole could see Sandow perform. His weak, flickering image could be seen flexing, lifting two dumbbells, and then turning a brisk, neat somersault. The entire film ran only a few moments, but it was long enough to thrill the patrons of the parlor.

Edison was not convinced of the invention's viability, but he was eventually goaded into developing a screen projector by a person who had greater faith in the coming age of moving pictures, William K. L. Dickson. Dickson was the chief photographer at the Edison think tank, and he had done much of the actual work on the motion picture project. He and Sandow struck up an acquaintance that was later to be beneficial for both men. This friendship is confirmed by the inscription that Sandow wrote in a copy of his newly published book, *Sandow's System of Physical Training,* that he gave to Dickson a few days after he was filmed. It reads simply, "To my dear friend, Mr. Dickson."[16] Sandow thus verified that he was the first bodybuilder ever to star in a movie (brief and primitive though it was). But in the meantime, he sought immortalization of a different sort—the kind that comes with wide public exposure.

Sandow, Ziegfeld, and the Trocadero Company soon headed west to the sunny, ripe-for-picking climes of California. Their destination was San Francisco, a city that had long cast covetous eyes on Chicago and its extremely profitable Columbian Exposition. The city planners decided that it was about time the City by the Bay should get a little piece of the action too. Consequently, they arranged for a lavish "Mid-winter Fair," drawing attention to California's balmy climate as well as its ambitious pleasure domes. San Francisco's Golden Gate Park was filled with attractions designed to lure thousands of wide-eyed spectators—the more exotic the building the better. There was a magnificent Hawaiian Cyclorama portraying the eruption of the Kilauea volcano, there were Chinese pagodas and Ceylonese tea gardens, and there was even something called the "Moorish Mystic Mirror Maze." Everything was calculated to dazzle the eyes and loosen the purse strings.

One of the most popular sections of the fair was a re-creation of a Central European amusement garden called the "Vienna Prater." It was here in the Kaiser Franz Joseph Hall, that Sandow was slated to appear on April 23. San Franciscans had heard of the marvelous athlete because of his many popular performances in Chicago, so they were eager to see him in person.

When Sandow finally arrived in the Bay City, he was met at the train station by the Prater manager and driven triumphantly through the streets of San Francisco in an open barouche drawn by four coal black steeds.[17] If his desire was to cut a romantic and dashing figure, he couldn't have succeeded more. He was to stay at the plush Palace Hotel in a luxurious suite of rooms overlooking the famous inner courtyard.

The next evening Sandow held a private reception for one hundred of the city's prominent physicians and members of the press. This was an effective ploy the strongman was to use whenever he arrived in town for the first time. Thanks to Ziegfeld's deft manipulation of the media coverage, Sandow was able to garner a great deal of free and useful publicity. The young athlete entered the packed Maple Hall of the hotel clad in a heavy ulster, but when that was cast aside he was revealed in a blaze of incandescent lights to excellent effect. "His massive frame was bare to the hips," recorded one newspaper reporter. "A pair of pink tights covered his lower extremities without detracting from the symmetry of his perfectly molded hips, thighs, and calves." No wonder the men broke into spontaneous applause when Sandow threw off his overcoat.

Then in his heavily accented English, Sandow gave selected details from his official biography, taking care to gloss over or sweeten up the unpleasant patches. After this, he walked among his audience, giving them the chance to feel his biceps—"firm and hard as wire cables," one of them pronounced. He then lay on his back, contracted his abdominals, and allowed any doctors and reporters who wished to do so to punch him in the stomach. When they were satisfied he was as well built as his posters proclaimed, the young man amazed them by turning a midair somersault. "He's a thoroughbred," a spectator remarked sotto voce as the men filed out of the room.[18] Sandow's first appearance in San Francisco could be counted a public relations success.

Five days after his press conference, Sandow opened at the Vienna Prater along with the Trocadero Vaudeville Company. Almost overnight they became the talk of the town. Together with Little Egypt, who had also chosen to go west, Sandow had become one of the sensations of the Mid-winter Fair. And once again, thanks to Ziegfeld's publicity, Sandow kept amassing more fame and greater fortune. Anything that got Sandow more notice was desirable.

The crafty Ziegfeld even used an incident created by a fifteen-year-old boy to superb advantage. Youthful Jackson Hines had been to see Sandow at the Prater and was so struck by the strongman that he worked his way backstage after the performance to pay Sandow his own particular homage. "It always seemed to me that he was painted with a pink powder," he wrote later. "He smelt of sachet. He would stand there in all his glory while the girls gave him the onceover with their beautiful soft hands." But it would not have been very manly of young Master

Hines to have done the same. He felt it more appropriate to give the strongman a playful jab in the ribs. But when he did so, the mighty Hercules yelped and burst out in his familiar high soprano giggle. Despite Sandow's vexation, Ziegfeld conspired to pay the boy two dollars a night to tickle the strongman after every performance, a ploy that became a huge attention getter.[19]

Hines was not the only one who observed Sandow's skin tone. Alan Calvert, editor of *Strength* magazine, wrote that Sandow's dramatic stage presence was helped by the look of his body under the lights. "He was not a 'Baby-pink,' but looked a deeper hue—almost a terra-cotta. Various men (all of whom claimed to have been either his associates or assistants) claim that for ten minutes before his act started Sandow would have himself rubbed with rough towels so as to bring the blood to the surface."

Calvert admits, however, that Sandow probably used cosmetics to achieve his body coloration. He describes a technique of makeup application that was most likely used by the great strongman. "The athlete stands at ease and relaxed while the entire surface of his body is dusted over with a reddish powder. Then he will lean over and flex his abdominal muscles. An assistant will then lightly pass a towel down the front of the athlete's body, wiping the powder off the high spots." When the strongman straightens up, there will be lines of powder left in the crease between the horizontal bands of muscle across the abdomen, thus making the athlete look very muscular.[20]

After the superbly powdered muscleman finished his opening run at the Mid-winter Fairgrounds, he moved his act closer to the heart of the city. Sandow began a second engagement on May 1 at Stockwell's Theater on Powell Street as their principal act. He continued to draw large crowds and to proclaim himself "The World's Most Perfect Man." In reaction to this last claim the *Examiner* ran a series of articles attempting to settle that specific issue. Dr. F. Leverett Sweany of Market Street was adamant in his views that the athlete was certainly "the most perfect specimen of manhood that exists today." But others were not so quick to agree. "His figure lacks dignity or artistic contour," reasoned a local artist. And Miss Evelyn McCormick ventured the opinion that Sandow should ideally be slimmer and taller. "He could not have been a model for Donatello," she proclaimed archly. Finally, a professor from Stanford University tried to settle the question by agreeing that Sandow could be considered perfect, but only if one preferred the Farnese Hercules to the Apollo Belvedere.[21] And while the issue was batted back and forth in the press, Sandow's ticket receipts continued to grow.

But other, even better publicity ploys were brewing in the cool, gray city of love.

Shortly after they arrived in San Francisco, Sandow and Ziegfeld had the police arrest and lock up a young scoundrel by the name of Irving Montgomery. The prisoner was an Englishman by birth and a charlatan by profession. The tangled web of connections which linked him to the strongman and his manager stretched all the way back to Sandow's victory over Sampson and Cyclops.

In 1889, after Sandow had so soundly beaten his two opponents, Sampson and his hulking pupil, Cyclops, continued to play the provincial music halls. Early in 1890 they found themselves in Birmingham performing at Day's Music Hall. Incredibly, Sampson was still using a nightly challenge tactic, but lately no one had taken him up on it. In order to spice up their act, the phony athlete consulted with a local weightlifter and coach, Edward Lawrence Levy. Sampson wanted to find a local strongman (but, of course, not *too* strong) in order to take up the weightlifting contest that he offered regularly. Levy suggested Irving Montgomery, a Birmingham lad who was "well-made, and with natural gifts in the strength line." This suited Sampson perfectly, for not only was Cyclops almost certain to defeat the young man but in case he could not, Montgomery was more than willing to throw the match for a five pound note.[22]

As it turned out, Montgomery was easily beaten, but his good looks, strength, and willingness to deceive made him a natural candidate for the role of professional strongman. Shortly after this, Sampson and Cyclops disbanded. Cyclops decided to team up with Montgomery, and the two eventually took their strength act to North America. In order to cash in on another's fame, Montgomery took the further expedient of changing his name. In a magnificent display of brass, he decided to call himself Sandowe.

The strongest man in the entire world at that time was a massive French Canadian named Louis Cyr. Cyclops and the newly rechristened Sandowe could not possibly hope to defeat Cyr in a theatrical weightlifting contest, so they decided to do the next best thing: they issued insolent challenges to the Canadian, taking great care that he was always out of town when they did so. In 1891 at the Lyceum Theatre in Montreal this plan backfired, for Cyr had been warned about the situation ahead of time. Just as Cyclops was shouting out sarcastically, "Where is this Cyr who has fled from Cyclops and Sandowe?" the door to the theater burst open and the strongman strode in bellowing, "Je suis ici. Je suis arrivée! [Here I am. I have arrived!]" Cyr consequently made very short work of the two, beating them quickly and soundly. Shortly after this, Cyclops packed his bags and returned dejectedly to Europe. Many years later the chastened strongman admitted to a crony that he had never witnessed such awe-inspiring strength as Cyr's.[23] But defeat had no such effect on Montgomery, for he turned his attentions south of the border to the United States. There he found bookings under his assumed name. Eventually, fate led him to San Francisco at the exact time the real Sandow was scheduled to appear.

Nearly a month before Sandow and Ziegfeld were to arrive in California, posters began appearing all over San Francisco announcing the appearance of Sandowe at local theaters. The *Dramatic Mirror* got wind of this and reported the fact to Ziegfeld. He responded by firing off an angry telegram to the manager of the Palace Hotel where they were to stay: "Notify papers that Sandowe, who is advertised to appear in San Francisco, is an imposter. His right name is Montgomery."[24] But all parties concerned had to wait until the real strongman arrived in the city. One of the first things Ziegfeld did was to make sure Montgomery was arrested and thrown in jail, then he sought an injunction restraining him from using Sandow's name. Montgomery then brought suit against his two rivals, asking $50,000 in damages and a legal order to get Sandow to drop the use of his name. Sandow then countersued for exactly the same compensation. Only two things appeared certain from all this: it promised to be a legal nightmare and a public relations goldmine.

The newspapers had a field day as they recorded the particulars of the case in loving detail. "Men of Muscle Meet" read the headline on May 18, and the attention they showered on the proceedings showed they knew what kind of stories sold newspapers. But the bemused and tongue-in-cheek tone they adopted indicated their willingness to milk every drop of entertainment they could from the show people and the legal process.

The hearings were held in the court of Judge Slack, and from the beginning it was obvious this was not going to be a run-of-the-mill trial. The room was packed with interested spectators, lady admirers, and colorful witnesses. At one point, "the mob grew so dense and noisy that a deputy was placed on the door to admit only those who had business inside." But the witnesses were singled out by the press as being the most interesting of all. "Athletes and acrobats, song-and-dance ladies, comedians, jugglers, musical freaks, and flying men of the air arrayed in boisterous garb and sparkling gems also took part in the proceedings." Judge Slack must have seriously considered early retirement even before the trial got under way.

Fortunately, though, he stuck by his post. The first to take the stand was Sandow. He recounted the story of his life up to that point, telling how he had used the name Sandow all over the world. His rival, he swore, "is a base imitation of the original," and should not be allowed to profit from the name it took him so long to build. The young German athlete confessed that Eugen Sandow was a pseudonym, and that his real name was "Frederick Wilhelm Eugene Sander"—a patent lie, but convincing to those at the trial. He had taken the name Sandow "because stage people were in the habit of doing such things."

Another thing that stage people habitually did was to keep clipping files, and Sandow next brought these out, attempting to prove that he had taken his name long before Montgomery had ever dreamed of stealing it. But there were so many (it took four large volumes to hold them all) that a recess was called in order for him to fish out the appropriate ones. Montgomery, ever cool and audacious, had pulled out his clippings, which he kept in a small envelope. It was reported that Sandowe seemed to be "enjoying the discomfort of his rival who could not find what he wanted."

A long line of "character" witnesses was called after this. They included theatrical people who had known Sandow for some time. The tone was set by the first person to take the stand. She was Mrs. Alice Juliet Shaw, described as "A large, handsome woman who smiled incessantly." She admitted that she was an artiste. "What do you do?" inquired the attorney.

"I whistle," she replied sweetly.

"Oh you do?" responded the lawyer ingenuously, causing the spectators to snicker slyly.

Not surprisingly, no one seemed to take the trial very seriously. The only ones who appeared to be affected by the gravity of the situation were the two principals who glared and scowled at each other like alley cats. Sandowe showed a remarkable lack of restraint when he began directing his withering stares at members of Sandow's group. As the cross examinations were going on, one nervous little man leaped to his feet and yelled, "Your honor, Sandowe is making threatening faces and shaking his fist at me." When reprimanded, Sandowe merely smiled grimly and said he wasn't trying to kill anyone.[25]

The situation did not improve much when Montgomery got on the stand. As expected, he claimed that he was the one, true, original Sandowe, and that the other was attempting to cash in on his fame. At one point, Sandow's lawyer asked the Englishman, "Do you remember receiving a photograph from Sandow?"

"Yes, sir."

"Did you not then curl your hair and endeavor to copy it?"

"No, sir," he shouted indignantly. "I'd rather suffer death first." But mortification of a different sort was in store for him. The next day the newspapers enjoyed themselves immensely, reporting the exchange under the headlines, "He Copied Sandow's Curls."[26]

After several days of such testimony, San Francisco must have seemed a calmer place when a decision was reached. Judge Slack fined Montgomery $25 for contempt of court, but the graver issue of the $50,000 seems never to have been settled.[27] No great matter, though, for both men got more than their money's worth in free publicity. Imitation may be the sincerest form of flattery, but Montgomery had gone too far. He was forbidden once and for all from using his stolen name. Sandow's honor had been protected, and he was free to pursue his career unimpeded by ersatz strongmen sporting his own name. In summing up, the *Chronicle* reflected the common sentiment: "The trial furnished amusement and instruction for everyone, including the attorneys."[28]

Poor Montgomery took advantage of whatever notoriety he could garner from his court battle, and he managed to obtain a few engagements under his rightful name. But like others of his ilk, Montgomery gradually faded from view. Lawrence Levy, the man who had unwittingly started him on his ill-fated show business career, reported in 1903 that the last he had heard, Montgomery was "playing in some comedy or tragedy wherein weightlifting was dovetailed."[29] For an athlete of any quality, it was a sad end to a sad career.

In the meantime Sandow was playing to packed houses at Stockwell's Theater. Small wonder, since it was almost impossible to open any of the three San Francisco papers and not find an article about him. Ziegfeld was working overtime keeping Sandow in the public eye. One of the most surprising methods he used to accomplish this was described in the *Chronicle* of May 17, 1894.

In an era of sexual liberation and burgeoning feminism, it is perhaps surprising to discover that some people were enjoying freedoms of this sort many years ago. This is evidenced by the special performance that Sandow put on at Stockwell's Theatre. This novel matinee was sponsored by the Sketch Club of San Francisco ostensibly so that the young strongman could use his unclad muscles to illustrate a lecture by an artist, Solly Walter, on the decline of modern art. The performance was for ladies only—no gentlemen, save members of the press, would be admitted under any circumstances. That afternoon the reporter from the *Chronicle* was surprised at the total absence of men. Even the ticket taker was a woman.

Promptly at 2:30 Mr. Walter began his talk. He started with references to Praxiteles and the Venus de Milo. He explained that modern art had fallen on bad times, not because of the artists but because they lacked a good model. On and on he droned, while some of the ladies were showing distinct signs of boredom. "In spite of its polite interest in the lecture," the reporter noted, "the audience was impatient for the show to begin. Every eye wandered frequently to the red plush curtains at the back of the stage." Sensing their impatience, Walter finally signaled for the curtains to part, and "Sandow stood revealed in the blaze of light just as he does in his regular performances—only with a difference. The athlete had put off his belt, tights and shoes, and wore but a single garment, a strip of silk not much bigger than a handkerchief."

The ladies obviously liked what they saw, for after a great intaking of breath, there began an insistent patter of gloved hands. In response, Mr. Walter pointed out Sandow's various muscles and had him flex each one in turn, revolve slowly, and display himself to the admiring group. It was noted that "There were some suppressed giggles, but it was mercifully dark in the house and the offenders had no need to hide the consequent blushes; no one could see them."

At last, after a forty-five-minute display, the curtain rang down, but the applause was so loud and persistent that both Sandow and Walter came back out for another bow. One enthusiastic lady was so excited that instead of clapping with her hands, she banged two large books together. As the audience reluctantly exited, the ticket taker gave away souvenir photographs of Sandow. It was also reported that several of the ladies hung about the stage door in hopes of waylaying the athlete for something more than a modest look. He may not have been a proper model for Donatello, but that did not seem to faze the ladies in the slightest.

Up to this point, Sandow's San Francisco visit had been a publicist's dream, but his most magnificent triumph in that line was yet to come. "Perhaps the greatest, certainly the most thrilling, of all my experiences," wrote Sandow in 1910, "was my fight with a lion in San Francisco."[30]

The story begins shortly after Sandow arrived in California. Colonel Daniel Boone was the owner of a menagerie of trained animals that performed at the Mid-winter Fairgrounds. Boone acquired an 850-pound California grizzly bear whom he named Siskiyou. He cruelly arranged to pair off the bear with one of his trained lions, Parnell, in what he termed a "Catch-as-catch-can Wrestling Bout—No Hold Barred." Actually, it was to be a bloody fight to the finish. The garish orange and black posters announcing the match went up all over town. Understandably, the prices were extremely high: tickets ranged from ten to twenty dollars.[31]

Fortunately, the Society for the Prevention of Cruelty to Animals got wind of the bout and, in conjunction with the police, put an end to it at once. When Ziegfeld heard of the canceled match, it set his ever-acquisitive brain working. Why not substitute Sandow for Siskiyou? There was no law against that.

Much has been written about the strongman's lion fight, but very little of it can be believed, and the trail of falsehood and exaggeration can be traced directly to Sandow and Ziegfeld. Naturally, Sandow's version of the fight shows him to have been heroic and high-minded, but the newspapers tell a different story.

Parnell, Sandow's prospective opponent, was a truly ferocious, 650-pound beast who was himself no stranger to the front pages of local papers. Nearly a month earlier he had attacked an inattentive trainer, lacerating the man badly enough to send him to the hospital. Shortly after that, he mauled and killed Boone's prize Great Dane, Nero.[32] Plainly, the animal was not to be trifled with.

Also resident at the Boone menagerie was Commodore, a mangy, bedraggled, superannuated beast who had had all the fight knocked out of him years ago. It took very little ingenuity for Ziegfeld to transfer the man-eating attributes of one lion to its more docile neighbor. Here was a perfect opponent for Sandow's match. But strong as he was, Sandow was not fool enough to go into a lion cage unarmed, even if the beast in question was the hapless and nearly toothless Commodore. If the contest was to be a struggle between brute strength and human strength, something must be done to even up the score. Boone suggested cutting off the animal's claws and pulling out his teeth, but the specter of the SPCA hanging over them moved him merely to apply large leather mittens and a muzzle to the lion.[33]

For his part, Sandow agreed to get complete control of the lion. If he failed, the match would be awarded to the lion. It was reported that a great deal of money was being wagered on both sides. "Colonel Boone has implicit faith in his protege," one journalist reported, "while Ziegfeld is willing to stake his last dollar on Sandow." But whatever the outcome, both Boone and Ziegfeld seemed assured of making money. They had done their publicity work well, and stood to gain a great deal from the dollar-a-head admission fee that they charged. The man who brought the world the Dancing Ducks of Denmark and the Invisible Brazilian Fish was poised to strike again.

Sandow's fight with the lion was billed as "The Event of the Century," and as one reporter was forced to admit after the fact, "Nothing like it has ever been witnessed in this or any other century." A large tent was put up in Golden Gate Park, complete with sixty-one boxes and a special tier of seats for the press. In the center of the arena a large cage had been hastily erected for the performance. It was here at 9:30 in the evening that Sandow battled with the king of beasts.

It was reported by the *Chronicle* that "many ladies of wealth and fashion sat in the boxes, burning with eagerness to see Sandow, the modern Samson, twist the daylights out of the four-footed athlete." Long before the show began, Sandow had emerged into the arena and had cheerfully greeted the lovely creatures, "bowing and lifting his lid to the ladies." Win or lose, Sandow was a hit with at least this part of the audience.

As the eager spectators entered the arena, they were routed past a cage where Parnell snarled and roared ferociously. Their anticipation was carefully built to high intensity by the time six men carried out a portable cage containing the strongman's opponent and warily opened the door. But the crowd must have realized that something was amiss from the beginning. As four powerful calcium spotlights focused on the enclosure, they revealed a scene that portended the evening to come: Commodore refused to come out of his cage. Finally, after much jabbing and poking from behind, "the aged, time-worn and weary beast came limping out."[34]

As soon as the lion was out of his iron box, it was apparent that he was at a disadvantage. The huge, uncomfortable gloves that covered his paws and the muzzle on his jaws were so large and unwieldy that the audience immediately began to sympathize with the beast rather than the man. "The moment the spectators detected the size of the gloves that Commodore wore," wrote the *Morning Call,* "there were murmurs of disapproval heard from all quarters."[35] There was also the matter of the lion's infirmities. "Commodore," one reporter facetiously noted, "limped on all four of his legs simultaneously." No wonder the sporting instincts of the audience were offended.

But the crowd had paid good money to see the "Sensation of the Century," and Sandow attempted to make the best of things. The athlete entered the cage and boldly walked up to the lion, eyeing his opponent sternly. Commodore's reaction was to bury his nose in the sawdust. In an attempt to get some action from the beast, Sandow then roughly tweaked the animal's ear. "A whine was the only response." Next Boone gave the animal a strong whack with this whip, at which the lion struggled to his feeble feet and then promptly fell down again. Something was very wrong here.

"Before the terrific one-sided struggle for life and further arenic fame had progressed two minutes," wrote the man from the *Chronicle,* "some of the spectators yelled 'fake.'" Desperate to provide some sort of a contest of strength and to forestall any further outcries, Sandow brusquely grabbed the lion by his mane and began shaking him. The animal's reaction was to flick sawdust in his adversary's face with his flailing tail. Finding that the only signs of life emanated from the nether end of the creature, Sandow came around, grabbed the tail and dragged and flung him around like a sack of potatoes. Then he grabbed a handful of whiskers and yanked. Still no reaction other than a few pathetic whimpers. Some smart aleck in the crowd then yelled, "Throw in the box and let him wrestle with that."

Rightly feeling that his reputation was on the line, Sandow then picked Commodore up and carried him around the ring, but the lion seemed to enjoy being lifted like a lap dog. In disgust Sandow put down his beastly burden near the edge of the cage. But at that moment, a photographer emboldened by the lion's passive behavior inched closer to the bars, focused, and exploded a powerful flash. This finally infused a little life into Commodore, for he jumped up in a fright and trembled mightily. But it was a short-lived revival, and he soon lapsed into his former condition.

By this time the crowd was getting ugly. There were yells and insults flying constantly. Desperate, Boone started whipping the poor beast viciously. Then Sandow tried again. "He yanked and hauled and mauled Commodore and rolled him around in the sawdust till the lion's tongue hung out through the muzzle." Finally, the local representative of the SPCA stepped in and mercifully put an end to the charade.

Boone declared Sandow the winner and presented him with a medal that Ziegfeld had earlier purchased at Shreve's jewelry store in the city. The colonel made a little speech in an attempt to mollify the angry crowd. "It is not what Sandow had done," he announced nervously, "but for the way he did it, and for his gallantry in entering this den of wild beasts."[36] But no one seemed convinced. Sandow left the arena hastily, angrily vowing for a rematch—next time with Parnell. This time, though, the strongman had been made to look very foolish by his excessively mercurial manager.

The next day Colonel Boone spoke to the press. He denied vociferously that the animal had been chloroformed, but he did not seem able to convince many other people of that fact. Ziegfeld, on the other hand, probably had the right idea. Shortly after the contest began, he grabbed his share of the $3,000 take for the evening and prudently spent the night in Oakland, safely across the Bay.[37]

Perhaps the poor beast had been drugged—the men involved were certainly capable of such a stratagem. But more likely there were simpler reasons. Commodore's advanced age would have been reason enough in itself, for as one perspicacious observer remarked, "Were there such a place as an old lion's home, Commodore should have been an inmate instead of indulging in the giddy sports of the arena."[38] But there were also the unwieldy mittens that were placed on him; they caused him to teeter and fall more than once. When the lion found himself thus handicapped, perhaps he simply gave up.

Sandow and Ziegfeld came up with an elaborate and fanciful excuse for the evening's fiasco. The lion, they announced, had been frightened by an earlier drubbing he received at a rehearsal. He consequently had all his leonine ferocity knocked out of him. "At heart, you know, most beasts are cowards," Sandow later wrote smugly, "and having met his match at the rehearsal, the lion had no appetite for another struggle."[39]

But the people of San Francisco were not so easily convinced—nor so forgetful. Some eighteen years later Ziegfeld returned to the city, this time with a different attraction: The Follies. But the newspapers were quick to point out to their readers that this was the same man who brought them the lion fight back in 1894. Those with long memories were probably a little relieved when they witnessed his glorification of the American girl rather than another highly suspicious animal show. Thankfully, the only beasts present in the theater that evening were the wolves in the audience.

Shortly after his infamous fight with the lion, Sandow, Ziegfeld, and their entire Trocadero vaudeville troupe left San Francisco. Much to the consolation of everyone, there was no more talk of the strongman's fight with Parnell. Sandow's lion-fighting days were over for good. But his days as a performing strongman were far from over.

After a brief run in San Jose, the company set their sights on southern California. "Well do I remember our arrival in Los Angeles," Sandow was quoted later. "Thousands and thousands of people came to meet our coach, the children smothering us with roses as though it were some battle of flowers."[40] With all the shenanigans in the north keeping Sandow's name in the papers in the south, it is no surprise that Los Angeles eagerly awaited his visit; however, the thousands of people that he described so eloquently were nothing more than a Ziegfeld fabrication.

Ads had appeared in the newspapers announcing his performance at the New Los Angeles Theater. The firm of Jacoby Brothers, Clothiers, even ran a special sale for boys' Sandow suits, "The strongest suit in the world."[41] He finally arrived on June 1, 1894, to a modest welcome. "What a lovely country is that," he wrote of southern California, "a country of perpetual summer and blue sky, of bright flowers and delicious breezes."[42] And with Ziegfeld carefully planning his every move, it also proved to be a land of wealth and profit.

On the evening of their first day in Los Angeles, Sandow and Ziegfeld called their usual press conference at the swank Hollenback Hotel. The reporters were greatly impressed with the strongman. "When the muscles are relaxed," one of them wrote, "his flesh is soft as a woman's, but when he brings his muscles into play, his person is as solid and unyielding as iron."[43]

One of the most important things Sandow did while he was in Los Angeles was to pose for a famous series of photographs. Long before the area became known for glamorizing celebrities on film, southern California was the home of one of the finest studio photographers in the land, George Steckel. He turned out a classic series of poses with Sandow clad only in an artificial fig leaf. Highly regarded by collectors today, these shots have become valuable and elusive trophies, some of them fetching hundreds of dollars each.

Sandow's stage performances in Los Angeles were typical of those he gave throughout his long tour of America. There were many talented vaudeville performers in the company. Elsie Adair, a serpentine dancer, was first on the bill. She undulated and glided sensually for a while, much to the delight of the customers in the balcony. As she danced a rousing finale, the lights dimmed and a magic lantern shone brilliantly colored beams on her swirling mass of skirts. Abruptly, the picture of Democratic president Grover Cleveland was projected on the skirts. The crowd broke into raucous boos and hisses. Then the features of ex-president Benjamin Harrison appeared. The people began to cheer and hurrah. It was a bizarre political tribute, but it appealed to the crowd's violently partisan views.

Next on the program was Rosalind Thrall, the "Whistling Prima Donna," who warbled some stirring and sentimental airs. Fortunately, she was on and off quickly. A balancing trapezist, a singer, and the Hardellas doing their "grotesque athletics" rounded out the bill. The last person to appear was the great Sandow himself.

Conductor Sieveking struck up a stirring fanfare, and the curtain went up revealing Sandow on a pedestal. The strongman was dressed in tights and turned around as colored lights were flashed upon him. He then flexed his muscles, exhibiting his amazing muscle control by making them jump and flutter to music. Next he dismounted from his pedestal and took up two 56-pound dumbbells and turned a backward somersault. As if this were not enough, he next performed the same trick blindfolded and with his feet tied. More weightlifting and work on the Roman Column followed this. As a grand finale, he supported three horses while in the familiar Tomb of Hercules position. Gauged by the thunderous applause that broke out after the curtain had fallen, Sandow had scored another triumph.[44]

On Sunday afternoon, June 4, Sandow was interviewed for the last time in Los Angeles by the gentleman from the *Herald*. The reporter wanted to know how one went about becoming strong. Sandow explained very patiently that the only way was to work out with weights, suggesting light dumbbells and high repetitions, and to be persistent. "Use your willing power," he suggested. Then in a rare moment of candor, the strongman added, "I know very well that I am not a perfect man as my manager frequently has for purposes of advertising said, but I know also that by the application of certain broad principles I have acquired almost perfect physical control over myself."[45]

After his run in Los Angeles, Sandow and the company took a brief respite from their nightly performances. This afforded them a good opportunity to view the many sights of the area. A charming photograph has survived which shows the entire company en route to one of these attractions. The members of the Trocadero Vaudeville Company, together with Ziegfeld and its star, pose stiffly on an old-fashioned "Tally-Ho" coach in front of the Hotel Green in Pasadena. The picture provides a rare, almost informal, glimpse of a group of theater people on holiday.[46] But underneath the lighthearted frivolity certain tensions were developing between the star and his manager, and their holiday also helped defuse some of the impending contretemps.

After his week's vacation, Sandow returned to Los Angeles for a couple more performances. At that point he had completed all his engagements in the West, but he had one more duty to perform before he headed back east, though it meant returning briefly to San Francisco. While he was in the Bay City, he had become great friends with a German wrestler, George S. Miehling. As a special favor to him, Sandow agreed to be godfather to his infant son. In return, the father named the child after his fellow countryman, calling him George Sandow Miehling. Sandow presented his little godchild with a silver goblet, and on it he had inscribed the motto Strength Be Your Treasure. An appropriate sentiment considering his athletically minded family.

Earlier in the day, however, Sandow had discovered much to his chagrin that the little Miehling baby was not the only one who was named after him. Just as he was taking the cable car to get to the christening party, he heard someone calling, "Sandow! Sandow!" When he saw that it was a comely young lady, he immediately dropped off. "You know how shy I am about the ladies," he explained with mock seriousness, "and I saw I was not acquainted with her. But I stepped up to her and said, 'I beg your pardon.' She flushed all up and answered, 'I beg your pardon; I wasn't calling you—I was calling my dog.' Then I noticed a big Danish boarhound."[47]

Sandow left for the East shortly after his encounter with the eponymous canine. By this time, the strain in the friendship between Sandow and Ziegfeld had become quite apparent. No one seemed to discover the reason—perhaps it was because each was such a strong personality that they simply chafed under any constraints at all. Sandow and Sieveking would often huddle in conversation on trains and elsewhere, leaving Ziegfeld to amuse himself as best he could (most often in the compliant arms of the nearest chorine).[48]

The monotonous journey was broken briefly when they stopped in Omaha and were nearly fleeced by a few Nebraska sharpies in a gambling den.[49] Ziegfeld remained in Chicago, Sieveking went back to Europe, and Sandow sailed for England. While there, he arranged a different kind of engagement that was to startle the world.

On August 8, 1894, the major newspapers in both England and America carried the announcement that realized Ziegfeld's worst fears and caused immediate grief to many of the muscleman's fervent female admirers. "Sandow the professional strongman," one of them read, "was married this morning in Manchester to Miss Blanche Brookes."[50] The two had carried on a trans-Atlantic courtship by letter, but since Sandow was performing almost constantly they had to postpone their wedding until a more propitious time. That time finally arrived after the very lucrative American tour. Blanche had kept herself occupied in various moral and educational pursuits—in fact, she had just returned from an extended stay in Germany where she was attempting to learn her fiancé's mother tongue. Blanche Brookes was a very proper young lady, and she had very definite ideas about what constituted proper behavior for a gentleman too. This high-mindedness was to cause no end of strife later on, but for the moment all was rejoicing and unalloyed bliss.

In the meantime, back across the Atlantic, Ziegfeld was anything but blissful. He was working gamely to keep Sandow's marriage a secret for as long as possible. At the same time he attempted to keep the strongman's name in front of a fickle and forgetful public; with Sandow out of the country, this was not always easy, but somehow he managed. Late in the summer a report was circulated (almost certainly by Ziegfeld himself) that linked the strongman with lovely Lillian Russell once again. Mere mention of the American beauty was enough to spark interest, and this time was no different. "The rumor that Mr. Sandow's tour in this country will be abandoned," reported one newspaper, "and that he will join Miss Lillian Russell's company is entirely without foundation." Sandow, the article continued, would go on tour for thirty weeks. Ziegfeld slyly covered up the real reason for his absence by explaining that he was busy engaging new artists for the organization in Europe—after all, why break the bitter truth to all those admission-paying young ladies?[51]

When the season finally began, all hopes of keeping a lid on the muscleman's wedding had to be scrapped: Mrs. Sandow had decided to accompany her husband on his tour of America. Big changes were apparent in the troupe from the beginning of Blanche's sojourn with it. Sieveking was noticeably absent, but then so were Sandow's famous postperformance posing sessions where young ladies were invited to feel his muscles. Sandow's flirtations with his admirers had to be either eliminated or carried on very discreetly. Still, there were other compensations. Bringing along a wife must have given him a more respectable position and perhaps a few social invitations that he might otherwise have missed. His wife was also quite lovely in her own right. She was described as "Manchester's reigning belle" by one journalist.[52]

Her beauty and charm were confirmed by an article that appeared in the *Chicago News* describing Blanche's first appearance in that city. "In a box close to the stage sat Sandow's lovely young wife. She is tall, slender, and exquisitely beautiful. Her eyes are large and soft, black as night, and very sensitive. Her hair is just as black, and curls naturally about her oval face. She is one of the prettiest women of the season, and was dressed in a scarlet and white striped silk, with black skirt, and wore a heavy combed lamb's wool cloak and broad screening hat."[53] From the sounds of it, her husband was not the only one who gathered ardent admirers.

Her beauty is also attested to by an anecdote told by Ziegfeld. "We were in the Cafe Martin in New York," he recalled. "One of a group of fellows at another table kept ogling Mrs. Sandow. Finally I said to him, 'Don't do that.' I guess he had been drinking, for he replied, 'I'm satisfied with what I'm looking at.' "

When he persisted in his unwelcome attentions, Sandow stalked over and grabbed him by the scruff of the neck. The startled masher wouldn't let go of the table, so Sandow tossed both into the street. "In about ten minutes," Ziegfeld concluded, "the waiter came to me and said there was a gentleman outside to see me. I went out. It was the victim. He said, 'Say, who was that bird? I was in a vise.' "[54]

Sandow and company began their seven-and-a-half-month tour of the United States on October 1, 1894. It would be an arduous job, trekking across the heartland of America, stopping at towns and cities on the secondary vaudeville circuit. Starting in the Northeast, they traveled then to Lima and Columbus, Ohio. Cincinnati and St. Louis were next. Then on to the towns of the Great Plains like Kansas City, Missouri; Lincoln, Nebraska; and Sioux City, Iowa. Just about any metropolis big enough to have its own opera house or theater saw the company for a least a few days.[55]

Sandow always worked at a fever pitch no matter what he was about. For a man who touted a healthy life, Sandow's day-to-day schedule was potentially debilitating: he was fond of working inordinately long hours, smoking, consuming rich hotel food, and traveling constantly. It was a dangerous and difficult regimen even for a man in perfect condition. Unknown to everyone, including Sandow himself, it was a schedule that would eventually cause the athlete to slow down whether he wanted to or not.

For a man who passed himself off as a paragon of fitness, Sandow often indulged in distinctly unhealthy recreations, but perhaps this was due as much to ignorance as it was to intemperance. Reporters who pestered Sandow for advice on diet and life-style often received confusion and contradictory replies. In 1893, for instance, the strongman made some unusual assertions. "Sandow does not believe in training," announced *Pearson's Magazine*. The reporter quoted Sandow as saying, "Under my system of getting strong, a man need but follow the ordinary course of life and take reasonably good care of himself. No dietetic regulations are needed. Let him eat and drink whatever suits him. As for sleeping, I don't think it makes any great difference when he sleeps, provided he gets sleep enough. I myself go to bed anytime between midnight and three o'clock in the morning. I eat whenever, whatever and as much as I please. I drink all I can get. Yes; beer, ale, wines, champagne, cognac—everything. But I never drink to excess."[56]

One year later in *The Cosmopolitan*, Sandow was more conventional in his dietary counsel. "I abjure everything intoxicating," he piously averred, "and never suffer myself to touch tea or coffee." Sandow also advised his readers to get at least nine hours of sleep each night—to do otherwise would be the same as "burning their lives at both ends."[57] Ironically, Sandow must have found it difficult to follow his own advice since he was leading a life that encouraged sensual excess and monotonous labors.

The arduous obligations and the duties of dulling sameness were broken briefly and unpleasantly when the Sandows reached Omaha, Nebraska. Still wary from the last visit to the midwestern state when he had been cheated at cards, the strongman and his wife cautiously settled into the best hotel in town. But their worries were justified when, during the middle of the night, two daring burglars broke into their room and robbed them as they slept. The next morning Sandow discovered that he was missing several $25 gold pieces and the fine watch that had been presented to him by the penitent count de Furnimbac many years previous. As luck would have it, that night was one of the few when Sandow's famous beer-drinking dog, Sultan, had not been present in the room.[58]

By spring of 1895, the Trocadero company had worked its way east and was performing in New York and Boston. The basic composition of the group changed from time to time, but it was still a strong and varied conglomeration of variety performers. There were dancers, singers, whistlers, and even Scottie, a "calculating collie," in addition to the acts that had remained with the company from the previous season. By the time the season came to an end that summer, the Trocadero troupe had covered a great deal of territory, made a great deal of money, but had also worn themselves down considerably.

The strain was especially apparent in Blanche. The star's wife was growing restive and homesick. The life of a nomad did not suit her at all; she needed permanence and respectability to be happy. More importantly, she discovered that she was pregnant with their first child. So after thirty weeks of packing and unpacking, of staying in strange cities, and living in temporary hotel rooms, Blanche decided to return to England, leaving her husband behind.

There were other stresses coming to the surface too. During the later phase of the tour, the marked rift between Sandow and Ziegfeld had grown deeper. Both men were acquiring different interests. The friendship, and with it the partnership, was beginning to cool even more than it had before. As soon as the season closed, Ziegfeld went off to Chicago to conclude arrangements for a new deal he had in the works. He was attempting to raise money for a grand, English-style music hall to be built on the plans of the Empire in London. He had managed to wheedle $50,000 out of Sandow, and was reportedly ready to sail for Europe where he would search for talent for both the new theater and the Trocadero company. Unfortunately, the plans for the theater soon fell through, and the European performers he found were decidedly second-rate.[59] Somehow a bill was put together, however, and the program opened in early 1896 in New York City. Since those acts proved lackluster and unappealing, Ziegfeld decided the only thing to do was to convince Sandow to undertake a series of one-night stands. The producer wanted to book smaller towns, as Sandow had appeared many times in the major cities. Reluctantly, Sandow agreed to the scheme.

Despite their differences, Sandow and Ziegfeld purchased a luxurious "Pullman Palace Car" which they would use to take a party of friends on a pleasure trip to the continent's edge at San Francisco. The two had then planned to sail to Australia and the Orient from the Golden Gate, but fate was to intervene.[60] Their burgeoning feud, which had lain just under the surface, broke out in the open and became too intense for the men to continue as partners. Though the breach was no surprise to close associates, the theater world was caught unawares when the trade papers dramatically announced the split. "Sandow and Ziegfeld were supposed to be inseparable," the *Dramatic Mirror* reported. "They are still great friends, however, and the separation is merely a matter of business."[61]

Though their business relationship was at an end, they decided to part on fairly amicable terms. A few weeks after the break, each man went his separate way. Sandow laid plans for a fall tour with a new manager and a new company. Ziegfeld signed on as agent for a winsome young wire walker named Virginia Aragon. A short time later he convinced the sexy French chanteuse, Anna Held, to come to America, and he began her glorification. Thereafter, Ziegfeld and Sandow were too busy to see each other, and communication between them came to a halt.

Neither man had much to complain about, really. Ziegfeld had made a phenomenal quarter of a million dollars out of the tours, and Sandow even more. Typically, the strongman invested his profits in various money-making ventures, while Ziegfeld frittered away most of his share at the gaming tables of New York.[62]

When Sandow and his manager parted company, both men were at pivotal points in their careers. The ambitious young Ziegfeld was able to parlay his talents at glorification to dizzying heights of success. But sadly, when the great stock market crash of the thirties came, Ziegfeld, who was then living in New York, lost nearly everything, including his health. At last in 1932, sick and weak, he decided to go west to California one final time. According to Billie Burke, Ziegfeld's actress-wife, the ailing Flo was delirious for most of the long train ride from New York to Los Angeles. He kept rambling about Chicago and Sandow as he tossed and turned in his Pullman bed.[63] Once he arrived, Ziegfeld did not have long to suffer, for on July 22, 1932, he died. He was laid to rest at Forest Lawn Cemetery, far away from the sparkling lights of Broadway.[64]

In her autobiography, Billie Burke remarked truthfully that Sandow would never have attained his fame without her husband's exuberant showmanship. "It is an odd thing, come to think of it," she mused, "that in later years Flo completely reversed this theory of exploitation. He never indulged in stunts with his *Follies*, but always sought distinction."[65]

Perhaps so—but it was a different time and a different show, and it called for different tactics.

To talk about Ziegfeld is to totter constantly on the edge of hyperbole. He was one of those curiously larger-than-life figures of the past whose likes we will never see again. He was variously a scoundrel, a philanderer, a cheat, a liar, and many other equally unsavory things, but he was also a genius. And it was thanks to his genius that Sandow made a name for himself.

Though he had rather unceremoniously cut himself loose from Ziegfeld, Sandow took immediate measures to secure his personal future. He engaged Charles B. Jefferson as his new manager, and he arranged for a tour to begin that autumn with a group of supporting players billed as "Sandow's Olympia Company."[66]

The muscleman received a disappointing shock when he opened at the Alvin Theater in Pittsburgh in September. A certain electricity seemed to have vanished from the audience. He was greeted listlessly and applauded mildly. The frenetic excitement he was accustomed to generate had gone. Had Sandow gone stale with American audiences? Jefferson worried and wondered. Unfortunately, Sandow was no longer a sensation and had begun to be taken for granted. He was familiar enough to the readers of the humor magazine *Judge* that they could poke gentle fun at him in a cartoon where the strongman (called "Slamdown") metes out some well-deserved comeuppance to a carousing cowboy.

This was just one in a series of jesting references to Sandow and others of his profession. As figures of ponderous mock dignity, strongmen had long been natural targets of satire. Humorists had frequently lofted cruel but often hilarious arrows at the stage Hercules. Many cartoons appeared in humor magazines around the world that poked fun at the bombastic strongman whose phony feats of strength were revealed by mistreated underlings. Since Sandow was the single most famous strongman of the time, many of the caricatures have a striking resemblance to him.

Several well-known cartoonists also turned their attention to Sandow. In 1902 humorist Tom Browne, produced "Sandow in the Days of His Youth," showing the golden-haired young hero picking up a German schoolyard bully by the collar. Six years later, the great English wit Max Beerbohm used the strongman's recognizable persona to poke fun at the increasing commercialization of Academia. Among other "idols of the market-place," he portrays a beefy and incongruous Sandow receiving an honorary degree at Oxford's yearly Encaenia.

One of the funniest of the many Sandow parodies appeared one

THE TOUR OF AMERICA   97

year after the athlete's death, in the 1926 film *The Strong Man*, starring Harry Langdon. The title role is a burly but good-hearted giant called "Zandow," played by Arthur Thalasso. The pasty-faced Langdon plays "The Great Z's" assistant, who is inevitably forced to perform at short notice when the strongman is indisposed.

Unfortunately, Sandow's situation late in 1896 was nothing to laugh at. In order to stem the rising tide of indifference, Sandow and Jefferson came up with what they hoped would be a rejuvenating, money-making idea. About a week after they had opened, the *Pittsburgh Post* ran an excited review: "Manager Kirk of the Alvin sprung a surprise on the big audience last night at the close of the performance by the Sandow troupe." The reviewer went on the explain how the theater had secured one of the new-fangled motion picture projectors that actually showed huge, clear, and lifelike movies. As the curtain rang down on Sandow's live performance, a screen was lowered and a motion picture of the strongman flickered magically before the rapt audience. Afterwards, this was heartily applauded by the crowd.[67]

Motion pictures were neither startling nor novel in 1896; what was extraordinary about Sandow's film was that it was projected onto a screen for everyone to see. People had been conditioned to think of movies as brief, dim peep shows, but here were larger-than-life images moving jerkily across a huge screen. Sandow had stumbled onto an exciting innovation whose time had come.

The movie shown to the patrons of the Alvin had been filmed by W. K. L. Dickson for Biograph Studios, a spinoff of Edison's prolific group. Actually, Biograph made four films of Sandow, all relatively uncomplicated and shot from a single camera position. The titles of these extremely brief works were listed as follows: "Sandow (no sun)," "Sandow (sun)," "Sandow (breathing)," and "Sandow (not breathing)." All these films showed the strongman posing and demonstrating his excellent muscle control and development; at the end of two of the films, he performs a crisp, quick backflip. The breathing referred to in the last two titles involves the deep respiration required to display chest expansion. Simple as they were, the movies impressed the critics and the Pittsburgh audience.

Sandow was already something of a "movie star" since the rival film company, Edison's Vitascope, was also pursuing him to appear in their productions. Agents Raff and Gammon wrote to Ziegfeld on April 29, 1896, asking Sandow to perform for Edison's cameras: "[Sandow] was good enough to go there [Edison's studios in East Orange] two years since and permit us to take photographs of him in his 'act' for exhibition on the Kinetoscope. The original negative is worn out, and we would like to secure a new one for exhibition on the Vitascope. We believe it would result in a big advertisement for Mr. Sandow, and we will endeavor to reproduce him in one of his 'acts' life sized, and it would probably be exhibited throughout the world." Despite the offer, Sandow threw in his lot with Dickson and Biograph.[68]

Thankfully, these motion pictures put some much-needed vitality back in his act, and Sandow's popularity as a showman grew faster than ever. It must have seemed as if fate had once more laid out a banquet of prosperity for him. But the feasts of the gods are often poisoned, and such was the case this time, for the strongman found himself performing day in and day out, often twice nightly, with matinees several times a week. It was a grueling schedule that Sandow had kept up unfailingly for three long years. Inevitably, it caught up with him, and despite Sandow's highly vaunted strength, his hectic way of life came crashing down upon him. His enthusiasm for performing "took wings that outsped even my physical strength," he wrote later, "and though I never had a day's illness or suffered from any disease in my life, I had at last a very serious nervous collapse." Though it sounds incredible, the muscleman claimed that his weight sank from 15 stone (210 pounds) to 8 stone (112 pounds). His muscles "seemed almost to fade away." His skin became sallow and seemed to hang loosely on his frame. He had come to the end of his tether. The strongman had been rendered feeble and helpless.[69]

"There is a breaking strain," Sandow wrote in 1919, "with the toughest physical material, mental and physical, beyond which even the most perfectly developed and balanced man or woman may fail. Any tremendous and unexpected crisis may cause the best physical structure to collapse, just as a violent earthquake will bring down the strongest building and uproot the deepest and most firmly-laid foundation."[70] Sandow had experienced just such a cataclysm. But what was this "unexpected crisis" which afflicted him? One authority has stated that his *crise de nerfs* came about because of his many amorous liaisons; but perhaps a better explanation is that it was caused by simple overwork.[71]

Sandow had come from a very modest background, and perhaps it was the fear of poverty that eventually brought about his crack-up. Whatever the cause, the effects were devastating. He was forced to cancel the remainder of his stage appearances in America and to return to England, where he spent many months gradually recuperating. "I made myself as strong and healthy again in every way as I was in my youthful prime," he reported later. "I restored myself entirely by increasing my income of nervous energy and restricting my expenditure."[72]

Skeptics have argued that there might have been another reason for Sandow's "crisis." Possibly it was simply a convenient way to get out of an unsatisfactory business arrangement. Sandow had tarried too long in the halls. Ziegfeld saw it, but Sandow preferred to avoid the truth for as long as possible. Perhaps the breakdown therefore was invented or exaggerated in order to allow him a convenient exit before an even more humiliating failure in his career.

Whatever the cause, the result was the same: the magnificent Sandow was burned out. Even he conceded that he needed time to himself—months away from the hectic hurly-burly of vaudeville—a quiet spell in the country with Blanche and the baby daughter he had hardly seen. Sandow returned to Britain with fame and fortune in the palms of his hands, but he also carried with him physical disability and mental fatigue. He sought breathing room from his demanding public; he required time to heal his wounds.

A Growing Business

1897–1901

Sandow had returned to England broken in health but not in spirit. Debilitated though he was, the now internationally famous star was determined to put in motion long-term plans to share his knowledge of physical culture with the rest of the universe and to reap the financial benefits that this would entail. Sandow had become wealthy, famous, and a respected sports figure in the amazing space of six years. The triumph had cost him a temporary setback in health. Thanks to his naturally strong constitution, however, he easily pulled himself out of his crisis. All it took was a few month's rest with his wife and his baby girl, Helen. After this short interval of quiet domesticity, Sandow proceeded to activate the ambitious plans that had been brewing in his mind.

As early as 1887 Sandow had taken on occasional pupils, but never on a regular basis.[1] When his American audiences saw him, many people were stirred to transform themselves into stronger, shapelier, healthier beings just like Sandow. They might not dare to become perfect men, but they could certainly improve their physiques. Sandow was impressed by the depth and fervor of this interest in physical culture, for everywhere he performed he reported an avalanche of appeals from people who wanted to build their bodies. It likewise cannot have escaped his notice that here was a vast opportunity for turning his reputation into hard cash. So he began experimenting with various exercises and teaching techniques. He began detailing a system of exercises which would be adaptable to different ages, sexes, and states of health. Gradually, it occurred to him that some sort of school was needed in order to take care of the growing number of people clamoring for instruction.

Thus in 1897 Sandow opened his first Institute of Physical Culture at 32a St. James's Street, London.[2] Here he was able to conduct his own exercises and use his own special equipment. The instructors were trained by Sandow himself, and he made sure that every exercise was lucidly described and clearly demonstrated. It was a healthful and fashionable retreat from the grinding routine of urban life.

Before Sandow opened his institute, weight training and muscle building were both considered "proletarian" occupations by the class-conscious British bourgeoisie. Most of the bodybuilding gymnasiums in London were in the south and east ends of the city, deep in the working-class quarters. Young men who were anxious to perfect their bodies would usually work out three times a week. Since the average work week was sixty hours, further free time to exercise was out of the question. Very few upper-class "gentlemen" would touch a barbell; it was too much like manual labor, and of course gentlemen didn't engage in hard work.

Wishing to draw upon the desire for exercise but avoid the class connotation, Sandow created a luxurious "Institute of Physical Culture" rather than a lowly gymnasium. Significantly, Sandow placed his institute in Piccadilly rather than in other, less prestigious areas, thereby appealing to middle-class snobbishness. Thus Sandow clearly realized where his best financial prospects were to be found, and he conscientiously sought them out.

At this distance in time, it is really impossible to get a precise demographic picture of who responded to Sandow's message of physical fitness since all the records of his enterprises have been long since destroyed. We can, however, piece together the workings of similar operations. In the first half of the twentieth century the American writer and weightlifting theorist Mark Berry (1896–1958) revealed the makeup of a large group of weight trainers. In 1926 Berry became editor of *Strength* magazine and director of the venerable Milo Barbell Company. From its founding in 1902, this institution was the first to advocate heavy weight training. Fortunately, Berry was an excellent businessman, and he kept precise records.

Berry presented a breakdown of Milo's customers, and it is safe to assume that Sandow's clientele would not have been too different. About one-fourth of those who enrolled as Berry's pupils were blue-collar workers. In this category he included farmers, mechanics, policemen, soldiers, or other laborers. Another quarter was made up of college and high school students. But by far the largest group of those interested in improving their bodies were white-collar workers; one-half of all Milo's customers were in this category. Within this group Berry listed office workers, clerks, executives, teachers, and members of the professions such as doctors, lawyers, and clergymen.

Like Sandow, Berry was clearly proud that he could count so many members of the middle and upper classes among his customers. "The reader may then readily understand," he explained rather archly, "how mistaken the impression is that bar bell users are comparable to the class mostly associated with pugilism or as they are otherwise known, 'rough necks.'" Both Berry and Sandow understood that to be successful they needed to tap into the great mainstream of the Anglo-Saxon public, and this meant making weightlifting more palatable to genteel society.[3]

Sandow's school was originally a sort of luxurious clubhouse, with baths and training rooms, where the exercises could be learned and practiced. Throughout its long existence, the institute managed to retain its rich, wood-paneled, clubby atmosphere. There were plush waiting rooms filled with potted palms and Victorian clutter. There were sumptuous bathing rooms where a sweaty athlete could choose between a sit-down or a shower bath. There were oak-paneled smoking rooms, consulting rooms, and even a music parlor. But it was primarily a place for working out. The exercise room was a large, airy hall with high ceilings and hardwood floors. An individual oriental carpet marked each exercise station. The athlete would stand or lie on the carpet and work with the weights which were neatly racked on the wall behind him.

Most of the teachers in the institute were former army men, and all of them were made to study anatomy and to pass a rigid examination before they could become full-fledged instructors. These instructors, and occasionally Sandow himself, would circulate, answering questions and helping out. It must have been a very gentlemanly way to pursue bodily perfection.[4]

The institute's first manager was Warwick Brookes, Jr., Sandow's brother-in-law. Much like Sieveking before him, Brookes, Jr., was a reformed weakling who was termed by Sandow "the best pupil I have ever had." When Sandow first met him in 1891, he was described as "exceedingly delicate," and able to walk only by the use of crutches. But by sheer will power and Sandow's exercises, he strengthened himself so that he became a new man.[5] Certainly, if this former invalid could regain his vigor, then anyone could. Thus Sandow and his disciples at the institute were ready to throw out the lifeline of health to the weak and peaked of the world.

Soon the institute was accepting more and more students. "Ladies quickly realized the benefits resulting from systematic exercise," Sandow noted, "and so great was the increase in number of persons of both sexes and all ages desirous of taking up my system that additional accommodation became a matter of absolute necessity."[6] Surprisingly, at the height of its popularity, there were twenty Sandow Institutes all over the British Isles, six of them in London alone. New wings to the original building were also gradually added.

Sandow quickly discovered that ladies required more room than gentlemen. They wanted to exercise in complete privacy, so curtains were added to the women's section of the exercise floor, allowing them to work in perfect seclusion. "I have heard a lady exclaim," remarked the director, "that her dearest friend might be undertaking a course in an adjoining apartment for all she knew of her presence in the establishment."[7]

The reason for all this secrecy stemmed from an overzealous sense of modesty. Female exercises were considered a most intimate body performance, and thus the ladies had to be protected from the prying eyes of men. If this were not possible, then the woman athlete was expected to exercise while strapped in her corset despite the very real danger she ran of splitting the steel stays.[8] So Sandow's curtained rooms offered a place where his female customers could run through a set of movements while remaining uncorseted and unseen. It was the way the ladies wanted it.

Soon it became quite fashionable for ladies to take up a course of physical culture at a Sandow's Institute. In his autobiography, playwright Sydney Blow tells of a conversation that took place between his mother and a friend of hers, Constance Wilde, wife of ill-fated Oscar. When his mother asked Constance to go with her to Sandow's school of physical culture, Mrs. Wilde burst out laughing. "I really couldn't," she said. "I don't know how you can do exercises with that man. Don't you ever laugh at him?" Not only did Mrs. Blow *not* laugh at him, she was positively shocked at the very idea of snickering at Mr. Sandow at all. "She thought he was such a wonderful man," Blow explained, "he had improved her health so much."[9] Perhaps it was a mental comparison between Mrs. Wilde's soft and corpulent husband, then languishing in prison, and Sandow's hard muscularity that caused her to be amused. Besides, Sandow's defenders seemed to far outnumber his detractors—male or female.

Another significant event occurred in 1897—the publication of Sandow's second book, *Strength and How to Obtain It.* Unlike his first book, this was more of a training manual. There was also a great deal of very fanciful autobiography in it, but the principal thrust of the work was to give tips on effective exercising. Included in every copy was a large fold-out chart of exercises which could be detached and hung on the wall, enabling his readers to exercise at home. Thus physical fitness was made available to large numbers of interested people who might never have tried it before.

In order to encourage his pupils, Sandow included testimonial letters from former students as well as photographs of ordinary citizens who had brought themselves to a state of greater muscular development. He also offered advice on the proper way to do the exercises and how to receive the greatest benefits from them. He even included some elementary information on food and nutrition. In all, it was a valuable and useful addition to the physical culture bookshelf.

This was also the first book that was supposedly written entirely by Sandow himself. However, it is very doubtful whether he could have written this work, considering his limited command of written English. We can safely assume that Sandow's ideas were put into a more acceptable form of English prose by someone else.

In addition to his other activities, Sandow was also performing in music halls throughout the British Isles. One spectator remembered him at the Pavilion in the British capital about this time. After spending twenty minutes being absolutely cruel to himself and without turning one of his golden hairs, the strongman devised an interesting finale to his turn. A powdered lackey entered carrying a top hat, overcoat, and black ebony walking stick. Sandow took the stick and used it skillfully to flick the hat precisely on his head. The footman then held open his topcoat, and Sandow donned it suavely. From an inside pocket, the athlete then took out a cigar and silver matchbox. After putting the cigar in his mouth and spitting out the end onto the stage, he lit it. This was the cue for the orchestra to strike up a jaunty march. He swaggered off to his martial music as if he was just going to get into his private hansom and drive to a fancy French restaurant for supper. Only one thing marred the total picture; he might have looked elegant in overcoat and topper, but he was still wearing his pink tights and Roman sandals. They spoiled the picture. They simply did not give the effect he wanted to give: the perfect English gentleman.[10]

But while Sandow was attempting to emulate a dapper English gentleman on the London stage, three men were formulating a strongman act that was destined to give Sandow the most serious challenge to his career. The Saxon Trio, consisting of three supremely powerful men, Arno Saxon, Oscar Hilgenfeldt, and Arthur Henning, were relative newcomers to the British variety stage. They had formed their partnership in Leipzig, Germany, only a short while before coming to England. The linchpin of the act was Arthur "Saxon," as he soon came to be known. He was the strongest and came to be the most feared by rival strongmen. The act that the men took to Britain was somewhat novel in its approach, for they presented a real show of strength. There were no tricks or deceptions, no phony chain snapping or suspicious coin breaking, only a true display of great strength. But that was enough.

In 1897 the Saxons began a series of well-designed taunts intended to draw Sandow into a weightlifting contest. They regularly printed a challenge on their programs: "Arthur Saxon challenges Sandow or any other man in the world for any amount. A match can be ratified at the *Sporting News* office. Man and money ready." The trio gained a creditable reputation for strength, and by early 1898 Sandow could no longer afford to ignore their notices.[11]

On the night of Saturday, February 26, the long anticipated skirmish finally took place. Sandow was appearing at the Empire Palace in Sheffield while the Saxon Trio was at the Grand Theatre in the same city. At the finale of the act, Arno Saxon announced that Arthur would lift a barbell that even the great Sandow could not raise. After a suspenseful roll of the snare drum, Arthur advanced to the bell, rubbed resin on his hands, and then smoothly, almost effortlessly, bent pressed a 264-pound barbell. But as he replaced the weight on the floor, someone from one of boxes near the stage shouted, "Stop!" A man in evening dress stood and pointed at Arno. "I dare you, sir, to repeat that remark about Sandow being unable to raise that bell." Somewhat taken aback, Arno repeated his claim. After he did so, the man in the box removed a disguise from his face.

"Sir," replied the man in a measured, dramatic voice, "I am Eugen Sandow." This was what the audience was hoping would happen, and they immediately broke into waves of applause. Sandow jumped the stage much as he had done earlier with Sampson, but this time it was to protect his hard-earned reputation, not to make a new one.[12]

Perhaps in an attempt to intimidate Sandow, Arthur lifted first a 110-pound and later a 180-pound kettle bell to his shoulder, then he had one of his husky partners perch himself on the bell.[13] This he then bent pressed to full arm's length. Sandow would have nothing to do with these spectacular feats. He had come to answer the specific challenge and nothing more.

Because he was somewhat excited by the preceding events, Arthur had a little trouble lifting the heavy barbell to the correct position another time. But on the second attempt he was finally successful.

According to the *Sheffield Daily Telegraph,* this is what happened next: "Sandow raised the great weight up to his shoulder easily, but when he attempted to raise it higher with one hand the bar-bell swerved to one end. A further essay demonstrated the existence of the same difficulty, and an attempt was made to bring down the curtain. Sandow, however, insisted on another trial, and this time, finding the center, he raised the weight clean over his head with considerably less difficulty than his challenger had experienced."[14]

But a great controversy was brewing, one that would not be settled for four long years. Sandow's performance may have convinced the credulous reporter from the *Telegraph,* but those who knew something of weightlifting realized that he had not really completed the lift properly. After several shaky attempts, Sandow had managed to get the bell to his shoulder, but he could not stand fully erect to finish the lift. To the experts, it appeared that the mighty Sandow had been bested.

And so thought the Saxons, for in their posters and playbills they began publicizing Arthur as The Man That Defeated Sandow. However much this might have rankled Sandow, he must have felt that his case for proving otherwise was a weak one, for he did nothing about stopping the Saxons from advertising their victory for four years. And then, early in 1901, a way to ease out of this uncomfortable situation without losing face presented itself. Arno Saxon, the founder of the trio, was somehow forced out of the group entirely. Perhaps he did not come up to Arthur's high standards. Anxious to get even with the group, Arno engineered an effective revenge. He got in touch with Sandow and agreed to give testimony that the barbell used in the fateful match in Sheffield had been filled with quicksilver and that this was the reason Sandow had such difficulty raising it properly.[15]

Immediately Sandow contacted his solicitors and started legal proceedings against the Saxons and the circus where they were then performing. The charge was criminal libel in making the statement on their posters that Arthur Saxon defeated Sandow in a contest of strength. With the thought of an expensive lawsuit on his hands, the nervous manager of the circus printed an apology and a retraction of the alleged libel in the *Lancashire Daily Post* on January 5. But this was not enough. Sandow knew he had the Saxons where he wanted them, and he was out for blood. So the suit proceeded as planned.

Arthur Saxon was somewhat bewildered by the whole situation. When confronted with the circus owner's statement, he professed no knowledge of it at all, and added, "I have never apologized or withdrawn the statement"; and moreover, he was ready to meet with Sandow for a rematch. But this was not to be.

The complaint for libel was finally brought before Mr. Justice Bigham and a special jury in the city of Birmingham, where Sandow was then appearing. The lawyers for Arthur Saxon contended that Sandow had not been able to raise the barbell in question after four attempts—even on the fifth try he could not manage to raise it properly. Therefore they did not consider their advertising to be libelous at all.

In response, Sandow first called Lawrence Levy, the well-known Birmingham man who had discovered the dubious talents of Irving "Sandowe" Montgomery. The appearance of a local man who was willing to verify Sandow's strength was guaranteed to have its effect on the jury.[16] Next, it was Sandow's turn to testify.

He revealed in testimony what was perhaps the real reason for the litigation: the manager of the Empire Music Hall where he was performing "declined to continue his engagement unless he secured the withdrawal of the bill describing Saxon as having beaten him." It was only as "the strongest man on earth" that he was able to command such high fees. It also did not help his image as a teacher of physical culture. After all, who would want to be taught by the second-strongest man in the world?

Then Sandow dropped his bombshell. His lawyers called Arno Saxon to the stand. There he stated that there had been mercury in the barbell on the night in question, thereby rendering a successful lift impossible. He testified that after much practice, Arthur had been able to perfect a lift keeping the bell at a dead level. Since Sandow was unused to the weight, he was not able to lift it properly. He assured the court that his partner, Arthur, had won the contest not by strength but by craft.[17]

All the sincere and vociferous denials of the defendant seemed to have no effect, for the jury retired briefly. When they returned, they found for the plaintiff. Arthur Saxon was ordered to pay £25 in damages to Sandow, and galling though it must have been, the Saxons were forced to remove the offending statement from their posters and advertising.

Sometime later Sandow claimed to have obtained the original barbell and to have found the hidden compartment still containing the mercury, thus vindicating Arno's claim. But certain nagging questions remain. Many years after the event, Kurt Saxon, a later member of the group, claimed that the quicksilver story was nonsense. "What we always did for saving expenses was to fill our barbells with sand," he announced, "and that would not give any lifter trouble."[18] Since their partnership had just begun, the trio simply could not afford to fill the large bell with so expensive a substance as mercury. But perhaps even more damning is the fact that no matter how much he might practice, not even the great Arthur could keep such an unsteady liquid at a dead level. Eventually the bell would see-saw out of control. So the evidence suggests that Sandow invented the story in order to justify his inability to lift the weight, and then had the disgruntled Arno back him up.

Later analysts of the *Sandow* v. *Saxon* case have sided with Arthur Saxon, not the victor. In "Saxon vs. Sandow," Alan Carse gives both a description of the hearing and some strong criticism for the quality of the decision. From Carse's account it seems clear that Sandow based his case on a technicality. In order to complete a bent press correctly, it is necessary to stand erect holding the weight with straightened arm above the head. This Sandow had failed to do, but the strongman and his resourceful lawyer hoped to wiggle out through a legal loophole. Failing this, Sandow planned on obscuring the facts with a little show business glitter.

When it came time for him to testify, Sandow jumped up in the middle of the courtroom, tore off his shirt, and revealed his muscular physique. Next, an assistant brought a barbell into court. Then while Sandow's lawyer explained that this was exactly as Sandow had lifted Saxon's bell, the blond Hercules stood the bell on end, rocked it to his shoulder, tilted it, swung it around, and pressed it to arm's length. He did not stand up straight with the weight, but he did prove that he had lifted the weight above his head with one hand.

Anyone with even a smattering of weightlifting knowledge would realize that this was not proper form for the bent press. Unfortunately, Mr. Justice Bigham was apparently in the dark in matters athletic. He ruled that Sandow had indeed raised the bar over his head as the strongman had contended all along. The judge therefore granted an injunction restraining the Saxons from again repeating their claim of victory over Sandow.

Carse's remarks summed up the ruling nicely: "Learned as are judges and other minions of the law about many things, the result of the famous court case certainly showed that they knew nothing of the correct form in weight lifting."[19]

His reputation had been neatly, though none too nobly, rescued in the *Sandow* v. *Saxon* trial, but it only served to point out the vagaries of the strongman's life. Fame was fleeting, and there was always some Young Turk eager to snatch it away. He had long known that something else was needed to keep interest alive in his system and himself. So in the summer of 1898 he embarked on a bold new venture—one that would change both his life and the way the public perceived body-building. He decided to start a magazine. It was called simply *Physical*

Culture, and it was first published in July, edited and directed by Sandow. In his first editorial he explained his concept of physical culture and why it was important. The ultimate aim of physical culture, he announced, "is to raise the average standard of the race as a whole. That is, no doubt, a stupendous task, and one which it may take many lifetimes to accomplish. But everything must have its beginning, and unless we set about improving the physique of the present generation, we cannot hope to benefit those who come after us."[20] It was a tall order, but it was one that he grew increasingly to believe in. It was also a dream that began to have its effect felt all over the English-speaking world at an astoundingly rapid rate.

The first volume of *Physical Culture* was fairly typical of others that were to follow. There were athletic training tips and articles on individual sports. There were cartoons and frivolous pieces, and there was even a series of articles on common strongman feats and how to do them. Surprisingly, the quality of the writing was generally quite high for a sporting magazine. The editors had secured articles by such well-known authors as the American Hamlin Garland; the author of *All the World's Fighting Ships*, Frederick Jane; music hall comedian Dan Leno; and the humorist P. G. Wodehouse.

In April of 1899 the name of the magazine was changed to *Sandow's Magazine of Physical Culture*. It was by this name that it would be known henceforth. Almost from the start, the magazine was considered timely enough to be bound in more permanent covers, and during its heyday there was hardly a library in the country that did not have at least one or two of the familiar red volumes on its shelves.

Early as it was, *Sandow's Magazine* was not the first periodical to be devoted completely to physical culture and bodybuilding. Professor Edmond Desbonnet had founded a weekly journal, *L'Athlète*, in 1896. In the words of its founder, the magazine was "destined to bring the good news to France and to propagate the ideas of strength, health, beauty, and morality."[21] The publication, however, was geared to sports and athletics generally, not to physical culture alone. Unfortunately, bodybuilders would have to wait two more years for a magazine exclusively their own.

The honor of producing the first health and body culture journal was finally nabbed by Bernarr Macfadden. In 1898 he began to publish a magazine called *Physical Development*. Macfadden had come to England from the backwoods of Missouri just the year before in order to market a new rubber chest expander. He had the good fortune to team up with a British sporting entrepreneur, Hopton Hadley, and the two of them started the magazine. Eventually, they parted company, each to begin his own publication. The Englishman began *Health & Strength*, probably the best known of the early bodybuilding magazines, and the American continued with *Macfadden's Physical Development*. This later spawned a whole host of publications in the United States, most famous of which was *Physical Culture*. [22]

Many have concluded that the colorful Macfadden had only a tenuous hold on sanity, especially in his later years. But one thing is certain: he popularized health, strength, and bodybuilding in a well-intentioned though often sensational way. His principal downfall was his credence in just about every crackpot speculator and theorist who came along. He continually experimented with new and "advanced" ideas of health and hygiene, regardless of their logical content. He wore a hat with holes cut in it (for ventilation), and only rarely cut his unruly, frizzy hair. He walked five miles to his New York office every day barefoot, often carrying a forty-pound sack of sand if he thought there might be reporters lurking along the route. And through it all, he still had time for what one of his many wives called "a perpetual zest for physical love."[23] Compared to Macfadden, Sandow must have seemed as respectable as a Sunday school teacher.

One of the early innovations that appeared in *Sandow's Magazine* was the *Half-Crown Postal Course*. [24] The editor had received so many inquiries from subscribers about exercises that he decided to institute a mail order business. For the low sum of two shillings and sixpence, the correspondents got a table of exercises that was supposed to last them for one month. The course of exercises was drawn up depending on the particular wants or needs of the persons writing in. Sandow stated the aim of the postal course was "the proper and systematical development of the whole frame and internal organs" and "to strengthen the *will*, and thus to help them to fill their several vocations in life with a capacity and joy which are unknown in a debilitated frame."[25]

Partly because of Sandow's magazine, partly because of his correspondence course, and partly because of the popularity of his stage performances, the desire to become healthy and strong was beginning to catch on. Slowly at first, then later gathering momentum, a physical culture craze was sweeping the world. For the first time since the ancient Greeks, large numbers of people were starting to take stock of their health and their physical appearance. The wonderful possibilities of bodybuilding and exercise were suddenly dawning on the popular imagination, and Sandow was in on the ground floor of this movement.

Men, women, and children began hefting dumbbells, performing exercises, and swinging Indian clubs—unsure and creaky at first, they gradually became adept at the new movements. "Physical Culture," one prominent journal assured its readers, "is very much in the air just now, but not only in its aspect as an aid to beauty, but also as an avenue to health."[26]

It soon seemed as if a new and glorious age of physical perfection was dawning. This new era received an unpleasant and sudden impetus in 1899. In that year Great Britain and her colonies went to war against the stubborn little South African republics of the Orange Free State and the Transvaal.

Overnight, obscure geographic points at the other end of the world became household words. Magersfontein and Mafeking, Kimberly and Ladysmith, Spion Kop and Colenso all became bloody and terrible names—reminders of the boys in khaki on the veldt. But the Boer War had another subtler effect on life in Britain. When induction began and thousands of men joined the army, the medical inspectors found that a shocking number of the volunteers could not meet the standards set by the military. A frightfully high percentage of them were too weak and sickly to fight for queen and country. Great numbers of men were stoop-shouldered, emaciated, diseased, or just generally faint and infirm. Clearly, something had to be done—the defense of the kingdom depended on it. Sandow and people like him were soon there to see that the flower of English manhood grew strong once more. British fighting men may have had hearts of oak, but unfortunately many of them also had arms of rubber and chests of dough. The prophetic warnings of people like Aldershot's Fox had not been heeded, but with Sandow's help, that would all change.

Even without the war, however, the physical culture craze would have gathered adherents. It was not long since the Society for the Suppression of Vice had crusaded against any game playing on the Sabbath. Those who persisted in such physical exercise as "the shameful practice of rowing-machines and boat races" found themselves prosecuted in the courts. Starting midway through the nineteenth century, however, a fascination with sports gripped Victorian society. As a journalist in 1870 pointed out, young men of the day seemed "possessed by a perfect mania for every species of athletic contest."[27]

Bruce Haley in *The Healthy Body and Victorian Culture* has observed that this sporting craze was at least partly motivated by the Victorian spirit of self-improvement. This time, however, the desire to better oneself had shifted from the spiritual to the physical realm. According to Haley, "The March of Mind was giving way to the March of Body."[28]

It had suddenly become fashionable to engage in athletics, and both sexes were eager to participate in a little friendly sport. Only a few years before, the only game a well-bred lady could indulge in was croquet, but with the change in attitude, women were playing tennis and golf and many other sports that had hitherto been the exclusive domain of men. The men were also participating in athletics more than ever. There was hardly a city or village in Britain that did not have its cycling society, its cricket team, or its football club. In fact, at the height of the craze a certain reverend gentleman complained that the people of England were beginning to renounce St. George for St. Sandow.[29] For his part, Sandow wisely refrained from any claims of saintliness.

The combination of athletics and religion had long been linked in the English mind. Muscular Christianity, which was so stridently espoused in the public schools, was a potent force. It was an English gentleman's duty to use his God-given strength to good effect. It had been granted to him in order to be used, in the words of one authority, "for the protection of the weak, the advancement of all righteous causes, and the subduing of the earth which God has given to the children of men."[30]

From its beginnings in the mid-nineteenth century, muscular Christianity caught on with amazing rapidity all over the English-speaking world. Taking into account the Victorians' obsession with *force* as a philosophical tenet, muscular Christianity was an idea whose time had come.

Basically, the doctrine sought to reconcile physical vigor with spiritual sanctity. Many mid-Victorian religious men had been alarmed at the encouragement of "feminine" virtues in the church. Such qualities as humility, acceptance, and meekness were rotting the church from the core—or so they believed. What was needed was a more active role for robust members of the religious community. Many men of the cloth strove to become more physical and aggressive; they were tired of turning the other cheek. Aggression and strength were man's portion, and many were determined to act on this creed.

Perhaps the most eloquent spokesman for muscular Christianity was Thomas Hughes. Through his Tom Brown books, he influenced thousands of British and American readers with his ideas. In the author's works, aggression is touted as the central quality of all manly existence. "After all," he asks in *Tom Brown's School Days,* "what would life be without fighting, I should like to know? From the cradle to the grave, fighting, rightly understood, is the business, the real, highest, honestest business of every son of man.... I am as sorry as any man to see folk fighting the wrong people and the wrong things, but I'd a deal sooner see them doing that than that they should have no fight in them."[31]

From Hughes and others like him, gradually there grew up a cult of "manliness" that permeated sport and education in the late nineteenth century. Benjamin Rader points out that the term carries no connotation of what we know as *machismo*. "The manly youth, above all, practiced sexual continence and resisted the 'secret vice' [masturbation]. . . . The manly youth cultivated self-command and absolute candor; he abhorred display, pretension, sentimentality, and capitulation to pain. He insisted on justice and was quick to defend honor with physical prowess; he was physically active, striving to develop to the utmost robustness, animal energy, and personal courage."[32]

Sandow and others used popular theology to gather more adherents to their cause. As early as 1899 *Sandow's Magazine* ran an article titled simply "Muscular Christianity" by the Reverend G. P. Horne. In it the author assures his readers that becoming holy and becoming strong are nearly identical: "Between Muscular Christianity and Physical Culture is, at farthest, a short step: the praise of one is praise of the other, the apostle of one is also apostle of the other. . . . Muscular Christianity is Physical Culture from the point of view of the minister of religion."[33]

Not to be outdone, the rival magazine *Health & Strength* jumped on the religious bandwagon by encouraging its readers to go into the gymnasium and win over athletes to their cause. "Full-orbed manhood," wrote H. X. Yoxall, "with thorough-going consecration to Christ, is the only hope the Church has of winning back the great, growing, throbbing world of modern sports."[34]

Thus the physical culture craze had finally succeeded in joining health and holiness. Clergymen gradually came to see the body as an ally rather than an enemy in winning over the soul. It also opened up exercise and gymnastics to another large group of initiates who might not otherwise have considered it.[35]

Strength of body and strength of character were indissolubly connected. And so, whether he wanted it or not, the odor of sanctity descended uneasily upon Sandow. An important manifestation of this near canonization was a slim volume published in 1899. It was called *Hints from Sandow* and was written by the Reverend R. L. Bellamy, vicar of Silkstone. The book is presented in the form of a dialogue between two athletic chums, Ted and Charlie. They have finished their workout at Sandow's Institute, and as they rest, their thoughts turn to spiritual things. Though not strident or overly preachy, the book does make its points in a rather charming manner. One of the men compares Christianity to using Sandow's patented grip dumbbells in progressive weights. "Now, isn't that just our Lord's method?" he asks innocently. "Use what you have as well as you possibly can, and then more shall be given you. Faithfulness in little is the way to power over much."[36] Exercise thus becomes a metaphor for the acquisition of saving grace. It was an odd combination of ideas, but the book's sincerity and timeliness made it a favorite with the athletic set.

While others were attempting to use physical culture to save souls, Sandow was turning to other dividends of the fitness mania. One of the finest ventures that presented itself was the sale and marketing of exercise machines. In a move that has been adroitly emulated by many others, Sandow was able to cash in on his fame by pushing his apparatuses. As early as 1894, while he was still in America, he patented and sold an ungainly contraption for developing the legs. This "ingeniously contrived and useful machine" looked like it would be more at home in a torture chamber than a gymnasium.[37] It consisted of two posts about five or six feet apart to which were attached rubber cables with stirrups. The athlete sat in the middle and put his legs through the stirrups, attaching them about the knees. He was thus able to work the muscles on the inside of his thighs. Not surprisingly, the machine never really caught on.

Sandow's next venture was considerably more successful. On March 6, 1897, shortly after he had returned from his tour of America, Sandow entered into an agreement with the Whitely Exerciser Company. He was to act as European agent for the company and demonstrate and sell their popular product.[38] The Whitely exerciser was a chest expander which used a complicated series of rubber strands and pulleys to build the muscles. Sandow found that this device was so enthusiastically received that a year after he began work for Whitely he quit abruptly and established his own rival business in France. There he produced his particular version of the device and called it "Sandow's Own Combined Developer." He touted it as a combination of a rubber exerciser, chest expander, light dumbbells, and weightlifting apparatus. It was much like the Whitely exerciser except for some important improvements that he had devised. He did away with the complex pulleys and added light dumbbells to the handles. He made the weighted handles removable so the device could also be used as a chest expander. Sandow's developer was much more versatile than any other on the market, and it accordingly sold extremely well. By the time the new century turned, there seemed to be one in just about every household in the kingdom.

One of the principal virtues of Sandow's developer was its simplicity. It was attached to any closed door, with one rubber strand attached to the top and the other to the door knob. The user exercised by simply yanking vigorously on the weighted handles. Despite its ease of operation, however, attachment to doors must have made it very precarious at times, for there are many jokes and cartoons in the pages of *Sandow's*

Magazine showing the consequences of children or servants who open the door at inopportune moments. But the benefits far outweighed the drawbacks. "A few minutes' use morning and evening," remarked one advertising booklet, "will brace up the system, quicken the sluggish liver and do away with that tired feeling resulting from a sedentary life."[39]

Another of the developer's greatest selling points was its adaptability. The entire family could use it, and it was particularly recommended to ladies. "Its daily use," Sandow promised his adherents, "will drive away the Demon Dyspepsia and Insomnia." Sandow's combined developer was "weak enough for a child—strong enough for a Sandow."

Sandow's device continued to sell extremely well for a very long time—even after the death of its inventor. Eventually, the Sandow trademark and endorsements were purchased by rival firms and then sold and resold several times. Its last incarnation, the Sandow Appliance Company, estimated that over one million sets of developers had been sold all over the world. The apparatus has even crept into modern parlance, for to this day in France the word for any rubber cable has remained *un sandow*.

Building health and muscles at home had been an important part of physical education since the 1860s. Several companies had specialized in providing these "Parlor Gymnasiums" to households around the world. The American firm of Peck and Snyder advertised pulley machines, Indian clubs, dumbbells, and other devices that were designed to build the muscles and stamina of the users. The principal advantage of working out at home was that the user did not have to fear overdoing it. Peck and Snyder assured their customers that the home gymnasium "embodies all the virtues to be derived from attending a regular gymnasium, but far more beneficial in its results, as the tendency in a gymnastic school is to overdo, and thus neutralize the otherwise good results of judicious muscular exercise."[40]

Home exercise continued to blossom, and soon others were involved in selling their own brand of exercise to the public. By the turn of the century, A. G. Spaulding had taken over the field by merchandising many of the same items but on a much wider scale. Health & Strength in England and Bardou, Clerc & Cie. in France were purveyors of home exercise equipment on the other side of the Atlantic.[41]

By the time Sandow entered the business, there had been many others before him, but the great strongman had one major advantage over the others. None of his competitors had Sandow's name and reputation to help sell the equipment, and this proved invaluable as a marketing tool.

Inspired by his striking successes in the developer line, Sandow next turned to a rather more unique sort of device, the "Spring-Grip Dumbbell." One of Sandow's pet theories of muscle building was that one must concentrate carefully on the specific muscles that one worked while exercising. In order to aid in proper concentration, he invented the grip dumbbell. "The bell is composed of two halves," he explained, "between which a number of small steel springs are placed. The number of springs can be altered so that the power required to close the bell can be varied to the extent required, with the result that the pupil can regulate his progress to a nicety as his strength increases." In addition, the added mental energy that was needed to keep the bells closed added almost unconsciously to the concentration and will power.[42]

Sandow advertised heavily in his own and other magazines, claiming that the shining nickel-plated devices were "the greatest invention of the age." The ads proclaimed, "Ladies use them. City men use them. Children use them. Cricketers and footballers use them. Everybody should use them. SANDOW USES THEM."[43] In the early 1920s another improvement was added to the spring-grip dumbbells: a small bell rang when the springs had been depressed all the way, enabling the athlete to know when the dumbbell was completely closed.

As important as his inventions and business successes were, they were not enough to make Sandow forsake his stage career. An appearance that nearly wreaked havoc with Sandow's carefully molded reputation as an artist occurred in Paris. Thanks once again to Professor Desbonnet, we get a new light on Sandow's character. Unfortunately, it is an illumination that is not very flattering to the strongman.

One of the most important promotional techniques that Sandow had learned from Ziegfeld was to make himself as visible to the public as possible. It was a ploy that had always served him well in the past; however, Sandow's perpetual ballyhoo and shrill self-aggrandizement had seldom won him friends among his many jealous but less savvy competitors.

The strongman's unpopularity became baldly evident when he was slated to appear at the Casino de Paris in 1900. When a group of chauvinistic French athletes heard of his booking, they found their Gallic pride wounded to the quick. They quickly organized a *chahut*, that peculiar French reaction of booing, hooting, and whistling which is reserved for wildly unpopular theatrical acts. They intended to teach the invading *Godam* a lesson he would not soon forget.

The most formidable opponent in the cabal against Sandow was the massive weightlifter Apollon, known to his countrymen as "le Demi-Dieu de la Force." Sandow was well known as a flamboyant and extravagant figure who regularly appeared in the papers on both sides of the English Channel. Apollon and his cronies were angry and jealous that the Casino had imported a foreigner to perform feats of strength when there were plenty of good Frenchmen who were far superior to Sandow at lifting weights. They were therefore determined to prevent the Anglo-German upstart from sullying the stage of the theater.

That clear-eyed observer of the athletic scene Edmond Desbonnet soon got wind of this conspiracy, and when Sandow arrived in the French capital, the professor decided to warn his old friend of the impending disaster. The only solution seemed to be to get Sandow and Apollon together for a face-to-face meeting. This they both agreed to do.

Aware of his reputation as a man who threw about much money and even more rhetoric, Sandow wisely explained his situation to Apollon in humble and candid terms. "Listen, my friend," he begged. "I am not wealthier than you. On the contrary, I am in the same difficulty as you are. Like you, I am trying to earn a living. But there is a difference—I admit it: as a foreign athlete here, I am forced in particular to make myself well received. My ostentation might seem excessive, but consider that in order to make myself easily accepted I have to lead a showy life, to display an exaggerated generosity, and in short, to have many extra expenses. In thinking about this, can you believe that when all these expenses are deducted I make more than you?" Sandow then invited Apollon to watch him work. It was not his lifting that he intended to specialize in, rather he was concentrating on his artistic posing routines. There could not possibly be any rivalry about that. After some consideration, the "Demi-dieu" seemed mollified, but Sandow was still worried about the other volatile Frenchmen in the plot.

On the night of his debut, the Casino was packed. Even Sandow's wife, Blanche, came over for the event. At the appropriate moment, Sandow's turn was announced, the orchestra struck up "The Washington Post" march by Sousa, and the curtain should have risen. But nothing happened. Sandow, completely unnerved by fear of French insults, dithered fretfully behind the scenes and refused to go on stage. The orchestra came to the end of the march and started again, but the same thing happened a second time: the curtain did not go up.

Finally, Desbonnet, Blanche, and the manager of the Casino rushed backstage and confronted the nervous athlete. The group begged Sandow to go on. They assured him that nothing would happen to mar the performance, and if worse came to worst, the orchestra would drown out the boos and whistles of the audience. Everyone attempted to infuse the athlete with some much needed confidence. At last, Sandow agreed reluctantly to go on.

When the curtain finally rose, the impatient audience quickly calmed down. Sandow posed masterfully in his famous red velvet posing box, and almost at once the French crowd recognized the work of a true artist. Aside from a few initial catcalls and challenges, the evening ended triumphantly. Sandow's popularity in the City of Lights had been preserved. It was, however, the last time he performed in France. The stress of confronting a Parisian audience no doubt threatened another nervous breakdown.[44]

If Sandow had learned a lesson from all this it must have been that he was no longer considered an international weightlifting threat. From now on, Sandow had to rely on fancy poses and elaborate stage tricks rather than legitimate lifting feats to entertain his audiences. His record-breaking days were over. From now on, he must concentrate on artistic effects.

Later in the year Sandow was back home in England where his acceptance as a performer had never been in question. Perhaps his *succès d'estime* in Paris had encouraged him to create bigger and better things in London. Whatever the reason, one of the grandest, most elaborate, and flashiest performances that Sandow—or probably any other professional strongman—had achieved occurred at the newly opened Hippodrome in London.

This magnificent theater had a reputation nearly as great as Sandow's. The journalistic coverage of its construction and opening had been unprecedented in its detail. The opulent hall had a huge stage which could be raised or lowered by means of a hydraulic lift, and this lent itself well to the production of mighty spectacles. One of the first and most famous of these cast-of-hundreds stage epics was *Siberia*. It opened at the Hippodrome in June of 1900 and played for many months. At one point in the action, the stage was partially flooded and Cossacks on horseback chased escaped prisoners from the salt mines. The harried escapees were forced to jump into an icy river in a suicidal attempt to gain their freedom. "Nothing more ingenious or startling," wrote the *Graphic* breathlessly, "is to be seen in London than this scene, which raises the excitement of the audience to fever heat."[45]

In September of that year, also on the same bill with *Siberia*, was "Sandow, the Strongest Man in the World." His act included the usual posing and strength stunts—all thrilling in their own way, but hardly competition to the feverish excitement of a stage epic. But Sandow had not lost his theatrical flair; he too knew how to generate a little heat of his own. For the second half of his act, he had arranged for a special tableau invented and produced by the theatrical director Frank Parker. This was entitled "Tommy Atkins supporting the British Generals." The writer Shaw Desmond remembered the exciting performance vividly. Sandow as Tommy Atkins, the personification of the British soldier, came out on the stage "scarce to be recognized in the new khaki of the Boer War." When Private Sandow discovers that a bridge needs to be built in a matter of minutes in order to save horses, soldiers, and officers, he offers his own body for the task. Sandow gallantly assumed the familiar Tomb of Hercules position, and a heavy plank bridge was placed in position across his young, sacrificial body. The British army then moved across him to the stirring chords of "Rule Britannia." The scene was as timely and appropriate as it was magnificent, and it marked a high point in Sandow's career as a performer.[46]

The British public might have loved Sandow, but he was being eyed jealously by others. Luigi Borra, the athlete who had been discovered and renamed Milo Brinn by Attila many years previously, reported to his old mentor in New York on Sandow's latest presentation. He wrote in a letter dated September 24, 1900, that Sandow's new act was a tremendous success, though he added petulantly, "I don't see much talent or cleverness in his performance." In his somewhat idiosyncratic English, the Italian strongman continued, "Is the old weightlifting exhibition staged in a elaborate scale. Of course, the success is his posing under the light showing his muscles, but his body is not so good as many years ago. His muscles they are fat and not so big as before." Then, realizing he was sounding vindictive, he adds, "I don't say they [Sandow's muscles] are bad, but they don't come up to expectation for a man that passes as the most perfect body and the strongest man!!!"[47] Fortunately for Sandow, the opinions of his rivals bore little weight when it came to his theatrical drawing power.

Brinn's caustic comments to the contrary, by 1901 Sandow could claim with some justification that he was one of the most perfectly developed men of his era. It was because of his bodily perfection that he was approached by Professor Ray Lankester, director of the natural history branch of the British Museum. He wanted to mount an exhibit displaying examples of all the major races of the world—the first was to be the Caucasian race, and Sandow was to represent it.[48]

To do this Lankester asked the strongman to have a complete cast of his body made; this was then to be mounted on a pedestal and displayed like a magnificent work of art. According to the director, the cast would serve two purposes. "Firstly," he said, "it presents a perfect type of a European man, and secondly, it furnishes a striking demonstration of what can be done in the way of perfecting the muscles by simple means."[49] Thus Sandow's cast was to be a fitting monument to man's ability to mold his own body. And Sandow could not have been blind to the massive free publicity for his schools, mail order courses, and apparatuses that he would receive. Honor and potential profit—it was a perfect combination.

Making a cast of something dead or inanimate is not really a great problem, but troubles start proliferating when one is dealing with a living subject, and no one had ever attempted a complete body cast before. The firm of Messrs. Brucciani, who had been contracted to make the cast, openly expressed doubts about whether the project could be done at all. First there was the problem of remaining absolutely motionless for the time it took for the plaster to set—an excruciating fifteen minutes. Added to that was the even greater difficulty that Sandow had: he needed to keep his muscles flexed and tense the entire time in order to show off his body to the greatest benefit.[50] It was not going to be an easy task. Nevertheless, the lure of being immortalized in plaster was too strong to resist, so Sandow duly delivered himself into the hands of the Brucciani family.

The first step in the casting process was to pose correctly. Unfortunately, Sandow chose a stance that was neither graceful nor easy to hold. He flexed his right bicep, holding one of his grip dumbbells, his head turned toward his fist. His left arm was extended downward with another grip dumbbell in its grasp. Awkward though it was, the pose had one distinct advantage: Sandow could show off all his best features: his biceps, triceps, lats, obliques, thighs, and of course, his extraordinary abdominals.

Next, a carefully constructed paper pattern was made and a stand was built so that he could return to exactly the same pose day after day. After this, a wooden mold was placed around the section which was being cast, leaving a space of about an inch or two. Sandow's skin was then thoroughly oiled so that when the mold was pulled away the tissue would not come with it and a little cloth sack was carefully positioned over his private parts.[51] The final step was to pour liquid plaster of Paris into the frame. When it was firm, it produced an exact impression of Sandow's body.

Since it took fifteen minutes for the plaster to harden, one of the greatest problems that confronted the athlete was remaining still. Each body section had to be done separately in order to reduce many of the difficulties. Later the mold sections were reassembled and more plaster was poured into the cavity. When this dried, the mold was broken away and the cast was complete.

Even the great Sandow could only stand about half an hour of this torture per day. "I used to finish up after each piece was done fairly 'blown,'" he remarked, "perspiring and winded much more than after the most arduous weightlifting performance I have ever accomplished."[52] Between sessions he had to take long rests in order to smoke a cheroot and get his breath back before he began the torment anew. No one has recorded the number of times he had to start over because he moved or the plaster did not set properly or who knows what other reasons, but we do know that it took him one solid month of daily sessions before the cast was completed. No wonder Sandow considered this the greatest feat of endurance he had ever performed.

The craftsmen producing the cast began with the legs and then proceeded up the body, ending with the head. They solved the problem of reproducing the face by doing it one half at a time. But by far, the hardest part was taking the chest and midsection. This is the part of the body that moves the most, breathing in and out constantly. In order to overcome this difficulty, Sandow had to keep the muscles of his chest and abdomen as still as possible. He was forced to take small, quick breaths—just enough to keep air in his lungs but not so much as to destroy the outer contour.

When the celebrated cast was nearly completed, Messrs. Brucciani put a few finishing touches on it. They made sure Sandow's curly hair was rendered artfully. They even reproduced his dapper Kaiser Bill mustache, taking care that both ends stood up smartly. After the obligatory fig leaf was added, the cast was ready for viewing. A small plaque was attached to the base, marked rather unpoetically "Xanthochroic-Caucasian type—E. Sandow."

When queried later about the honor of having his cast in the renowned British Museum, Sandow stated the case quite frankly, "Of course, I was only too glad and proud to do it. I grudge no trouble and time in the cause of physical culture," he declared, but added in exasperation, "I don't think I'd go through it again for any amount of money."[53] Circumstances would soon give him several other reasons for making that statement.

The reaction which arose after the cast went on view must have caught Sandow off guard. Critics and fellow athletes began to attack it almost as soon as it appeared. To speak truthfully, the plaster cast was not a thing of beauty. It lacked proportion and symmetry. Part of the difficulty arose with Sandow's desire to flex just about every muscle he had to its greatest extent. Unlike the balanced and well-formed original, the cast seemed to bulge indiscriminately in all directions. Almost at once skeptics started comparing the proportions of the cast to Sandow's earlier, verifiable measurements.

These unflattering comparisons were occasioned by a medical examination that had been conducted several years earlier by an eminent American professor. While Sandow was in Boston, Dr. Dudley A. Sargent, the respected teacher and coach at Harvard University, carefully measured the twenty-six-year-old athlete. Many experts consider these statistics to be the most accurate ever taken of the young strongman. Eight years later people could compare those measurements with the cast for themselves. Among other things Sargent reckoned that his subject's right bicep measured 16.9 inches and his waist was 32.7 inches. The cast, on the other hand, sported an 18-inch bicep and an astounding 36.5-inch waist.[54] Even allowing for normal growth, it was evident that something was wrong somewhere.

Part of the answer might lie in the process of making the cast in the first place. It is nearly impossible to get an accurate impression of a living subject no matter how scrupulous one might try to be. Sandow obviously tried to give as careful a rendition of himself as was possible, but it just was not good enough. Even the slightest movement would smear and blur the plaster, so it seems that this was part of the reason for the failure of the cast. A human being simply cannot remain motionless for the length of time it takes for plaster to harden properly.

So after all the hardship and genuine suffering that Sandow went through to make the cast, it was an aesthetic failure. Although there were many who defended it, the majority tended to find it graceless and clumsy. "A monstrosity," one journalist called it, and he echoed the sentiments of many others.[55]

In all fairness, though, it has to be admitted that the public simply did not know what to make of Sandow's impressive physique. They were used to seeing statues of well-proportioned Greek athletes, but Sandow's body was much more massive than the classical ideals of perfect musculature. At least one person—Professor Lankester—came to the strongman's defense here: "Who is to say," he asked rhetorically, "what are the limits of muscular development—where the line is to be drawn where healthy development leaves off and monstrosity begins?" It was a question that was as perplexing then as it is today. Wisely, Dr. Lankester did not attempt an answer.[56]

Understandably, Sandow reacted defensibly to these "reptile attacks" as he termed them. A telling cartoon appeared in a 1902 issue of *Sandow's Magazine* that sums up his attitude to the whole situation. It shows the cast being pelted with mud and smeared with filth. Underneath is written the simple caption "The Penalty of Success." It was a penalty Sandow had not expected and did not fully deserve.

After a while, the cast was retired from its spot in the museum. Its very existence and the furor that it had caused were gradually forgotten. Today, the cast lies disassembled in one of the many cavernous storage facilities of the British Museum. On rare occasions it is put back together for special visitors, then returned to obscurity. Each time it is taken apart and reassembled, a little more of the fragile plaster flakes away and a few more hairline cracks appear. One of these days this precious link with bodybuilding's history will suddenly crumble into a powdery heap.[57]

At the turn of the century, many thought Sandow marked the ultimate limits of human body development—no one would ever go beyond him. And many people were proud that this anomaly had occurred in their own lifetimes. As one American journalist put it: "It is to be hoped that the scientists of the future who excavate this cast from the ruins of London will believe that every man was like him."[58] If Sandow had anything to do with it, that prophesy would come to pass.

Sandow had been immortalized in plaster, on film, and in the hearts and minds of his many admirers, but there were still other crusades to attract his seemingly boundless energy and to gain him even more recognition. Perhaps his most ardent quest at this time was for national physical education—a cause which Sandow fought for tirelessly. And well he might have fought, for Great Britain's record in the area of physical education was certainly a dismal one. She was the richest, most powerful nation in the world, the owner of an empire so vast the sun never set on it, the model for all civilized countries. And yet, Britain was also one of the least healthy lands in Europe. Illness and poor health were rampant, and not just among the poor. Disease spread among the swells of Rotten Row almost as easily as among the indigents of Seven Dials. Simple knowledge of sanitation was sadly lacking in all classes and conditions. Perhaps the most shocking example of this ignorance was found in the royal family itself. Prince Albert, Queen Victoria's beloved consort, died in 1861 from typhoid fever contracted from drinking water that had been contaminated by an open sewer that ran through the cellars of Windsor Castle. King Cholera and Queen Tuberculosis reigned throughout the land and claimed subjects from all levels of society.

Throughout most of Sandow's life the sanitary conditions of most British subjects were abysmal. Even so, the government had made some efforts to improve living conditions. In an attempt to halt the spread of disease, Parliment passed the impressive Public Health Act in 1875. This legislation was designed to consolidate all previous public health laws and to divide the country into urban and rural health districts with elected councils.

The new law caused a few localities to begin the massive job of cleaning up. For example, Manchester, which had 38,132 privy middens in 1871, had them reduced to 606 in 1883. The statistics on some diseases were also encouraging. The rate of deaths from fevers, 901 per million between 1861 and 1870, dropped to 374 per million in the decade from 1871 to 1880. The death rate from typhoid, which had been on a steady rise until 1869, when there were 371 deaths per million, leveled off and then declined dramatically, dipping to a rate of 47 per million between 1911 and 1915.

Despite these advances, the hygienic conditions of the country were generally quite bleak. A report made in 1885–86 and titled "On Sanitary Survey Made in Anticipation of Cholera" claimed that "In some towns the old sewering is so defective as to be almost more an injury to the place than an advantage.... Sometimes there were no sewers provided at all."

The report also detailed information about the overcrowded and filthy conditions of workers' quarters. There was special mention of the insanitary living conditions miners were subjected to. Landlords took advantage of the different shifts the miners worked. "It is found convenient," reported the survey, "to take into a cottage two sets of lodgers who occupy all the beds in the dwelling not at night only, but both by night and by day; one set entering and lying down to sleep in the same room and in the same bed that had been vacated just previously by other lodgers."

These infractions were unfortunately typical of filthy conditions all across the country. So although the passage of the 1875 Public Health Act was a great parliamentary victory for reformers, in practice it was a failure simply because the struggle had not been continued with sufficient enthusiasm. Despite the efforts of Sandow and others like him, preventable disease and poor health continued to plague England and, for that matter, the rest of the world.[59]

On the American side of the Atlantic the situation was hardly better. As early as 1850 the mortality rate in Boston, New York, and other large American cities had begun to exceed that in London; by 1859 one out of every twenty-seven inhabitants of New York City would die in that year alone. It was small wonder that the death rate rose, considering the squalid living conditions in most large American cities.[60]

The poorer quarters of most U.S. cities were scenes of overcrowding, filth, and disorder. Narrow, unpaved streets were turned into muddy open sewers when it rained. Tumbledown tenements swarmed with unwashed and frequently unhealthy occupants. Contributing to the stench and filth were outside privies bordering most streets and insufficient drainage systems which were not able to carry away sewage.[61]

Sandow at the age of ten. "As a child, I was exceedingly delicate," Sandow wrote in 1897. "More than once, indeed, my life was despaired of. Until my tenth year I scarcely knew what strength was." From *Strength and How to Obtain It*, in the author's collection.

Sandow at the age of nineteen. The athlete's rippled abdomen and thickly muscled thighs are the result of his work as an acrobat. Lifting heavy weights would soon put on the bulk that was the mark of a real muscleman. From the author's collection.

Professor Louis Attila. Sandow's friend and mentor was an early champion of progressive weight training. Thanks to Attila's knowledge and experience, many budding athletes become professional strongmen. Photo by the London Stereoscopic Company, in the author's collection.

Sandow by E. Aubrey Hunt. The Anglo-American artist painted this portrait of Sandow in 1889 while the two were in Venice. The picture supposedly represents the athlete as a gladiator in an ancient Roman arena. It was while posing for this portrait that Sandow claimed he learned of Sampson's nightly challenge. From the collection of Joseph Weider.

Sandow lifts his challenge dumbbell. The London Stereoscopic Company turned out an early series of photographs in 1889. This one shows the athlete surrounded by his weights. Thanks to Attila's guidance, Friedrich Müller had been transformed into a full-fledged strongman. From the author's collection.

Sandow and Goliath. Karl Westphal, a huge quarry worker from Aachen, poses in his stage costume with Sandow. Unfortunately, the giant's stage presence proved to be much less imposing than his stature. Photo by the London Stereoscopic Company, in the author's collection

Martinus Sieveking. Sandow's "great and inseparable friend" was a talented composer and pianist who accompanied the strongman on his trip to America. After a failed tryst, La Belle Otéro sent Sandow back to Sieveking. From *Sandow's System of Physical Training*, in the author's collection.

Trocadero program. Ziegfeld arranged for this noble portrait of Sandow to grace the front of the Trocadero Theater program. From the author's collection.

Sandow, Ziegfeld, and Sultan. The impressario, the strongman, and Sandow's 200-pound boarhound, Sultan, pose for B. J. Falk around 1894. From an unidentified magazine clipping in the author's collection.

Sandow by Falk. Theatrical photographer B. J. Falk of New York was used to posing his subjects dramatically. Here Sandow reproduces the attitude of "The Dying Gaul." The photographer took the picture in 1894. From the author's collection.

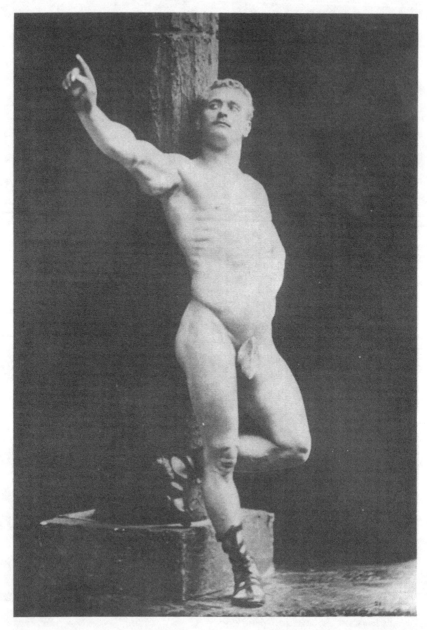

Sandow's famous column pose. B. J. Falk shot this masterful photograph in 1894, and it became a trademark pose that Sandow used on posters and other items. From the author's collection.

Sandow poses for Sarony. In 1894 Sandow presented himself to Napoleon Sarony at the photographer's New York studios. The series of pictures that he turned out helped define physique photography for the next several generations. Here the strongman poses in a classical Herculean mode with three props that were de rigeur: a weapon, an animal skin, and a fig leaf. From the author's collection.

The ladies idolize Sandow. "The Strong Man Exhibits His Form at Select Receptions to the Pretty Creatures" read the caption on the cover of the *Police Gazette* for Jan. 27, 1894. "I want you to feel how hard these muscles are," demanded the strongman. From the author's collection.

Strength and Genius. On Mar. 10, 1894, Sandow posed for this picture with Thomas Alva Edison shortly after the strongman had performed for the inventor's Kinetoscope. From *Sandow's Magazine*, 1902, in the author's collection.

Irving Montgomery, the False
Sandow. Exhibiting under the name
"Sandowe," Montgomery tried to
cash in on the real Sandow's appeal.
He was forced to stop imitating the
German athlete in a celebrated
court battle in 1894. From the
author's collection.

Blanche Brookes Sandow.
The strongman was married
in August of 1894 to the
daughter of a professional
photographer. She was
described by the press as
"tall, slender, and exquisitely
beautiful." For the moment
all was unalloyed bliss. From
Strength and How to Obtain It,
in the author's collection.

Sandow supports the Trocadero Company. The bare-chested athlete lifts nineteen performers (not counting Scottie, the "calculating collie"). Ziegfeld sits serenely above Sandow's head. From *New York Dramatic Mirror,* Dec. 21, 1895, in the author's collection.

Sandow in the days of his youth. Sandow gives a German schoolyard bully the old heave-ho in this humorous postcard by Tom Browne dated 1902. From the author's collection.

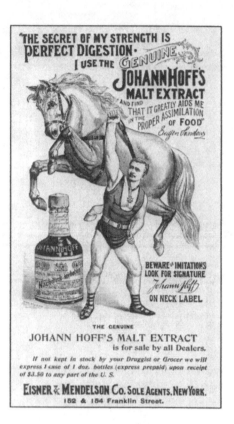

Sandow as a marketing tool. Because of his popularity, Sandow was called upon to endorse a number of products. Johann Hoff was probably the most aggressive in this regard. The strongman was used in posters and magazine ads in order to tout the benefits of malt extract. This engraving dates from 1895 and was featured in *Munsey's Magazine*. From the author's collection.

Sandow's Institute of Physical Culture. In an attempt to woo middle-class athletes into his institute, Sandow transformed the gym into a sort of luxurious clubhouse. "Rough necks" were not welcome at Sandow's Piccadilly headquarters. From *Strength and How to Obtain It*, in the author's collection.

Sandow's Magazine of Physical Culture and British Sport. For nearly a decade, this was one of the finest sporting journals in the world. Issue of Nov. 1901, in the author's collection.

Arthur Saxon. "The Man That Defeated Sandow" does a two hands anyhow lift in 1902. It was only through clever manipulation of the legal system that Sandow retained his reputation as a strongman. From *Health & Strength,* Jan. 1907, in the author's collection.

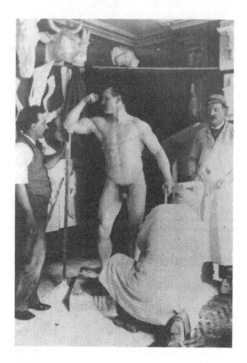

Sandow prepares to be cast in plaster of Paris. Cast makers, Messrs. Brucciani, attempt to reproduce Sandow's physique in 1901. Here he works on his pose with the technicians. Public Record Office, Kew, Richmond, Copy 1/451.

Sandow's cast. Unlike the well-formed original, the cast lacked proportion and symmetry. It was assailed as "a monstrosity" by some members of the press. It is currently stored far from public view in the British Museum. British Museum (Natural History); reproduced by permission.

Sandow in Australia. This photograph of Sandow was taken by D. Bernard, operator of the Swiss Studios in Melbourne. It shows the thirty-five-year-old athlete at the peak of his muscularity. From the author's collection.

Statuette of Sandow by William Pomeroy. Originally sculpted in 1891, this work became the trophy presented to victors in the "Great Competition" of 1901. Today, it is handed out to winners of the Mr. Olympia contest, bodybuilding's highest award. From the author's collection.

Young Sports Library. Sandow became the hero of dime novels as early as 1894. The cover of this flimsy opus shows the strongman bravely wrestling a ferocious lion. The story was as exciting as it was mendacious. From the author's collection.

Formal portrait of Sandow. A cravat and high collar give Sandow the proper dignity required of an Edwardian businessman. The photograph was taken by Warwick Brookes, the athlete's father-in-law, about the time Sandow returned from his world tour. From the author's collection.

Kate Sandwina. "Germany's beautiful herculean Venus" lifts two supers in her circus act. Sandwina was the most famous of the many entertainers who used variations on Sandow's name. From the author's collection.

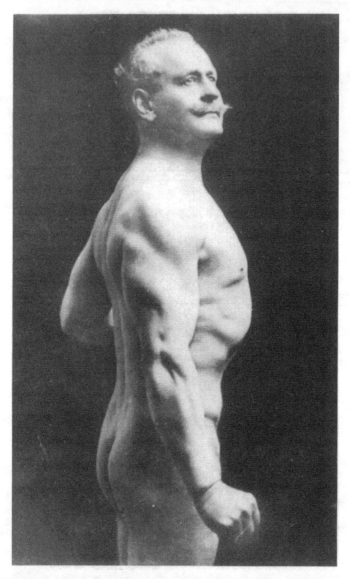

Sandow at fifty-two. Older but still energetic, Sandow longed for his past glory. "His weary eyes told the story of much glamor, color and adventure along the road of ten thousand yesterdays." Photographed by Brookes in 1919; in the author's collection.

Martinus Sieveking portrait. Aimé Dupont of New York City produced this profile photograph of the pianist in 1897. The artist has adopted a more bohemian look, perhaps to distance himself from his athletic friend, Sandow. From the author's collection.

La Famille idéale. Edmond Desbonnet's magazine *La Culture Physique* featured the Sandows on the cover of this issue from 1909. From the author's collection.

Sandow Pins Package. One of the oddest ways that Sandow's name was used by merchants was by this pin manufacturer from around 1895. The strongman's muscular body is prominently displayed as he attempts to bend one of the pins. From the author's collection.

The Dairymaids. A lavish set piece in this music-hall review from 1906 shows pretty girls exercising on a stage set made to look like a luxurious Sandow gymnasium. In addition to lifting weights and pulling on exercisers, the girls swing Indian clubs, fence, and swing on suspended rings. From the author's collection.

Athletik
Jllustrierte Wochenschrift für
Sport und Körperpflege

III. Jahrgang — Nr. 19   Frankfurt a. M., 11. Mai 1911

Der 1867 in Königsberg geborene Athlet Eugen Sandow, den obiges Bild in seiner Glanzzeit darstellt, kam 1889 nach England, wo er seit dieser Zeit lebt und sich durch den athletischen Sport ein grosses Vermögen erwarb.

Athletik Sport und Körperpflege. German magazines of the time tended to empha-size Sandow's athletic qualities rather than his gentler side. Here, Athletik, "the weekly journal for sport and body culture" from 11 May 1911 shows an early photo contrasted with a contemporary portrait of the strongman. From the author's collection.

Miss Carrie Moore. The star of *The Dairymaids* was Carrie Moore, a pretty Australian lass who discovered that if she wrapped her muscular torso in several yards of tightly stretched fabric, she could make a sensation. The barbell is an afterthought; it did not figure in her number. From the author's collection.

Patent application: Sandow toy, 1915. After yanking on the arms for a certain number of times, the child was rewarded with a little candy that rolled down a chute in the doll's head. The mouth popped open, and the sweet was obtained. From the author's collection.

Sandow bust. Hibbert C. Binney created this bust in 1908, and it apparently was destined for a niche somewhere in the Sandow Institute. Sandow is portrayed as a paragon of commercial rectitude and sober trustworthiness. He is a captain of business not a music-hall entertainer. From the author's collection.

Even among the wealthier classes, things were not much better. The average life expectancy of all Americans in 1900 was only 47.3 years. Ten years later that figure had risen only to 50 years.[62] The typical American, whatever his economic condition, worked too hard and played too little. Young Americans had been described in 1855 as "a pale pasty-faced, narrow-chested, spindle-shanked, dwarfed race."[63] That description is confirmed in the few statistics that were gathered at the time.

Most of the measurements relating to height, weight, and general stature were taken by the military. English anthropometrists recorded that in 1897 the average height of recruits in the British army was 67 inches and average chest measurement was 34 inches.[64] American statisticians were even more enthusiastic about recording the physiological measurements of their fighting men. This was part of an "anthropometry craze," as one writer terms it, that swept the country. All inductees were carefully measured before beginning service, and these figures were conscientiously recorded.[65]

One of the first such examinations was published in 1856, reporting on the troops that fought during the Mexican-American War. This revealed that American volunteers tended to weigh less than European or English recruits. Perhaps because of this, there were also nearly twice as many rejections of Americans for being "too slender, and not sufficiently robust" or for "malformed and contracted chests."[66] This analysis of American soldiers was fated to be confirmed over and over again whenever U.S. fighting men were scrutinized before a conflict.

In 1877 Dr. B. A. Gould compiled a table showing the stature of men who volunteered during the Civil War. These were broken down by state or country of birth. The group with the least impressive physiques were those from New England. Their average height was 67.834 inches and their mean weight was 139.39 pounds. This was contrasted with the Scandinavian-born soldiers who averaged 67.337 inches in height and weighed 148.14 pounds. The average height for all volunteers was 67.4 inches, and the average weight was 141.96 pounds. Clearly, the weedy stature of American men needed some serious attention.[67]

Surprisingly, the first one million American soldiers drafted into the army in 1917 showed measurements that were almost exactly the same as those who had fought half a century earlier. The average height of all U.S. doughboys was 67.5 inches and the mean weight had actually dropped slightly to 141.5 pounds.[68] From the Mexican-American War to the Great War, very little had been done to improve the skinny stature of Uncle Sam's troops.

If the men were scrawny and unimpressive physically, their sisters were even worse off. "In this country," fretted one nineteenth-century observer of female health, "it is scarcely an exaggeration to say that every man grows to maturity surrounded by a circle of invalid relatives, that he later finds himself the husband of an invalid wife and the parent of invalid daughters, and that he comes at last to regard invalidism- ... the normal condition of that sex—as if Almighty God did not know how to create a woman."[69]

Two things were patently obvious from these reports: first, that Sandow had his work cut out for him, and second, that he had a very large constituency to work with. Thanks to numerous reports and anecdotes, it had finally dawned on the general public that something had to be done to improve their own health and fitness.

Sandow and others like him insisted that the first step to improved health was regular exercise. As early as 1846 there had been a German gymnasium in Hyde Park, but it was forced to close soon after. Despite this initial attempt, there had only been a few random efforts to raise the physical standards of the nation's youth and to teach them the rudiments of sanitation, nutrition, health, and fitness.

One of the models in this crusade was the Oxford gymnasium of Archibald Maclaren, which had been opened in 1859. The *Illustrated London News* printed a picture of the interior and an account of Maclaren's techniques of diagnosis and treatment. Other gymnasiums soon opened throughout the kingdom, including one in Liverpool that cost £14,000 in 1865. A year later London still did not have a gym, and Lord Morely called for half a dozen halls like the ones Maclaren operated in Oxford. He argued that these "would make London a perfect sanatorium for hard-worked mortals who are compelled to live there the greater part of the year."[70]

This educational vacuum was soon apparent during the Boer War, and it occasioned a great deal of questioning and heart-searching among the powers that were. "Again and again," Sandow harped, "we have Colonel MacKinnon having to meet Lord Kitchener's orders to march by supplications for a few days' rest, as his men were thoroughly worn-out. This is, in a nutshell, the disadvantage which the British soldier has to face with the Boers."[71] But mere fatigue was the least of the problems faced by the entire British nation. The lack of proper physical education in state schools needed immediate attention, and Sandow thought he had the answer: adopt his system of physical training.

As the new century arrived, neither king nor commoner questioned the obvious need for a national fitness program. As usual in matters of state, however, there was much acrimony and infighting as to whose program should be adopted. Though the best-known proponent, Sandow did not have an open field ahead of him in Britain. Dr. Matthias Roth, a Hungarian who had come to the island as early as 1848, developed a practice as a therapist who attempted to remedy the many muscular and skeletal malformations common at the time. He used the Swedish method of exercise cure, quite different from Sandow's approach. Roth's regimen was originally devised by Per Henrik Ling and called the Lingian system in Scandinavia. Naturally, Roth believed his way was the best cure of all, and he became a tireless pamphleteer for the cause. He showered the British public with a torrent of words praising Ling and recommending the use of his system in British schools, just as it was compulsory for Swedish youth. When push came to shove in 1901, Roth had succeeded in building a very large and vocal constituency.

Obviously, Roth and his adherents were not entirely wrong. The Swedish exercises were well known all over the world for their thoroughness and effectiveness. They comprised a rigorous set of calisthenics carefully designed to work as many muscles as possible and to build endurance within a relatively short period of time. Both boys and girls in Swedish schools were examined by a specially trained physician three times a year, and all teachers had to study physical exercise and be in good health themselves.

A high point in Roth's campaign came in 1878 when his disciples on the London school board persuaded it to appoint a Swedish "Lady Superintendent of Physical Exercises." Her successor, Miss Martina Bergman, after a short spell with the board, opened a private physical education college for women in 1885. Her students eventually took the Swedish system into girls' schools and later to other educational authorities as inspectors and teachers. In addition, the Royal Navy and later the army sent officers to the Central Institute in Stockholm and they successfully pushed the Lingian system as instructors in the armed forces. By the time King Edward VII came to the throne in 1901, many groups were agitating for health education in the schools, though the Sandow and Swedish proposals remained at the forefront.[72]

It was into this disputatious fray that Sandow plunged. Editorials and articles appeared constantly in the pages of *Sandow's Magazine* as he railed against the lack of proper physical training for Britain's youth. "It passes the wit of man," he wrote in 1901, "to imagine the careless way in which people leave the physical development of their children to blind chance." What was needed was a sane and intelligent system, one that addressed itself to all the children. "When I speak of national physical education, I have more particularly in my mind's eye, not strong and robust children, but the weak and delicate, tainted, it may be, with hereditary disease—epileptic, rickety, anaemic, consumptive, or the rest—who will grow up, if they ever do grow up, to become a burden to themselves, their friends, and the nation."[73] And besides that, he believed that a child's physical well being had a direct influence on his intellectual abilities, for a frail or sickly child simply could not learn properly. "To force mental education on a weak or diseased body," he wrote, "is like offering a juicy beefsteak to a man without teeth or giving strong wine to a delicate child."[74]

After the Boer War, a royal commission on physical deterioration was formed to examine the British army's poor performance. They pinned a great deal of the blame on the lack of a system of exercises in state schools. Since the Lingians were in a powerful position after seventeen years of hard lobbying, they were able to sweep aside all opposition to the Swedish system. It was their system which was eventually adopted by the schools, not Sandow's.

Sandow had toiled long in the vineyards of physical culture, but there were two important reasons why his system was not chosen for state schools. First, he arrived on the scene too late. Others had begun before him, and by the time Sandow picked up the banner of national physical education, he was far back in the pack. But perhaps the most important reason for his failure was his lack of credibility as a serious educator. People had been conditioned to see him as a showman and music hall performer, not as the savior of British youth. Simply because he was a stage personality, his views, regardless of their merit, were automatically discounted by a great many people in power. To his credit, Sandow continued to fight for physical education in schools, and if not his system, then any was better than none. If he had lost this particular battle, Sandow was not ready to concede defeat in others. He would continue to make his presence felt in British society for many years to come.

7

Triumphs and Travels
1901–7

Despite his failure with the national physical education movement, Sandow was able to count more than his share of successes, too. One of the most striking and spectacular of these triumphs was the Great Competition of 1901. This was the world's first major bodybuilding contest, and since Sandow judged it from the beginning one of the culminations of his work in physical culture, he was determined to make it a memorable event. Most people agree that he achieved his lofty goal.

The ability to think big was something he learned from Ziegfeld, and Sandow had truly big plans this time. In the very first issue of *Sandow's Magazine* in July of 1898, he set his noble scheme in motion. He announced that there was to be a great competition open to all Sandow students in the United Kingdom. It would promote the spread of physical culture and "afford encouragement to those who are anxious to perfect their physiques." There would be tempting prizes amounting to one thousand guineas in all. The man who was judged to have the most perfectly developed body would be awarded a magnificent solid gold statuette of Sandow reportedly worth £500. The second-place winner would be awarded a solid silver statuette, and the third-place winner would receive one of bronze.[1]

Sandow's trophy-statue has a fascinating history in its own right. It was originally sculpted in 1891 by William Pomeroy when the athlete was on the music hall circuit. It shows a graceful but muscled strongman who grasps one end of a globe barbell in one hand and balances delicately with the other. Over the years, Sandow had several copies of his statue made in both bronze and lesser metals. Today, an original of this sculpture is one of bodybuilding's most sought-after relics. Small wonder, then, that there were many who were interested in winning it in 1901.[2]

Although there had been contests before Sandow's Great Competition, his was still the grandest and most comprehensive that had ever been mounted. Professor Desbonnet claimed to have organized physique contests (*concours de beauté plastique*) intermittently from 1892 to 1922, but these were primarily local events, with no attempt to attract a wide number of athletes. It was not until 1934 that the French began a regular series of nationwide contests.[3]

The English were not much more advanced when it came to bodybuilding matches. Professor John Atkinson, a bonesetter by profession, arranged the first British contest of this sort in 1898. At the conclusion of a regularly scheduled weightlifting meet, the professor presented a fine silver cup to the "Best Developed Man." The winner was Launceston Elliot, the brawny athlete who had been the weightlifting victor in the first Olympic Games in Athens two years before.

It is significant that the Atkinson contest was held after the main weightlifting event had taken place. At the time, and for many years to come, bodybuilding was considered the stepchild of weightlifting, and thus was kept out of sight for as long as possible. This makes Sandow's Great Competition all the more important, since the judging of well-developed physiques, rather than the ability to lift heavy weights, was the center of attention.

As soon as the announcement of the competition appeared in *Sandow's Magazine,* there was a flurry of activity among the readers. Applications began flowing in. It must have seemed as if everyone wanted to be a part of this contest. With a finger firmly on the British pulse, Sandow had determined that the public was ready for a competition, and he was ready to give it to them.

But much remained to be done before the contest could actually be mounted. One of the first things Sandow had to do was to devise some viable system of elimination, since nothing like that existed at the time—at least on the scale he wanted. His solution was a bold one: he would organize a series of local bodybuilding contests in each of Great Britain's many counties. In order to assure fairness, Sandow agreed to oversee each of these regional competitions. The individual county winners would receive gold, silver, and bronze medals, and then would be eligible to compete in the grand competition.[4]

Sandow made it clear from the beginning that prizes would not necessarily be awarded to men who had huge physiques. He was looking for symmetrical, even development. To press home that point he published a list of qualities that would be taken into consideration when the winners were being chosen. First, there was general development; second, equality or balance of development; third, the condition and tone of the tissues; fourth, general health; and fifth, the condition of the skin.[5] With judging criteria like these, it was not surprising that many contestants felt themselves qualified to enter.

After nearly three years of county championships, the date of Saturday, September 14, 1901, was finally settled on for the Great Competition. For weeks leading up to the contest, notices appeared all over London announcing the magnificent spectacle which was to take place. The site chosen for the judging was the Royal Albert Hall, a huge arena originally constructed as a memorial to Queen Victoria's late husband. As it turned out, it was an apt choice since it was the only place in the metropolis that could hold the overflow crowds that appeared that night.

By all rights, September of 1901 was not the most auspicious time to hold a public entertainment of any sort. It must have seemed that one disaster followed another in the world at large. Earlier in the year, the old and seemingly immortal queen who gave her name to the era had died at Windsor. Farther from home, the Boer War had been raging in the Transvaal region of South Africa for some time, and although the tide had turned in Great Britain's favor, it was undoubtedly in the back of nearly everyone's mind.

Worst of all was the shocking news that had reached England that very day from the United States: President William McKinley had just died from an assassin's bullet. Over a week before, a disaffected anarchist had run up to the president and pumped several shots into the startled man. Eight days later he was dead. Fortunately, none of these dreadful events totally dampened the spirits of the audience.

In a patriotic gesture, Sandow generously agreed to donate all the proceeds from the competition without any deductions whatsoever to the "Mansion House Transvaal War Relief Fund."[6] This was quite an offer, since the expenses of running an affair of that magnitude were considerable. Still, it gave the competition an air of legitimacy since those who attended it could claim that they would "both advance the cause of physical education and augment the funds of this most deserving charity," as Sandow's publicity flier put it. Once again he had found a winning combination: a plea for patriotism and a magnificent sports extravaganza.

It was reported that on the evening of the contest all the buses and hansom cabs for miles around were taken by people eager to get to Albert Hall. The organizers had made precautions against seating people in the aisles and the orchestra pit, but these had to be discarded because of the huge throngs trying to gain admittance. The hall was packed with 15,000 spectators on the night of the competition, and many hundreds had to be turned away at the door. The stage was set and the audience, anxious for what was to become bodybuilding's finest hour, waited expectantly.[7]

Promptly at eight o'clock, the band of the Irish Guards began playing Chopin's somber funeral march, and immediately the entire audience rose to its feet. This was a heartfelt tribute to the slain American president. There was a large American contingent in the house and it was reported that they were "unmistakably touched by the earnest and solemn demeanor of all."

Not one to lose a beat or to squander the feeling of drama that was in the atmosphere, Sandow quickly had the house light extinguished. Suddenly, twenty powerful spotlights burst out of the darkness and shone on the floor of the hall. There they picked out row after row of boys from the Watford Orphan Asylum as they marched out in perfect precision. These boys—fifty of them in all—performed their moves with such quickness and exactitude that they "aroused the audience to a great pitch of excitement."[8] The ovation they received was long and hearty.

After this, in quick succession, came various athletic displays. Wrestling, gymnastics, chest-expander drills, and even fencing were included in this part of the program. Sandow evidently believed in giving the audience its money's worth. Even so, many spectators must have wondered if the Great Competition would *ever* get underway. But at last the band struck up a lively march. It was in fact Sandow's own composition, "The March of the Athletes," and to its beat a stately procession of sixty competitors strode in.

It must have been a stirring sight to see all those athletes marching in cadence. Only one thing detracted from the solemnity of the occasion, and that was the costume the men were ordered to wear: black tights, black jockey belt, and leopard skins. Not only did the leopard skin and tights cover up the men's legs, but they just plain looked silly. However ridiculous the athletes may have felt, these proud men represented the flower of British bodybuilding, and as one journalist remarked, "to stand in their ranks was a distinction."[9]

Sandow was extremely lucky in his choice of judges, for he was able to secure the services of two of Edwardian England's most honored and respected men. One was a famous sculptor and amateur athlete, Sir

Charles Lawes. The other was the even more famous author Dr. Arthur Conan Doyle, creator of Sherlock Holmes. Sandow himself was to act as a referee in case of a difference of opinion between the two.

The presence of these two luminaries shows the depth of interest in bodybuilding that permeated its early years. The fact that neither man was a bodybuilder seemed to make little difference. What they lacked in judging expertise, they more than made up for in the prestige they lent to the competition and the sport.

After all the contestants had marched into the arena, the real judging of the evening began. Lawes, Doyle, and Sandow walked slowly up and down the rows of men, pausing here and there to inspect them at closer range. After some time, they made their decisions, and twelve finalists were picked from the group. When this was accomplished, the first part of the contest was over, and an interval was called.

When the event resumed, it was Sandow's turn to give a performance. He came out in the middle of the arena and went through his famous strongman act. He posed, tore a pack of cards in two, lifted weights, and generally impressed the audience with his strength and grace. The spectators showed their appreciation by giving him an ovation that lasted a full five minutes. They were obviously grateful not only for his performance but for all his labors on behalf of physical culture.

After Sandow's turn, the really important part of the evening commenced: the final judging. The twelve men each stood on a separate pedestal and went through a series of compulsory poses designed to display every set of muscles. The previous care and attention given to the contestants was nothing to what they were now to experience. Not a single aspect of their bodies was missed by the judges as they inspected the men, scrupulously looking for strengths and weaknesses. "Mr. Sandow," it was noted, "fairly went on his hands and knees to examine the nether limbs of the men." And all the time the audience watched and waited "with breathless interest."[10]

At last, their anticipation was satisfied and three winners were selected. The bronze statue for third place went to A. C. Smythe of Middlesex, the silver statue for second place was awarded to D. Cooper of Birmingham, and the solid gold statue for the best developed man in Great Britain and Ireland was presented to William L. Murray of Nottingham. The band struck up "See the Conquering Hero Comes" and a huge roar of approval arose from the thousands of spectators. And with that, the world's first bodybuilding competition ended triumphantly.

Sandow had done the seemingly impossible. He had made

bodybuilding—a sport in its infancy—a center of public interest. Even the reserved and respectable *Times* of London reported the competition favorably, calling it a "novel and interesting display." Though they characteristically warned their readers that "in some cases the development of the muscles appeared to be abnormal," and they questioned whether Sandow's system might be beneficial to everyone, since it produces "such extraordinary muscular deviation."[11] Still, people who would never normally have come into contact with the sport found themselves caught up in the enthusiasm that gripped athletic London. It suddenly appeared that thousands were willing to risk "muscular deviation" and give bodybuilding a try.

The proceeds from the competition amounted to over £500, and as promised, all of it was donated to charity. With unerring instinct, Sandow had struck a responsive chord in the British public. John Bull was ready for health and strong physiques, and Sandow seemed to know how to supply them. Bodybuilding had come of age almost overnight.

In the congratulatory rush that followed Sandow's coup, hardly a thought was given to the victor of the contest. Murray had apparently played his little part in the drama and then prudently vanished along with his precious golden statue. Over the years his trail had grown cold. He seemed to have disappeared into the cool English mists.

Murray had not vanished completely, however. After Sandow's contest, the victor decided to take advantage of the championship that he had won. He organized a minor strongman act of his own. This consisted of poses, mock gladiatorial combats, and heavy silver wands that were swung through the air in time to music. The high point of the act came during a sketch entitled "The Eve of Battle," in which Murray, arrayed as a Roman general, led a troupe of young athletes attired as soldiers.[12]

When the call to arms came for World War I, Murray gave up his act and enlisted. Unfortunately, he was the victim of a mustard gas attack while in the trenches, and this left him debilitated for the rest of his life. After the war he became the manager of a theater in the northern British city of Newcastle, and despite his grievous injuries, lived to the age of seventy-five.

Murray's golden statue remained with him throughout the years, though its existence had been forgotten to all save members of his immediate family. When a later historian tracked down this elusive trophy, it was in the possession of Murray's nephew. But at closer range, the statue turned out not to be solid gold, as Sandow's publicity had reported, but rather bronze with a thin gilt plating. The golden statue proved to be a gilded sham.[13]

All this certainly does not detract from the importance of the contest itself. Though Sandow's Great Competition bore little resemblance to a modern contest, it still accomplished three major goals. First, it brought together the top musclemen of Great Britain, then the sports superpower of the world. Second, it showed that improvement of the body was an attainable goal. And third, it proved beyond a doubt that a bodybuilding competition made a very entertaining show. One well-known weightlifting teacher of the time called the competition "a complete and glorious victory for physical culture," and added that Sandow could "claim to have accomplished a marvelous success towards the advance of the great cause we all have so much at heart."[14] That cause was bodybuilding, and thanks to Sandow and people like him, it continued to grow and flourish.

Although Sandow's was the first and the grandest, interest in physique competitons continued to build. After the 1901 contest, the next world-class bodybuilding contest occurred in New York two years later. Significantly, this was produced by promoter and publisher Bernarr Macfadden, Sandow's chief rival in America. The eccentric physical culturist promised $1,000 to "the most perfectly developed man in the world." His judging criteria were remarkably similar to Sandow's: "Remember," he warned in a brochure, "that this competition is not to decide who is the most wonderfully developed man, as we do not desire to select abnormal representatives or freaks from the standpoint of development; we wish the prize to be awarded to the most perfect specimen of physical manhood." In addition, the men had to be at least five feet four inches in height, subscribers to *Physical Culture* magazine, between twenty and fifty years of age, and submit a photograph to the judges. Contestants came from all across the United States and Great Britain.

The winner of this important contest was Al Treloar, the man who had assisted Sandow in Chicago and who later became athletic director at the Los Angeles Athletic Club. His title as "The Perfect Man" therefore started him on the road to professional and sporting success.

Both Sandow's and Macfadden's contests thus set the precedent for the myriad other "Mr." competitions from then on. Perhaps the most important innovation was that in both events the physique judging was at the center, not the periphery, of the action. There was also a fairly comprehensive search for contestants; these were not merely local contests. The two organizers drew athletes from a wide geographical area. From these two early competitions, therefore, all modern physique tournaments evolved.[15]

Spurred on by the triumph of the Great Competition, Sandow soon prepared for another sally into the limelight. Only a month after the Albert Hall contest, Sandow and his wife left daughter Helen with relatives and crossed the Atlantic to begin a new tour in America.

This was Sandow's first engagement in the United States in nearly five years, and he came with an entirely new and original act. The strongman's first foray into American vaudeville theaters had been brash, youthful, and spectacular—he had opened the eyes of many people on the subject of physical development. This new tour was different. Sandow no longer needed to make a name for himself; he was already famous. This time he would use artistic poses, special electrical effects, and fancy scenery. It was a mellower, more graceful performance as befitted one who was viewed as the undisputed monarch of muscles.

When Sandow came to America in 1901, however, he had more on his mind than simply showing off his muscles in elaborate style. He wanted to arouse the interest of Americans in health, nutrition, physical culture, and bodybuilding just as he had done in Great Britain. He was also exploring the possibilities of establishing a few Institutes of Physical Culture in the principal cities of the new world. So it was with much anticipation that he began his sojourn at Proctor's posh Fifth Avenue Theater in the heart of fashionable New York.

His new act could boast "elaborate and suitable scenery, effective costumes, and a cohort of supers dressed in Roman garb." In the first part of the performance, the house lights were turned out, the tableaux curtains drawn aside, and then a powerful electrical spotlight was directed onto Sandow who stood on a pedestal inside a posing box, a large cabinet lined with a rich plum-colored plush cloth. Sandow had used the cabinet before, but the new one featured different appointments. One of these was his rotating pedestal. He had a stage hand lie on his back at the rear of the box, concealed by the draperies except for his head and hands which were visible to the audience. The helpful grip then slowly revolved the pedestal while Sandow flexed and posed. The box also contained hidden incandescent light bulbs which allowed the athlete to work out a sophisticated lighting system with adjustable side illumination and an overhead spot in order to bring out the anatomical details of his well-developed body.[16]

The second half of the strongman's new American act consisted of weightlifting and card tearing, but the most impressive part was Sandow's work with a very affable white horse. The athlete hung off the animal's hind quarters and lifted weights of various sorts. But as one writer noted, "the cheerful equine deserved credit for supporting both Sandow and the weights."[17] At the climax of the performance, Sandow picked up one of the Roman soldiers who was standing about and threw him up in the air and onto the horse's back. The animal then reared up dramatically, and ran offstage at a frightful speed.

Despite the polish and showmanship that his new act demonstrated, many newspaper critics were less enthusiastic than they might have been. One reporter drew a few sarcastic comparisons between Sandow's earlier, more energetic shows and his present performance. "Even when he was with us last time," he wrote, "the strongman was prone to pose. Now he handles his hands as though he were a soubrette with a new diamond ring and shoots them out like a western congressman at a Presidential reception wearing his first pair of cuffs." He concluded derisively that far from hurting the act, the posing sequence "injects therein a brand of comedy that is better than any premeditated humor."

In fact, the papers generally viewed the strongman with a slightly more jaundiced eye than they had before. They were not able to resist poking fun at Sandow, however ill deserved it might have been. One reporter even took issue with the athlete's costume (or lack thereof). His skimpy attire caused the newspaperman to note that instead of giving tips on how to become strong, Sandow ought to reveal how not to develop pneumonia.[18]

Sandow's attempts at posing were not completely unappreciated, however. Some fans were clearly impressed with both his showmanship and his physique. "It was simply wonderful the way he did it," wrote one witness. "It was all seemingly spontaneous yet every breath, I believe, was studied, as I look back at it. The whole effect however was to give one the impression of seeing something extraordinarily beautiful. . . . [his body] was so beautifully proportioned and 'handled' that you just sighed over it and said that for once you had witnessed something about which you had formerly only dreamed but did not think could ever be attained by any mere man."[19]

Even the newspaper wits had to admit that "The act was beautifully staged," though they were quick to add that "the absurd array of petrified persons in togas and things make the Roman arena scene almost ridiculous."[20] Another reporter described Sandow's scrawny assistants as "several Roman guards who evidently belong to a race of elastic sided men, to judge by their wrinkled legs."[21]

Despite the snide critical comments, Sandow's famous posing box with its red plush lining and its sophisticated lighting made his act particularly well received by the public. The athlete had long since made his *poses plastiques* (literally, "physique" or "body" poses) the center of his act, rather than his weightlifting or feats of strength.

Although he was probably the best at it, Sandow was certainly not the first to employ physique posing in his vaudeville routines. That honor goes to the extraordinary Andrew Ducrow, an early-nineteenth-century circus performer who began his career as an acrobat and bareback rider. Incredibly, Ducrow originally began imitating classical statuary while flying around the circus ring on the back of a galloping horse. By 1828, however, he had discovered that he could get a much better effect by posing on a pedestal in the middle of the ring. Eventually, his "Living Statue, or Model of Antiques" turn became the most popular part of his show.

Ducrow had a lithe and sinewy physique. "His figure was a most perfect model for the sculptor's art," wrote one journalist after seeing his performance. The former horseman was a great hit as "The Dying Gladiator," "Mercury," "The Egyptian Mummy," and many other living statues. Unlike Sandow, however, Ducrow chose to wear flesh colored tights in order to simulate nudity without outraging the decency of his spectators.[22]

The art of *poses plastiques* became very popular in the later nineteenth century. Some poseurs chose to paint themselves all over rather than to wear a body stocking; these "men of marble or of bronze" imitated famous classical statues. This sort of thing was very popular in France in particular. In 1881, for example, the Théâtre Pietro Gallici exhibited several "Tableaux de marbres" and in 1895 the Théâtre des Arts of M. Ulmann offered twelve poses featuring "men of bronze" at each show.[23]

One of the finest uses of pure physique posing was to be found in Monte Saldo's 1906 music hall act called "The Sculptor's Dream." When the curtain is raised, a sculptor toasts his newly completed statue of a magnificent marble athlete. After downing his wine, the sculptor drops off to sleep, the lights dim, and a spotlight picks out the gleaming white statue. When screens open and close around the statue, the audience sees that the sculpture has changed its pose, interpreting a series of classical works. Saldo's artistry and beauty of physique put his act in direct competition with Sandow's own.[24]

Posing as a music hall turn survived up to World War II at least. Only it was not heavily muscled men the customers paid to see by then. Young ladies posed as statues, heavily powdered and nude to the waist, appeared at the Windmill Theatre in London. In order to be legal, however, they were forbidden to move a muscle.[25]

Unlike the later topless posers, Sandow was constantly on the move at this time, and when he took his popular act to Boston, the strongman made it a point to visit an old associate, Dr. Dudley Sargent, who taught physical development at Harvard University. Dr. Sargent took the opportunity to deliver a lecture on Sandow and his fine physique, which was given in the new Harvard Union. Like his regular performances, this too was packed with interested spectators. At the conclusion of the lecture, Sandow presented the university with a magnificent gift: the only copy of his cast made by the British Museum.

Partly in response to this fine gift, Dr. Sargent wrote the *New York Herald* in order to confirm Sandow's supremacy in the realm of bodybuilding. Sandow, he claimed, served as "a particularly valuable object-lesson to the young men of America. Sandow's visit to the university will stimulate great interest among the students. The fact is impressed upon them that what he has been able to do others may do." And finally, in a fit of adulation, he concluded, "Sandow is the most perfectly developed man the world has ever seen."[26] This was heady praise indeed from America's foremost physical education instructor.

In private, however, Sargent's praise of the cast was somewhat less than ecstatic. Writing in 1912, he admitted that the plaster image was accurate in some respects, such as Sandow's flat feet, and exaggerated in others—one can assume he meant the exceedingly large waist.[27] Still, the cast did go on exhibit in the Hemenway Gymnasium, and there it remained for many years. Eventually, like its British counterpart, it too was taken down and stored away. Gradually it was forgotten, and its present whereabouts are unknown. The celebrated cast has become a casualty of apathy and neglect. Fortunately, there was no time for Sandow himself to check on the reception of his gift. He was occupied with other business.

For six long, grueling months Sandow crisscrossed the East, packing in the spectators wherever he went. His tour took him as far west as Detroit, as far north as Toronto, and as far south as Richmond. Once more Sandow had engineered a theatrical and financial success. By all rights, when his second trip to America ended in late April of 1902, he should have returned to his home in England and rested. But Sandow was much too energetic and ambitious for that.

The Sandows returned to Europe in early May, and after a quick check on Helen, they departed almost at once on an even more extensive excursion. They left from the Mediterranean port of Marseilles aboard the Pacific & Orient liner SS *Orizaba,* bound for the Antipodes. Sandow was now going to perform and proselytize in Australia and New Zealand.[28]

Traveling with the often quarrelsome couple was Miss Edward, a British friend of Blanche Sandow's whom she found comforting and extremely compatible. Neglected by her husband in favor of numerous infidelities, the muscleman's wife might have sought consolation and understanding from her hired companion. If this is so, there is no doubt that Miss Edward had her hands full on the troublesome voyage.

No sooner had the ship reached Naples and the passengers been escorted ashore for a brief visit to the picturesque surrounding country-side than the eternal satyr in Sandow got the better of him. He started to flirt and dally publicly with an attractive lady he had met on the vessel, and she was not immune to his considerable attentions. Neither the tourists nor the guides were blind to what was happening. One of the guides hoped to profit from the incident by reporting it to Mrs. Sandow and Miss Edward. Sensing he had scored a bulls-eye with the furious consort, the Neapolitan went even further. He proposed to Blanche that she elope with him as the final revenge on the unfaithful Eugen. To the Italian this must have seemed only appropriate. The trifling circum-stance of the existence of his own wife and seven children appears to be of no concern. Blanche may have been tempted, but the cool head of Miss Edward undoubtedly intervened. If Mrs. Sandow had taken the fatal step, her husband would have retrieved her in due course, though no one would have blamed the long-suffering wife. Miss Edward must have dampened the raging fires.

Making light of the situation later, Sandow remarked that had he known what was going on between his wife and the Italian, "there might have been a vacancy in the corps of guides in Naples."[29] With a beginning like this, the voyage promised to be a stormy one indeed.

When the vessel left Italy for Egypt, there was a cooling-off period for all parties involved. The *Orizaba* made a quick coaling stop at Port Said, and then traversed the Suez Canal. After passing through the sweltreringly hot Red Sea and Gulf of Aden, they steamed toward Ceylon. After a stop in Colombo, the ship continued on the last and most unpleasant leg of the journey. Adding to her misery and discomfort, Blanche had to put up with yet another problem, seasickness. A terrific series of storms buffeted the *Orizaba* as it bobbed and pitched across the Indian Ocean. Nursed as best she could by her companion, Sandow's wife was almost constantly ill in her stateroom, leaving her husband free to amuse himself above decks.

To the considerable relief of Mrs. Sandow, at least, the West Australian port of Freemantle was sighted on July 11, twenty-six stormy and sultry days after leaving Marseilles. Sandow's Australian manager, Harry Rickards, met the ship at the port and then accompanied the group on the short train ride to Perth. Here they were impressed by the city's beautiful architecture and the gracious hospitality of its residents. The elegant Victorian storefronts and graceful cast-iron balconies must have seemed paradise after nearly a month at sea.

Almost as soon as he stepped ashore, the athlete was given much attention in the press—even before, since a crowd of eager reporters had come to meet the *Orizaba* aboard the pilot's boat. The papers were lavish in their praise and generous in their coverage. "Sandow in every respect justified all that has been said of his marvelous strength and of his great muscular development," wrote the reporter from the *Perth West Australian*. He added that Sandow performed his great feats of strength with such ease and absence of straining "that the onlooker wonders where the limit is attained."[30]

After a hasty recovery from her mal de mer, even Blanche was not immune from the attentions of the press. An illustrated journal, the *Perth Social Kodak*, published a photo of her and a short interview to go with it. In the article, the interviewer expressed the thought that Blanche must be a brave woman to have married a "modern Samson." "Oh, he is as gentle as a lamb," she explained gamely. "You see, I have been married eight years, and I don't look very bad, do I?" In a flowery avalanche of similes, the reporter answered her question: "If to look as sweet as a picture, as dainty as a rose, and as fresh as a lark be the outcome of eight years [of] married life with a modern Hercules, [then] certainly Mrs. Sandow does not look 'very bad.' "[31]

Sandow was still using the Roman Arena act that he had just taken to the United States. One drawback was that he needed a horse in order to perform some of the more spectacular lifting feats. Bringing one from America was out of the question, so he arranged to purchase one in Perth. Unfortunately, the animal he obtained did not take to training easily. In fact, in rehearsals it continually backed into the orchestra pit, sending the musicians flying. "Had suits of armour been available," Sandow remarked, "they would willingly have been donned by each member of the band as a protection against his onslaughts."[32] Eventually, the clumsy creature learned his part and the tour continued.

From Perth, the intrepid band went to the gold-mining region around the town of Kalgoorlie, deep into the forbidding interior. As the company traveled farther into the barren west Australian desert, the cool breezes and shady eucalyptus trees of Perth were replaced by the rocks, arid scrub, and ferociously hot winds of the outback. When they arrived at the rough and tumble community, the group discovered that the gold diggers were as warm in their appreciation as the climate. After every performance, these enthusiastic and boisterous miners "manifested their approbation in their usual vociferous and whole-hearted manner."

In spite of his favorable reception, Sandow admitted that it was hard to get used to the primitive conditions in that rowdy frontier outpost. "The theatre there is made on the sardine-box principle—built of tin. Consequently, apertures are numerous, and these are stopped in the primeval manner of stuffing them with rags." To make matters even worse, liquids of all kinds were scarce, precious, and devilishly expensive.

Most trying of all were the primitive hotel accommodations. The Australian bush is not renowned for its comforts, but at least Sandow did not have to share his room. Some of the assistants in the company were not so lucky, for the athlete noted wryly that a few of the players found their beds "turned into fowl-runs by chickens who evidently thought the assistants were intruders."[33] Everyone must have longed for Perth's opulent Hotel Australia, where the company had been lodging. Still, with all the difficulties, it must have seemed quite an adventure—and besides, the entertainment-starved miners were quite willing to pay dearly for their amusements.

After leaving the goldfields, the troupe returned to Perth, where they took passage on a mail steamer headed across the Great Australian Bight to Adelaide. Once there, the newspaper panegyrics gushed anew. "There have been strong men since the days of Samson," wrote the *Adelaide Advertiser*, "as there were great men before Agamemnon. But the thews and sinews which the far-famed Mr. Sandow exhibited to a select gathering last night must have distinguished him from the overwhelming mass of men had he lived in any age." Not to be outdone, the *Evening Journal* reported, "It does one good to meet and shake hands with Sandow. He is a nerve tonic, a veritable pick-me-up. To the frailest and weakest he holds out something more than hope. He gives everyone his absolute assurance that he can become strong."[34]

One enthusiastic correspondent from the South Australian capital felt the urge to break into verse. The "Ode to Sandow" was the result. It read in part:

> Hail, mighty Sandow! 'Tis thy mission great
> To preach to men—the body's highest state;
> That, since it is the temple of the soul,
> 'Twere well that we its beauty should extol.[35]

Fortunately, few others translated their raptures into poetic form.

Shortly after his arrival in Adelaide, Sandow held one of his press conferences for reporters and medical men. He answered questions, displayed his body, and let people feel his muscles. One claim that Sandow boasted about at this point was that he could make his own heart stop beating simply by willing. Sounding much like a snake oil salesman, he attempted to show that he had a perfect control over his own body because of the strenuous regimen of exercises he followed.

But after he made his extravagant claim, one scoffing Adelaide lawyer shouted out, "So can I."

"Yes," quipped Sandow, "when a nice lady comes along." Though it was a weak riposte, it neatly sidestepped the real issue and caused "roars of laughter." The meeting ended when a prominent medical man stood up and thanked Sandow for allowing them to attend, adding that there had never been a stronger man before, and probably never would be.[36]

After a fortnight in Adelaide, the Sandow company proceeded by train to Bendigo in the state of Victoria, and from there to Ballarat. There they were accorded another warm welcome from local athletes and city officials. While in the Victorian interior, Sandow not only performed nightly but also drummed up a little business by demonstrating and giving instructions in the use of his products to various civic groups. The clever strongman always made sure there were cameras and reporters near when he gave the police force or the fire brigade a few drills with his developers and dumbbells. A week of performing and public relations followed, and then the troupe left Ballarat for Melbourne, where they arrived on September 6, 1902.

After establishing headquarters at the Menzies Hotel, the Sandow company settled down to their month's stay in southern Victoria. They were afforded a mayoral reception which was reported with much ballyhoo in the press. The strongman, his wife, and the ever-present Miss Edward were also able to attend a concert by the famous operatic singer Dame Nellie Melba. Thanks to this social whirl, Sandow had very little trouble keeping his name before the public. He was lecturing on physical culture and performing in his music hall act on a daily basis. He had quickly become a nearly ubiquitous subject of conversation. Sandow's own name recognition was brought home to him in an amusing way. "I was sitting in a tramcar," Sandow wrote, "and commenced to cough. An old gentleman with whom I had entered into conversation advised me to be careful, and told me that I ought to practice the Sandow exercises, as they were very good things for toning up the system!"[37]

Sandow was also fortunate to have located an excellent photographer in Melbourne, Mr. D. Bernard, who operated the Swiss Studios. He turned out another masterful portfolio of photographs of the strongman, showing him to excellent effect. Many of Sandow's most famous later poses date from this time. These pictures are simple and stark homages to Sandow's physique. They show him clad in Roman sandals and leopard skin briefs, most often posed against a black background. They have remained graceful and stylish remembrances of the athlete at the apex of his physical development.

Mrs. Sandow was not being neglected at this time either—at least not by the Australian press. She seemed to receive almost as much coverage as her husband. Quite a stir was caused when she criticized local women in a Melbourne newspaper interview. "Your Australian girls are so pretty," she remarked. "Such sweet, lovely faces I have seen in the streets, but they walk horribly. They stoop, they do not carry themselves, they seem to burden themselves. It seems such a pity, for, no matter how beautiful a woman's face is, if she waddles or stoops she spoils it all, doesn't she?"[38]

Perhaps after her comments about the gawky carriage of Australian women, Blanche and Miss Edward thought it best to leave. So after a short stay in Geelong, the Sandows departed by sea to Sydney, where they arrived on October 4. As soon as they steamed into the lush, island-dotted harbor and disembarked at the Woolamaloo Docks, their enthusiastic reception began. Australia's oldest, most cosmopolitan city opened its doors to the famous athlete, and it soon seemed as if everyone was clamoring to get a look at the great Sandow. His reputation as a fine showman promised to keep the theaters full every night, but his reputation for curing the sick had also preceded him to New South Wales. This was attested to by a letter the strongman received from a Sydney woman asking him to send a free pass to the theater for herself and her three children who were just recovering from a bout with the measles. "Out of consideration to the Sydney public," he remarked, "and to prevent the spread of measles, I decided *not* to send the pass."[39]

After performing and lecturing widely in New South Wales, Sandow booked passage for Brisbane. Blanche had gotten her fill of traveling, so she and Miss Edward elected to stay in Sydney while her husband went on to the wild, tropical north by himself. When he arrived at his destination, Sandow found that the usual reception awaited him. Local athletes, city officials, and even the prime minister of Queensland were eager to greet the famous strongman.

Sandow gave several highly successful medical lectures while in the city. The *Brisbane Courier* of October 31 noted that, "As Mr. Sandow stood upon the stage, he indeed looked the embodiment of perfect manhood." His presentation was obviously quite an eye-opener for the Brisbane audience, since the reporter admits that "many of those present were astonished to observe highly trained muscles of whose very existence they had previously had no suspicion." What they lacked in anatomical expertise, they more than made up for in unfeigned enthusiasm.[40]

When he had completed his weeklong engagement in Queensland,

Sandow returned to Sydney and from there sailed on to their next destination, New Zealand. The group arrived at Auckland on November 17. Here their greeting was not a lively as they had hoped. There were no official receptions, no fêtes, no garden parties as there had been in Australia—only a pervasive indifference. After a few days of half-filled theaters and lukewarm applause, it must have come as a relief when they were able to leave Auckland and visit the rest of the North Island. At Wanganui they inspected a school run on the Sandow system. This was one of the first to adopt the strongman's ideas, and he was very proud to note that the school had earned a reputation for producing healthy, well-adjusted children.

Eventually, the company worked its way south, performing in Palmerston North, Napier, and other communities. Finally, they reached Wellington, the bustling capital of the colony. When the entourage arrived at the Wellington train station, they were relieved to see a modest crowd of admirers who had come to greet and have a look at the "Modern Hercules." Not everyone in the crowd was won over by Sandow's claim to be a paragon of strength, for one young lady, obviously expecting some giant of superhuman stature, was overheard to exclaim disappointedly "Why, he's just a MAN!"[41]

After a short run in the city, the troupe traveled across the Cook Strait to the South Island. In Christchurch Sandow met F. A. Hornibrook, one of the founders of the physical culture movement in New Zealand. He had long been a correspondent for *Sandow's Magazine* and had founded a school built upon Sandow's principles. "I have no hesitation in saying," remarked Sandow, "that the work performed that day was the best, and the physical culture the finest I had seen in Australasia."[42]

Only Auckland refused to pay him much attention, for throughout the length of New Zealand Sandow was greeted warmly and appreciatively. He had succeeded in raising the interest in physical culture among the inhabitants of the colony. "He is playing the part of a showman just now," wrote the *Timaru Herald* of December 29, 1902, "not because he likes it, but as the best available method of extending a knowledge of his system of obtaining health and strength; and it follows that his exhibitions are feats of strength."[43] But Sandow *did* like being a showman, and he *was* changing the way people viewed their health and their bodies. He had succeeded in delighting and instructing his audiences wherever he went—few entertainers or educators could claim to have done either with such panache.

When Sandow and his associates finally departed Invercargill at the southern tip of New Zealand, he must have felt satisfied that his mission had been a profitable one from many points of view. His stated reason for visiting Australasia was to educate the colonial populations there. "It was not as a 'strongman' that I wished to pose to the inhabitants of this Western Continent," Sandow explained, "but rather as a pioneer of health."[44] A great portion of his time had been taken up in lecturing and demonstrating the theories of his system to municipal bodies and groups of medical men. He had been very free with his offers to initiate local firemen and policemen in the use of his apparatuses, and all across Australia and New Zealand he had spent many days working with large assemblies of public servants. Undoubtedly, much of his motivation was from financial profit—after all, a whole new continent of potential customers was suddenly opened to him. But there must have been more to it than that, for there were certainly easier ways of making money that would not have taken him so far from home.

The large numbers of medical men who were shown the extent of physical development must also have helped spread the idea that well-built young men were not just a few random freaks. In his lectures, Sandow used a muscular young model, James Young, to help him illustrate his speech. The youth demonstrated that Sandow was not just a fluke; others could attain beautiful development.

If Australians and New Zealanders were impressed by Sandow and his methods, then the reverse was also true. "I fully realized the immense vitality of the Saxon race," Sandow admitted, "and the splendid future that must be in store for such a people. Not the least factor in the evolution of this future will be their steady and undeviating adherence to the cult of the body."[45]

Sandow's trip to the southern continent brought about some real changes in Australasia. His greatest legacy was the fact that others were inspired to follow in the strongman's wake, and thus they began an interest in physical culture and a healthy life-style that has persisted to the present. Those inspired either directly or indirectly in Australia have included some of the finest athletes who have emerged from the southern hemisphere.

Two men who were most instrumental in putting Australasia on the world bodybuilding map were John A. Rice and Clarence Weber. These two met at school in Melbourne and both soon began muscle building using Sandow's method. Shortly thereafter, the men were teaching informal classes in physical culture and slowly gaining valuable experience. But they were soon destined for bigger and better things.

"When the great Eugen Sandow came to Melbourne," Rice wrote, "Clarence and I obtained an interview with him and he gave us a lot of encouragement." Fired by their meeting with the visiting strongman, the men started the first bodybuilding gymnasium on the continent in 1903, "The Victorian Health and Strength College" (later changed to "Weber and Rice's Health and Strength College"). Rice became a champion strongman and Weber earned a reputation as Australia's most famous early strongman and wrestler. At six feet tall and weighing two hundred pounds, Weber was considered by many to be the finest proportioned man in the world.[46]

Another important Australian physical culturist who claimed to have gained inspiration from Sandow was J. M. Hendry. Before the author and champion weightlifter emigrated to Australia, Hendry admitted that his "first efforts at bodily improvement were sponsored by the Sandow Institute, St. James, London." He later put this and other experiences to good use and was proud to acknowledge that he had won the title of "Australia's Leading Record-Breaker" after he had demolished 155 world and Australian records.[47]

Several other important strength athletes came to Australia, at least partially influenced by Sandow's warm reception there. Weightlifter Milo Steinborn found himself in the country at the beginning of World War I. He had come to perform and compete, but since he was a German citizen, he was soon packed off to a concentration camp where he was forced to wait out the hostilities. There, he was able to train with a makeshift barbell and, despite a diet which consisted almost entirely of mutton, managed to remain strong and in good health.

Launceston Elliot had a much pleasanter reception down under. The Olympic weightlifter and physique champion decided to emigrate to Australia in 1923 since he had family there, and so this athletic pioneer lived his last years in the southern continent in peaceful seclusion. He was buried in Melbourne, the same city that saw the formation of Weber and Rice's groundbreaking college of physical culture.[48]

New Zealand was initially less enthusiastic about physical culture and its stars. Nevertheless, there were several important proponents of bodybuilding. As early as 1900, Hornibrook, Sandow's great advocate in New Zealand, had written to *Sandow's Magazine* with a photograph showing the first Sandow team trained in the colony. "Judging by the great interest taken here in Mr. Sandow and his splendid work," he wrote in the accompanying letter, "there is every reason to expect that, in a short time, [Sandow's] name will become as household a word as it is at home."[49] Another backer of bodybuilding was Dr. F. B. Hutchinson of Wellington, described as "a keen student of body culture and its benefits." He devoted much time, effort, and money to the promotion of bodybuilding at the turn of the century. In spite of the enthusiasm, however, most of the early physique athletes of New Zealand were unimpressive when compared to their brothers across the Tasman Sea.[50]

With these successes behind him, Sandow exercised a little of his own immense vitality and returned not to London but to the United States. While her husband went back to America, Blanche and Miss Edward traveled in a different direction. Sandow's wife had had enough of the gypsy life; she was ready to return to her daughter, her family, and her home. But there was an even more pressing reason for her trip back to England: Blanche was pregnant with their second child. She could certainly not be expected to keep up with her dynamic husband while in such a delicate state of health.

In the meantime, Sandow was giving birth to a few schemes of his own. On his last visit to Boston, the athlete had set in motion some ambitious plans, and in 1903 he returned to marshal those forces and make sure they headed in the right direction. Sandow arrived in New England around the first of January, for on that date Sandow's College of Physical Culture opened its doors. It was one of the best-equipped gymnasiums in the country. It occupied the entire upper floor of the New Century Building on Huntington Avenue, and like his British schools, the college gave lessons both individually and in large classes. There were also ample facilities for both men and women. Although Sandow's new American school was a bold and risky venture, it still offered a great potential for profit.

Sandow made sure that he was on the premises regularly, always ready to be consulted on physical problems. He was happy to enroll students who were unable to attend his school personally in the successful postal course. As in England, this correspondence course gave instructions, exercises, and advice by mail. It also allowed Sandow to reach many other potential customers in the American hinterland. He planned to open schools like the one in Boston in all the principal cities of the United States.[51] The former circus acrobat from the backwaters of Europe was on the verge of creating a vigorous new empire of physical culture. This, after all, was an era of grand schemes and daring plans—a perfect time for Sandow and energetic men like him. There was money to be made and glory to be grasped. Sandow wanted both.

One particularly effective means of aggrandizing his growing empire was to found the American version of *Sandow's Magazine*. Though it was heavily dependent on its British counterpart for its appearance and structure, the new magazine catered more to distinctly Yankee culture and tastes. There were articles on the Yale and Harvard football teams, the exciting indoor sport of basketball, and a wealth of other health and strength articles.

Another reason for founding the magazine was to take advantage of the physical culture craze which was just beginning to catch on in the United States. "There is evidence on every hand," Sandow wrote in the introduction to the January 1903 issue, "that great numbers of people are awakening to the importance of the establishment and conservation of health through the practice of physical exercise, indulgence in recreation, and attention to hygienic conditions."[52] If there was to be a fitness mania in America, Sandow wanted to be in on it.

Unfortunately, the latest version of *Sandow's Magazine* proved to be much more ephemeral than its British model. It survived for only four monthly issues. In April of 1903 it ceased publication altogether. The Yankee public was simply slower to warm to crazes, especially imported ones, and the physical culture movement took a great deal longer to travel the vast distances in this country than it had in Great Britain. There were also several other magazines on the market already, the most prominent of which was Bernarr Macfadden's *Physical Culture*. These had taken quite a slice out of the proposed readership. It would seem that Sandow and his Boston-based organization simply came too late to woo readers to his particular brand of bodybuilding.

The majority of Americans, however, recognized Sandow's name and face immediately—to many he was as familiar as the Indian on their pennies. Smokers could puff on Sandow cigars and read about his comings and goings in the newspapers. Like such fictional heroes as Frank Merriwell and Fred Fearnot, Sandow had even become the model for several romantic dime novels. Thus the great strongman left his mark on American literature as well as athletics.

One of the first places Sandow's literary presence was felt was in the stacks of dime novels that inundated American boyhood. As early as 1894, Sandow had become the star of one of these works. The *Young Sports Library* produced a highly romanticized biography of the strongman: *Eugen Sandow, the Strongest Man in the World; or the Thrilling Life and Adventures of the Most Famous of All Athletes*. The cover illustration is indicative of the book's tone and veracity. It shows the strongman bravely wrestling a ferocious lion while horrified onlookers gasp in amazement. This was a patently untruthful account, but then factual reporting was never a strong point in the popular press.

Several years later, probably inspired by Sandow's second visit to America, *Wide Awake Weekly* published a volume entitled *Sandow, Junior; or, the Boy Who Looked Puny* by Prof. Oliver Owens (1906). The hero of this flimsy opus is Thomas Preston, described as "a puny enough looking boy, not more than five feet three in height, nor did he look as if he would weigh more than a hundred." Like his namesake, who was supposed to have been born weak but achieved greatness, Sandow, Junior's frail appearance belies an inner strength. When the young man arrives in Blissville, he immediately rescues a farmer whose leg is trapped under an overturned wagon. As well as revealing his amazing strength, this act also wins the gratitude of the townsfolk as well as a new name for the main character. "Three cheers for Sandow, Junior—a boy of grit!" they exclaim. But the quiet boy earns the jealous enmity of some. So it is not until Sandow, Junior saves the rich but scornful Miss Elsie from certain death that he is finally accorded a permanent place in the hearts of both Miss Elsie and the Blissvillians.

Thus Sandow became a ten-cent hero—a model for strength and courage for a generation of boys. The earnest writers of this sort of book attempted to show that the muscular Christian virtues of manliness, purity, and participation in athletics would yield up a harvest of moral improvement and almost certain material success. The unwritten message of all these books was that what had happened to Sandow (both Junior and Senior) could happen to the impressionable young readers.[53]

Another obvious place to search for Sandow's influence on American literature is in the work of an author who made a virtual cult of manly strength, Jack London. A careful reader can find glimpses of Sandow-like characters throughout the works of London. The writer's fascination with strong, muscular, aggressive men is certainly well documented.

In a boxing story, "A Piece of Steak," however, one character seems to have been drawn almost literally from Sandow's image. Tom King, the aging hero of the story, is forced to fight a youthful, well-built opponent named, significantly, Sandel. King's adversary in the ring is described as "youth incarnate, deep chested, heavy thewed, with muscles that slipped and slid like live things under the white satin skin. The whole body was acrawl with life. . . . His face was strongly handsome, crowned with a curly mop of yellow hair." Just about all that is necessary to make the description complete is Sandow's distinctive mustache and leopard-skin trunks.

Though London never actually met Sandow, he was obviously cognizant of his presence, and aware that his readers would see the similarity between the real and the fictional character. Sandel/Sandow represented for London strength, manly beauty, and vigor. When he created Sandel to represent these qualities, the author knew that his audience would make the connection easily.

"A Piece of Steak" is not one of London's best works, yet there is a primitive power about it that makes it memorable. Sandel is not delineated as a character as much as Wolf Larsen, the perplexing antihero of *The Sea Wolf* (another Sandow-like figure), but perhaps the writer felt that it was unnecessary since he had already plugged his character into a preexisting set of values that would make further description superfluous.[54]

Sandow had been imitated, admired, and satirized. Thus, by the time of his latest visit, he had been firmly entrenched in American folklore. He had even been accorded the signal honor of meeting with President Teddy Roosevelt to discuss the topic of the American physique and how it could be improved.

It was perhaps inevitable that Sandow and Roosevelt should meet. The energetic president had become the foremost embodiment of the American muscular Christian, and as such he represented everything that Sandow admired most. He was, in fact, a political Sandow.

Sport for Roosevelt was a metaphor for life itself. Woe betide anyone who did not play fair according to the president's rules. Busting the trusts was one way Roosevelt showed his adversaries what happened when they did not play honorably. Roosevelt's "Strenuous Life" became a popular and timely catchphrase that helped physical culture advocates like Sandow snare new acolytes to the cult of the body.[55]

Sandow was clearly impressed with the energetic American president. In their meeting together Roosevelt "showed a marvelous grip of [physical culture], and did much to encourage [Sandow] in his mission to bring about an improvement in the physique of the English-speaking race."[56] Together, the two men would mold American society to fit their own ideals, but in very different ways.

The strongman had been performing seriously for little over thirteen years. Surprisingly, he had been in the New World for nearly seven of those years. He had built up a considerable reputation among the citizens of North America. Taking advantage of his fame, Sandow arranged for one final tour of the land that had almost become his second home. After two months in Boston, overseeing the College of Physical Culture, he and his supporting company went on the road again. Boston, Philadelphia, Cleveland, Detroit, Pittsburgh, and finally New York all saw him one last time. He had a hectic schedule in each of these places, giving lectures on physical culture in the mornings and then performing in the evening. By late spring he was ready to return to England. As usual, his tour had been a success, but his ambitious plans for a chain of institutes and popular magazine both folded about the same time.

In mid-May of 1903, Sandow returned to England for the first time in nearly a year of traveling. He rested briefly with his family in London, and there he saw his new daughter, Lorraine, for the first time.

But after several weeks with Blanche and the children, he was on the road once more. He began a provincial tour, again lecturing in the morning and performing in the evening. This journey took Sandow to the North of England, the Midlands, and Wales. Then after a week's rest, he commenced the whole thing over again in the suburban music halls of the London area. He was also making the rounds of his many schools, trying to drum up even more interest in them.[57] Clearly, Sandow found it difficult to adapt to the life of middle-class urban domesticity that a family demanded. The life of the vagabond was more to his liking, and it would take several more years of married life to break him of this love.

In between engagements, Sandow also had the opportunity for other amusements. He had long been fascinated by automobiles, and from time to time he would escape for a little motoring. He kept a small fleet of motorcars and often championed races and other similar events in the pages of *Sandow's Magazine*. Like many other Edwardians born on the brink of the mechanical era, he retained an almost childlike interest in engines and mechanisms of all sorts. He was never so happy as when behind the wheel of his beautiful Winton Special Touring Car, flying down the road at the precipitous speed of thirty or more miles per hour. What better toy was there for a born wanderer?

Sandow also had time to spend in his offices occasionally. A reporter from *Tit-Bits* recounted an incident that happened about this time in the London headquarters of Sandow's developer company. "My life is in danger," the athlete announced cooly one day. He pointed toward one of his rubber exercisers. "There," he said, "is the secret of all my trouble." He explained to the journalist that earlier in the week a swarthy oriental gentleman burst into his office. The man explained in heavily accented English that he had just arrived from Constantinople. He laid before the startled strongman a written order for several developers to be sent to an address in Turkey. He explained that the developers were for the ladies of his master's harem. The next day a note arrived warning him not to breathe a word about sending the apparatuses to the wives of his master, or the Turkish pasha would send an assassin to murder the strongman. Thus by the very act of revealing all to the reporter, the intrepid strongman was risking a scimitar in the back. Yet Sandow did not seem unduly nervous. As the journalist noted, "The man who can lift an automobile containing four passengers smiled and smiled."[58]

But Sandow was not willing to let the green grass of England grow under his feet for long. No matter how many threats of murder might punctuate his day, he still found the life of a businessman dull and unexciting. So in early May of 1904, almost a year to the day since he had returned from his last tour, he departed once more. This time he was headed toward the most exotic parts of the world. This was to be a grand tour of South Africa, India, and the Orient. One major difference marked this trip: Blanche refused to accompany her husband on his globe-trotting junket. The reasons for this refusal are not hard to fathom: she had two small daughters to care for, and Eugen was planning a visit to some of the most primitive, fever-ridden places in the world. It was no place for a young mother.

Sandow gathered together another company of performers and they set sail for southern climes. They would not return to England for another eighteen months. The group's first stop was the newly pacified colony (formerly the independent republic) of the Transvaal. They arrived at Capetown and then proceeded immediately to the rich interior region. On May 27 Sandow and suite arrived by train at their destination, Johannesburg. There they were met at the platform by a big reception of reporters and well-wishers. The *Rand Daily Mail* praised Sandow as one who "has done more for healthy physical development in the last years than all other strong men together, and has proved that strong men can be as intelligent and clever as the weaker man who devotes all his time to brain development."[59]

Wisely conserving the strength that had been so recently lauded, Sandow decided to shorten his South African itinerary. For the first time since his severe illness, he exercised some caution in taxing his vigor to the limit. He prudently restricted his appearances to the two largest cities of the colony, Capetown and Johannesburg. Accordingly, Sandow was booked for his first appearance at the Empire Palace Theatre in the Transvaal capital on May 30. As usual, his traveling routine remained the same; he lectured on physical culture to doctors and other interested parties at the matinees, and he gave his regular performance in the evening.

When Sandow first strode majestically on stage, his carefully nurtured reputation as a clever and talented artist had preceded him. There was standing room only at the Empire Palace on his opening night, and he was greeted with wild and enthusiastic cheering before he had flexed a single golden muscle. The newspaper reviews of his performance were ecstatic in his praise: "It was a marvelous exhibition. . . . His agility was no less remarkable than his strength. . . . His body is the perfection of symmetry."[60]

Despite the glowing notices, some South Africans were not so willing to accept Sandow's strength on faith. The strongman had long enjoyed showing off his power by an extra tight handshake—if the other party winced, Sandow let out with his familiar, high-pitched giggle. But he apparently got more than he bargained for backstage in Johannesburg. Morris Jones, Sandow's press agent, was brusquely accosted in the Empire lobby by an uncouth, burly individual who asked, "Say, are you de bloke wot's with Sandow?" When Jones admitted that he was, the other man introduced himself as Michael Williams, champion heavyweight of South Africa and England. He wanted to talk to Sandow about a possible match.

When taken backstage, he was first formally introduced to Sandow, and then the two clasped hands. Both men immediately tried to squeeze the other into submission. "The strain was terrific," reported Jones, "but neither flinched for several minutes." Finally, Williams let go and took his hand away. Jones must have realized that something was amiss when the usual soprano giggle failed to appear. After a bit of serious discussion, Sandow rejected Williams's challenge—the purse was not big enough to justify the match. Just as the fighter was about to leave, he asked pathetically, "But say, who's goin' to pay fer me hand?" Upon inspection it was found that the small bones were all broken across the back and it had begun to swell alarmingly. Even Sandow did not escape completely unscathed: his wrist and forearm had been badly sprained, and he was forced to cut out part of his act for more than a week.[61]

Fortunately, his injuries did not curtail his nightlife. On June 10, 1904, he was the guest of honor of the Johannesburg Amateur Gymnastic Society at Frascati's Restaurant. It was a lavish affair with a fancy French menu and a seemingly endless list of toasts and responses. Even the chef contributed to the festivities by concocting a special dessert which he dubbed "Sandow's Pudding."[62]

Despite all the sweet homage paid to him by the gymnastic society, there was little excitement among the defeated Boer inhabitants of the Rand. Understandably, most of the Afrikaaners were still reeling from the recent war, licking their wounds and eyeing the English-speaking invaders suspiciously.

Though Sandow was faced with sullenness at every turn by the freshly defeated Boers, a thoughtful act by a British soldier considerably brightened his African outlook. As the strongman was traveling from one former Boer stronghold to another, a lance sergeant of the Coldstream Guards mailed him a photograph he had found on a South African battlefield several years earlier. Though torn, stained, and faded, the image was clearly that of Sandow in a muscular pose. The sergeant wrote that the print had been dropped accidentally on the veldt by a retreating Boer fighter in the heat of action. Sandow was heartened by the anonymous infantryman's interest in himself and physical culture, and the gesture softened the muscleman's hardening attitude toward the dour Afrikaaners. As for the photograph, Sandow kept it as a bizarre souvenir of one of Queen Victoria's most unfortunate wars.

Unlike Australia, South Africa took longer to warm to physical culture and the arts of the strongman. One possible cause for this was that Sandow's stay was briefer than his earlier Antipodean visit. Perhaps another explanation was that to the Boers Sandow undoubtedly represented the hated conquering power of Britain, and they wanted none of him or his country. Thus, for a variety of reasons the strongman's ideas never really flourished on the rocky veldt of South Africa. Even so, there were a few places where Sandow's legacy could be detected.

Among the Afrikaaners, one young man did heed Sandow's call; he was Tromp van Diggelen. Cursed with a frail constitution, the Boer lad began training with Sandow's method at an early age, but soon found that he was not getting the results he wanted. After inventing his own exercises, he soon became stronger. Eventually, van Diggelen became a professional strongman himself. Later when he wrote of his experiences with Sandow, he was quick to praise his mentor and to admit Sandow's power of inspiration.[63]

Sandow had done athletes of the region another good turn: he had made the public aware of strongmen and their stunts. Thus another South African who benefited indirectly from Sandow's tour was William Pagel. This massive strongman was most famous for carrying a horse up two vertical ladders about twelve feet high. Pagel would stand between them and mount the ladders to a height of about nine feet. The horse, said to weigh a thousand pounds, was suspended from a harness which fit over the man's neck and around his waist.[64]

With his own act as a centerpiece, Pagel operated a circus which toured South Africa from the turn of the century to the 1930s. Today Pagel is remembered primarily as the employer of an even more remarkable strongman, Hermann Goerner. In all, the German-born Goerner made five tours of South Africa from 1922 to 1938. In that time he performed such feats as wrestling with an elephant, supporting a merry-go-round on his feet while eight men rode the contraption, supporting a bridge on his shoulders while a fully laden touring car drove overhead, and many other equally spectacular stunts.[65]

Despite the early apathy, South Africa has since produced quite a few remarkable strength athletes. C. G. "Milo" Pillay, a weightlifter of East Indian extraction, competed effectively in the 1932 Olympic Games. He later opened a gymnasium in Port Elizabeth, where he attracted many prominent lifters and bodybuilders from the region.[66] Today, South Africa is remembered by strength historians as being the home of two magnificent bodybuilders: Roy Hilligenn and Reg Park. Thus the work Sandow began nearly a century ago is being carried on by other equally able men and women. But in 1904, Sandow's impact was just beginning.

From Johannesburg, the Sandow company returned to Capetown on July 18. After a relatively brief run in South Africa's port city, they left for the next leg of the journey: a tour of the exotic ports of the Orient. The group visited the largest cities in Japan and China, constantly arousing interest among the native and European populations for Sandow's brand of physical culture.[67] Java and Burma were also on his itinerary, and since these and other countries in the area did not have adequate theatrical facilities for his exhibitions, Sandow brought along his own. He had a great tent put up that would shelter six thousand people, thus assuring him of a venue. In addition to his usual company, he also took along twenty-nine athletes from many different countries who performed and inspired the local populations.

As an additional testimonial to his abilities at transforming ordinary men into athletes, Sandow collected a native inhabitant from every country he visited. They were all weaklings whom he would make into real men. Presumably, after they had been changed into he-men they would be returned to their native lands in order to gather adherents to Sandow's system of physical culture. It was the kind of scatterbrained experiment that only a supremely self-confident Edwardian gentleman would attempt.[68]

The tradition of returning to civilization with a collection of natives is an old one indeed. Captain Cook returned to England in the eighteenth century with a number of South Pacific islanders, and before him Columbus brought back a group of Carib Indians. These aborigines could then be "civilized" by their hosts and returned to their homelands to teach their fellow countrymen. Sandow was simply one of the last in a long line of European pioneers who came home with a cargo of strange brown men. This placed the strongman firmly in the tradition of the missionary spreading the Good News to the savages, but this time it was the gospel of strength and health. The techniques and the rhetoric that he employed, however, were remarkably similar to the Christian propagandists of another age. Sandow had thus learned to evangelize for the body, not the soul. Fortunately, in late autumn of 1905, Sandow was about to preach to the biggest congregation ever: India.

The British Raj had been firmly entrenched in the subcontinent for many years, but even the redoubtable English had been unable to make life more bearable there. It was a land rich in potential, celebrated by armchair chauvinists as the jewel in the imperial crown. Perhaps the greatest monument to the British in India was the capital city of Calcutta. This huge, sprawling, inelegant metropolis was the country's nerve center. From the administration buildings and the viceregal palace, the decrees that kept the far-flung crown colony running efficiently were issued. Here squalor and wealth, Hindu and Christian, nabob and coolie coexisted uneasily. Like so many other travelers and adventurers before him, it was here that Sandow came first.

The strongman arrived at the port, and then took the short train ride to the center of Calcutta. Howrah Station, a great, ugly, flyblown pile that served the mighty city, was alive with excitement as Sandow stepped down from the train. He found the platform crowded with hundreds of people waiting to greet him—there were Europeans and natives of all castes and creeds. The perfumes and stenches, the curious faces, the babble of a hundred unfamiliar tongues all told Sandow that he had truly arrived in a strange and distant land.

Sandow had come to India in order to explain his system and to assure those who were interested that anyone could attain virility and vitality. In order to encourage his many devotees, he began almost immediately to appear in local theaters. One of the first of these was the Theatre Royal. Here the tattered punkahs beat back and forth ineffectively as Sandow performed in the sweltering hall. Far from being dissuaded by the heat, there was a standing-room-only crowd of enthusiastic spectators.

Sandow cleverly gathered adherents to his cause by a series of articles he wrote for the *Indian Sporting Times.* "The native Indians have a fine foundation for the building of large, physical men," he assured his readers. He explained that it was only the lack of proper diet and systematic exercise that made them so thin and haggard. In answer to his critics' charges that India's ferocious climate was simply too unhealthy for exercise, he announced that "seldom have I found a country where I want to exercise as much and often as I do here." All the same, he preferred to work out in the early morning, before the heat became unbearable: "Fifteen minutes before *chota hazri* [the early, pre-breakfast snack] does you as much good as three days' exercise in England."[69]

Sandow was also receiving much attention from the native Indian population. A lead article in *The Bengalee* of Calcutta explained his system clearly and expressed appreciation for Sandow's presence in the region. The *New India* went even further in its praise, citing passages from the *Upanishads,* India's holy book, to prove that interest in physical culture was religiously sound.[70] Sandow was given the honorific title

Sando Pahlwan, and then promptly challenged to a wrestling match with the famous native pugilist Gamun Baliwala. "Pahlwan," as he thereafter learned, was a term applied to athletes, specifically wrestlers. Wisely, Sandow declined to meet the Indian in the ring.[71]

India, like Japan, has a long history of traditional wrestling. To the adherents of this ancient discipline, wrestling is a lifetime profession. All the men who participate in the sport must be born into a family of *pahlwans.* These men usually come from the Punjab, a mountainous region where climatic conditions are more favorable for developing the fleshy physiques that these men possess.

Their training is rigorous. One authority has witnessed the wrestlers doing 2,000 *dunds* or push-ups and 2,500 *baithaks* or deep knee bends. With this remarkably strenuous workout lasting all day, it is amazing that the men are not as thin as whippets, but that possibility is effectively removed by their prodigious eating habits. When the athletes are well rested from their exercises, they begin the daily feast. Each man reportedly consumes several chickens, two gallons of goat or buffalo milk, and pounds of nuts and dates.[72]

Europeans were awakened to the prowess of these athletes in 1910 when an enterprising English promoter, R. B. Benjamin, took a troupe of Indian wrestlers to Britain in order to pit them against the best men Europe had to offer. The unqualified star of that tour was a huge Punjabi named "Gama." At the age of twenty-two Rustam-e-Zama Gama had already become something of a national hero in his native land because of his great ability as a fighter.[73]

As he grew older and more powerful, Gama became virtually unbeatable. His greatest triumph over western opponents occurred in 1928. In that year he fought the massive Polish wrestler Stanislaus Zbyszco, and in a humiliating defeat the Indian was able to pin the European champion in only ten seconds. The great Gama died in a Lahore hospital on May 22, 1960.[74]

When he was not performing or being challenged by massive native wrestlers, Sandow was mixing with the English community. Fortunately, the Anglo-Indian Army was particularly interested at this time in encouraging exercise and sport. Despite the torrid climate, there was a widespread conviction among the officers that violent exercise was the key to staying healthy in the tropics. In the opinion of Lord Frederick Lugard, governor general of Nigeria, men who played polo regularly rarely fell ill. General Willcocks, commander-in-chief of the West African Frontier Force, attributed his good health to running a mile before dinner every day. This was all the more remarkable since the general had only one leg.

Perhaps the strongest argument for the type of regular exercise that Sandow advocated was to keep the men away from more dangerous temptations. By the time Sandow arrived in India, the army had seen a terrific rise in cases of venereal disease. In 1897 alone, over 50 percent of all men in uniform were treated for the disease. Drink and idleness were said to be at the root of the problem, but most conceded that the real cause was the closure of the official military brothels where the epidemic could be controlled.

By the time Lord Kitchener became commander-in-chief in 1902, the problem had only gotten worse. He attacked the problem with threats and sermons. Kitchener instructed his officers that it was their duty to keep the men busy by instilling a love of games and outdoor sports. By 1909 the problem had apparently been solved, but the improvement was probably due more to the discreet reopening of the brothels than anything else. Nevertheless, it was into this dispute that Sandow stepped during his visit in 1904, but at least it assured him a serious hearing among the long-suffering military men.[75]

Sandow arrived in India and the other tropical colonies at a time when he would have been most appreciated. The strongman represented a perfect specimen of vigor and fitness, and to make things even better, he advocated lots of exercise and a healthy life-style. Sandow offered physical and moral salvation just as he had in Europe, but his message was accepted much more avidly in the remote colonies.

While he was inspiring the army, Sandow was being lionized by the native population, too. The strongman seemed to make the best impression on middle- and upper-class Indians, and he had several interesting experiences with them. Far from being secretive or inscrutable, Sandow found his native Indian friends to be extremely solicitous and generous—sometimes excessively so. At one point in his trip, the strongman was staying with a well-known native figure. His host learned of Sandow's love of motoring, and thus graciously insisted on driving to a remote town some forty miles distant. "We had not gone far before I noticed that at regular intervals on the route various carriages and pairs were stationed. At first I could not make out whether they were there by accident or by design, but later on I heard that for fear the motor might, perhaps, break down my host had ordered a carriage and pair to be waiting at every mile on the route." Sandow concluded that such kindness is "convincing evidence of the innate courtesy of His Majesty's loyal subjects in India."[76]

Generosity of a different sort was offered to him by a wealthy Parsee contractor. Dhunjibhoy Bomanji had been afflicted with a dread tropical disease, elephantiasis, and he came to Sandow as a last resort.

By the use of his curative physical culture, Sandow was able to bring down Bomanji's grotesque swelling, and to restore him to good health. The Parsee was extremely grateful and paid Sandow a handsome sum outright. He further offered the visiting strongman £10,000 if he would stay with him in India. Sandow tactfully refused.[77]

While he was in the Punjab, Sandow was given a rare and amazing opportunity to visit the harem of a local potentate. The ladies wished to know something of physical culture, and they wanted the perfect man to teach them. Sandow jumped at the chance. Visions of menacing, half-naked eunuchs and sensual, reclining odalisques must have danced in his head. The reality, however, was somewhat less than stimulating as he found when he was ushered into a large room in the palace. Running down the middle was a thick, beaded curtain. The room was well lighted on Sandow's side, but dark on the ladies' side—thus they could see the athlete, but he could not see them. Nervously, Sandow ran through a few exercises, but he could not view his students—he could only hear the rustle of silken saris as they repeated what had been shown them.

At the end of his session, the wives asked through an interpreter if they might feel the great man's biceps. Sandow was willing. He therefore approached the beaded curtain, bared his arm, and as he flexed, slender brown hands snaked through the curtain and caressed his stony muscles. It must have been more than even a strongman could endure.[78]

Long after Sandow had left the harems and hovels of India, he was not forgotten. Although there had long been a tradition of strength building on the subcontinent, many Indians were quick to take up Sandow's ideas. Thus there was a remarkable surge of interest in physical culture after Sandow's stay. One author has noticed a particularly fervent attention to strand pulling that he traces directly to the strongman's Indian sojourn.[79]

Despite the impetus given by Sandow's visit, western bodybuilding did not really take off in India until the 1930s. It was then that gymnasiums and athletes began to proliferate at a rapid rate. The most important Indian physical culture instructor of the time was Professor K. V. Iyer. He established the Hercules Gymnasium in Bangalore City about 1935, and soon had a membership that reached several hundreds. He also began India's first correspondence course, and he later became one of the physicians to the maharajah of Mysore. Iyer attempted to blend Yoga, Hindu mysticism, and occidental physical culture into something uniquely his own. He must have been successful, for his photographs reveal him to have had an excellent physique by the standards of any nation.[80] Without Sandow's pioneering work, these men might never have gotten started.

Sandow left India rich not only in experience but also in the money that he had made. All of his tours had been successful, but this one was especially so. It was also to be his last extensive trip to foreign parts. He eventually gathered up all his company and they left India in August of 1905. They were returning to Europe after an absence of a year and a half, and they were going back to stay this time.

On September 18, their ship, *Le Nord,* steamed into Dover, and there it was greeted by a large crowd of people. A special train had been chartered by the Sandow organization between Charing Cross Station and the Dover platform. A few days earlier, Blanche had crossed over to Calais so that she could greet her long-absent husband in advance, and together they could make a triumphal reentry onto British soil. After their ship had docked, the Sandows stepped off the gangplank and a brass band immediately struck up "See the Conquering Hero Comes." Helen, their little nine-year-old daughter, ran up to her papa and embraced him excitedly. It was reported that one of the first things she wanted to know was if her father had brought back "any little nigger boys for her to play with."[81]

Perhaps she had caught sight of the group of native weaklings as they exited the ship. Chinese, Hindus, Kaffirs, Punjabis, all looking exotic and mysterious, disembarked with their teacher. How they must have felt at being brusquely transplanted to England can only be guessed at. Yet they, like many of their white brethren, placed their trust in Sandow.

When the initial excitement of his return subsided, the Sandows settled into a house at 61 Holland Park Avenue in the London borough of Kensington. The elegant row residence was largely purchased through the generosity of the grateful Indian patient whose health Sandow had restored. In return, the strongman named the manse "Dhunjibhoy House" after his benefactor. The Sandow family occupied these premises for the next twenty years.

Comfortably ensconced in Kensington, Sandow conceded that he was ready to settle down, give up the exhausting tours, and leave center stage to others. While there is little doubt that Blanche had constantly urged him to retire from public exhibitions, there were other compelling reasons for the momentous decision.[82] At forty years of age, his body was showing signs of wear, tear, and sag. He was no longer the world's most perfect man and the once-adoring public knew this undeniable truth. Sandow had also become absorbed with the institute, his magazine, and his mail order businesses. Plainly, these concerns took up his waking hours.

Sandow was not a sedentary person. He thrived on the adulation and attention that he received from his music hall appearances. Unfortunately, Blanche did not share her husband's love of the theater. She refused absolutely to be present at any of his performances—she had traveled with him all over the world, but she could no longer bring herself to see her husband on the stage.[83] Perhaps she was jealous of the praise and attention, perhaps she was insecure about the many opportunities for petty infidelities, perhaps she loathed the free and easy morality of the theater or the matinee girls who lined up at the stage door. Whatever the reason, something gradually caused her transformation from gentle dove to quarrelsome shrew. Over the course of time, Sandow and his wife settled into an uneasy partnership. A truce was called between them, and henceforth he would increasingly leave Blanche to herself while he pursued the discreet attentions of others.

Sandow's discord at home seemed to presage the troubles he was having elsewhere. The year 1905 marked the beginning of the end of the physical culture craze. As fads go, this one had hung on a remarkably long time, but it was inevitably doomed to extinction. People began to lose interest in Sandow and bodybuilding; they had been attracted to other forms of exercise and amusement. Most notably, bicycling had grown in popularity, and the new craze had one distinct advantage over bodybuilding: boys and girls could do it together. So for this and a variety of other reasons, Sandow found interest in fitness slowly waning.

As the popularity of his sport and persona dropped off, attendance at the many Sandow schools fell dramatically. This was perhaps the cruelest cut of all, since it affected Sandow's ego as well as his bank balance. To hedge his losses, the master teacher ordered most of the studios closed.[84] Sandow did retain a semblance of dignity, however, by continuing to operate the chain's palatial centerpiece near Piccadilly Circus.

It must be admitted that Sandow fought hard to keep public interest alive in fitness and exercise. One of his expedients was to change *Sandow's Magazine* from a monthly to a weekly format.[85] The editors and writers tried everything to spark more interest. They offered articles on foreign places—India and Japan; they gave helpful health hints—avoid breathing "used air" even if it causes a row; they even offered moral advice—vice is a disease to be avoided like others.[86] But these were only stopgap measures, and they could not turn the rising tide of indifference. In 1906 the magazine became visibly more interested in promoting health and nutrition rather than bodybuilding, and it tended to take on a decidedly preachy tone.

When preaching did not work particularly well, the editors tried something at the other end of the moral scale. One of the most titillating types of music hall turns at the time was the living statuary acts that were appearing frequently. In the guise of high culture, a nubile young lady would pose in imitation of classical sculpture wearing little but her makeup. Perhaps the most popular of these acts was the one belonging to Mlle Olga Seddon. She had a risqué tableau vivant act at the London Pavilion where she appeared nearly nude along with her three so-called brothers as statues. Miss Seddons's powdered body was shown in all her topless splendor in the pages of the tabloid.[87]

One shapely cover girl known only as "La Milo" is pictured as "The Bathing Girl" in a later issue. She appears posed coyly in a long but form-fitting bathing costume, safely encircled by an oversized life preserver, and poised on the brink of a dive. La Milo had already caused the suicide of one rejected suitor—a fact that was gleefully reported in *Sandow's Magazine.* Later the publication reported another of this femme fatale's daring exploits: she had been chosen to portray Lady Godiva in a Coventry festival. Her costume—pink tights and a very, very long wig.[88] *Sandow's Magazine* had discovered cheesecake and yellow journalism.

In the long run, though, it was all in vain. For on June 25, 1907, Sandow sadly told his readers that the magazine would cease publication. He promised to send each faithful subscriber a large portrait of himself, but the magazine that had begun the physical culture craze eight years earlier had gone under from want of interest.

Despite the failure of the schools and the demise of his journal, Sandow was not ready to retire. In the next few years, Sandow would confound the doomsayers and once again find success. Like his beloved Winton Special, Sandow simply shifted into another gear.

8

The Final Years
1908-25

Freed from the demands of his former enterprises, Sandow had discretionary time to devote to new interests. Among other activities, he began the promotion of physical culture for women. There had long been lady athletes who had appeared on the music hall stage. They sported formidable sounding names like Athleta, Vulcana, or Herculina, and made a career of impressive feats of strength. Perhaps the strongest of these music hall amazons was Katie Sandwina (née Brumbach). She was billed as "Germany's beautiful herculean Venus, possessing the most perfect female figure" and "the female Sandow." And if we are to believe the posters that announced her performances, "It would be futile to attempt a description of this sensational feature. It is beyond the power of words."[1]

Sandwina was the most famous of the many entertainers who used variations on Sandow's name to further their own careers. Unlike the others, however, she was a genuinely talented performer in her own right.

The strongwoman married a man named Max Heymann who took over the job of managing the career of his amazonian spouse. One of his first changes was to rechristen his wife after the more famous strongman. Even with this transformation, success was not a certainty. After several attempts, Sandwina finally caught the imagination of the vaudeville audiences with an act that was first presented in 1918. In this Kate clattered on stage in a Roman chariot wearing a tight fitting gladiator's costume. Leaping adroitly from the chariot, Sandwina juggled cannon balls, broke horseshoes, twisted iron bars, and broke chains. The climax of the act came when she supported a bridge on her chest upon which stood over a dozen people dressed as Roman soldiers.[2]

Katie Sandwina was a much-loved performer and athlete. Her fame and popularity were both increased when she and her husband moved to New York City and opened a German-style tavern and restaurant. It quickly became the haunt of nearly every strongman in the area. They were drawn at least in part by the entertainment, for Sandwina would display her celebrated strength in nightly shows, performing the feats that had made her famous.

When she died in 1952, many writers were quick to point out that despite her great height (over six feet) and girth (usually over two hundred pounds), she was as soft-spoken and feminine as many of her less-muscular sisters.[3]

No matter how Sandow and his associates viewed these pioneering women, it was crystal clear that the public regarded them as little more than sideshow freaks. There was a strong prejudice against any sort of female fitness program at all, for it was commonly believed that exercise would make a woman awkward, graceless, and manly. It was against this prevailing attitude that Sandow fought, and it was largely thanks to him that women began to take an interest in their own bodies and their health.

"A woman," Sandow wrote in 1911, "was not meant to go through life a tremulous mass of disease or weakness."[4] Robust good health was a woman's birthright just as it was a man's, and Sandow meant to do something about correcting the situation. "Every woman ought to exercise," he announced, "it is not merely a question of getting rid of 'salt-cellars,' of fleshiness, or scragginess; it is a question of health and happiness."[5]

A generation earlier, the poet Byron had satirized the genteel women of northern climes: "How poor their forms appear! How languid, wan, and weak."[6] The frailty described by the poet had a simple cause. Virtually all exercise except for dancing was forbidden to women of fashion, most of whom "recline upon our sofas murmuring and repining at every claim upon their personal exertions."[7] This situation had largely improved by the turn of the century, but the average woman's constitution was still far from sturdy.

Surprisingly, as late as 1890 a prominent journal, the *Union Standard*, criticized physical activity because it was not ladylike. "A girl must simply, because she is a girl, refrain from taking part in certain healthy recreations. They must not forget they are young ladies."[8] But despite the reactionary beliefs of some so-called experts, many advancements had been made in the realm of female health. Thanks to new developments in contraception, women were finally freed from the difficult and dangerous cycle of constant pregnancy and childbirth. Women were also slowly pushing their way into the formerly all-male dominion of sport. There were ladies' archery associations, bicycling clubs, tennis teams, and natation societies springing up almost daily. But it was not enough. Something further had to be done to raise the physical state of women's health. Their days as hothouse flowers were coming quickly to an end; it was time to breathe the fresh, bracing air of fitness and health.

Sandow had always devoted a large section of his institute to use by ladies, and at the Ebury Street branch of the school he had a very large and faithful group of female members who worked out regularly. Over the years, he gradually devised a series of exercises that would help women to tone up and trim down. In 1911 he published these in *Strength and How to Obtain It* as a special large fold-out chart just as he had done for the men. Women were starting to liberate themselves from the strictures of male domination, and as they gained moral and intellectual strength, they also gained physical strength.

Despite his pioneering work, it cannot be said that even Sandow was in the vanguard of female liberation. "It is a woman's mission to look beautiful," he announced, echoing the sentiments of his age.[9] But he differed from the others in his idea of beauty. Sandow preferred the bright flush of health and the pliant spring of muscle, and he continually railed against the cruel dictates of fashion. "It passes the wit of man," he complained, "to discover how self-respecting women can employ the various deceptions so commonly used with a view to heighten their attractions." The high-heeled shoe, the pointed toe, "gay deceivers," and a thousand other articles of clothing that distorted the figure and caused discomfort, or even disfigurement, came in for his wrath. "Any arrangement of dress which does not give free play to the body is bad," he wrote. And at the beginning of the new century, everyone knew exactly what article of clothing was the worst offender—the whalebone corset.[10]

For thirty years the villainous corset had been one of Sandow's bugbears. He complained about the garment on a regular basis in highly colored terms: "Any contrivance, the wearing of which induces bad circulation, digestive troubles, and nervous complaints is assuredly to be condemned vociferously."[11] However, it was all to no avail. No matter how much he deplored or adamantly condemned it, women simply did not stop their tight lacing. So Sandow decided to try a different tactic.

With all the planning and secrecy of a Prussian general preparing a military campaign, Sandow investigated the corset problem. "Most carefully I went into the question, studying it closely in conference with the greatest corsetières and corset manufacturers all over the world, and as the result of years of experimenting, I succeeded in producing a corset which has not only met with the entire approval of members of the medical profession, but has also been acclaimed the ideal garment from the modistic point of view by the leading dressmakers of Europe and abroad."[12] Thus did Sandow's Patent Health and Perfect Figure Corset come into being.

In spite of his claims of uniqueness, Sandow's wonderful invention was not as novel as he might lead us to believe. There had been many other so-called health corsets which had gradually taken over the market since about 1900. The makers of these had claimed—as Sandow did—that they allowed for freedom of movement and were of hygienic design. The principal difference between the regular corsets and the new health corsets was the characteristic shape they gave to the female torso. The health corset pushed the wearer's bosom forward and the buttocks back, contorting the body into a different—though hardly healthy—position. The hourglass figure of the old corset had yielded to the "S" shape of the new. It was true that the new undergarment displaced fewer internal organs, but it still could cause severe spinal curvature if worn for prolonged periods of time.[13]

Nevertheless, Sandow touted his new invention proudly, claiming that it was made of the daintiest of materials, was highly fashionable, and was guaranteed to be pleasing to women of the most fastidious taste. The corset was still potentially dangerous, however. So for those ladies who chose not to truss themselves up in whalebone, and for those whose ample proportions refused to be tamed by even the tightest lacing, Sandow offered an alternative—good old-fashioned exercise.

Despite Sandow's advocacy, female exercise still was not a universially accepted concept. "*What has the average girl to do with a gymnasium?*" demanded one contemporary commentator in outraged italics. "Sweeping and scrubbing a floor and dusting out a room is infinitely more beneficial than going to a sanctified room to turn somersaults."[14] According to like-minded male critics, a woman's place was in the home, preferably on her knees with a scrub brush in her dainty hand. But for those women who were able to escape, Sandow was there to provide the sanctified room as well as the specialized equipment to fill it.

Even so, when Sandow seriously took up the question of improving the female physique by regular and scientific means, he discovered that not much work had been done in the field. There had been exercises for women before, but very little had been done to compensate for the obvious physical differences between men and women. He noticed that in the earlier systems of physical culture, "Women had simply been treated as a man of inconsiderable physical strength, and had been given the same exercises, but fewer of them, and the same apparatus to work with as men. This, of course, was utterly wrong, and undoubtedly mischievous in its effects."[15] So with his usual eagerness, Sandow set about remedying the situation. The result of his labor was a contraption he called the "Symmetrion."

This new device was really just a refined version of his developer, but it was specially designed to produce a symmetry of form. The apparatus consisted of a wide adjustable band which the lady placed around her waist; this was connected to elastic cords and pulleys which were attached to doors or bedposts. There were two handles so that the user could work her arms and hands also. He included with it a chart of special exercises which were devised not only to beautify the figure but also to cure indigestion and to tone up the nervous system. Among the many claims that Sandow made for his symmetrion was that it developed the bust, removed double chins, made the waist slim, strengthened the ankles, and perhaps best of all, it did not disarrange the hair in any way.[16]

Thanks to Sandow and his innovations, the modern woman in the new century did not have to despair if her figure was not ideal. His symmetrion could shape and mold her body, and his health corset could cover the remaining physiological flaws. Thankfully, the twentieth-century woman did not have to complain of creeping obesity as did a Gilbert and Sullivan peeress twenty or so years earlier:

> Stouter than I used to be,
> Still more corpulent grow I—
> There will be too much of me
> In the coming bye and bye![17]

While he was being hailed as a benefactor of womankind, Sandow was not neglecting his own interests. In 1902 Sandow had begun experimenting in other marketing ploys. His first foray in this line was "Sandow's Embrocation." This was a liniment designed to keep an athlete's muscles supple during exercise and free from pain afterwards. Ever eager to claim extravagant benefits, Sandow also alleged that the rubbing oil would help cure cases of rheumatism, lumbago, sore throat, and other ailments.

Around 1910 the strongman made another attempt at mass marketing when he introduced "Sandow's Health and Strength Cocoa." This was touted as a beneficial dietary supplement, helpful especially to athletes. The chocolate powder was advertised as being perfectly pure, possessing a delicious aroma and flavor, and because of its richness in albumen, having a particularly high food value.

The driving force behind the marketing of Sandow's cocoa was Warwick Brookes, Jr., the strongman's energetic brother-in-law. Almost from the start, young Brookes saw the huge potential for profit in Sandow's many business enterprises, and he did not hesitate to pursue those avenues aggressively. He was, as one commentator put it, "a wild and venturesome lad." In his shrewdness and adventurous spirit he was every bit the equal of that other exploiter of Sandow's persona, Florenz Ziegfeld.

Brookes, Jr., moved quickly up the ladder at his brother-in-law's firm. First he became head of Sandow's Institute, but he soon took over the Sandow Grip Dumbbell Company and guided it successfully for several years. His next brainstorm arrived in the form of Sandow's cocoa.

The young man discovered that if he went to Germany, he could purchase a kind of cocoa waste from which the fat had been extracted. He arranged with a company called Reichardt to ship great quantities of this residue to England where he packaged it in attractive tins. Apparently the product did, in fact, have some merit since it did not upset the digestive systems of those customers who were unable to deal with fat.

In 1911 Brookes opened a cocoa factory in London's New Kent Road, and then he instituted a massive advertising campaign touting the benefits of Sandow's Health and Strength Cocoa. On the day that the cocoa was introduced, Brookes arranged for a lavish banquet for newspaper executives and eminent publicists. To ensure a favorable reception for the new product, each guest received a gold hunter watch valued at thirty guineas. There was apparently more to drink than cocoa, however, for soon the banqueters were engaged in a raucous competition of sliding their expensive new timepieces along the carpet like curling stones.

Despite the hijinks, the banquet and attendant ad campaign produced the desired results, and sales of the chocolate drink began to grow dramatically. Brookes had originally planned to produce a maximum of ten tons of Sandow's cocoa per week, but because sales were rising rapidly, he was overruled by his fellow directors. In order to satisfy the greater demand, a new Sandow's cocoa factory was begun in 1913 at Hayes in the London borough of Bromley. Here the managers hoped to turn out fifty tons of chocolate power each week.

Trouble began almost as soon as production started up. As Brookes had probably foreseen, the big cocoa companies perceived little danger in a competing firm that produced ten tons a week, but one that turned out fifty tons was a different story entirely. So Cadbury and others cut their prices, and Sandow's cocoa company quickly discovered that they were being forced out of the market. By 1914 Sandow's company was losing money at a disastrous rate, and its chairman, A. W. Gamage, was consequently forced to resign. To make matters worse, the country by then was in the throes of World War I, and there was a great deal of consumer resistance to using a German product as the base for the chocolate. The managers of Sandow's Ltd. had to scramble to find another more politically correct source for its cocoa. Eventually they did so, but the increased expense and the bad publicity did not do much to endear the drink to the British public. Finally, by 1916 it was all over. Sandow's Cocoa, Ltd., was forced into bankruptcy. Toward the end of its existence, the company's total liabilities had soared to £20,438 before the directors decided to call it quits.[18]

Despite the cocoa debacle, Brookes, Jr., continued his position at the Sandow organization. He made sure to ingratiate himself with his business partners and other associates in the City. After leaving Sandow in the 1920s, Brookes became a prominent businessman and sportsman. He even won a seat in Parliament for a time. Brookes, Jr., was "a natural exploiter" who was clearly at home in the rough and tumble world of Edwardian commerce.

Part of the reason for Sandow's business and marketing successes were people like Brookes who knew how to make the public want Sandow's products and services. As evidenced by the cocoa fiasco, not every campaign was equally triumphant, but the sheer number and energy of these commercial maneuvers kept the strongman's name before the public. It was little wonder, therefore, that the Sandow organization continued to grow and prosper.[19]

In addition to all his other enterprises, Sandow was also acquiring an ever-increasing circle of satisfied patients and staunch supporters. One of the most avid of these disciples was Tromp van Diggelen, a young South African athlete. As a young boy in Johannesburg, he had been afflicted with weak lungs, and in an attempt to cure him, van Diggelen's mother took the boy to London where he was examined by Sandow. Van Diggelen was instructed to start working with one of Sandow's developers in order to build up his system. Unfortunately, even after a year of work, there was no appreciable improvement, so the Boer lad decided to make up his own set of exercises. Luckily, these had the desired effect.

When he had built up his constitution to an appropriate level, van Diggelen returned to Sandow and reported that he had used his own ideas for development. "I admire enterprise in such a young boy," Sandow graciously replied, "I advise you to keep on as you have been doing and I want to see you now and then as I am interested." Not only did the Boer youth continue to develop, he eventually grew strong enough to go on the stage as a professional strongman. He billed himself as the "South African Apollo" and even edited his own sports magazine for a while. Unfortunately, van Diggelen never really had the talent or the temperament to be a top-notch strength performer, and as time went by he reluctantly gave up his stage career. Eventually, he had to be content with promoting the talents of others, and it is thanks to him that later athletes like Max Sick and Hermann Goerner were introduced to music hall audiences.

Van Diggelen continued to be devoted to Sandow, and would praise him in extravagant terms whenever possible. He often betrayed a near-Freudian fascination in his descriptions of his one-time mentor: "His muscular development was actually *beautiful* to a connoisseur of the male physique.... That handsome face (very much like that of my own father) set the wonderful body off."

It was probably because of this rather worshipful mood that Sandow consented to let van Diggelen measure his arm in 1908. The only catch to this uncharacteristic liberty was that the South African Apollo had to promise not to publish the results. It was just as well, for the forty-one-year-old strongman's arm measured a relatively flabby seventeen inches.[20]

Despite the hero worship and lavish praise that Sandow enjoyed, not all the recognition he received was flattering. Anyone as successful in as many different areas was bound to take his share of stinging barbs too. Not surprisingly, most of his criticism came from former or present rivals. One of those was William Bankier, a brawny and handsome Scots strongman. Bankier had been known by several stage names; when he began in the business, he called himself "Carl Clyndon, the Canadian Strong Boy." But it was the title suggested by the famous painter Sir John Millais by which he was best known, Apollo. In 1900 he published a book titled *Ideal Physical Culture,* and in it he issued harsh criticisms and strident challenges to Sandow in an attempt to get him to test his strength. Much to his discredit, Bankier grew more and more shrill in his name-calling, accusing Sandow of being a coward, a charlatan, and a liar. "He fondly imagines his figure perfect," Apollo sniffed, "which is by no means the case. He has three very grave faults, viz., sloping shoulders, small calves and flat feet, common to all the German athletes."[21]

In 1903 Apollo started his own magazine, and thus had a whole new forum for his small-minded rantings. One of the most extraordinary and vitriolic articles in this vein appeared in May of 1904. It purported to be a piece by Sandow's one-time nemesis, Cyclops, though the work was almost certainly penned by someone else. The evidence points to Apollo as the real author. The article attempts to point out all the flaws in the popular conception of Sandow's athletic prowess, but it very quickly deteriorates to a great deal of petty and peevish vilification. "Picture to yourself a good-looking man tripping on the stage with the short pitter-patter of a fussy little woman with sore feet trying to avoid treading on a companion's dress, and forcing herself to look amiable. That is exactly how Sandow walks upon the stage."[22] To his credit, Sandow simply ignored the ungentlemanly defamations.

Sandow may not have convinced Apollo and Cyclops of his integrity, but there were many others who took an opposite view. Sandow had long derived great satisfaction from his philanthropic work, and with typical flourish, he proclaimed himself "Amicus Humani Generis," a friend of the human race; then with equally typical bravado, he attempted to live up to his self-appointed title. His work with unfit men was well publicized and had met with much success, and his assistance to women had turned many a porker's ear into a silk purse. But he also helped the poor by contributing heavily to orphan asylums and other deserving charities.

Happily, the underprivileged were not the only recipients of Sandow's largesse, for he always seemed ready to help when there was a worthy cause to work for. When the explorer Ernest Shackleton was fitting out an expedition to the Antarctic in 1908, Sandow helped him by donating the hefty sum of £1,000.[23] That same year the Olympic Games were to be held in London, but due to fiscal problems there was not enough money to house the foreign athletes properly. Once again Sandow was approached, and once again he generously contributed £1,500 toward the housing and entertainment of the visiting contestants.[24]

However noble and generous all these gifts to the nation were, they would not have been possible without the great success of Sandow's Curative Institute. It was this organization that gained for him the undying regard of many sickly and weak patients. The curative treatments that Sandow offered at his institute in St. James's Street became well known for their effectiveness. Sandow achieved remarkable results for his followers by giving them simple but serviceable exercises and dietary advice. He had discovered that the whole person was involved in medical treatment and that a healthy body was more disease resistant.

These are precepts that modern man takes as a given, but it was bold new thinking to many at the turn of the century.

The ability to cure diverse ailments by exercise was one of the most dramatic of all Sandow's claims. Exercise had long been recognized as an important road to health, but physical culture had mainly been pursued as a prophylactic rather than a solution to disease and deformity. Sandow's innovation was to turn exercise into a means of healing existing conditions. He published a long list of booklets, *Sandow's Health Library,* detailing the problems that he was confident of curing. These pamphlets—twenty-four in all—promised to cure such maladies as indigestion and dyspepsia, constipation, liver troubles, obesity, rheumatism and gout, anemia, kidney disorders, deformities, speech defects, skin disorders, insomnia, and neurasthenia.

As with most innovations, however, there were several precedents, and Sandow's brand of curative physical culture was no different. As far back as the 1860s manufacturers of parlor gymnasiums were touting their products as panaceas for virtually all health problems. A contraption called "Mann's Healthlift," for example, promised to cure neuralgia, rheumatism, problems of blood circulation, and torpor of the liver, among other things.[25] John E. Ruebsam's "Home Gymnasium" similarly promised that "By a systematic use of the muscles the circulation will be increased, and many chronic ailments will disappear." If we are to believe his brochure, the home gymnasium would cure infantile paralysis, chicken breast, anemia, paralysis, hemiplegia, dyspepsia, rupture, and a host of other troubles.[26]

Soon other physical culturists had discovered the profit-making benefits of the exercise cure. Professor D. L. Dowd professed the ability to cure a variety of orthopedic troubles through calisthenics; these included bowed or knock-kneed legs, wry neck, and curvature of the spine. Anthony Barker thought he could clear up problems such as indigestion, weak lungs, nervousness, and headaches through light dumbbell use. One innovative thinker even believed that he could smarten up idiots by physical exertion. "People naturally stupid" he claimed, could be made "comparatively intelligent by prevailing on them to take gymnastic exercise."[27]

Curative physical culture reached its apogee in the first decades of the twentieth century when mail-order muscleman Lionel Strongfort (Max Unger) declared that anyone could cure drug, tobacco, or alcohol addiction, increase height, return lost sexual potency, and vanquish the common cold all by exercising according to his system.[28]

Though he was a little less extravagant, Sandow claimed his system could cure everything from stooped shoulders to stammering by diet and exercise, nor was it startling that this aroused the skepticism of many people. One of the most famous investigators who swooped down upon him was the reporter from *Truth*. Henry Labouchere, the muckraking journalist and sometime member of Parliament, had founded this well-known magazine many years earlier, and as time went on it had acquired a reputation for hard-hitting investigative reporting. So when Labouchere sent a representative to interview Sandow and take a look around the institute, the reading public sat up and took notice. A brief favorable account of the institute was published in 1907, but four years later *Truth* was back again, this time determined not to let a single detail escape them. If there was any quackery going on at Sandow's clinic, the sleuths at *Truth* would certainly uncover it.

The first thing the magazine's investigator did was to meet Sandow himself. The reporter later admitted that he was a little bemused at the director's appearance, for he half expected "some modern variant of Hercules, draped in lion-skins and leaning on a club made of a tree trunk." Instead, Sandow greeted him in proper business attire, and after a while Sandow had thoroughly charmed his guest. Despite the strongman's smart morning coat, starched collar, and stylish cravat, the writer ended up praising his host for his superb physique. The reporter was then told of the procedures used to help the patients who came to Sandow.

Mr. Sandow personally saw and diagnosed each person who walked through the door—he left nothing to his deputies. In fact, in order to speed up the process, there were five separate consulting rooms so that the director could shuffle back and forth between them, seeing a maximum of ailing patients in a minimum of time. As soon as the problem had been diagnosed, the "prescription" was given. The invalid was instructed in a series of exercises which were designed to fit the ailment he suffered from. These were written down and put together into a little book, so that one could consult them at any time. The visitor was then directed to the exercise room.

The main part of the gymnasium was on the second floor. It was a large, light, airy room about sixty-five feet in length. The reporter was surprised at the utter lack of gymnastic equipment and heavy weights. Most of the treatment carried on in the institute consisted of calisthenics and light dumbbell work. There was nothing more—Sandow was attempting to build up the muscular system and to improve the circulation. A serious bodybuilder would be out of place at the Curative Institute.

The exercising hall was divided into cubicles and each patient was thus able to work out in total privacy, away from the prying stares of others. There were several trained attendants who hovered about, ready to answer questions or help out whenever necessary. To the gentleman from *Truth,* it seemed to run as smoothly as a Swiss clock.

After the weary patient finished his exercises, he could take advantage of the luxurious bathing facilities. The clients could have their choice of hot, cold, or shower baths. Medicinal baths along the lines of the famous resorts at Harrogate, Carlsbad, and Marienbad could be had at no extra charge. Since this was the heyday of opulent but extremely expensive spas, this feature was a compelling inducement to participate in itself.

The many mysteries of the body and its proper maintenance were perplexing to most Edwardians, as, indeed, they are to all of us. One of the most common solutions to these physical infirmities has long been to spend time at a spa. At these retreats, a patient could relax, undergo a water cure, or engage in other healthy physical activities. Sandow, therefore, was in the mainstream of popular thinking when he declared that he could cure an amazing variety of ailments by his system of exercise and diet.

Unlike Sandow's Institute, most of the other famous spas of the day were located away from the cities. In America, Macfadden led the rest in the establishment of curative resorts. His "healthatoriums," as he termed them, were located in upstate New York, on Long Island, in the New Jersey Pine Barrens, in Chicago, and in Battle Creek, Michigan. These establishments resembled Sandow's in their regimens of therapy and judicious exercise, though Macfadden laid more emphasis on a healthful diet than did his English competitor.[29]

Of course, the rich surroundings were all very impressive, but did Sandow's treatment actually work? That was one of the primary questions that the man from *Truth* wanted to determine. Sandow allowed him to see anything in his files that he wanted, and he accordingly dug out letter after letter attesting to the effectiveness of the system. Then he was shown testimonials from just about every doctor in Harley Street, praising Sandow and his system. After it was all finished, the results boiled down to nothing less than a resounding success: 44 percent of his patients reported dramatic improvement in their conditions, 52 percent reported slight improvement, and in only 4 percent of the cases was no improvement reported. It certainly seemed that Sandow was onto something good. *Truth* was convinced.[30]

Admirable though they were, these surprisingly high statistics only told part of the story. Before any potential patient was admitted to the institute, his case was carefully screened by Sandow. If his ailment was treatable, he was admitted; if not, he was directed to the nearest medical specialist. Sandow was shrewdly aware of the limitations of even the best diet and the most carefully supervised exercises, and so he avoided all those cases where successful treatment was in doubt. With the instincts of a born athlete, he only played to win.

Sandow received much satisfaction from his curative work, and he spent ever increasing amounts of time and money to promote it. He published hundreds of pamphlets and books touting his system and calling attention to his successes. He received glowing testimonials from many celebrities. The flamboyant pianist Paderewski and the celebrated tenor Ben Davies had both taken the Sandow cure. So had Sir Arthur Conan Doyle who had worked in the system for many years and was reportedly a "firm believer in the efficacy of judicious systematic light exercises." But without a doubt, Sandow's greatest coup in getting celebrities to endorse his system came about in 1911. In that year he was appointed by royal warrant to be "Professor of Scientific and Physical Culture" to King George V.[31]

Journalists the world over made much of this new position. "Sandow to Make George the Strong Man of Europe" read one of the headlines. Although as Prince of Wales, George had visited Sandow's Institute on one or two occasions and had used Sandow's developers as a means of keeping fit on a state visit to Australia, the appointment was largely an honorific one. George hardly had time to spare on exercise. Nevertheless, the papers speculated that the king might be building his muscles in order to use them on his "dear first cousin, Billy Hohenzollern" in order to "chuck his cousin over his shoulder."[32]

Although the reports of the king's athletic prowess and his desire to trounce the kaiser were meant to be comic, it still portended an ominous malaise. This uneasiness in England and Europe was reflected in the gradual rise of nationalism and militarism. The winds of a terrible war were beginning to blow, softly, almost unnoticed at first, but soon whipped up to hurricane intensity. The devastation that would follow in its wake was thankfully unimaginable.

Sandow responded to the early public interest in soldiery and armed force in a characteristic way. He offered a contest with tempting prizes. Perhaps the most effective of his military competitions was the one that arose out of an appeal by Lord Esher for more troops. The London County Corps of the Territorial Army was charged with protecting the home front, but enlistment had sunk to a shocking state. Viscount Esher had to raise eleven thousand new recruits in a hurry in order to insure the nation's safety in the event of war. Esher had long been a champion of modernization in the British army, and he must have viewed with alarm the deterioration of the home forces. In order to raise the large number of troops that he needed, the viscount had to resort to a few less conventional tactics. In this he was aided by the *Daily Mail,* which made his crusade their pet cause. To show his patriotism, Sandow also agreed to help out. He volunteered to provide physical training at his own expense for all the recruits who were too puny to pass the physical examination. Then, at Lord Esher's request, Sandow agreed to give three months of free physical training to each of the eleven thousand men who came forward during the appeal. He further presented £1,000 in cash prizes to the men who made the greatest physical improvement under the training. This did the job, for it was reported that "an immediate influx of recruits made itself manifest."

Even the *Times* of London seemed amazed at the dramatic progress made by the men. "Each of the 104 prize winners added no less than 12 inches to their combined neck, chest, arm, and leg measurements, while the winner of the first prize of £500 obtained in all an improvement of 27½ inches, 5¾ inches being added to his chest girth." So Sandow had saved the national honor and helped bring up the home guard to its full compliment. He well deserved the praise that was showered on him in the press: "Mr. Sandow, by his patriotic action, gave every one of the 11,000 young men the opportunity of improving his physique."[33] And had they but known, those young men would be called upon to serve their country sooner than they might have expected.

There was never any real question of Sandow's own patriotism. He had married a British woman, had lived in England for many years, and in 1906 he had renounced his German citizenship and had become a loyal British subject.[34] But when the fateful and tragic summer of 1914 arrived, no one of Teutonic extraction was free from suspicion, so during the Great War Sandow found it best to keep a low profile.

Throughout his life Sandow continued to speak with a heavy German accent, and his once stylish Kaiser Bill mustache must have had the effect of a red flag in front of a bull whenever he was in public. On the other hand, he had gained many friends in Britain. He had become physical culture instructor to the king himself and had hobnobbed with government and society leaders for quite some time. There could never be any doubts about where his political and national sentiments lay.

Despite Sandow's undoubted loyalty to king and country, rumors of his persecution flew about as thick as blackbirds at sunset. One of the most persistent was that he had been imprisoned and even executed in the Tower of London. These were especially popular in American newspapers of the time. They were difficult to disprove at that distance; they called up images of the athlete's decapitation like an Elizabethan traitor; and they were all as thrilling as they were mendacious.[35]

One concession to the prevailing low opinion of Germans was that Sandow was prepared to make was his clever switch of national origin. In a notice in one of his books, he lists his nationality as "Russian, born Königsberg, naturalised British."[36] He thus deftly changed his background in one fell swoop—though it must be remembered that his mother was truly Russian. Sandow was not the only one to arrange such a conversion, however; even the British royal family traded names from the German house of Hanover to the English Windsor. Aside from this single transformation, Sandow preferred to let his work and enthusiasm be his protection against the Hun haters. And so he continued his labors, spurred on by the desperate cataclysm of total war.

The burning issues of military preparedness and national survival were addressed by Sandow in what was probably his most ambitious book, *Life Is Movement.* Though it was published in 1919, one year after the armistice, it was written during the last couple of years of the war. The book was meant to be a culmination of his life's work in the field of curative physical culture, and in it he expounds many revolutionary and novel ideas. The whole project grew out of the poor condition of Great Britain's recruits in the recent unpleasantness. Just as he had warned of the poor state of the British physique during the Boer War, Sandow found that the situation had not improved very much since then. Far from being a whining jeremiad, Sandow's book offered some solutions to the problems which he presented.

There were several classifications in the British army for new recruits, ranging from A–1 to C–3. Those who were judged A–1 by the medical men who inspected the inductees were best fitted for service. The eye-opening catalyst for Sandow's book was the appalling number of men who failed to make the A–1 grade. The situation was no better in America. According to Sandow, no less than sixty-six out of every hundred men who volunteered for the United States Army had to be rejected because they were physically unfit. Speaking in 1918, just one month before the hostilities ceased, British prime minister David Lloyd George, summed up the state of Anglo-Saxon health: "I solemnly warn my fellow-countrymen that you cannot maintain an A–1 empire with a C–3 population. Unless this lesson is learned the war is in vain."[37] At long last Sandow's Cassandra-like warnings were heeded.

Under pressure of war, the powers in government and education were finally ready to listen to Sandow and men like him. Fortunately, Sandow had a distinguished record at getting men up to fighting strength. In addition to his assistance to Viscount Esher and the territorials, he had given free training to another fighting group, the Church Brigade.[38] He had also long specialized at his institute in bringing prospective officers up to required levels of physical strength to obtain their commissions. No wonder one public figure complimented Sandow on being "the greatest 'recruiting sergeant' the Army ever had."[39]

When general mobilization was called, Sandow's system was not forgotten. Many regiments had Sandow to thank for whatever physical prowess they possessed when they went into action. The captain of a Worcestershire regiment wrote to him in 1915 to tell of the great benefit the men had experienced since they started using Sandow's exercises. "I may add," the officer noted proudly, "that the C.O. has been complimented three or four times by different generals on the apparent hardiness and fitness of his men."[40] In the dark days of 1915, those men would need all the strength and staying power they could muster when they arrived at the front and were forced to put up with the filth and horror of the trenches.

Life Is Movement is much more than just an instruction book for training soldiers, though—it is a manual for conduct of life. Sandow's book grew out of an earlier work that was burdened with the cumbersome title of *The Construction and Reconstruction of the Human Body,* first published in 1907. The later work enlarged and put into popular terminology his ideas from the previous book. From its introduction by Sir Arthur Conan Doyle, it is clear that this was a book for the general public. It has the glib, facile tone of a lecture, and in fact it might well have grown out of Sandow's many public addresses in the cause of physical culture throughout the world. He uses many quaint and interesting metaphors in order to make the mysteries of the human body more fathomable to the common man.

Exercise and general well-being he presents as "torpedo nets" against disease. He suggests the establishment of a "Scotland Yard of Health" which would seek out unhygienic dwellings and workplaces and punish the owners. There are times when Sandow seems genuinely overcome by his subject and waxes poetic in his crusade to raise the sanitary standards of the nation: "The spirit or soul that occupies a bodily dwelling filled with the divine music of health makes a little heaven on earth within its body. Vicious cravings, passions and tendencies cannot tarry long there. This is real re-formation and re-education of man, from whom all social reformation must spring."[41] It was a glowing, utopian society that he foresaw, and at its root was the improvement of the exercise and dietary habits of an entire people.

But he had other messages, too. Sandow explained in clear and understandable terms the complexities of cell structure and basic nutrition. He was one of the most vocal forces in the early twentieth century to warn modern man of what we would call *stress* and what he called *neurasthenia*. He advocated exercises for pregnant mothers in order to make them and their children stronger and to reduce the suffering that accompanied childbirth. He even supported a healthier attitude toward pubs and bars. These should be open to all he felt—they should be clean and open meeting places for the sexes. Even children should be admitted, in that way they would foster a cleaner outlook and rid the tavern of its sordid atmosphere.[42]

So in the spirit of the great reformers, Sandow wanted to change society for the better. He wanted to make people healthier and happier. He wanted to eradicate sickness by strengthening the body. His was the dream of a disease-free world, where fresh air, light, and health flourished as they had in the days before omnibuses, express trains, and suffocating office or factory work. In his interview in *Truth*, the reporter correctly diagnosed his subject as "an idealist with a very practical side to his nature."[43] Nowhere is this more apparent than in his curative work. Sandow was always ready to support enthusiastically the improvement of the race and the betterment of mankind. He wished to create an Elysium out of the ruins of the great conflict that had just devastated Europe.

In addition to making the world safe and healthy for its progeny, Sandow was also keeping his hand in business. In 1922 he came out with another edition of *Strength and How to Obtain It,* and he also made some important modifications in his spring-grip dumbbells. This time a bell would ring when the two sides of the apparatus had been completely compressed. "The user both hears and feels the signals," he announced, "and his mind is kept concentrated and alert to carry out the exercises that bring him physical and mental fitness."[44]

Although he had his share of successes, Sandow's business ventures were, on the whole, adversely affected by the war even after the armistice. The principal customers for his exercise products were young men, but as the casualties began to mount, it became clear that a huge segment of eighteen- to twenty-five-year-olds had been wiped out by the fighting. Those who survived from that generation were often intent on enjoying themselves rather than indulging in the discipline and hard work involved in Sandow's system of exercise. It must have been with considerable uneasiness that Sandow and his directors watched their profits edge ever lower.

Fortunately, Sandow's interests did not completely center around the vicissitudes of his business. He was also watching his family grow and flourish. Helen, his oldest daughter, was interested in the theater. Several years earlier she distinguished herself in London by taking over the principal part in a musical comedy after the lead fell ill. At that time she was described as "a good looking girl, with thick fair hair," who "resembles her father in appearance." But as the article pointed out rather coyly, Helen was prettier and could sing.[45]

Photographs of Lorraine, his younger child, appeared in *Life Is Movement*, in which she wears a Grecian gown and looks as if she was filled with the vitality of youth. She is shown at fifteen, and is described as "proud of her fine physique" and "as keen an enthusiast on health and fitness as the author himself."[46] Sandow had been called a man of strong domestic interest.[47] This seems to be borne out by the many expressions of pride that he showered on his children.

The situation was not quite so idyllic with Sandow's wife. Blanche chose to remain out of the spotlight, rarely appearing with her husband in public. The woman who had turned heads in America and charmed reporters in Australia sulked moodily in Dhunjibhoy House, ignored and forgotten by the press and the people. The loneliness and resentment that must have accompanied her self-imposed solitude gradually found a vent through their daughters, so that gradually the girls' love for their father was replaced by their mother's gall and bitterness.

Fortunately, few people outside the family were aware of this widening rift, for Sandow made sure all the proper appearances were scrupulously maintained. When Lorraine Sandow was married in 1924, her father even went to the expense and trouble of mailing a piece of her wedding cake to a friend in America. The friend was Earle Liederman. Mercifully, history is mute on the condition of the cake when it arrived at its destination, but the partnership it helped to cement was a significant one for both men.

Liederman had built up a very successful mail order exercise business starting in 1916 and was quite well known in the realm of physical culture. In order to escape the constant demands of his correspondence courses, he decided to take a vacation in Europe. After he disembarked from the *Aquitania* at Southampton, he went straight to London, where he decided to meet his longtime idol, Eugen Sandow. His description of that visit and of the subsequent business dealings he had with the older master are important records. Liederman was a very observant young man and his account yields many interesting details about Sandow and his motivations.

Liederman recalled that an iron fence enclosed an emerald green lawn which fronted Sandow's Institute. On either side of the door were two large bronze statues. When he entered the building, the thing that first caught his eye was the large gold-framed portrait of Sandow by Aubrey Hunt that had been painted over thirty years before. There was also plenty of Victorian furniture: leather divans, carved mahogany furniture, several desks, and a great deal of comfortable clutter.

After almost an hour of waiting, during which Liederman had the distinct impression he was being spied upon, he was finally ushered into Sandow's office. Liederman recognized Sandow at once. He was "erect, heavy-set, medium height," and sported "a mass of iron-gray hair, grayish mustache, heavy tired-looking eyes, full face, frock coat, striped trousers, white lining to his waistcoat over which hung a black ribbon." At the end of the ribbon was a pince-nez which Sandow twirled nervously. He resembled a fastidious diplomat rather than a former music hall performer.

"How do you do, Mr. Liederman!" greeted the older man cordially. Sandow held out his hand, and Liederman clasped it. It was a strong, confident grip. "In grasping Sandow's right hand," he wrote, "I felt its thickness. It was not large, but very thick, especially where my fingers touched the lower part."

The young man then began telling Sandow of his admiration for him. When Sandow replied to this, Liederman was startled to hear Sandow speak with a thick German accent, "Vell, I haf heard so much about you, too." All the years in English-speaking countries had done little toward improving his pronunciation. Sandow then obliged his visitor by showing off his muscular prowess. He took off his coat and rolled up his sleeve. "His forearm was full and wonderfully shaped," Liederman reported. "Thick at the wrist, thick at the elbow, but much thicker around the central part because of magnificently developed pronator muscles." Sandow then flicked his bicep, making it jump and flutter just as he had done on stage in the old days. But alas, his body had not completely escaped the ravages of time, for Liederman noticed that his tricep seemed a little slack. He added that "The skin was not firm, nor were the minor muscles or ligaments in clear definition." Then, slapping the bottom of his thigh, the aging muscleman announced excitedly, "Here iss a good vun—feel dot!" Liederman happily complied, noticing that "the curve and bulk was pronounced" and that it possessed a "youthful contour as well as size."

But there were other telltale signs of age. Sandow's neck betrayed his advanced years, for when it was viewed from the side it looked too large because of flabbiness under the chin. In order to cover up the wrinkles in the front of his neck, he wore a stiff Gladstone collar and flowing tie. However, the young man was impressed with Sandow's absence of a bay window—his waist was just about right. Clearly, he was in good physical shape for a man of his age and background. "My aim is to be in as good condition as you are when I reach your age," Liederman said genuinely. Sandow replied warmly, "You will."

In spite of Sandow's veneer of formality and reserve, Liederman began to perceive his real character. Every now and then the older strongman would reveal flashes of enthusiasm that were not consistent with his dignified position. Despite the inevitable ravages of age, Sandow's heart remained young and zestful. In a moment of insight, Liederman grasped the situation. "His weary eyes told the story of much glamor, color and adventure along the road of ten thousand yesterdays, and his soul seemed to hunger for that which was forever gone . . . glory, applause, excitement and youth!" Sandow still yearned for the old wandering days in the music halls and vaudeville theaters of the world. Despite his obvious success, he was ready to try one last fling at touring, and he must have seen in young Liederman a valuable associate in that plan.[48]

Artfully, Sandow began to court Liederman and to play upon his obvious hero worship. The first step in that process was Sandow's endorsement of Liederman's system of bodybuilding. "Dear Mr. Liederman," Sandow wrote, "I have tested your system of physical culture, and I do not hesitate to express the opinion that it is a perfect health and muscle building system, both from a medical and a practical point of view, and one which, if honestly practised, cannot fail to produce the best possible result."[49]

This was quite an extraordinary move; for obvious reasons, Sandow had always been extremely reluctant to endorse any rival system. Liederman was elated when he left the Sandow Institute that day. "I was to get a real bona fide endorsement from this great authority! And without even asking for it! I confess that I was inwardly thrilled at the time and feebly tried to express my thoughts and appreciation in fumbling words of thanks."[50] But was the guileless young Liederman's system really that much better than many others on the market? Or might Sandow have had an ulterior motive in his generous testimonial? Whatever the reasons, to the young American it must have seemed too good to believe.

From this auspicious beginning, their partnership escalated. During 1924 letters flowed back and forth across the Atlantic. Sandow sent his new American friend a barrage of expensive gifts. A match case, a complete desk outfit, and other things arrived from England—and everything reportedly made of solid gold and engraved "To my friend Earle Liederman from his friend Eugen Sandow." The unsuspecting Liederman was being groomed for big things.[51]

Gradually a plan began to emerge from the exchange of correspondence. Sandow would come to the United States for one final tour and Liederman would be his manager and financial backer. Sandow would conduct a nationwide lecture tour to promote physical culture, then he would return to New York and establish there another Sandow's Institute. After the institute was in operation, Liederman would take over the running of this gymnasium, allowing its founder to return to England. In the following years Sandow would only visit America occasionally.

Liederman jumped at the chance to collaborate with the great Sandow. Aside from the honor that would accrue to him, a partnership with the older strongman would enhance his own name and lend greater credence to his work in physical culture. He foresaw great profit in the plans. Since he was especially busy that year, Liederman had to send an associate to London in order to clear up a few remaining contractual difficulties with Sandow. When his representative arrived back in the United States, he brought with him a contract whereby Liederman was to pay Sandow the astounding sum of $10,000 a year for twenty years. Even the normally pliant Liederman balked at this expensive arrangement, however. Eventually a more realistic contract was hammered out, granting Sandow $7,500 a year for five years.[52]

So in late 1924 Sandow received the first installment in the form of a bank draft for £1,500. The contract was thus set to go into effect on January 1, 1925. But before he was to come to America, Sandow sent Liederman a note inviting his new friend to accompany him on a brief automobile tour of England, Scotland, and Wales. Liederman was forced to refuse, but Sandow went anyway. According to all published reports, it was on this trip that Sandow was injured severely, and as a result died shortly thereafter. So the fine plans Sandow and Liederman had put together came to naught. Their partnership was ended by a final and incontestable force, death.

On the morning of October 15, 1925, readers on both sides of the Atlantic were shocked when they picked up their newspapers and saw the startling headlines: "Eugen Sandow, Stage Hercules, Dies in London." They learned that the great strongman had died the previous day due to the bursting of a blood vessel in his brain. This had been caused by the shock and strain he received when he lifted, single-handed, a car from a ditch. "He knew he had injured himself," wrote the *New York Times*, "but thought he was getting better until a few weeks ago." He had been feeling poorly for the past three weeks according to the *Times* of London, and was under the care of the eminent Harley Street physician Sir Thomas Horder. But all had been in vain. In the end the strongman succumbed to his last great foe.

Almost at once, people began drawing moral conclusions from the great man's death. The *Union* of Springfield, Massachusetts, editorialized the day after he passed away that Sandow's pupils need not necessarily fear the pernicious effects of exercise just because their teacher died. "Even if in his own case death ... was the result of excessive exertion, it does not follow that disciples who followed his system without trying to duplicate his feats were incurring any serious risk."[53] Several years later, Desbonnet was still peeved at Sandow for being so foolish as to die in a reckless manner. "Sandow has a right to the fine title of educator, and even his premature death serves as a lesson for us. It is an example of that which one should not do: work to excess and break records. It is sad to think that because of petty vanity a beautiful human machine lies forever six feet underground."[54]

However disappointed others were, it must be admitted that Sandow's death as reported in the newspapers of the world was a romantic—even heroic—way to die. He strained himself in an attempt to rescue one of his beloved motorcars. In some versions of the story there is even a passenger trapped in the overturned vehicle. It was the stuff of legends, and had he been there, Sandow would surely have enjoyed it.

Despite the suspicious sound of the whole affair, the evidence appears to confirm that Sandow was indeed involved in some sort of car accident prior to his death. Physical culturist Joe Assirati reported that a distant relation of his was a servant in the Sandow household in the mid–1920s. She verified that her master came into the house one day complaining of a severe headache. Sandow claimed that the pain had developed as a result of righting a car after an accident.[55] Unfortunately, the exact chronology of events has been lost, so we will never know with any certainty when this mishap occurred.

Morally satisfying though these stories are, there remain certain nagging questions concerning his death. First, there are serious discrepancies and ambiguities in the date of the alleged accident. According to the *Times* of London it occurred "two or three years ago," but in Liederman's account the accident happened in 1925, the same year as his death. If the earlier date is correct, would Sandow have agreed to appear in an extensive tour of America knowing he was not well? Second, and most damning, is the evidence presented on Sandow's death certificate. There the cause of death is given as "aortic aneurysm." It does not take a skilled physician to determine that a burst blood vessel in the brain is quite distant from the aorta. An autopsy could have cleared up these questions, but curiously this was never permitted.[56] When all the evidence is compiled, a different story begins to emerge— one not so romantic or heroic. The facts lead to the almost incontrovertible assumption that there was a cover-up surrounding the famous man's death.

Some perceptive persons had smelled a rat from the start. Immediately after Sandow's death, W. A. Pullum was warning readers of his magazine, the *Strong Man,* about the story. "We do not recommend anyone to take too literally the statement which has appeared in the press that Sandow died as a result of lifting his motorcar out of a ditch, singlehanded." He was suspicious since it would have been impossible for anyone, let alone a fifty-eight-year-old man, to lift a one-ton car out of a ditch without assistance. Unfortunately, Pullum offers no speculation on the reasons for this deception.[57]

A possible clue for the mysterious and circuitous trails in the story is found in two accounts of Sandow's last days from widely diverse sources. The first comes from Liederman. In discussing his relationship with Sandow in 1925 he stated, "He wrote me many letters wherein he mentioned trouble with his throat and other general reverses, and further mentioning that he was forced to cancel his immediate lecture tour in Great Britain."[58] Clearly, Sandow's health was slowly deteriorating. He was being laid low by disease, and Liederman undoubtedly knew more than he admitted.

As early as August 28 of his last year, Sandow was reported to be seriously ill, for on that day he was visited for a final time by an old friend whom he had not seen in many years, Florenz Ziegfeld. He and his family had been on vacation in Europe that summer, and before they left they decided to call on the ailing strongman. Fortunately, Ziegfeld's nine-year-old daughter, Patricia, was taken along on the visit, and she recalled it many years later. "The day before we sailed for home," she wrote, "Daddy hired a car and we drove out through the rain to see Eugen Sandow, the strongman who had started Daddy on his career, and who lived in a nice little house outside of London. He had been ill, and he received us wearing a brocade dressing gown. He was still divinely handsome, just as Daddy had always described him." Sandow and Ziegfeld embraced emotionally, "they were so genuinely glad to see each other that there were tears in their eyes. They spent a long, happy afternoon reminiscing, and when we left, they embraced again."[59] It was the last time the two men were to meet, and perhaps they both sensed it.

Sandow was obviously very ill at the time, for he greeted his guests in his dressing gown. This must have been a considerable embarrassment to the normally fastidious Sandow, whose sartorial correctness was well known. Perhaps the tears that Sandow shed that day were doubly painful, for he might have felt that his own end was near. One and a half months later, those feelings were realized. He was dead at the age of fifty-eight.

Many have speculated that Sandow was forced to pay the price of a premature death because of what used to be called the "follies of youth," or more plainly, venereal disease. It is a well-known fact that one of the causes of an aortic aneurism is syphilis. If this was the case with Sandow, it might also account for the family's bitter reaction after his death.

Thus, like a pack of cards that has been shuffled and reshuffled, the facts of Sandow's demise can be dealt in a variety of combinations. But we can never really be sure that we possess a winning hand, for we lack one important element—the ace of truth.

Shortly before their father died, Sandow's children had rushed to Blanche's side. Helen took over many of the chores after her father's death, such as writing notes of thanks to the many people who sent their condolences.[60] Even with this help, there was much for Blanche to see to.

The funeral services were held on October 16 at St. John the Baptist Church in Holland Park near the family's home.[61] According to a witness, the obsequies were not particularly emotional. Most of the mourners were business associates who sat through the memorial services stiffly and dispassionately. Olympic weightlifter Launceston Elliot may have been there, as was W. G. Hunt, director of Sandow's Institute. But grief, if there was any, was efficiently concealed.[62]

After the public ceremonies, Sandow's mortal remains were interred at the lovely rustic cemetery at Putney Vale, near London. A sad and ironic difference distinguishes Sandow's burial place from those around it: there was not then, nor has there ever been, any stone to mark the grave of the father of bodybuilding. He lies just as he has from that autumn day in 1925 when he was laid in the earth—in an unmarked plot in a forgotten corner of the graveyard. In the years that followed his death, there were several attempts to raise some sort of a monument over Sandow's last resting place, but always with the same results: the family would not allow it.

An outraged letter from H. W. Couzens that appeared in the November 12, 1932, issue of *Health & Strength* is indicative of others in the campaign. He asked, "I wonder how many of your readers know that Sandow, who died on October 14, 1925, is buried in Putney Vale Cemetery? Unfortunately, his grave remains quite bare: nothing in the shape of a stone has been erected to his memory, at least there wasn't up to a year ago."[63]

The editor promised in a note to look into the allegations with a view to remedying the situation. In a later issue, the editor admitted to failure, since Sandow's widow could not be located. Ironically, she was found by the magazine seventeen years later, but still refused permission for a grave monument.

In 1962, Eric Moorhead of Victoria, Australia, was similarly appalled by the state of Sandow's grave, and he agreed to donate a sum of money to keep the overgrown grave tidy. Unfortunately, this was the only attention the grave has received since Sandow's funeral. Currently, Sandow's grave is just as neglected as it has been for the past seventy years.[64]

Blanche's adamant refusal to erect a marker on her husband's grave was almost certainly the revenge of a woman who had been neglected and deceived throughout her life, perhaps even been the innocent victim of venereal disease. It is not so difficult to believe that the family concocted the story of Sandow's death in order to still the gossiping tongues of others. We shall probably never know for sure. The only thing that is obvious is that Blanche and her daughters wanted Sandow to lie in disgrace for all eternity, unknown except for the few.

Less than one month after his death, Blanche put Dhunjibhoy House, their furniture, all works of art, and Sandow's beloved automobiles up for auction. She was certainly not destitute, for according to the records, her husband left an estate of the gross value of £9,565, with net personalty of £5,271, so this unseemly haste was not motivated by poverty.[65] Shortly after this she slipped from public view, and from then on neither she, nor after her, her daughters, would have the slightest thing to do with Sandow or his memory. All invitations, all requests for interviews were curtly refused. The hatred that they bore him roiled and festered to the end of their days.

To a superstitious mind, it might seem as if the entire family had been cursed by the hatred between Eugen and Blanche even to the next generation. The elder daughter, Helen, married a man named Joe Strong and soon disappeared from sight. Blanche moved back to Manchester after her husband's death, and apparently lived there in bitter obscurity until her own death.

Sandow's beloved younger daughter, Lorraine, was especially unlucky. She married James Douglas Brown, a wealthy Manchester department store owner. Although he was a successful businessman, Brown's real love was botany, and he gradually came to spend more time in the greenhouse than with his pretty young wife. It should have been no surprise, therefore, when Lorraine ran off with Brown's protégé, a young Oxford undergraduate who boarded with them. Henceforth, she was never seen or spoken of by them again. To the family, she was as dead as her poor forgotten father.

Eventually, the two settled in Wimbledon. Lorraine reportedly retained her good posture, attractive figure, and classic beauty long into old age. Her new husband gave up his academic career and was forced to drive a taxi to make ends meet.[66]

Sandow's many business enterprises suffered a similarly sad fate. After he died, Sandow's many companies were gradually sold. His institute was taken over by Mr. Hunt, who kept it alive for a while. His mail order system of curative physical culture survived the longest, continuing to prosper on the value of Sandow's name. Eventually, it too faded away, and Sandow was superseded by other, more aggressive entrepreneurs.

But it should be remember that Sandow's legacy is really more permanent than all these. His accomplishments are not so easily forgotten in some circles. One of the most important ways his influence reaches beyond his unmarked grave is in the undeniable inspiration he gave to an entire generation of athletes. By their own admission, many first-rate sportsmen saw Sandow perform and then were later encouraged to build bodies similar to his. After Bernarr Macfadden and Al Treloar saw Sandow in Chicago, they both decided to follow the physical culture star. Alan Calvert and Mark Berry, early bodybuilding authors and theoreticians, were inspired to begin writing and publishing about muscle building based on Sandow's example. Olympic weightlifting champion Launceston Elliot and athlete Monte Saldo were equally encouraged to go on the music hall stage in emulation of their model. Furthermore, it should be remembered that these men represented only a tiny percentage of the many people who were inspired by Sandow to become stronger, shaplier, and healthier.

The inspiration Sandow provided others was soon translated into more commercial terms. The strongman's name suddenly became synonymous with strength itself. This was especially true among marketers of clothing. There were boys' "Sandow Suits" (the strongest suits in the world), Sandow stockings, Sandow "Gentlemen's Garters," and a host of other products. The promoters of these commodities sought to cash in on Sandow's immediate name recognition. The fact that the strongman neither gave his permission nor even knew about the garments was of little concern to them.

In addition to pure strength, Sandow also came to represent raw virility for his generation. According to one anthropologist, David D. Gilmore, masculinity consists of three main ingredients. These are physical strength, sexual prowess, and economic success.[67] Using these criteria, it is clear that Sandow qualified easily in all three areas.

Sandow's strength was unquestioned, and his ability to attract willing partners of either sex has been well documented. The strongman's wealth was very much in evidence, too, since he took pride in spreading it around with little apparent care. Gilmore notes that " 'real' men are those who give more than they take; they serve others. Real men are generous, even to a fault."[68] When Sandow distributed his largesse to both military and civilian charities, he was unwittingly partaking of these ancient masculine traditions.

Interestingly, violence played little part in Sandow's persona. He certainly does not qualify as a kind of Edwardian Rambo. On the contrary, Sandow's masculinity was of a relatively gentle variety. His destructive rampages were either faked (as with the lion fight) or simply boyish hijinks (as with the spoon bending and chair smashing).

Another more material legacy of Sandow's success was his effect on the business of bodybuilding. He and his associates virtually pioneered the industry that others now control. Sandow's company marketed equipment, food supplements, and gym memberships long before any of the other entrepreneurs had become active. Perhaps more importantly, Sandow knew how to make muscle building palatable to all classes, and he used that knowledge to further his own career. He encouraged women and children to exercise and lead healthier lives; he was of course not alone in these crusades, but it was his marketing genius that allowed his ideas to be disseminated and popularized among the public at large.

According to the sports theorist Donald Mrozek, the great message of Sandow and other turn-of-the-century physical culturists was that man was no longer fated to keep the body he was born with. The body could at last be molded to fit an ideal form. Just as the hand of God had fashioned Adam, so now the human form could be shaped anew, this time with carefully supervised exercise and a healthy lifestyle. Doubting Thomases needed to look no further than Sandow himself; what he had achieved others could emulate.

Mrozek points out that thanks to the new scientific studies of the human body, physical perfection was theoretically possible. "As with marble so with flesh, man could sculpt and finish a form that actually perfected the physical characteristics that were potential genetically."[69]

Finally, it was this very physical perfection that gave Sandow an added importance in his society. In effect, he defined the parameters of masculine beauty. His much-touted good looks provided the beau ideal certainly for his own generation, and many would argue that his paradigm is for all ages. Sandow's obvious athletic physique represented an ideal that gradually caught on with succeeding generations of young men. Sandow's arrival on the social scene signaled the banishment of the thin, pale, intellectual model as well as the stout, prosperous model of masculine perfection that had prevailed before.

Despite his unquestioned importance, Sandow's relative position among modern athletes is a little less clear. It is always a dangerous pastime to compare the athletic stars of one generation to those of another. There is little to be gained by this exercise and much to misinterpret. Sandow has even less in common with today's bodybuilders than, say, Babe Ruth has with Henry Aaron. The steroid-induced muscles and monomaniacal focus of contemporary physique athletes would have been completely foreign to Sandow and the bodybuilders of his generation.

Nevertheless, these comparisons are inevitable. Starting as early as 1926, magazine writers were beginning to place Sandow side by side with modern athletes.[70] These first comparisons were initially very flattering, but as bodybuilding techniques became more sophisticated, the contrasts were not always favorable. Sandow's weightlifting prowess had been challenged during his own lifetime, so it was only natural that this was the first area where his abilities were questioned.

In the early 1930s writers were beginning to see Sandow in a more realistic light, not as the superhero that the strongman preferred in his own lifetime. "The great assets of Sandow were his grace and strength—particularly in his arms," wrote J. H. Nurse in 1932. "*He was never a big man,* and no one seems to realise this fact. If he ever weighed 15st. [210 lbs.] (as he stated in his book *Life is Movement*) it was when he put on flesh—meat pure and simple."[71]

By 1960 Sandow's dethroning as a weightlifting superstar was complete, but he was still being revered as a physique star.[72] By the late 1970s, however, the Anglo-German athlete was no longer admired as a model of physique excellence, but rather as a pioneer who had popularized a sport that had grown beyond anything Sandow himself would have recognized.

Today, Sandow's physique would not qualify him even to a minor place in contemporary competitions. His only presence at a Mr. Olympia contest is in the form of the gracefully modeled statue that was created by Pomeroy a hundred years ago. The victor of the bodybuilding contest receives a replica of Sandow's image as a trophy. However, even this has been updated, for the contest organizers have chosen to hire a sculptor to "muscle up" Pomeroy's balanced design to make Sandow's musculature accord better with modern tastes. Still, the award is symbolic of Sandow's reemergence as an important figure in the bodybuilding world.

So despite his unmarked grave in Putney Vale Cemetery, Sandow's real monument is to be found in every bodybuilding gymnasium in every country of the world. He acted as an evangelist for healthy and strong bodies. By his example, he pointed the direction that others would follow.

Perhaps the best summation of Sandow's effect on his own generation is found in the obituary published in the *New York World.* "Sandow was no mere dumb-bell lifter," it notes, "he was the personification of the transcendental muscular aesthetic. It booted little how much he could lift, or whether he could lift anything at all; one attended his exhibitions to look and be exalted by pure beauty."[73] Today, after nearly a hundred years, that beauty still exalts us.

Afterword

Sport history is a rapidly evolving species, and a decade can make a huge difference. It took me thirteen years to research and write my biography of professional strongman, physical culturist, and Edwardian businessman Eugen Sandow, and in the intervening decade between the book's first appearance and the present edition, there has been much work done by me and others on Sandow's life, career, and significance. For instance, there have been thoughtful analyses of physique display, physique photography, masculinity, femininity, and the sexuality of bodybuilders. All of these wonderful works were naturally not around when I wrote my book, but I hope that my contributions have in some way inspired my colleagues to produce their own works. I have included a list of the best of the best in a bibliography that follows this essay.

When I first wrote Sandow's biography, I stated that the strongman had been all but forgotten, that no university courses were taught that mentioned him, and that the ultimate sign of his ephemeral fame was that his grave in London's Putney Vale Cemetery was unmarked and unvisited. I am happy to say that all of these situations have now been rectified. Sandow is now in the sights of a surprising number of sport, theatrical, and social historians, and I am aware of several courses in which Sandow is not only mentioned but featured prominently. Although Sandow has not achieved the status of a universally recognized icon, he is increasingly well known by the general public. Most gratifying of all, the strongman's grave finally has a suitable marker. The black marble stone in Putney Vale Cemetery is inscribed in gold letters "The Great/ Eugen Sandow/ 1867–1925/ The Father of Bodybuilding."[1] So there is much to be optimistic about.

In addition to the new respect for Sandow, much new information has come to light that helps flesh out the bones of Sandow's professional life. The essay which follows is an attempt to bring Sandow's life and career into sharper focus by the addition of these newly found sources; unfortunately, it can only give the outlines of the man's outer life, not the core. Unlike eloquent writers, effusive talkers, or those lucky enough to find themselves a Boswell, Sandow's inner feelings continue to elude even the most patient researcher. The facts of Sandow's life are plentiful, but the man himself remains the same mysterious conundrum he has always been.

Sandow always claimed that just as his life began in weakness and ill health, his professional career started in anonymity and poverty. Although he may have exaggerated the first part of that equation, the latter part is most certainly true. Fortunately, a few tidbits of information about the strongman's early years as a performer have surfaced, and they confirm the estimation that this was a very trying time in his life. One of the scraps of information from this period comes from the Belgian magazine *Le Biceps*. In January 1900, a brief, unsigned anecdote attests to Sandow's poverty while he was in the Belgian capital: "We knew Sandow in Brussels several years ago when he had no other profession but as a model for sculptors, principally for Jef Lambeaux and for Gaspard. At that time Sandow earned three francs every third day. There is no doubt that 'union makes strength,' and when its properly used, strength makes a fortune."[2] Sandow was living in miserable poverty, and earning an occasional three francs was hardly enough to encourage an athletic career. Eventually, the young man was forced to perform as a busker in a public square; there can be no doubt that Sandow was desperate.

A later article in the French magazine *La Culture Physique* by its editor and publisher, Edmond Desbonnet tells of another incident that confirms the strongman's early, unhappy days in Belgium. The date of the incident is somewhat unclear, but apparently it happened around 1908 after Sandow had earned glory and a fortune in England and America. He decided to go to Belgium once more, "the country that had taken him in, helped him and put him on the right track." The now wealthy man revisited the places where he earned his meager living in the past: the circus where he once performed, the rooms on the Boulevard de la Senne where he lived with Professor Attila, the old gym run by Attila, the studios of Jef Lambeaux and others, and finally to Place Rouppe where Sandow had been forced to perform as a sidewalk strongman. It was here that he earned a few coins before the artists had hired him, but to his surprise the spot that he had occupied years before was taken by a family of acrobats. Sandow could see at once that they were desperately poor, and he was determined to help them. He gave the astonished father of the troupe a £100 note in memory of the strongman's early poverty. Desbonnet's comment points out the contrast between Sandow's youth and his maturity: "What a deal of soul searching he did while comparing what he had become with what he had been before."[3]

Another important time in Sandow's early career were the months he spent in Italy. The chronology of his sojourn (or more likely, sojourns) is hard to pin down, but it appears that, aside from a holiday or two on the peninsula, Sandow spent large parts of 1888–89 in Italy. A few things are apparent from the stories that have recently emerged: Sandow's stay was remunerative, he was well known to the Italian public, and he concentrated on wrestling more than weightlifting.

"I can well remember when I was in Milan, competing against the Italian champion." Sandow reminisced in 1892. "There were lots of ambitious youngsters who wanted to make matches with me, and when I did compete, I took 40,000 francs in two days. Not a bad gate for such a poor country, was it?"[4] Indeed, it was not. Since Sandow often played fast and loose with the specifics, readers should not accept the exact sum mentioned, but clearly he had made good money. There is no mention of what his adversaries were champions of, but it is pretty fair to say that it was probably wrestling. It is hard to imagine any athlete making that kind of profit on a lifting match.

Another story from this time concerns the great Roman wrestler Basilio Bartoletti. This wrestler is mentioned specifically in *Sandow's System of Physical Culture*, but little additional information is given about their match. Bartoletti was described by a contemporary in frank terms. "His stature was small but quite sturdy, and he tended to obesity. More than the vigor of his muscles, he valued dexterity and training."[5] He must have been a competent fighter because his career lasted an extraordinary fifty-two years, and he is credited with inventing the name "Greco-Roman wrestling" to indicate his preferred style.

The dates of his life are not clear, but his best years were probably 1870–90. By the time the aging Italian wrestled with Sandow at the Teatro Manzoni in Rome, neither dexterity nor training could help him since he was past his prime; still, he had the courage to wrestle with the young and handsome German. Poor Bartoletti was quickly and decisively defeated, and he recalled the event many years later. "There was nothing I could do with this murderous lion: his hands tightened around me like pincers of iron. I could either beg for mercy or be squeezed to death."[6] It was undoubtedly with the five hundred

franc purse from this and the other contests that made Sandow reluctant to leave Italy. It was only the promise of an even greater reward
as well as the chance to hit the big time that convinced Sandow to go
to London in late 1889 and challenge Sampson and Cyclops in a duel
of strength and daring. The experience as well as the profits of his
Italian adventure allowed him and Attila to survive and to flourish in
the greatest sporting nation in the world: Great Britain.

As we have seen, after his initial success with Sampson and Cyclops, Sandow's life improved significantly. He received regular bookings and his fame grew quickly, but there were only a few descriptions
of his music-hall act at this time. One of the best appeared in 1891
in *The Daily Graphic* of London, and it mentions that the strongman
had to keep innovating in order to stay at the forefront of his profession. "Even strong men," confirmed the article, "if they would retain
popular favour, must emulate the Hercules they attempt to rival by
finding themselves fresh ordeals of endurance." Thus, Sandow's act
at the Tivoli Hall of Varieties marked a turning point for the young
athlete because he shifted from lifting mainly iron weights to other,
more interesting items. When he bent backwards while doing his Roman Column feat, Sandow picked up not a barbell but a fully grown
man; he later lifted an attendant overhead and held him aloft with
one hand "almost as easily as a nurse would 'dance' an infant."

The climax of the act came when the strongman lifted a pony.
"The chestnut steed, a spirited little animal is slung by ropes in the
centre of the stage. Grasping a strap handle on the near side with
the right hand, and pin the animal's near hind leg with his left hand,
Sandow bears his novel burden steadily off the stage." The athlete then
supported a grand piano on a platform in the Tomb of Hercules position along with a pianist and three other musicians all belting out the
strains of *Rule Britannia*. Sandow was clearly honing his show-business
skills as well as refining many of the stunts that he would later perform
on his many world tours.[7]

Sandow's reputation and fame may have been on the ascendant,
but his was still far from being a household name. Desbonnet tells
another story which he must have heard from Sandow himself and
which demonstrates a mischievous aspect of the strongman's character.
It also shows the control that he could exercise over his body because
of his muscular development. Desbonnet dates the episode around
1887 in London, but a more accurate date must be 1889 after Sandow
had arrived in London in order to challenge Sampson. Sandow was
not yet well known in the British capital, thus when he went to order
a suit of clothes, the clerk suggested that he choose from some of the

ready-mades that he had on hand. "It must be said that when he was dressed in street clothes, Sandow did not look like an athlete; he was an ordinary gentleman and only one who was well acquainted with the world of physical culture could guess the strength of this Hercules."

Sandow thus refused the *prêt-à-porter* suits, saying to the tailor, "It is impossible for me to find clothes that are ready-made, since my physique is not one that is normally encountered, and to be more precise, a suit that fits my measurements is not available for sale." The experienced tailor was loathe to let a customer tell him that he could not find adequate clothing on the store's racks, and he expressed that opinion. So the strongman decided to play a trick on the clerk. He allowed himself to be measured by the man, but Sandow expelled all the air from his chest while this occurred. The salesman promised to have a newly altered suit available for him if the athlete would return a bit later. When he came back, Sandow expanded his chest to its greatest dimensions, and the astonished tailor could not believe his eyes. He re-checked the label to make sure that he had the correct one, and then he apologized and promised to supply another suit to the correct dimensions the next day.

Naturally, when that day arrived, Sandow came back and assumed his normal dimensions once more, and the oversized suit hung on him in folds. "I warned you that my measurements were not available on the market." The distraught tailor was at his wit's end. "Sir, I give up trying to find a suit that fits, and rather than redoing the suit, I would prefer to give you some money along with the request that you visit my competitor who is located just across the street."

Sandow then replied, "You can deliver two suits; I'll wear the small one on the days when I go to the theater and the big one when I wander about Whitechapel; the ruffians will think twice before attacking me." The tailor did as he was told, but gave Sandow a substantial discount.[8] Episodes like this helped Sandow build his status as a mythic personality, and it also shows his rather cruel sense of humor at the expense of the poor clothing salesman. Perhaps he wanted to show his superiority both physically and intellectually over the lowly clerk, thus increasing his stock as a bonafide member of the middle class.

Another of Sandow's favorite stunts is reported in the British press at this time. It was previously assumed that Sandow's private "anatomy lessons" were innovations of his cagey American manager, Florenz Ziegfeld, Jr., but new evidence suggest that the audiences came earlier than this. Another article in *The Daily Graphic* from later in 1891 describes one of these all-female art lessons in some detail. Mr. Osborn, a fellow of the Royal College of Surgeons lectured some attentive students at Mrs. Jopling's School of Art on "The Superficial Muscles."

According to the *Graphic*, "There was a flutter of expectation as Sandow, wrapped in an enormous coat, entered the studio." There was even more fluttering after the athlete threw off his covering and climbed up on a table; the interesting development was that (as later in America) Sandow did not wear the tights that covered him in his stage performance. For all intents, he was naked. As Sandow flexed and preened his well developed body, Mr. Osborn pointed out the principal muscles, and the ladies sketched away furiously in order to remember and profit from the event. "The lecture and demonstration," confirmed the reporter, "was followed with the closest interest by the audience."[9]

Sandow's fame and comfort before audiences clearly increased at this formative time in his career, and under the tutelage and guidance of his mentor Attila he continued to keep himself in the public's eye. Sandow had not as yet sloughed off the role of traditional strongman (rather than physique star), and this is confirmed by his continued interest in proving his strength. In February of 1892 Sandow broke the world's record for the bent press by lifting 269 pounds, thus besting the record of Louis Cyr.[10] Since the French-Canadian strongman was just then performing in London, this was meant to be a direct challenge to Cyr.

There was enough interest in Sandow's challenge that a reporter from *The Sporting Life* was dispatched to Sandow's home in Warwick Street, Pimlico, to interview him. What resulted was an interesting encounter for many reasons, not the least of which was that the reporter was greeted at the door by "Mrs. Sandow." It is unclear who this woman was, but she was almost certainly not the strongman's lawful wedded spouse, since he was legally and publically married in August of 1894 to Blanche Brookes. At one point, the reporter refers to the woman as "Nelly," but it is uncertain whether this was her real name or not; however, lacking any further verification, this name is as good as any.

Nelly described a little spat that she and Eugen had been carrying on for a few days. Nelly went to see Louis Cyr's performance against Eugen's wishes. The strongman explained, "I did not want anyone to think that I had sent spies to find out what manner of man this Louis Cyr is." Adding fuel to the fire, Nelly had been talking about the Canadian frequently ever since, and things only got worse after the women mentioned that Cyr "had a very pleasant face." She explained, "Ever since that time, Eugene [*sic*] has twitted me on having a partiality for the Canadian. Whenever I speak, it is Louis this and Louis that. He is like a big boy." It is apparent from this exchange that "Mrs. Sandow" was well-enough known that she was recognized on sight as Sandow's mate.

The reporter was invited to dinner, and despite a few jibes at one another, Sandow and Nelly seemed to enjoy the experience. Sandow was curious about the reporter's opinion of Cyr, and he was told that the American editor Richard K. Fox had offered £1,000 to anyone who could duplicate Cyr's feats. Sandow was apparently convinced that he could do so, and he hinted that most of the stunts were probably tricks. This indicates that he had not had an opportunity to size up his opponent carefully, because he would have discovered very quickly that there was no pretense or trickery in the mighty Canadian's lifting abilities. When Sandow discovered the extent of Cyr's true power, he had the sense not to challenge the Canadian strongman to a lifting contest.

The evening's happy domesticity was ended when the reporter confessed that he was forced to retreat after inhaling the "perfume of Sandow's ten shilling cigars." The first "Mrs. Sandow" apparently retreated, too, but only after her common-law husband abandoned her in 1893. Perhaps Sandow had more than one reason for accepting the offer to come to America on such short notice and in the middle of New York's unattractive summer season.[11] Significantly, in the passenger records for Sandow's date of arrival in New York on June 6, 1893, there is no indication of his marital status.[12]

Sandow had little time to think of marriage after he arrived in America for the first time. A mere six days after he disembarked from the *Elbe*, he appeared at the Casino Theater. There were over five hundred people in attendance at a hot and humid performance on the sultry evening of Sandow's first tour of the U.S. Time and again, the reviewer in the *New York Times* referred to the oppressive heat of the theater: Sandow's poses were accompanied by "slow music and much perspiration"; and again, "as it was rather warm, Mr. Sandow refreshed himself by turning a few somersaults with his eyes bandaged and his legs tied."[13] The next day, the paper reported on the athlete's first public show in equally glowing terms. "Sandow is a wonderful creature," the reporter bubbled. "Such a development of biceps may not be unusual, but the man's back and chest have surely not been equaled since the golden prime of Samson."[14] It was clear that even in the midst of a heat wave, Sandow could draw in a respectable crowd, but if Florenz Ziegfeld, Jr. had not been at the Casino Theatre on a trip to New York, the course of both men's lives would have been drastically different.

It was Zeigfeld who took Sandow out of the ranks of strongmen and thrust him into superstardom, but it was not at all a sure thing that this would happen when the strongman and his future manager first encountered one another. The young impresario was skilled at gauging the public's likes, dislikes and curiosities, but he was still young and untested in the theatrical world. Sandow must have sensed Ziegfeld's competence, but he remained under contract with Henry S. Abbey when he left New York for the Trocadero and the Chicago World's Fair. Abbey, however, did not understand the new style of management that his younger rival was involved in, and he sometimes misread a situation. This is clear from an episode that occurred shortly after Sandow began his run at the Trocadero. Hjalmar Lundin was a brawny Swedish lad who had just arrived in the Midwest, but aside from energy and great strength, he had little in the way of assets. Thus when some friends pointed out to him an ad in the Chicago papers promising one thousand dollars to anyone who could duplicate Sandow's stunts, it sounded like a great idea. He had everything to gain and nothing to lose—with Sandow it was just the opposite. When the brawny Swede showed up at the theater, and Abbey had a look at him, Lundin realized that he was "as welcome as a case of smallpox!" Abbey reluctantly agreed to let the contest continue, but he would act as referee. Sandow must have been confident when he lifted 270 pounds (almost certainly in a bent press) that no one else in Chicago could equal this record-breaking lift. Their amazement was therefore great when Lundin had little trouble duplicating the lift. However, Abbey declared that the Swede had not done the lift in as perfect a form as his adversary, so he was not entitled to the thousand dollars. Despite the protests of the spectators, Lundin left as poor as he had arrived.[15]

Sandow was beginning to understand that his real chance to become a star lay not in showing what he could lift, but in how he looked. A rival American strongman, J. Walter Kennedy, summed up Sandow's claim to fame very aptly when in a newspaper interview he stated that "Sandow would rather pose than compete any time. As a poser he is probably without a peer, but as a strong man, there are many men who can give him points and best him."[16] Unfortunately, Abbey did not grasp this essential fact, and he was unable to market Sandow appropriately. Perhaps Sandow himself did not quite understand his own appeal and charisma, but that was destined to change very soon.

When the Columbian Exposition ended, Ziegfeld was still uncertain about what he should do next. He wanted to keep the Trocadero going as a permanent theater, and he tried to convince Sandow to stay in Chicago, but the strongman did not want to be tied down. Besides, Sandow was eager to return to England, and he departed shortly after his run at the Trocadero ended, anxious to continue wooing his future (and this time legitimate) wife in Manchester.[17] Romance was on Sandow's mind, and he hastened back to Britain in order to court Blanche Brookes, the daughter of a prominent photographer whom he had met in a very interesting way.

According to an article by Edmond Desbonnet, Sandow was performing in Manchester before coming to America. During his music-hall act, he happened to catch sight of a very beautiful young brunette sitting in one of the boxes. The lady watched Sandow's performance with great attention, and the athlete stole more than a few glances at the charming spectator, to the point where "his performance was a bit distracted because of her." As soon as his turn had ended, Sandow could not discover the lady's name despite his best efforts.

The next day Sandow was strolling in Manchester when he saw a carriage pulled by two galloping horses that was madly careening out of control. The helpless driver was clearly incapable of stopping the runaways. Inside the carriage there were several women who screamed pitifully for help. Heedless of the danger, Sandow jumped in front of the horses and brought them to a halt after being dragged for a few hundred meters. The strongman then opened the door to the carriage and two older ladies descended, but then—surprise—out came the beautiful unknown from the previous evening. The young lady blushed deeply on discovering who had risked his life to save her as well as the two other ladies (who turned out to be her aunt and her mother). The young brunette then invited Sandow to return with them to her home "and soon began an idyl which resulted in the marriage of Eugen Sandow and Miss Brookes."[18] As with all of Sandow's anecdotes, we must wonder if it really occurred. There is little doubt that the original source of this little story was the strongman himself, and Desbonnet would never have recounted a story that was invented from whole cloth, but it still does not mean that Sandow was telling the unvarnished truth. More important than accurate history, Sandow was concerned with his image as a larger-than-life figure: one that would jump in front of a runaway carriage in order to save damsels in distress.

After this quick visit with Blanche, Sandow returned to America in December of 1893, and Ziegfeld was finally able to persuade the strongman to leave Abbey and let the Chicagoan manage him, but not in his hometown. Ziegfeld took Sandow and the troupe that he had assembled to Koster & Bial's Vaudeville theater in New York for a run of eight weeks. After playing to great acclaim in New York, Sandow and his company departed for San Francisco, the Midwinter Fair and the notorious fight with Commodore the lion.

Accompanying the troupe was the pianist Martinus Sieveking, the Dutch musician who traveled and lived with Sandow for a while. Sieveking was born in Amsterdam on March 24, 1867, and after studying the piano, he became an accompanist for the Lamoureux Orchestra in Paris. Sieveking toured extensively in the United States both as a soloist where he became famous for his massive reach of an octave and a half and later as the accompanist for the famous soprano Adelina Patti. In the latter part of the nineteenth century, Sieveking published several works for the piano, some of which were produced by the prestigious New York music publisher Schirmer. Sieveking retained a love for physical exercise throughout his life. A few tantalizingly brief letters from the pianist have survived, and in them he discusses his dedication to physical fitness.[19]

The Dutch-Jewish musician resided in Paris and eventually emigrated to America in 1916 while World War I ravaged Europe. Shortly after this, he opened his own piano school in New York City. His "dead-weight system" of teaching piano achieved a degree of recognition. Sometime in the 1920s Sieveking moved to Pasadena, California where he lived for the rest of his life. Sieveking was famous enough to be mentioned by name in the book *Lost Horizon* (1933), by James Hilton. The novel's narrator is traveling in the East on his way to Shangri-la, but he states that among the passengers on board ship leaving Yokohama was "Sieveking, the pianist, en route for a concert tour in the States." He gives a report of an onboard recital: "He [Sieveking] played well, of course, some Brahms and Scarlatti, and a lot of Chopin." After a long teaching and concert career, the pianist died on November 26, 1950.[20]

The question of whether Sieveking was Sandow's lover will probably never be resolved fully, but at the very least, we can be certain that the two men shared an intense friendship. Part of the problem is that from our perspective in the twenty-first century, it is difficult to speculate on the subtexts of their relationship; when we read, for instance, that two men from the 1800s "lived together" or even "slept together," we should not be quick to attribute meanings from the 2000s. Neither the term nor the concept of homosexuality had wide currency in the late-nineteenth century, and same-sex "romantic friendships" flourished both with and without physical intimacy.[21] Sandow was a highly attractive man who clearly enjoyed the company of women; we should be aware that while he was associating with Sieveking, he was also carrying on a long-distance courtship with his future wife. Whether Sieveking was the love of Sandow's life, simply a good friend, or a brief infatuation is ultimately something that the reader must decide for himself.

While Sandow, Sieveking, and Ziegfeld were traveling across the continent, the strongman's name was growing increasingly familiar to the public, but one of the drawbacks of that situation was that others used his face, figure, and identity to their own ends. There was at least one "Sandow" who crisscrossed the United States before the real athlete's appearance. A herald from 1894 for Washburn's Circus announces that "Mr. Sandow, the Great American Samson. An Adonis in Form! A Hercules in strength!" will perform with the exhibition. Since the strongman is referred to specifically as an American and nearly every day of Eugen Sandow's tour can be accounted for, this is almost certainly an example of a counterfeit.[22] Another example of this deception was confirmed by Sandow in an interview held in Milwaukee, Wisconsin in 1894. The reporter was a little confused because the strongman was reported to have played in the city two years previous, but there was a simple explanation for the mix up. "This is my first engagement in Milwaukee," Sandow stated; "the report that I was here two years ago probably arose from the appearance here of 'Sandowe,' a man named Montgomery, who uses my name with the letter 'e' added. He was in London when I was there, and I had a warrant out for his arrest, but he left the country to avoid it."[23] Sandow and Ziegfeld would catch up with Montgomery in San Francisco, and the resulting trial/circus would provide much amusement and free publicity.

Another example of free publicity was Ziegfeld's arrangement to have Sandow pose for Edison's Kinetoscope. The driving force behind the early cinema was W. K. L. Dickson, and in the book that he produced a year after Sandow's appearance, he devotes several pages to the filming. Most of the copy is lifted directly from Sandow's program notes, and is thus virtually useless as a reference, but it is clear that Dickson recognizes Sandow as a major vaudeville star of the time.[24] It soon became fashionable to have one's name associated with the handsome, young athlete, even if the connection was questionable or illusory. Mrs. Isabella Stewart Gardner was one of Boston's richest and most original hostesses in the 1890s, and it is said that on a visit to Boston, Sandow and the eccentric art collector met briefly at one of the strongman's post-performance receptions. "While timid society matrons flutteringly felt his biceps," the journalist Lucius Beebe reported, Mrs. Gardner gave his muscles "a dig with her fingers that made the great ape let out a grunt of astonishment."[25] As entertaining as it might be, it is highly unlikely that the incident occurred as it was described. The jab in the ribs and resulting yelp was an old story that had been told before (see pp. 78–79). The author gives no source for his anecdote, so there is no telling where he heard it. Another reason for the story's suspicious pedigree is the descriptor "ape"; no one who had actually seen the blond-haired Adonis is likely to have used that word. Perhaps the word is Beebe's and not Mrs. Gardner's; if so, the effete and sensitive Beebe might well have considered any man with muscles to be an ape.

Sandow's tour of 1894 was a triumph for everyone involved. It also provided the strongman with an opportunity to encourage his own particular brand of fitness advice; he demonstrated the exciting potentials of the human body, and his example was not lost on his audiences. "Sandow's appearance at his performances," confirmed one newspaper report, "has done more to encourage physical development than any other known performer."[26] No matter where he went, Sandow was always happy to give advice to eager reporters on the secrets of his great strength and muscularity; unfortunately, most of that advice was perfectly useless, but it did not stop him from giving it. Although, as some papers pointed out, Sandow's methods were not unusual and he was not an anomaly, but they emphasized the necessity of following the athlete's specific regimen: "Sandow can in no way be regarded as a *Lusus Naturae*, his magnificent development is nothing but the result that may be obtained . . .by anyone who will spare the time and make the effort required to take the course of training along the lines laid down by Mr. Sandow for physical development."[27] Still, readers were anxious to know the "secret" of Sandow's great power and beauty, and the strongman had enough sense not to disappoint them.

"It is the mind—all a matter of the mind. The muscles really have a secondary place. If you lift a pair of dumb-bells a hundred times a day with your fixed attention on some object away over in Cambridge, it will do you very little good." If you concentrate your mind on a single muscle for three minutes each day, the results will be immediate.[28] As for the best equipment to use, there was little doubt: "Dumb-bells are what I pin my faith to."[29] These were usually the five-pound variety. He also insisted that one should plunge into a cold bath after a workout. No one seemed to notice or to care that this was all a lot of humbug. Sandow had known since his early days with Attila that the only way to build massive muscles was by exercising with progressively heavier weights. Still, it kept the fans and the newspaper men happy.

Another area that Sandow commented on was women's fitness

and how to obtain it. A rather extensive article in *The Baltimore Sun* encapsulates many of his theories on female health and exercise. Women, Sandow believed, should exercise for health and endurance not necessarily for muscularity. He recommended three-pound dumbbells for women, not the pulley weights that were found in most gymnasiums of the time. Sandow insisted that walking and horseback riding are the best forms of outdoor exercise for women, but he noted that women must ride sidesaddle because he considered it "much more natural and less dangerous." Riding astride the animal is fine if the horse is quiet, but if there is jumping or jolting involved, then the risk of injury is great. He was reluctant to recommend bicycle riding for similar reasons, but also because "there is a tendency to slope the shoulders and contract the chest," but "with moderate speed, riding is easy and graceful, and I do not think injurious."[30]

Perhaps one of the reasons for his interest in female athletics was the presence on the tour of Blanche Brookes Sandow, Sandow's new wife. The press was eager to mention the beautiful wife of the handsome muscleman; the fear that Mrs. Sandow might put a crimp in the style of the matinée girls had not gone unnoticed, either. "The young 'Greek God' is accompanied on this trip by his lovely wife, a matter in which the sentimental admirers of the 'Perfect Man' may feel a subsidiary interest." Spectators who hoped to see La Sandow in action, however, are cautioned that "she doesn't lift anything; not even her Samson's hair."[31]

This did not mean that Sandow's wife was idle or that she neglected her health. "I make my wife take a cold bath every morning and walk ten miles or so," the strongman declared. He continued by explaining, "That's because she has no house keeping to employ her time. In the afternoon she plays on the piano for several hours."[32] It sounds like a tedious honeymoon for a young lady just two months after her marriage. Blanche, unlike her husband, never seemed to enjoy the spotlight, and she would take the first opportunity to return to England as soon as the season was over.

Eugen, on the other hand, thrived in the public eye. He enjoyed wearing elegant or eccentric clothes and appearing suitably sporty. When he first arrived in Baltimore, the reporter was impressed enough to give a description of the man's attire. "When this modern Hercules reached the hotel, he was garbed in a most picturesque costume, consisting of a Norfolk jacket and a pair of knee pants." He later received the reporter in "the latest style Prince Albert suit, and looking for all the world like an ideal Beau Brummel."[33]

Sandow's appearance was only one of the things that fascinated the public; they also wanted to know about his habits. Moderation, he claimed, was the key to his health; this ran to both food, drink, and (surprising to modern readers) smoking. "I began to smoke when I was twelve years old," he announced, "and I have smoked ever since. Sometimes I smoke a dozen or fifteen cigars a day, and then I don't smoke again for days. If I want a short smoke, I don't see any harm in a cigarette."[34] Since these "short smokes" were considered bohemian at best, effeminate at worst, and unhealthy even in Victorian times, Sandow's words are all the more remarkable.

Another quality that the press remarked upon was Sandow's elegant appearance, so unlike the common run of strongmen that they had learned to expect; here was a man who was mentally acute and not overly muscular. The reporter from Philadelphia remarked that Sandow was "not merely a strong man, as that term is applied to brute force, but a conspicuous representative of the intelligent development of the muscular energies to the highest point."[35] Sandow's combination of brains and beauty was a characteristic that Dr. Dudley Allen Sargent of Harvard University had noted as early as 1893. Sargent declared that Sandow combined "the characteristics of Apollo, Hercules and the ideal athlete." Sargent was also impressed with Sandow's comportment while being measured and inspected by the Harvard scientist. "His behavior under the tests was admirable." Even more impressive was the strongman's education: "He has a considerable knowledge of anatomy, and can call the muscles by their proper names. I should be glad to have him come and lecture before the students of Harvard."[36] According to contemporary author Carolyn Thomas de la Peña, Sandow presented himself to Sargent as "an educated, gentleman strongman who embodied the best of brute strength and scientific erudition."[37] By means of his contacts, his appearance and his brain power Sandow was consciously making himself acceptable to all classes of American society.

Sandow's tours of North America had been successful, so the reasons for ending it are all the more mysterious. What really happened will perhaps never be known, but the nervous breakdown story seems to be as convenient a reason as any. The only thing that is known for sure is that Sandow's last performance with Ziegfeld was on February 29, 1896.[38] If the athlete did suffer from a nervous collapse, it was of a remarkably short duration, for by the end of the year Sandow was performing once again on the London stage. It is more likely that a variety of reasons mitigated against Sandow's staying in America any longer: the relationship with Ziegfeld had soured, he had saturated the major vaudeville theaters of North America, he wanted to start working at his magazine and gymnasiums, and perhaps most pressing of all Blanche Sandow was pregnant with their first child.

Sandow had almost single-handedly begun a fitness movement that soon swept around the world. The situation is confirmed by an extensive article in *The Sketch* that appeared late in 1896. "As the craze for physical exercise of all kinds seems to be now at fever-heat," it reported, "Sandow's return to England, after a considerable absence in America, is most opportune." The purpose of the article was to report on the strongman's new music-hall turn at the London Pavilion, and to testify to its great success. The audience was primed to greet Sandow with the kind of wild enthusiasm that he had first encountered in America. The reporter was eloquent about the performance despite the fact that the strongman was performing alone for the first time in several years. The showmanship and suavity of Sandow's act impressed the reporter most of all. "What is particularly 'fetching' in the performance of everything he does," writes the author, "is the singular grace of carriage accompanying each, while every gesture is totally devoid of the affectation usually to be met with in strong men." Mrs. Sandow was also in the audience, and like the Americans, the British press reacted favorably to her; she also brought along the couple's newborn child, Helen.[39]

Sandow was doing more than just starting a family at this time; he was also starting a business—or more accurately, several businesses. The professional athlete was demonstrating a remarkable ability to forge a business empire, too, and soon Sandow schools, equipment, and other products were launched on the worldwide market. Most of the enterprises were in the English-speaking world, but Sandow had also begun to make his ideas available in other countries. Not surprisingly, his courses, books, and products were very well known in his native Germany.

The occasional article had appeared in the German sporting press while Sandow was making a name for himself in America and the United Kingdom, but it was not until the first years of the twentieth century that Sandow's influence began to be felt in Teutonic countries. Part of the reason for this relatively late arrival in the German heartland was the existence of a sporting tradition that was already very well established. The Turnverein had a head start in the realms of physical fitness and exercise, but eventually Sandow's fame abroad and his Teutonic roots allowed him to make some important inroads into the closed world of German athletics. Sandow long maintained that his countrymen were physically superior to all others. "The best race, physically—and I speak now altogether apart from any bias in favor of my own country—is the German. The reason of this is that the conscription system has compelled a certain amount of attention to physical training. Many young men, otherwise weakly, having been brought out and made strong by the drill they had to undergo."[40] It is ironic that Sandow would attribute German physical superiority to the military considering his own evasion of duty (even more ironic that he thought of Germany as "his own country"). Perhaps because he considered Germans better than other nationalities, this led him to devote more time and energy to raising their standards. Thus, Germany was one of the first places where Sandow's system was marketed outside of Britain and the United States.

An early article in *Kraft und Gewandtheit* [Strength and Skill] describes the first German athletic school begun by Theodor Siebert, and in it the author compares the cost of the two gymnasiums. A one-hour workout in Sandow's school cost eight marks (an outrageous price in those days), and a one-hour workout in a *Sandow-Volkskurs*, i.e. a group lesson, cost each pupil 2.7 marks. This is contrasted with Seibert's charges: 20 marks per week including food and accommodation. Little wonder that Sandow grew ever wealthier and that poor Siebert went bankrupt after only a few years of operation.[41] Part of the reason for his success in Germany and elsewhere was that Sandow understood the value of mass marketing. It was this that allowed him to charge higher prices for his courses and equipment.

Nowhere is Sandow's advertising genius more apparent than when he arranged for the respected German publication *Kraft und Schönheit* [Strength and Beauty] to publish a special booklet in 1901 dedicated entirely to Sandow and his methods. *Das Sandowheft* [The Sandow Handbook] went through several editions, and each time it sold out almost immediately. By 1902 the booklet proved to be such a glowing success that a further expanded edition of ten thousand was released; this later edition lasted only one and a half years before it was superseded by another edition of ten thousand. The publishers wisely decided to keep the notebook priced fairly at fifty pfenning "in the hopes that the *Sandowheft* might become a true handbook of the people." It is not known how many editions this brief overview of the Sandow system went through, but there were at least thirty thousand copies of the booklet in circulation.[42]

It was heartening for Germans to learn of Sandow's success abroad, and in one of the articles, this is brought to their attention quite clearly. "Our fellow countryman Sandow has enjoyed an uncommonly great popularity in England for years, and he is still extraordinarily popular today. He himself or his manager gladly talk at length about his feats. As for his personality, a whole string of legends has been woven about his wondrous strength."[43] This intense interest contributed to Sandow's popularity and prosperity in his German homeland, and his most popular book, *Strength and How to Obtain It*, was translated and first published in Germany in 1905, only a few years after it had appeared in English.[44] At least six thousand copies of the book were printed. Sandow showed his former compatriots that it was possible to create a business out of the desire for fitness, assuming that a high enough tuition was charged.

Despite the high cost of a Sandow course, there was apparently great interest in following his regimen. Remarkably, a document has survived from 1906, the *Verzeichnis der jenigen Herren, welche sich an Sandow-Kursus beteiligen* [Table of men who participated in the Sandow Course], which gives an amazing amount of information on the type of people who felt that they could benefit from a regimen of exercise as directed—albeit from a distance—by the most famous athletic teacher in the world.

The results of the listings give a wealth of demographic data. Of the twenty-four who are listed, the majority are soldiers (eleven); other professions include merchants, grocers, office or bank clerks, and one is listed as a *Gymnasiast* or high-school student. The men's ages range from sixteen to forty-two, with the majority (fifteen) in their twenties. Height and weight are next recorded, and then the question "Do you have a heart disease?" All have answered, no. "How many hours do you sleep at night?" (between seven and a half to nine). "How much wine, beer, or water do you drink?" (most drink between half a liter to two liters of beer; eight of the men profess to be teetotalers). "Are you a vegetarian?" (none). "Which part of your body do you particularly want to exercise?" (everyone has answered "all parts"). "Are you a member of a sports organization?" (most of them (thirteen) are members of a *Turn- und Sportverein* [gymnastics and sports club]). Which kinds of sport do you want to do after completing this course?" (most have answered gymnastics; the rest prefer running, rowing, soccer, a few do not know). "Do you promise to exercise with the Sandow system every day until April 1?" (yes). Finally, "Do you wish to take part in a muscle competition?" (eight men say yes, the remainder, no).[45]

Several conclusions can be drawn from this document. First, Sandow's course was considered sufficiently effective for bringing men's physical state up to snuff that it was used by military men; the rest are sedentary workers. Although the cost of the course is not listed, we can be certain that it was high, so even if we did not know the men's professions, we could assume that they were at least from the middle class. Most of the men are in good health and they already belong to sporting organizations. Perhaps the relatively low number of participants represents a careful selection process. It has already been established that Sandow would reject pupils whose cases were too far gone to obtain any dramatic benefits. It is unfortunate that Sandow's records from his other schools have been lost; this is our only known listing of students, and even these are tantalizingly brief and incomplete.

Bodybuilding and physical culture were clearly international phenomenons, and the success of Sandow's system is confirmed by its popularity in Germany and its triumphs in the Anglo-Saxon world. Sandow's exercise equipment was sold in a variety of countries, and his works had been translated into many major European languages. The fitness craze was clearly set to expand throughout the world.

Sandow's Institutes in Britain were also experiencing a period of prosperity, and his books sold well. The decade from approximately 1895 to 1905 represented the height of the fitness craze, but even after the initial excitement had worn off, the public continued to come to exercise and restore their lost health. But did Sandow's methods really work? One of the most thorough and balanced critiques of Sandow's system was that which appeared in *Cassell's Physical Educator* by a bright and dedicated physical educator, nutrition expert, and tennis teacher, Eustace Miles. Most contemporaries who evaluated Sandow's courses had some very dull axes to grind, and their comments are not necessarily accurate or fair, but Miles was not promoting a particular brand of exercise (at least not at the time he was writing).[46]

Miles begins by pointing out that "Sandow is not an athlete in the Anglo-Saxon sense" (280); nor do his exercises try to produce sportsmen.[47] His system is designed to build up the strength of invalids and weaklings by using rubber strand apparatuses and light spring-grip dumbbells, but the critic points out that all but the most disciplined users would find the routines quite boring after a while. "While the system is simple, it has the disadvantage of bald simplicity" (285). There were countless variations on the way one could tug on the exercisers or swing the five-pound weights, but they are all so similar as to be virtually indistinguishable. Those hoping to build up strength in order to play most sports will find nothing here but disappointment. "The chief original feature of the Sandow system is that the person must grip the dumbbell with his hand *all the while*," Miles complains. He adds rather sarcastically, "This seems a very small contribution to Physical Science, and a very fatal one in many cases" (282).

The system is so popular because its inventor is such a muscular and obviously well-developed man, and he must practice what he preaches. Miles praises Sandow by admitting that, "at least we must give him full credit in being a living exponent of what he urges others to become" (284). At the same time, Miles warns his readers that, like most self-promoters, Sandow promises more than he can possibly deliver. Sandow's system "claims disastrously too much. That is its weakness, as it is the weakness of nearly every system that we have ever heard of or seen" (288). Miles has acutely divined that Sandow's system has been culled from other sources: "he has done little more than gather exercises from the Continental and British storehouses . . . and then to add the use of dumbbells, grip-dumbbells, and exercisers" (289).

When all is added up, Miles declares that Sandow is the great popularizer who has drawn in those who might not otherwise have given physical culture a try. He has used his appearance and his reputation to help others, but he has only taken the first steps toward the regeneration of mankind. "Sandow has not founded physical culture himself, but he has lent to it interest for the masses. He has lent to it cheap apparatus and an undeniably imposing figure. Implements and a personality—these are his main contributions, these are what we praise" (289).

The more Sandow appeared in vaudeville the more popular his institutes and other products became, so in order to satisfy his worldwide fans, the athlete decided to go on another even more ambitious tour. In 1901 he toured in North America and traveled to many of the continent's major cities, but one of the places which he visited for the first time was Montreal, Quebec's principal metropolis. Like Germany, Quebec had a great respect for physical strength, and the principal exponent of that strength was the mighty Louis Cyr. By late 1901 when Sandow arrived to play at Proctor's Music Hall, the great French-Canadian had retired to his farm and was no longer a threat to Sandow, but many in the province felt resentment towards someone who claimed to be "the strongest man in the world" when this was patently untrue. The Anglo-German's appearance became therefore a cause of "a deep commotion in the world of sports"[48] between the English speakers who supported Sandow and the French-speakers who championed Cyr and others. *La Presse,* the city's main French newspaper, published a simple report of Sandow's act and repeated the claim that he was "one of the strongest men who exists."

After this, the newspaper published an angry letter from J. E. Rousseau which announced, "Today as always, I do not recognize a man stronger than Louis Cyr, and being [French-] Canadian the same as Mr. Cyr, I do not like to see men claiming the title of world's champion without having deserved it."[49] Even more pointed was the reaction of Horace Barré, Quebec's then reigning champion of strength. He came to the offices of the newspaper and announced bluntly, "I am the only world's champion, and I am ready to defend the title against all comers—Sandow as well as any others—I am ready to meet him anytime in a real contest of feats of strength. Let Sandow come on; he will be welcomed. I don't want to make a noise in order to advertise myself, but in circumstances like these, I believe that my duty is to show myself, to face up to those who proclaim themselves champion without really being so, and to let him know that I do not fear him."[50] In all likelihood, Sandow did not even know of the hornet's nest that he had stirred up since it occurred mainly in the French press; still, it points out the dangers of calling oneself "the world's strongest man" when such was patently not the case. It also indicates the growing rift between the two cultural groups in the region: the French and English-speakers. The Francophones were loathe to allow any usurpation of their rights or insults to their heroes.

After a relatively brief tour of North America, Sandow returned to Britain and made arrangements to depart on his most ambitious tour yet: to the Antipodes. Fortunately Dr. Bob Petersen has done some excellent work in recording Sandow's Australian tour as well as the reactions of the audiences. For the most part, the public in Australia reacted as it had in other parts of the world: they were amazed at Sandow's unique combination of strength, masculinity, beauty, and grace. According to *The Bulletin* of Melbourne, "The women watch him with half fear, and seem to be speculating on him as a husband; the men regard him with an envious admiration, for physical strength is still the most prized of all gifts in this world despite its civilisation."[51] Sandow's sex appeal as well as his strength are singled out as being remarkable.

The strongman was doing a good deal more in Australia than just impressing the girls and making the men envious; he was also giving them advice on how a real man behaved and what he looked like. *The Sunday Times* of Melbourne published a large illustration and a two-column article in which the visiting athlete gave his opinions on many subjects related to his host country. The interviewer posed this question: "Do you think that any superiority we possess in Australia as compared with the people of some other countries is due to the admixture of foreign blood? . . . Do you think the crossing of the German, British and other European breeds has produced the result you mention to any extent?"

Sandow's answer was reasoned and fair: "Muscular strength is not so much a matter of breeding as of cultivation. I have noticed the very weakest men, with apparently no breeding at all, develop into the very strongest men by adopting a scientific system of muscular education, and the possibilities in this respect are not confined to young and growing people. It is never too late to mend, says the proverb, and I might say similarly that it is never too late for one to start the work of physical development." As a modern spin doctor might say, Sandow was staying on-message. He wanted his readers to understand that anyone could attain strength by using his system—breeding, race, or even physical weakness was no hindrance to becoming a stronger and shapelier person.

Another issue of great interest to residents of the southern continent was the consumption of strong drink. Sandow demonstrated that he was no teetotaler or prude. He delivered his perennial message: drink, eat, smoke, and do all other things in moderation. "Do you drink much water?" followed up the interviewer. "I don't remember having drunk water in my life," replied the athlete. "Except by accident, while cleaning my mouth."[52] This is advice that might have been said in jest, but it must have assuaged the consciences of many a larrikin.

While he was in Australia, Sandow wrote and published one of his rarest books, *The Gospel of Strength*. Most of the work is dedicated to outlining the strongman's ideas for transforming humanity through physical culture, but it is divided into nineteen "talks" or mini-lectures. By giving the book an evangelical-sounding title, perhaps Sandow was trying to point out the connection between physicality and spirituality that had been at the core of the YMCA and Muscular Christianity movements; perhaps he also felt that it would be an easier sell to those who considered athletics to be a lot of useless frippery. Not surprisingly, the author adopts the style of a missionary as he begins to warm to his subject. "The deliverance of the Gospel of Strength," Sandow writes in the first talk, "in other words, the teaching of Physical Culture, I regard as my life-work, and my aim is to teach men how they may arrive at that condition in which they will be best able to carry out their life's work, whatever it may be."[53]

A little later in the first talk, Sandow emphasizes once more the work's religious tone by quoting from a real sermon that was delivered by the Rev. Henry Howard of Adelaide. "Those of you who have seen Mr. Sandow perform, know what a wonderful power he has of controlling his muscles," Rev. Howard intones. The minister explains that this will improve the will power, and that this is definitely something that

Australians might profit from. "Though I do not take much notice of phrenology," Mr. Howard avers, "I believe the phrenologists when they say that colonials lack powers of concentration; that they like change and do not care to be fettered down to a thing; that they are desultory in their studies, and soon grow weary. If Sandow's method can help them, by concentrating the mind on the particular sets of muscles they wish to exercise, it will eliminate this weakness in the next generation or two, and have a lasting effect on the Australian race."[54] If one were to believe the Rev. Howard, the Australians are a nation of dithering do-nothings, but he seems to see a way out of their troubles in Sandow's system of physical culture. This harsh estimation of the Australian character was hardly correct, and the proof can be found in a number of places, most prominently in the number of adherents and students that Sandow acquired in his tour of the southern continent.

After introducing Australians to his brand of physical culture, Sandow attempted to do the same for New Zealanders. Once again, a fine scholar has traced the strongman's tour of this country in an excellent book. By searching carefully through contemporary newspaper and magazine accounts, Caroline Daley has traced Sandow's tour and shown his effects on New Zealand. One of her conclusions is that although it was a remote nation, the islands were linked quite closely and quickly with European and North American cultures thanks to their place within the empire. Dr. Daley shows how Sandow's brief visit affected the proliferation of gymnasiums, beauty and muscle contests, swimming, sunbathing, and nudism.[55]

Sandow's tour of Australia and New Zealand had been a rousing success. He had inspired the colonials with the same enthusiasm for athletics and muscularity as he had elsewhere in the world. While he was in the Antipodes, he had set up schools and instructors to continue his work, and he had promised to open a string of gyms all across the region. These never happened; and although he continued to sell his home exercise, mail-order courses quite well, it was apparently not profitable to open a string of schools as Sandow had done in Britain. Despite this setback, there was another part of the world where Sandow could still generate excitement and (perhaps more importantly) money: North America.

The strongman's third and final tour of the United States was very different from his previous ones; this time, he was older (thirty-five) and the pace of his performances was slower and more stately as befitted someone who had risen to the top of his career. There was a different focus of this visit, too. Sandow wanted to establish in the

United States a number of gymnasiums and schools as he had in the United Kingdom, so he was using his theatrical success to promote commercial enterprises rather than to build a career.

Sandow arrived in the United States sometime in early 1903, and he immediately went to Boston where he began to work on his institute headquarters and the American version of *Sandow's Magazine*. As soon as those tasks had been completed, he could then go on a brief tour of a few eastern cities and return to England after the theatrical season had ended. The job must have been substantial because the strongman did not begin to perform until early April when his act appeared at Keith's Vaudeville Theater in Boston. The papers reported that Sandow's turn was a little different this time; the posing and demonstrations of strength were still there, but this time he added a brief lecture on physical culture. No doubt he was trying to rustle up some business for his burgeoning institute and magazine.[56]

Before he left Boston for the next leg of his tour, Sandow was forced to clear up some problems related to his new magazine. He had left a deposit with the Boston postmaster in order to send his publication via first-class mail since it was more reliable, but the post office had refused to honor this arrangement. Sandow consequently brought suit against Boston's Postmaster Hibbert in order to get the despute resolved. Niggling little problems like these might have eventually convinced the strongman that it was simply not worth the effort and constant vigilance that a sporting empire in America required.[57]

After his New England opener, Sandow then went on to engagements in Cleveland and Detroit. The most successful part of his brief third tour of America came in Pittsburgh where the *New York Dramatic Mirror* reported that there was "SRO, and the bill fully merited it."[58] As in previous stops on his tour, Sandow's emphasis had switched subtly in his appeal to the audience; this time he was touting the health benefits of physical culture to an older demographic, and he concentrated on more obviously commercial targets. For instance, the strongman was scheduled to appear from May 4–9 in the Steel City, but he also made time for a special appearance at Wannamaker's Department Store in Philadelphia where he gave a lecture and a demonstration in an attempt to sell his Sandow dumbbells to the public. The store's ad mentioned that "It seems to be the usual salutation now to say 'Good morning! Have you used Sandow dumb-bells?'" So the strongman's attempts were apparently quite successful.

In an interview that appeared in conjunction with his appearance, Sandow deals more thoroughly than ever before with the issue of older people. Is it ever too late to take up exercise? Sandow's answer is a predictable, no. "Cato learned Greek at 80, did he not? And the late Queen of England mastered Hindustani in her 75th year, I believe. Age has nothing to do with progress if the enthusiasm and will power are still there."[59] One might argue that learning languages is different from pumping iron in one's old age, still the point is made. As Sandow grew older, he began to think of prolonging vigor and activity. Unfortunately, his efforts to establish a chain of gymnasiums were not rewarded with equal success. After a brief run at a vaudeville theater in Brooklyn, Sandow sailed for home sometime after May 16.

By the end of the year, Sandow had returned home to London, and the Christmas season of 1903 saw him in Edinburgh where he performed in the annual holiday carnival show. There was no sign of aging or weakness in the strongman's physique according to the press reports. "This great and now well-known athlete," reported *The Scotsman,* "seemed to be in the pink of condition, lithe and muscular, and the feats of strength he essayed were such as might well entitle him to the name of the Modern Samson."[60]

Although he would visit South Africa and India in 1904, Sandow concentrated his energies increasingly on his business enterprises, and one of the most important markets that Sandow wanted to exploit was that of women's physical culture. The concept that women should (or could) work out with weights was a controversial one, but Sandow was always emphatic on the subject; women could gain just as much benefit from exercise as men. This attitude was given a fresh impetus in 1906 when *The Dairymaids,* a musical review, opened at London's Apollo Theatre. The plot of this "farcical comedy" is unimportant, but its most popular and spectacular set piece was the elaborate staging of the song "The Sandow Girl."

At one point in the play, the curtain rises on a group of twenty-three girls in tights and short athletic skirts who perform gymnastics, boxing, fencing, swinging Indian clubs, and other exercises under the watchful eye of a professor of physical culture. After the group of girls retire, five lovely young women come on stage and begin the song which would become something of a hit—although it was not the music that most intrigued the men in the audience. They were more interested in the shapely singers. The soloists were led by Miss Carrie Moore, a pretty Australian lass who had come to England just three years previously. Almost at once, the press was hailing her as "the life and soul of *The Dairymaids,*" and there is little mystery why.[61] Although she was in a long dress made from many yards of crêpe-de-chine, she and her little group appeared as if they had been melted and poured into the tight upper reaches of the dresses. One reporter noted that the women's draperies "assume voluminous proportions about the feet, but . . .vanish into nothingness as they approach the shoulders." There was little left to the imagination as far as the girls' lithe and athletic forms were concerned, and the journalist could only conclude that Miss Moore "had been trained by the high priest of physical culture (the great Eugen) himself." Her muscularity and confidence are confirmed in the lyrics to the song.

> Oh, the Sandow, Sandow girl!
> She is smooth and slim and supple,
> And compared with any couple of other girls,
> The Sandow, Sandow girl
> Is a priceless, peerless pearl.
> Even Sandow I think would be frightened to wink
>   at his Sandow girl.[62]

In order to confirm Carrie Moore's muscularity, she was photographed by Dover Street Studios lifting a large globe barbell. Ironically, this stunt was not in the play, but invented by the photographer or his model to show off her muscles and her form-fitting dress. She was adamant in her interview about the importance of avoiding corsets and tight lacing of any sort (although tight dresses seem to be quite acceptable). Miss Moore was also quick to praise the glories of exercise. According to the reporter, she plays tennis, rows, punts, rides a bicycle, walks, and plays cricket. Exercise, not tight lacing is the route to beauty, and it was Sandow's appliances that offered the best means for this. "I think that we Symmetrion girls should be looked upon as a sort of practical illustration of a great and natural theory that the feminine human form can—even in the twentieth century—look quite pleasant and up-to-date without the help of a squeeze in trellis work surrounding the middle of the body and reducing it to the proportions of an egg-cup."[63] Once again, the combination of sex appeal and health had brought more recognition and (presumably) more customers to the Sandow Institute at 32 St. James's Street.

When he was not involved in running his institute, Sandow was looking for other means to make money based on the public's desire for strength and health. In the first part of his life, Sandow had a string of successes in the theatrical, sporting, and business worlds, but after his touring days had ended, it would seem that his fortunes shifted. The former strongman suffered from a series of bad decisions, misplaced trust, and jealous rivalry. The first problems arose from the British Medical Association, which lodged a complaint against Sandow's Institute in 1911 claiming that Sandow was practicing medicine without proper training.

From the very start of his theatrical career, Sandow had sought the acceptance of medical men. Whenever he appeared in a new city, he would invite prominent citizens and doctors to a pre-performance explanation and demonstration. At first these shows were intended to raise interest in the press and keep the public's attention at a sufficiently high level that they would come to his vaudeville performances. Gradually, however, they came to be a justification for Sandow's brand of physical culture, and after his triumphal Australasian and 1903 American tours, he gave fresh impetus to the medical implications of his training. Sandow wanted to demonstrate that health, strength, and beauty were all possible with the judicious use of physical exercise. The body, he believed, could repair itself by exercise, and Sandow would be the great messiah of health who would lead mankind out of the darkness of pestilence and debility and into the light of a disease-free world. Sandow had learned his advertising techniques from Ziegfeld, and he should have shown more restraint.

When the British medical establishment looked at his claims, they became very suspicious. Sandow's promises reeked of snake oil to them. It was one thing to offer cures for corpulence, insomnia, and knock knees, but when Sandow began to claim victory over such diseases as liver complaints, nervous disorders, rheumatism, and skin troubles, the doctors went on the offensive. They believed that they had to put an end to what seemed to them to be sheer quackery. The articles in *Truth* (pp. 174–75) were a direct result of Sandow's counter offensive, but it would not be enough. By March 1911 Sandow seemed to have won the day when he was appointed professor of physical culture of King George V, but just two months later that triumph was forgotten when a renewed attack came. Suddenly, it seemed as if every doctor in Harley Street was arrayed against Sandow and his Institute of Curative Physical Culture.[64]

The first salvo in the battle was aimed at Dr. J. Robertson Wallace, the staff physician at Sandow's Institute, who was accused of "infamous conduct" and was threatened with having his name expunged from the Medical Register, making it impossible for him to practice medicine in Britain. The conduct that Wallace was charged with consisted of two offenses: first, allowing his name to be used in advertisements that were taken out by Sandow's company. This was a serious breach of medical etiquette because doctors at this time were forbidden to solicit patients. Secondly, and more seriously, the Medical Association believed that Dr. Wallace had lent his tacit support to the claims of miraculous cures by exercise that Sandow had touted in his advertising. Sandow's barrister

Lord Robert Cecil insisted that Wallace and two other medical prac-
titioners on staff were present simply to evaluate patients who might
not be fit for exercise or to assist if some emergency arose. "Is it not
a requirement for every passenger ship to carry a surgeon aboard?"
asked Cecil. They are not there "to protect the captain and owners
from responsibility for having perhaps shipped a man physically unable to undergo the voyage, but to ensure that the passenger should
have proper attention in the case of unforeseen eventualities." The
medical men, he insisted were in a similar situation.

Dr. J. Smith Whitaker, medical secretary of the BMA, thought that
this analogy was nonsense. "If the ship were advertised as a hospital ship
and the captain and crew claimed to be able to treat disease, and if the
surgeon shipped with the intention of aiding them, he would be guilty
of infamous conduct in a professional respect." After deliberating for
three-quarters of an hour, the Council agreed with Dr. Smith, and Dr.
(soon to be Mr.) Wallace was told that he would have six months to
reform his actions, and if at the end of that time he could not, then
his name would be erased from the Register.[65]

Exactly six months later, two letters appeared in the *London Times*,
one from Wallace and the other from Sandow, himself. The staff physician informed the public of the circumstances of his hearing, and
announced that he had no intentions of "reforming" because it was
not he who needed to reform. If the Medical Council wanted to erase
his name, then so be it. Sandow's letter was a good deal angrier. "For
upwards of 12 years I have met with the greatest success in my methods
of curing illness by my exercise treatment without having doctors to
assist me," he wrote. When medical men began prescribing Sandow's
cures for their patients, he wanted to express his gratitude to the medical profession by hiring a physician as a consultant. He now realized
the kind of jealousy this engendered in the medical profession. He had
inadvertently "offended the antiquated traditions of what is perhaps
the most jealously governed profession in the world." Indeed, his only
"crime" had been "making known through the medium of the British Press the health advantages procurable by my system of physical
exercise treatment."[66] The doctors whom he had courted for three
decades had turned against him, and the sting of their rebukes must
have been sharp. Even when he was a music-hall strongman, Sandow
had taken pride in his knowledge of anatomy and had impressed
many with his mastery of physiology. He might have made an excellent doctor if circumstances were right. Despite the setback, Sandow
continued to make his claims of medical treatment for as long as his

institute existed, and (perhaps as a bit of revenge or justification) in many of his brochures he made it a point to publish scores of names and testimonials from medical men all over the country.

If advertising caused him trouble with his Curative Institute, it was destined to plague Sandow in other enterprises, too. Not even his corset company was immune from problems as was amply proved when Miss Vera Jane Wood brought charges against The Sandow's Health and Perfect Figure-forming Corset Company in 1914. Miss Wood, an aspiring actress complained that a photo of her appeared in an advertisement for Sandow's Corsets making it appear that she wore Sandow corsets (which she did not); she consequently sued for copyright infringement and libel. The case is interesting for several reasons, most obviously because it gives an insight into the practices of both advertisers and photographers at this time.

Miss Wood testified that some weeks before, she went to Dover Street Studios in order to have her picture taken; since she was a pretty young lady and an actress, the photos were done for free and she was given a few proofs of the sitting. The court was then asked to imagine her embarrassment and chagrin when several friends came to her a bit later asking how much she got paid for wearing Sandow's corsets. It seems that they had seen ads in several London papers implying that Miss Wood's perfect figure was due at least in part to Sandow's corset. The actress was mortified to see her image and a brief statement endorsing the product in question, and she was certain that this picture would do damage to her burgeoning stage career. She claimed that it was she who owned the copyright to her own image, and since she most certainly did not wear a Sandow's Health and Perfect Figure-forming Corset, this constituted libel. She sought unspecified damages from both the photographer and the corset company.

After the plaintiff gave her testimony, one Mrs. March of the corset company was called to the box. She stated that her job was to go through a book of photographs sent to her regularly by the photographer and pick out pictures of pretty young starlets. After paying a use fee of £4 4s. to the photographer, the pictures would then be used in the company's advertisements. Most aspiring actresses found this system to be an excellent method of publicity, and there had never been any complaints before.

The judge heard the case, and the jury deliberated briefly. The ruling concluded that since she was an actress and her photographic sitting had been complimentary, the photos belonged to the photographer. Miss Wood had no grounds to protest. As for the issue of libel, the jury thought that since she was suing as an actress, the publicity could hardly have done her any harm; in fact, quite the opposite was almost certainly the case. Her actions were subsequently denied, but was the poor young lady really the loser? She had loads of free publicity, and Sandow's corsets were in the news in a way that they might never have managed otherwise, so it is unlikely that anyone protested the decision very heartily. This frivolous case was a boon to all.[67]

The court case involving Miss Wood points out a truism of the times: the person who controls the images wields great power. Eugen Sandow had known for many years that it was important to have the right kind of photographs, drawings, and other visual aids before the public at all times, especially if one made his living by his appearance (as Sandow did). Sandow's portrait had been executed by Aubrey Hunt, his photograph had been taken by Sarony, van der Weyde, and many others, and the beautiful statue by Pomeroy had become well known even in Sandow's lifetime.[68] Recently, however, several other previously unknown representations of the strongman have been revealed, and they shed light on Sandow and how he wanted to be remembered. The first is a bronze statue of the standing strongman that stands twenty-six inches tall and which is signed on the base "Hibbert Binney 1907." Sandow is nude except for a figleaf, and he raises his bent arms as if to flex his biceps; his head is turned in profile to the right. A fluted ionic column rises behind the athlete. Unlike Sandow's first statue, this one shows the man in his maturity, but his musculature is not emphasized. He is toned and fit, but not the superbly muscular, music-hall entertainer of the 1891 work.

The second statue is a life-sized bust of Sandow also by Binney which was completed in 1908, and it depicts the subject as a business man in suit, wing collar, cravat, waistcoat, and jacket. There were two versions of the work, one in rich, white marble on a green marble base, and the other of bronzed copper over a plaster form. Neither of these works depicts Sandow as a brash, muscular athlete in his prime; these are mature men. In the bust he is presented as a paragon of commercial rectitude and sober trustworthiness; he is a captain of business and a proud and successful man of affairs.

Not much is known of the artist except that in 1893 Hibbert C. Binney lived at Snaresbrook in Essex, and then in 1894 he moved to London. He exhibited at the Royal Academy from 1893 to 1921. The two statues were produced within a year of one another, and were probably commissioned by Sandow for his institute on St. James's Street. The large bust probably occupied a niche somewhere in Sandow's office, and it was meant to show the man's solidity, permanence, and a firm upholder of British, middle-class values.[69]

Those bourgeois ideals which Sandow aspired to so assiduously would be sorely tested in the coming years. He was destined to embark on a venture that for the next five years would try his patience and empty his bank account. This was to be the strongman's last great enterprise: Sandow's Cocoa and Chocolate Company Ltd. which ended disastrously for nearly all concerned. Sandow had been considering the idea of marketing chocolate for several years, but it was not until late 1911 that he was able to gather together the requisite financing for such a huge enterprise. In September of that year, his company purchased a building in the New Kent Road in south London in order to start manufacturing his own brand of cocoa.[70] But as soon the word got out about Sandow's Health and Strength Cocoa, the trouble started. Thorne & Co., Ltd., a rival company from the Midlands, brought suit against Sandow for copyright infringement, claiming that they had produced "Health Cocoa" for years and that the new brand would confuse consumers. This case was quickly decided in Sandow's favor, but the court case was a portent of worse things to come.[71]

Despite the lawsuit, Sandow's Cocoa and Chocolate Company, Ltd. was able to find sufficient investors who were willing to purchase shares in the company. There never seemed to be enough money to keep the company going. The report of the first shareholder's meeting in June of 1914 showed the business with its financial head barely above water. The problem was that the company's directors had spent too much on advertising the first year, and it left them short for other expenses.[72] With such ravenous competitors like Nestle and Cadbury's, it was necessary to carve out a market as soon as possible. That the company survived at all is largely due to the value of Sandow's name on the tin. Customers recognized the name and face of the famous strongman, and they were willing to dole out a few extra pennies for a chocolate drink that they believed would help them attain health and strength. The fact that it contained a little more dried albumin than other cocoas was not going to increase anyone's desire to purchase the mixture in an effort to improve one's vim and vitality.

Throughout the next year, there were constant problems with the company's management; nothing seemed to prosper, and no one could improve a situation that was rapidly going from bad to worse. Sales were constantly increasing, but so were expenses. Under normal business conditions, the company might have survived and even prospered, but the times were not normal. The Great War had begun in August 1914, and Britain's interest and energies were directed toward this great endeavor. Manpower was short and inflation was high, but still Sandow's cocoa struggled on. By 1915 an ugly rumor had began that the chocolate drink was manufactured by enemy workers in Germany and then presumably smuggled into the country in order to subvert good English chocolate makers. Thus when a customer went into a shop in Brighton and requested a tin of Sandow's Cocoa, he was told by the proprietor, Mr. F. Moseley, that there was none to be had in his shop. "I do not sell cocoas made in Germany," he explained bluntly. The confused customer contacted Sandow, and thus a lawsuit for libel ensued.

It took little time to prove beyond a doubt that the chocolate was made in Hayes near London, and to force Mr. Moseley to admit in court that he had been mistaken and that he would withdraw his statement. The judge in the case went even further. He opined that "at the present time it is a serious trade libel to say that a trader's goods here were made in Germany. A statement of the kind was calculated to cause great hardship to the trader, and an injunction ought to be granted in such a case."[73] Once again, we must wonder if this was not another instance of using the courts to disseminate a message that could be delivered in no better way. It all seems so neat and clean. The unnamed customer in Brighton was perhaps put up to his job, and it was all very convenient and very artificial.

In the end, it did little good to try to convince people that Sandow was producing good, English cocoa. The company sank deeper in debt, but stocks continued to sell reasonably well, at least in the first years.[74] Desperate to turn a profit, the directors of the company were willing to try almost any means possible to help sell more tins of cocoa. Shortly after the Great War began in 1914, Sandow's company made an "Offer to our Brave Lads at the Front!" by agreeing to donate five hundred silver-plated cocoa sets free to the families of any British soldiers who drove the Germans back from France into their own country. Unfortunately, most British soldiers in the expeditionary force were bogged down in the trenches of northern France, so it is unlikely that Sandow ever had to deliver a cocoa set.

This slightly mad appeal to patriotism was enough to save neither Tommy Atkins nor the Sandow Cocoa Company, and the factory lost a great deal of the owner's and the public's money. It went into receivership on June 24, 1916 and its remaining assets were liquidated to satisfy creditors. In all, the enterprise lost in the region of £70,000, the vast majority of which was borne by Sandow himself. The factory at Hayes in Middlesex near London was purchased by the Hayes Cocoa Company, and this in turn was sold to Nestlé in 1929.[75]

It has always been something of a mystery why Sandow permitted himself to make such obvious blunders. There may never be a satisfying answer, but one possible response is that Sandow needed adventure in his life; he chafed under the restraints of an ordinary life, and his constantly active mind bubbled over with plans and projects. Unfortunately, toward the end of his life, most of these ideas were slightly harebrained. One of the oddest problems that Sandow attempted to address at this time was children's exercise. When he pondered this issue, Sandow devised a novel solution late in 1913: he would create a doll that could be used as an exerciser. The resulting invention consisted of a jolly looking figure in a sailor's uniform; concealed inside the figure was a complicated series of pulleys and other mechanisims which would offer some resistance to children who pulled on the doll's arms and legs. There were miniature grip dumbbells instead of hands and stirrups where the feet would be, thus allowing for maximum usage. The purpose of this apparatus was "to provide a toy for children (for example those between the ages of one and seven years) which will require some physical effort to play with, or with which some physical effort may be exerted, so that the child may unconsciously be provided with a means for developing and maintaining its physical perfection and health." In order to provide the child with some further incentive to use the doll, Sandow decided to include a clockwork device in the doll's head that would provide a treat. After yanking on the doll's arms and legs for a predetermined number of times, the figure's mouth would automatically open and a small candy would roll down a tiny chute and pop out of the sailor's mouth.[76]

Perhaps this invention was simply too complicated or the idea of rewarding children with an unhealthy treat was incompatible with Sandow's goals. Whatever the reason, the former strongman could not find enough backers to put the doll into production. Despite the setback, he continued to work on the problem, and two years later, he had devised another solution. This time the doll was simpler with stout springs that spiraled down the sleeves and trouser legs of the figure. When the springs were squeezed and released, there was enough resistance to work the child's muscles, "thus forming a ready means of turning an ordinary doll or play figure into a useful and beneficial unconscious exercising medium for a child."[77]

Sandow was apparently convinced that he had at last hit upon the best combination of muscle builder and plaything, so in June 1915 he went to an associate, Harold Morris, a professor of physical education, and asked him to devise a series of exercises using his patented spring doll. Morris was asked to train a group of children and to give a public exhibition in addition to sending out circulars and do everything that was necessary to make the sale of the doll a commercial success. The professor prepared a series of fifty-five exercises, arranged them to music and trained a troupe of children who gave a public performance at the Savoy Hotel. Unfortunately, he was never paid for his efforts, and thus he sued Sandow for the sum of three hundred guineas. Unfortunately, nothing seemed to flourish for the strongman at this time.

Sandow had long wanted to manufacture the dolls, but he could not find sufficient financial backing. Sandow's own daughter Helen was named as head of the company formed to market and manufacture the dolls. It was not to be, however. The judge in the case ordered Sandow to pay Mr. Morris the money that he wanted. It was just one more disappointment in a long string that occurred at this time. Perhaps one of the reasons why Sandow did not pay Morris at once was because of the eminent collapse of the cocoa company (a time when money was in particularly short supply). Sandow, it would seem, was closer to financial ruin than he had ever been, and although he would live for another decade, these fiascos and debacles must have had an unfortunate effect on even a strong man's health.

Sandow's premature death at the age of fifty-eight evoked several poignant testimonies, but one of the most eloquent of these appeared in the *New York Times* two days after the great man's death. The author implies that Sandow and others of his kind are not fated to grow old. "The titans of history and legend have rarely attained advanced age," writes the editorialist. "They die the victims of accident or guile. How long would Samson have lived if he had not gone philandering in Philistia?" Athletes, he surmises, live no longer than the rest of us, but it is a pity that Sandow was not able to help more of us to attain a healthy life. And yet he has inspired countless people to take up strength, health, and beauty. "Sandow was the first of the men whose musculature heaves so mightily yet so easily in the advertising pages of the magazines, summoning young men from late hours and bad habits to the glory of the body and worldly success. The point left undemonstrated is whether the heroic human form is also the most long-lived."[78]

Sandow's body might have perished, and for a while after his death, Sandow's message seemed lost to the world. A mere fourteen years after Sandow's death, a French woman, Thérèse Pagès wrote of a pilgrimage that she took from Paris to London in order to visit the city that was most closely associated with Eugen Sandow. Pagès had practically grown up in Edmond Desbonnet's gymnasium in Paris, and her father had been a medical doctor who wrote often for *La Culture Physique* and other publications on the subject of physical culture, so she was very familiar with both Sandow and his reputation. She had heard many tales of the handsome strongman, and so her trip would be a sort of personal homage to the man. When she arrived in the British capital in 1939, she quickly learned that all of Sandow's schools had been closed; only his appliance business was still in operation. All of the great man's achievements had melted away quickly after Eugen's death. When she inquired about the institute at 32 St. James's Street, she encountered uncomprehending stares and complete ignorance; even though the man had died only fourteen years before, she complained, "it was as if I were speaking of something that happened before the flood."

Pagès laments that unlike Desbonnet, Sandow had not taken steps to perpetuate his instruction or his teaching methods, so when the great man passed away, his schools, his system, and his dreams died with him. Besides that, Sandow had fallen prey to the English disease of pursuing competitions and breaking records, which was the opposite of physical culture. Sandow, she complained, "had not become an educator in the fullest sense of the word, for he inclined too much toward spectacles and record breaking." Sandow had become a tool of the money men who controlled him and his business behind the scenes. The author claimed that since Sandow "was under the domination of capitalists, he was not independent, and he was forced to obey these men and to heed their orders. But these men looked no further than their balance sheets, and so this association limited Sandow's initiatives." If only Sandow had avoided strength stunts, competitive sports, and his rich backers he might have reached the age of 100, "but vainglory killed him at the age of 57."[79] Clearly, the author overstates her case to make a point; Sandow was never quite the forgotten man that Pagès claimed; she was attempting to point out the superiority of the French system over that of the British, and Sandow was the sorry representative of all that was wrong with exercise on the other side of the channel.

Eugen Sandow had not been completely forgotten, thanks in large part to the reputation that he had built so carefully over the years. Both before and after he died, the former strongman entered the language and culture of several countries. References to Sandow appeared in the works of writers, both minor and major: James Joyce in *Ulysses* (1922) has Leopold Bloom remind himself to take up Sandow exercises again; one of the characters in Robert Hichens's *The Woman with the Fan* (1904) relieves his frustration by working out with a Sandow's exerciser; Ambrose Bierce uses Sandow as an example of hyper-masculinity in his bitterly satiric poem "An Offer of Marriage"

(1903); and Saul Bellow's title character mentions his reluctance to putting in hours on the Sandow exerciser in *The Adventures of Augie March* (1953).

There has been something of a minor renaissance in Sandow studies, and he is being discussed in quite a few works that deal with art, photography, gender studies, sport, and other topics. There are two extensive and constantly updated websites dedicated to Sandow, and when his name is Googled, over twenty pages of references appear. It would truly seem that Sandow's significance as an exponent of beauty, masculinity, and physique display is finally being recognized and respected. If his contributions to the science of exercise and nutrition are largely discounted today, Sandow is still credited for his innovations in the exercise and fitness business. The numerous gym chains that dot the urban landscape today are run and organized essentially the same way that Sandow pioneered a century earlier. Sandow remains the great popularizer that he always was; he showed that a previously apathetic public could be persuaded to exercise for the sakes of their health and appearance. Sandow went out and wandered in Philistia, but rather than slaying the ignorant and untutored, he converted them.

Acknowledgments

I relied on the help of many friends who assisted me in various ways to learn more about Sandow and his activities. When they came across anything interesting about the man (usually while doing their own research), they would send the information to me. Many of the early newspaper articles were sent to me by David Horne of Sheffield, England and Dr. Bob Petersen of Sydney, Australia. I was aided in many ways by Michael Murphy of Westerly, Rhode Island; Dr. Caroline Daley of Auckland, New Zealand; and Josh Buck of College Place, Maryland. It was due to the kindness of Mr. Tom Lincir of the Ivanko Barbell Company that I have the patents for the Sandow dolls as well as other inventions. I am also very grateful to Dr. Bernd Wedemeyer-Kolwe of Göttingen, Germany; Daniël Christiaens of the Antwerp Muscle Archives; Gilles Janson of Montréal, Québec and to Sandra Bordin of Seattle and Biagio Filizola of Sapri, Italy who both helped me decipher some tricky examples of Roman dialect.

Chris Davies of Morecambe, Lancashire, Sandow's great-grandson has been of inestimable help to me in supplying details of his family's history. He has done much research on his famous relative and has discovered many hitherto unknown facts. Most dramatically, Davies has recently discovered evidence in Germany and Eastern Europe that calls into question the previously accepted story of Sandow's origins in Königsberg.

The Internet has been a great boon to researchers everywhere, and I must thank three people who maintain a couple of excellent sites dedicated to Sandow. The first is Christian Anderson of Palm Springs,

California; he has been very kind in forwarding messages and queries and in supporting my work from his Sandow Museum. Roger Fillary and Gilbert Waldron from the UK share duties on the SandowPlus site and have made research on the early days of British bodybuilding much easier by posting scans of entire books from the period.

Glossary of Weightlifting Terms

Back Lift: Weight is placed on a platform which is supported by two high wooden sawhorses. The lifter gets underneath the platform in a stooping position and has a support for his hands. He then straightens the arms and the legs and partly straightens the back, and lifts the platform which thus rests upon his shoulders.

Barbell: A round steel bar usually 5 feet in length and approximately $1\frac{1}{16}$ inches in diameter. Weights are attached to the ends of this bar.

Bent Press: Lifter takes a barbell in one hand, raising it first to the shoulder and then pressing it to arm's length overhead. The athlete "pulls in" and then bends the trunk sideways, resting the elbow upon the thigh prior to standing erect.

Block Weight: A rectangular weight with a ring attached on top. These were originally used in farm scales and were later appropriated by athletes.

Chest Expander/Strands: Exerciser consisting of one or more rubber or metal spring strands connected to handles at either end. The object is to pull the strands to full arm's length, thus working the pectoral muscles.

Clean: Lifter brings the weight in one clean, continuous movement from the floor to the shoulders.

Clean and Jerk: The weight is lifted to the shoulders in one clean movement, and then jerked to arm's length overhead. This lift was performed in both the one-handed and two-handed versions in Sandow's day.

Continental Jerk: This curious lift utilizes the sturdy belts that German lifters were fond of wearing. The performer raises the barbell high enough so that it can be dropped behind the buckle of the lifter's belt. Then standing with the feet in line, the performer takes the bell to the shoulders where it may again rest. Finally the weight is jerked overhead to arm's length.

Crucifix: Dumbbells or ring weights are taken clean to arm's length overhead and then lowered (with the lifter's palms up) until the arms are level with the shoulders.

Curl: Weight is grasped with both hands (palms front) hanging at arm's length across the lifter's front. From this position it is lifted to the shoulders by bending the forearms completely on the upper arms.

Dead Lift: To modern athletes, there is only one definition of this lift: the barbell must be lifted from the floor until the lifter is erect with straight back and legs. In Sandow's day, however, it was quite different: the performer stood on two chairs, grasped a handle that had been attached to the weight in both hands. He then raised the weight one or two inches from the ground by simultaneously straightening his legs and back.

Dumbbell: Essentially, this is a short barbell. Dumbbells usually measure 12 to 18 inches and are used mainly to work the arms individually.

Globe Bell: Barbell or dumbbell in which the weights on the end are spherical in shape. The globes can either be solid or hollow.

Harness Lifting: The athlete stands on top of a specially built platform. Another square platform is placed on the ground from which chains run up and attach to a collar fastened around the lifter's neck. The weight is placed on the lower platform, and then with a tremendous effort the lifter straightens his arms and legs, bringing his body to an erect position. By doing so he raises the lower platform and the weight an inch or two from the ground.

This lift was practiced almost exclusively by professional strongmen because of the expensive apparatus that was required. Additionally, because the platform was so complicated, with chains and struts going everywhere, it was a perfect mechanism to conceal trickery. It was a favorite of Charles Sampson's for this very reason.

Indian Club: A wooden club usually about 25–30 inches long, shaped like a tenpin and swung in the hand for exercise.

Jerk: The quick, lunging movement of arms and legs that a lifter uses to raise a weight from his shoulders to arm's length overhead.

Kettle Bell: A round or cone-shaped weight with a ring or handle attached for one-arm lifting.

Living Bell: Oversize barbell with wicker or papier-mâché bells at the ends used by vaudeville strongmen. Two of the strongman's assistants would conceal themselves in the bells. After working with the weight during a performance, the athlete would lower the bell to the stage and the assistants (usually pretty girls) would emerge. This was a famous feature of Sandow's act.

Muscling Out: The lifter grasps a kettle bell or ring weight in each hand and holds them out from the shoulders with the arms horizontal and the palms up. This is also know as holding bells "in the balance."

Plate-loading Barbell: Disc-shaped plates of iron are attached to the bar by means of a collar. This innovation meant that weight could be added or taken away quickly and easily.

Press: Lifter pushes a weight steadily and smoothly until the arms are fully extended.

Press on Back: Lying directly on the floor, the lifter reaches back and draws the barbell over the chest with the upper arms resting upon the floor. The bell is then pressed to arm's length overhead. Neither legs, buttocks, nor shoulders should leave the floor during the lift.

Progressive Weight Training: Building muscle mass and endurance by gradually increasing the amount of weight one lifts and the number of repetitions.

Ring Weight: Any weight with a ring on top. This type of weight is used as an alternate to the dumbbell. See Kettle Bell.

Roman Column: Metal pole approximately ten feet high that was used in Sandow's stage performances. The athlete climbed about halfway up the pole and inserted his legs around perpendicular supports, thus enabling him to bend backwards. In this way, the performer picked up various heavy objects with his hands and teeth. The use of this device required a very strong abdomen, and this was a way for Sandow to show off his well-muscled midsection. Supposedly, the column was invented by Sandow's mentor, Professor Attila, although he may have borrowed the prop from an even earlier strongman, Felice Napoli. Later Sandow expanded the concept of the Roman Column to include the "Roman Chair" and even the "Roman Horse." In both instances, he hung backwards over the chair or horse and performed lifting feats.

Sandow's Developer: Exerciser consisting of several rubber strands that could be used as a chest expander or wall exerciser depending on how it was set up. Instead of simple wood and metal handles, Sandow's patented developer had detachable dumbbells that were used as hand grips.

Shot-loading Barbell: The hollow globes at the end of the barbell can be filled with shot, sand, or some other suitably heavy material so that their weight can be varied.

Spring-grip Dumbbell: Another Sandow invention. A 5-pound dumbbell was split in two laterally and several springs were attached in the middle. Thus the athlete could exercise with weights and squeeze the dumbbells to increase wrist and hand strength. In later models a bell would ring when both sides of the dumbbell were completely depressed.

Strands: See Chest Expander.

Symmetrion: Sandow's version of his developer that he marketed for women. It contained a few variations: a stomach strap for working the abdomen and a head harness for exercising the neck muscles.

Tomb of Hercules/Human Bridge: The athlete supports himself on his hands and feet with his abdomen up. A specially prepared board which is heavily padded on the underside is then rested upon his knees and on the points of his shoulders. At right angles to this board, and resting upon it, is a long plank, and on this plank are assembled the weights which the athlete has to support. Although it is a supporting feat rather than a "lift," it was very popular with stage athletes.

Two Hands Anyhow: The athlete needs two separate weights to perform this curious lift. Usually these consist of a barbell and a ring weight. As the name implies, both weights are lifted to arm's length overhead "anyhow"; getting the weights up is all that matters. The most popular strategy for accomplishing this lift is to take the barbell to the shoulder with two hands, then jerk or press it overhead, and finally lean over and pick up the ring weight and put it overhead, too. Sandow preferred to bent press the barbell and then pick up the ring weight while he was in the lowest position of the lift. He would then straighten up, finishing the bent press with the barbell. After that, he would concentrate on pressing the smaller weight overhead, thus completing the lift.

Sources

Calvert, Alan. *The Truth about Weight Lifting*. Philadelphia: by the author, 1911.
Hoffman, Bob. *Weight Lifting*. York: Strength & Health, 1939.
Pullum, W. A. *Weight Lifting Made Easy and Interesting*. London: Athletic Publications, n.d. (c. 1925).

Notes

Preface

1. H. Allen Smith, *Let the Crabgrass Grow* (New York: Bernard Geis, 1960), 72.

Chapter 1: The Early Years, 1867–89

1. Francis J. Grund, quoted in Lois W. Banner, *American Beauty* (New York: Knopf, 1983), 227.

2. Quoted in Robert Farquharson, "The Influence of Athletic Sports on Health," *London Lancet* 7 (American ed.) (July 1870), 369.

3. George Beard, quoted in Banner, *American Beauty,* 232.

4. For an account of early French physical culture see Edmond Desbonnet, "Les Origines de la Culture Physique," *La Culture Physique* 31.449 (Sept. 1927), 262. MacLaren's story is summarized in Peter McIntosh, *Physical Education in England since 1800* (London: Bell, 1952), 91–96.

5. Quotes from Bruce Haley, *The Healthy Body and Victorian Culture* (Cambridge, Mass.: Harvard University Press, 1978), 167.

6. Rudolph Aronson, *Theatrical and Musical Memoirs* (New York: McBride, Nast, 1913), 208.

7. Eugen Sandow, *Strength and How to Obtain It* (London: Gale & Polden, 1897), 89. This work proved to be Sandow's most popular book, thus accounting for the reprinted and revised editions that were published in 1900, 1905, 1911, and 1922. Unless otherwise noted, all quotations are taken from the first edition of 1897.

8. Siegmund Klein, "Sandow—Truth and Fiction," *Strength & Health,* Dec. 1948, 14.

9. G. Mercer Adam, *Sandow's System of Physical Training* (New York: J. Selwin Tait & Sons, 1894), 23.

10. Eugen Sandow, "My Reminiscences," *The Strand Magazine* 39.230 (Mar. 1910), 164.

11. Sandow, *Strength and How to Obtain It,* 89.

12. Ibid., 90.

13. An anonymous obituary writer in the journal *D'Excelsior* claimed that early in his career Sandow was employed as a model by a Parisian professor of physiology, and that "he knew how to profit so well from the lessons and the lectures which he attended, that he acquired sufficient anatomical knowledge to allow him to establish an entire system of physical culture" (Edmond Desbonnet, "La Mort de l'Athlète Sandow," *La Culture Physique* 29.427 [Nov. 1925], 287).

14. Adam, *Sandow's System of Physical Training*, 25.

15. Undated holograph letter from Sandow to Attila (ca. 1890) in the author's collection.

16. Brief, unsigned announcement, *Health & Strength* 78.16 (Aug. 11, 1949), 13.

17. A concise history of the Turner movement can be found in Emmett Rice, *A Brief History of Physical Education* (New York: Barnes, 1930), 99–106. See also Deobold Van Dalen and Bruce Bennett, *A World History of Physical Education* (Englewood Cliffs, N.J.: Prentice-Hall, 1971), 230–31.

18. See the notes Edmond Desbonnet appended to a translated article by George Jowett, "Eugène Sandow, le Sans-Pareil," *La Culture Physique* 32.464 (Dec. 1928), 356.

19. *San Francisco Chronicle*, May 19, 1894, 12.

20. Holograph letter from Edmond Desbonnet to Gerard Nisivoccia, Mar. 15, 1949, in the author's collection.

21. Adam, *Sandow's System of Physical Training*, 26.

22. For further information on Attila, see Leo Gaudreau, *Anvils, Horseshoes, and Cannons: The History of Strongmen*, 2 vols. (Alliance, Kans.: Iron Man, [1978]), 1:160–64.

23. For further information on Napoli, see David Webster, *The Iron Game: An Illustrated History of Weight-lifting* (Irvine, Scotland: by the author, 1976), 143.

24. Siegmund Klein, "Strongmen I Remember Best: Professor Attila," *Strength & Health*, Mar. 1959, 25.

25. Siegmund Klein, "My Quarter Century in the Iron Game, Part VI," *Strength & Health*, Aug. 1944, 35.

26. Quoted in Gaudreau, *Anvils, Horseshoes, and Cannons*, 2:38.

27. Klein, "Sandow—Truth and Fiction," 35.

28. David Webster, *Barbells and Beefcake: An Illustrated History of Bodybuilding* (Irvine, Scotland: by the author, 1979), 15.

29. Mark Berry, "The Rising Generation Indebted to Attila," *Strength* 15.1 (Mar. 1930), 31.

30. For further information on Batta, see Edmond Desbonnet, *Les Rois de la Force* (Paris: Berger-Levrault, 1911), 281–89.

31. Unidentified clipping showing the St. Michael statue with brief explanatory caption in French, probably from *La Culture Physique*. The translated caption reads in part: " 'Satan Trampled under the Feet of St. Michael' was posed by the athlete, Sandow, in 1888 when he was a pupil of Attila" (from the author's collection).

32. On Lambeaux and "indecipherable symbols," see E. Benézit, *Dictionnaire Critique et Documentaire des Peintres, Sculpteurs, Dessinateurs et Graveurs,* 12 vols. (Paris: Grund, 1976), 6:399.

33. Quoted in Gaudreau, *Anvils, Horseshoes, and Cannons,* 2:38.

34. Holograph letter from J. Diericke of Uccle (near Brussels) to Mr. Vissaguet, dated Sept. 5, 1948 (from the collection of Robert P. Stull).

35. Adam, *Sandow's System of Physical Training,* 29.

36. Ibid., 30–31.

37. Klein, "Sandow—Truth and Fiction," 34. Klein also calls into question Sandow's ability to destroy the machines single-handedly, and he implies that the cabman probably was his partner in crime.

38. Adam, *Sandow's System of Physical Training,* 32.

39. Sandow, "My Reminiscences," 166.

40. Details of Crauck's career are in Benézit: *Dictionnaire Critique et Documentaire,* 3:261.

41. Adam, *Sandow's System of Physical Training,* 35–36.

42. Ibid., 36–37.

43. Ibid., 37–38.

44. For further information on Crown Prince Frederick, see Theo Aronson, *The Kaisers* (London: Cassell, 1971), 129–96.

45. A photograph of the ring appears in Sandow, "My Reminiscences," 172.

46. Adam, *Sandow's System of Physical Training,* 113. Writing as far back as 1622, the Englishman Henry Peacham had confirmed the snobbish disdain for pugilism. Throwing and wrestling, advised the writer, are "exercises not so well beseeming nobility, but rather soldiers in a camp or prince's guard" (quoted in Haley, *Healthy Body and Victorian Culture,* 209).

47. Adam, *Sandow's System of Physical Training,* 40–41.

48. Sandow, *Strength and How to Obtain It,* 93.

49. For details of Hunt's career, see Benézit, *Dictionnaire Critique et Documentaire,* 5:673. Also see Ulrich Thieme and Felix Becker, *Allgemeines Lexicon der Bildenden Künstler von der Antike bis zur Gegenwart,* 37 vols. (Leipzig: Seemann, 1925), 18:146.

50. Sandow, "My Reminiscences," 167.

51. William Pullum in *Health & Strength* 59.4 (July 17, 1937), 112.

52. Peter Gay, *The Bourgeois Experience: Victoria to Freud,* 2 vols., vol. 1: *Education of the Senses* (New York: Oxford, 1984), 390. Perhaps the closest one can come to resolving the exact nature of Sandow and Hunt's relationship is to examine a similar situation mentioned in a biography of Arnold Schwarzenegger. The author quotes the contemporary physique athlete Ronald Matz: "When a bodybuilder is very short of money, he will do anything to survive. Some very rich gay men invest in athletes and say, 'I'll give you a thousand dollars just to pose.' Sometimes gay men watch the bodybuilder pose, then, after more money is exchanged, photograph them" (Wendy Leigh, *Arnold: The Unauthorized Biography* [Chicago: Congdon & Weed, 1990], 61).

53. Sandow, "My Reminiscences," 167.

54. Photograph in the author's collection. The Hunt portrait was apparently sold by Sandow's wife after the strongman died. After being lost for many years, it finally turned up for auction, and it was purchased by publisher Joe Weider, who keeps it at his headquarters in Woodland Hills, California. A fuller account of the painting can be found in David Chapman, "Sandow: Portrait of a Strongman," *Muscle & Fitness* 47.6 (June 1986), 209.

55. Desbonnet, "Eugène Sandow, le Sans-Pareil," 358.

56. The silver medal is in the author's collection.

57. The count de Furnimbac episode is detailed in Gaudreau, *Anvils, Horseshoes, and Cannons,* 2:48–50. See also Adam, *Sandow's System of Physical Training,* 100–102. A search of the *Almanach de Gotha* reveals no listing for the count de Furnimbac. This can be interpreted in one of three ways: Desbonnet uses a pseudonym, the count was from a very obscure family, or the entire story is spurious.

Chapter 2: The First Triumph, 1889

1. Even with these precautions, many a stage Hercules was occasionally caught unawares. Later in his career, Sandow himself fell victim to this tactic. In 1893 he offered a prize of $1,000 to anyone who could duplicate his lifting feats. Unfortunately, a burly Swedish lifter, Hjalmar Lundin, took him at his word, jumped onto the stage, and reproduced every lift. A nervous and embarrassed Sandow declared that the lifts were not done in "as perfect form" as he had done them. Thus the prize was denied the challenger despite the vociferous hoots of the audience (Klein, "Sandow—Truth and Fiction," 32). Also see David Chapman, "Gallery of Ironmen: Hjalmar Lundin," *Ironman* 51.10 (Oct. 1992), 146.

2. C. A. Sampson, *Strength: A Treatise on the Development and Use of Muscle* (Chicago: Rand McNally, 1895), 38–42.

3. Gaudreau, *Anvils, Horseshoes, and Cannons,* 1:165.

4. Ibid., 1:167.

5. Gordon Venables, *Mighty Men of Old* (York, Pa.: Strength and Health, 1940), unpaginated [22].

6. Ben Weinreb and Christopher Hibbert, eds., *The London Encyclopaedia* (London: Macmillan, 1983), 535.

7. William Pullum, "Strong Men over the Years," foreword to *The Amazing Samson as Told by Himself* (London: Samson Institute, 1926), 12–13.

8. Ibid., 13–15.

9. Quoted in Adam, *Sandow's System of Physical Training,* 49.

10. Ibid., 50.

11. Pullum, "Strong Men over the Years," 17–18.

12. Ibid., 18.

13. Quoted in Adam, *Sandow's System of Physical Training,* 55–56.

14. Ibid., 56.

15. Sandow, *Strength and How to Obtain It,* 96–97.

16. Adam, *Sandow's System of Physical Training,* 58.

17. Ibid., 58–60.

18. Unidentified clipping in Attila scrapbook dated July 2, [1893], in Todd-McLean Collection, University of Texas.

19. Pullum, "Strong Men over the Years," 21.

20. Sampson, *Strength: A Treatise on the Development and Use of Muscle,* 49.

21. George Hackenschmidt, "Charles Sampson: King of Showmen and Knave of Strongmen," *Mr. America* 5.1 (June 1962), 68–72.

22. Sandow, *Strength and How to Obtain It,* 98–99.

Chapter 3: A Growing Reputation, 1890–93

1. W. Parsley, "No Other Strong Man Looked like Sandow," *Health & Strength* 57.16 (Oct. 19, 1935), 466.

2. Adam, *Sandow's System of Physical Training,* 63.

3. Gus Macdonald, *Camera: Victorian Eyewitness* (New York: Viking, 1979), 143.

4. Herbert M. Schueller and Robert L. Peters, eds., *The Letters of John Addington Symonds,* 3 vols. (Detroit: Wayne State University Press, 1969), 3:436.

5. Phyllis Grosskurth, *John Addington Symonds: A Biography* (London: Longmans Green, 1964), 276.

6. Adam, *Sandow's System of Physical Training,* 67–68.

7. Ibid., 68.

8. Ibid., 69–70.

9. Sandow, "My Reminiscences," 169.

10. Adam, *Sandow's System of Physical Training,* 75.

11. Undated (ca. 1890) fragment of holograph letter from Sandow to Attila in the author's collection.

12. Gaudreau, *Anvils, Horseshoes, and Cannons,* 1:181–86.

13. Adam, *Sandow's System of Physical Training,* 99.

14. Ibid., 77–88.

15. For further information on the bent press, see Siegmund Klein, *How to Bent Press,* published by the author around 1936. This is a slender booklet that discusses the history and techniques of this lift. Also see "Klein's Kolumn" in *Strength & Health,* a series of articles that began with the July 1936 issue and ran through April 1941. This monthly column was designed to popularize the bent press and to call attention to those who still practiced it.

16. Unidentified English newspaper clipping in the collection of David Webster in Irvine, Scotland.

17. Adam, *Sandow's System of Physical Training,* 103–4.

18. Ibid., 89–97.

19. McIntosh, *Physical Education in England since 1800,* 104.

20. Quoted in Byron Farwell, *Mr. Kipling's Army* (New York: Norton, 1981), 81.

21. Ibid., 146.
22. Ibid., 151.
23. Adam, *Sandow's System of Physical Training*, 90–94.
24. McIntosh, *Physical Education in England since 1800*, 139.

Chapter 4: New York and Chicago, 1893–94

1. Adam, *Sandow's System of Physical Training*, 105.
2. Sandow, *Strength and How to Obtain It*, 119.
3. Rudolph Aronson, *Theatrical and Musical Memoirs* (New York: McBride, Nast and Co., 1913), 82–83.
4. Quoted in Adam, *Sandow's System of Physical Training*, 111.
5. Ibid., 115–16.
6. "Reign of Sandow, 'Perfect Man,'" part 2, *National Police Gazette*, Mar. 17, 1928, 14.
7. *Harper's Weekly*, July 1, 1893, clipping in the Billy Rose Theatre Collection, New York Public Library.
8. Quoted in Adam, *Sandow's System of Physical Training*, 109.
9. Quoted in Sandow, *Strength and How to Obtain It*, 129.
10. Quoted in Adam, *Sandow's System of Physical Training*, 110.
11. Arthur H. Lewis, *La Belle Otéro* (New York: Trident, 1967), 102–4.
12. L. F., "Anecdote Athletique: Le Grand Chapeau de Sandow et le Petit Doigt d'Émilienne," *La Culture Physique* 30.431 (Mar. 1926), 413. As with the episode with Otéro, it is uncertain whether this incident actually occurred or not. L. F. assures us that this story is entirely true and widely known among the old-time athletes of Paris. But since this hoary and ribald tale has been told many times and in many guises, its authenticity is very suspect.
13. Unidentified newspaper article dated July 2 [1893] in Attila's scrapbook at the Todd-McLean Collection, University of Texas.
14. "Sandow Assaulted by Sarah E. White [*sic*]," *New York Times*, July 25, 1893, 9, col. 2.
15. Unidentified newspaper article in the Attila scrapbook in the Todd-McLean Collection, University of Texas.
16. "Attila, World Famous Athlete," *National Police Gazette* 93.1623 (Sept. 19, 1908), 6.
17. For many years Siegmund Klein (1902–87) was the grand old man of American bodybuilding. Through his many articles, his intelligence, and the direction he gave others at his noted gymnasium, he became an authority in the sport. He knew many of the physique pioneers, and fortunately he was eloquent enough to write down his remembrances. He delivered training advice and set down historical reminiscences in hundreds of magazine articles and in his own publication, *Klein's Bell* (1931–33). He is thus one of the most important chroniclers of the iron game.

For further information on Siegmund Klein see his autobiography in *Strength & Health*, "My Quarter Century in the Iron Game," in seventeen monthly installments beginning in March 1944. See also David Chapman, "Gallery of Ironmen: Siegmund Klein," *Ironman* 49.7 (July 1990), 90.

18. Jessie H. Hirschl, "The Great White City," *American Heritage* 12.6 (Oct. 1960), 9.

19. Ibid., 18.

20. Ibid., 9.

21. Walter Besant, "A First Impression," *The Cosmopolitan* 15.5 (Sept. 1893), 533.

22. Charles Higham, *Ziegfeld* (Chicago: Regnery, 1972), 2–4.

23. Ibid., 11.

24. Ibid., 7–9.

25. Ibid., 11.

26. Patricia Ziegfeld, *The Ziegfelds' Girl: Confessions of an Abnormally Happy Childhood* (Boston: Little, Brown, 1964), 35–36.

27. Higham, *Ziegfeld,* 12.

28. Trocadero program, July 24–27, 1893, in Chicago Historical Society.

29. Ibid.

30. Higham, *Ziegfeld,* 13–14.

31. *New York Dramatic Mirror* 30.763 (Aug. 12, 1893), 4.

32. Ibid., 30.769 (Sept. 23, 1893), 14.

33. John Burke, *Duet in Diamonds* (New York: Putnam, 1972), 86.

34. Sandow, *Strength and How to Obtain It,* 130.

35. Burke, *Duet in Diamonds,* 87.

36. The photograph is in the author's collection.

37. Higham, *Ziegfeld,* 14.

38. Louis A. Pike, "Al Treloar: Iron Man of Strength and Health," *Strength & Health,* Feb. 1949, 37.

39. Earle Liederman, "Episodes of Eugen Sandow's Private Life," *Muscle Power* 16.4 (Oct. 1953), 54.

40. Al Treloar, quoted in Ernest E. Coffin, "The Great Sandow," part 4, *Your Physique* 4.6 (Feb./Mar. 1945), 50. For additional biographical information on Al Treloar, see Webster, *Barbells and Beefcake,* 42–43.

41. Quoted in Harry Paschal, "Behind the Scenes," *Strength & Health,* Feb. 1946, 35.

42. Paul Bourget, *Outre-Mer: Impressions of America* (New York: Scribners, 1895), 61.

43. James Laver, *Manners and Morals in the Age of Optimism, 1848–1914* (New York: Harper and Row, 1966), 197.

44. Haley, *Healthy Body and Victorian Culture,* 137–38.

45. Roberta J. Park, "Physiology and Anatomy Are Destiny!?: Brains, Bodies and Exercise in Nineteenth Century American Thought," *Journal of Sport History* 18 (Spring 1991), 55.

46. Benjamin Rader, *American Sports: From the Age of Folk Games to the Age of Spectators* (Englewood Cliffs, N.J.: Prentice-Hall, 1983), 102–3. For additional information about Jack Johnson, see Randy Roberts, *Papa Jack: Jack Johnson and*

the Era of White Hopes (New York: Free Press, 1983). Comparisons with that other manly paragon, John L. Sullivan, were perhaps inevitable. In 1893, an early practitioner of sports medicine, Dr. Ramon Guiteras, was quoted as saying that Sandow was "so far as mere strength is concerned, far superior. He is also much quicker than the pugilist, but he has not the knowledge of boxing that Sullivan has, and it is a question whether he has the mental qualities and nervous strength that combined to make Sullivan a fighter." Quoted in "Reign of Sandow, 'Perfect Man,' " 14.

47. W. Arthur Long, "The Sandow Story," *British Amateur Weightlifter and Bodybuilder,* Apr. 1951, 14.

48. Hunter McLean, quoted in Paschal, "Behind the Scenes," 36.

49. Otis Skinner, *Footlights and Spotlights* (Indianapolis: Bobbs-Merrill, 1924), 209.

50. Liederman, "Episodes of Eugen Sandow's Private Life," 54.

51. Roger Austin, "Flo Ziegfeld's Blond Bodybuilder," *San Francisco Sunday Examiner/Chronicle,* June 4, 1978, magazine section, 32.

52. Liederman, "Episodes of Eugen Sandow's Private Life," 54.

53. Higham, *Ziegfeld,* 15.

54. Henry Adams, *The Education of Henry Adams* (New York: Modern Library, 1931). Although the dynamos made the greatest impression on Adams at the 1900 Paris Exhibition, he also mentions wandering among the machinery at the Chicago World's Fair. "One lingered long among the dynamos," he wrote, "for they were new, and they gave to history a new phase" (p. 342).

Ironically, Sandow and Adams might have crossed paths in Paris once more, for Sandow was again performing there. This time the strongman was at the Casino Music Hall while the historian was devising his theories and philosophies.

55. *New York Dramatic Mirror* 30.776 (Nov. 11, 1893), 7.

Chapter 5: The Tour of America, 1894–96

1. *New York Dramatic Mirror* 30.776 (Nov. 11, 1893), 7.

2. *New York Times,* Aug. 9, 1894, 5, col. 1.

3. For further information on the origins of vaudeville, see Peter Leslie, *A Hard Act to Follow: A Music Hall Review* (New York: Paddington, 1978).

4. For more information on the day-to-day operations of a vaudeville theater, see Marian Spitzer, "The Business of Vaudeville," *Saturday Evening Post* 196 (May 24, 1924), 125.

5. Robert Taft, *Photography and the American Scene* (New York: Macmillan, 1938), 346ff.

6. Ben L. Bassham, *The Theatrical Photographs of Napoleon Sarony* (Kent, Ohio: Kent State University Press, 1978), 14, 20.

7. Unidentified clipping (probably from a Pittsburgh newspaper), dated Oct. 8, 1894, from New York Public Library collection.

8. H. P. M., "The Latest Society Fad," unidentified clipping (*Harper's Weekly*?) from New York Public Library collection.

9. *Police Gazette* 63.891 (Jan. 27, 1894).

10. For a discussion of matinee girls and their male counterparts, stage-door Johnnies, see Banner, *American Beauty,* 179–80.

11. Otto Arco, "A Tribute to Bobby Pandour—Part II" in *Strength & Health,* Feb. 1942, 28; also see David Chapman "Gallery of Ironmen: Bobby Pandour," *Ironman* 50.7 (July 1991), 74.

12. Lionel Strongfort, *Do It with Muscle!* (Newark, N.J.: Strongfort Institute, 1924), 44.

13. *New York Dramatic Mirror* 31.897 (Mar. 17, 1894), 4.

14. For an excellent account of the earliest days of motion pictures, see Paul C. Spehr, *The Movies Begin: Making Movies in New Jersey 1887–1920* (Newark, N.J.: Newark Museum, 1977).

15. Quoted in Gordon Hendricks, *Edison, Motion Picture Myth* (Berkeley: University of California Press, 1961).

16. Dickson's copy now in the author's collection.

17. *New York Dramatic Mirror* 32.901 (Apr. 28, 1894), 3.

18. Austin, "Flo Ziegfeld's Blond Bodybuilder," 31.

19. Ibid., 32.

20. Alan Calvert, "Eugen Sandow: An Appreciation," *Klein's Bell* 2.1 (June 1932), 4.

21. Austin, "Flo Ziegfeld's Blond Bodybuilder," 32.

22. E. Lawrence Levy, *The Autobiography of an Athlete* (Birmingham: Hammond, [1913]), 47.

23. Edmond Desbonnet, "Comment Louis Cyr prouva à Cyclops et Montgomery qu'il était réellement champion du monde," *La Santé par les Sports* 3.32 (Jan. 8, 1913), 249.

24. Oscar Lewis and Caroll Hall, *Bonanza Inn* (New York: Knopf, 1949), 305.

25. *San Francisco Chronicle,* May 18, 1894, 12, col. 2.

26. Austin, "Flo Ziegfeld's Blond Bodybuilder," 33.

27. Ibid., 33.

28. *San Francisco Chronicle,* May 19, 1894, 5, col. 1.

29. E. Lawrence Levy, "Reminiscences of a Strong Man," *Apollo's Magazine* 1.5 (Nov. 1903), 198. Irving Montgomery was born Aug. 21, 1864, in Edgbaston, near Birmingham. In 1882 he joined the Coldstream Guards, and in 1884 he was ordered to Egypt with his regiment to try to rescue General Gordon. When he came back to England, Montgomery became an instructor of gymnastics to the officers and privates of the Guards. He left the service in 1887 and returned to Birmingham, where he eventually fell in with Sampson and Cyclops. This according to an undated clipping from the *National Police Gazette* (?) in the author's collection.

30. Sandow, "My Reminiscences," 170.

31. The announcement is in the Posters collection of the California Historical Society, San Francisco.

There had always been a strong interest in California in bizarre animal combats. Probably the most notable fight of this sort occurred in 1851. A grizzly bear and a bull were let loose in a ring at San Jose, and the resultant excitement ran so high that the entire state legislature adjourned to witness the slaughter. See John Rickards Betts, *America's Sporting Heritage 1850–1950* (Reading, Mass.: Addison-Wesley, 1974), 25.

32. *San Francisco Chronicle,* May 21, 1894, 14.
33. Ibid., May 22, 1894, 14.
34. Ibid., May 23, 1894, 14.
35. *Morning Call,* May 22, 1894, 10.
36. *San Francisco Chronicle,* May 23, 1894, 14.
37. Gaudreau, *Anvils, Horseshoes, and Cannons,* 44.
38. *San Francisco Chronicle,* May 23, 1894, 14.
39. Sandow, "My Reminiscences," 171.
40. Sandow, *Strength and How to Obtain It,* 141.
41. *Los Angeles Times,* June 3, 1894, 10.
42. Sandow, *Strength and How to Obtain It,* 141.
43. *Los Angeles Herald,* June 2, 1894, 3.
44. *Los Angeles Times,* June 4, 1894, 8.
45. In a later bout of self-criticism, Sandow was quoted by *Strength* magazine in June 1917 as remarking wistfully, "If my legs were an inch and a half longer, I would be the finest proportioned man in the world" (clipping in Todd-McLean Collection, University of Texas).
46. The photograph is in Hoblitzelle Theatre Arts Library, University of Texas.
47. *San Francisco Examiner,* June 20, 1894, 16.
48. Higham, *Ziegfeld,* 16.
49. Sandow, *Strength and How to Obtain It,* 141.
50. *New York Times,* Aug. 9, 1894, 5, col. 1.
51. *New York Dramatic Mirror* 32.816 (Aug. 18, 1894), 3.
52. Quoted in "Notes of the Month," *Sandow's Magazine* 6 (1901), 445.
53. Ibid., 445.
54. Quoted in "How the World Went Mad over Sandow's Muscles," *Literary Digest* 87.5 (Oct. 31, 1925), 48.
55. Itinerary can be traced through the pages of the *New York Dramatic Mirror* for 1894–95.
56. Quoted in "Reign of Sandow, 'Perfect Man,'" 14.
57. Eugen Sandow, "How to Preserve Health and Attain Strength," *The Cosmopolitan* 17 (June 1894), 175. The truth about Sandow's attitude toward diet is probably best recorded in Arthur W. A. Long's article "The Sandow Story," part 2, *British Amateur Weightlifter and Bodybuilder,* June 1951, 23: "Sandow never dieted. He ate what and when he fancied and applied a good knife and fork. He was fond of his glass of wine, too, but as in most things he was moderate, so he was in this."
58. Sandow, *Strength and How to Obtain It,* 146.
59. *New York Dramatic Mirror* 32.807 (June 16, 1894), 4.
60. Ibid., 35.895 (Feb. 29, 1896), 19.

61. Ibid., 35.902 (Apr. 11, 1896), 19.

62. Higham, *Ziegfeld*, 18.

63. Ibid., 218.

64. Several decades after his burial, Ziegfeld's body was moved from California to New York, where it currently rests.

65. Billie Burke, *With a Feather on My Nose* (New York: Appleton Century-Crofts, 1949), 139.

66. *New York Dramatic Mirror* 35.905 (May 2, 1896), 20.

67. Quoted in Gordon Hendricks, *Beginnings of Biograph* (New York: Beginnings of the American Film, 1964), 40.

68. Terry Ramsaye, *A Million and One Nights: A History of the Motion Picture* (New York: Simon and Schuster, 1926), 255. Sandow was destined to pose for one further set of motion pictures. According to Professor Edmond Desbonnet, in 1900 Sandow and he both took the opportunity to be photographed by Dr. Étienne-Jules Marey's Chronophotograph. This was a wicked looking invention that resembled a large rifle. It was actually a harmless photo-gun that took sequential pictures when the trigger was pulled. In this way, the photographer was able to register motion. The images that were thus recorded were crude to say the least. The moving subjects were bunched together in a series of multiple exposures giving the illusion of motion. Unfortunately, Sandow's portrait has never surfaced, so it is impossible to say what he was doing while being chronophotographed (holograph letter from Edmond Desbonnet to Gerard Nisivoccia, Aug. 29, 1948, in the author's collection).

69. Sandow, *Life Is Movement*, 425.

70. Ibid., 426.

71. Harry Paschal, "Behind the Scenes" in *Strength & Health*, Oct. 1945, 22.

72. Sandow, *Life Is Movement*, 426.

Chapter 6: A Growing Business, 1897–1901

1. Adam, *Sandow's System of Physical Training*, 27.

2. Sandow, *Strength and How to Obtain It*, 2d ed. (c. 1900), 35.

3. Mark Berry, *Physical Training Simplified: The Complete Science of Muscular Development* (Philadelphia: Milo Publishing Co., 1930), 219–20. Not all working-class lads had access to gymnasiums, and often those who did could not afford even the most modest fees. The answer was to work out on one's own using whatever material was available. This was not very satisfactory, so many young men banded together to form weightlifting clubs, and by pooling their resources, they were able to purchase equipment and supplies. For more information on working-class clubs and their formation, see F. W. Rabenau, "The Plaistow Physical Culture Club: Its Origin and Growth," *Strong Man* 1.4 (May 1923), 77–78.

4. "Sandow Curative Treatment by *Truth*'s Investigator" (London: Sandow's Institute of Physical Culture, c. 1911), 18.

5. Sandow, *Strength and How to Obtain It*, 2d ed., 30.

6. Eugen Sandow, *Body-Building, or Man in the Making* (London: Gale & Polden, 1905), 42.

7. Ibid., 42.

8. Bernard Rudofsky, *The Unfashionable Human Body* (New York: Prentice Hall, 1986), 182.

9. Sydney Blow, *Through Stage Doors* (Edinburgh: Chambers, 1958), 64.

10. Blow, *Through Stage Doors,* 64–65.

11. Gaudreau, *Anvils, Horseshoes, and Cannons,* 2:11.

12. William Oliphant, "Arthur Saxon, Strong Man of Germany," *Strength & Health,* May 1936, 11.

13. Gaudreau, *Anvils, Horseshoes, and Cannons,* 2:11.

14. "Sandow and the Saxons" in *Sandow's Magazine* 6 (1901), 149.

15. "Sandow and the Saxons," *Sandow's Magazine* 6 (1901), 149–50.

16. Levy, *Autobiography of an Athlete,* 112.

17. Gaudreau, *Anvils, Horseshoes, and Cannons,* 2:13.

18. Ibid., 2:11.

19. Alan Carse, "Saxon vs. Sandow," *Strength & Health,* July 1942, 13, 35.

20. Editorial, *Sandow's Magazine* 1 (1898), 7.

21. In 1902 Desbonnet began *L'Education Physique;* in 1904 he established his most famous magazine, *La Culture Physique;* and in 1911 he started *La Santé par les Sports.* Later he claimed to have produced physical culture magazines since 1896, though this was not strictly true. For a fuller account of Desbonnet's career, see Georges Dardenne, *Historique de la Culture Physique* (Ayeneux, Belgium: by the author, 1986), 29–39.

22. David Webster, "Bernarr Macfadden," *Muscle Mag International* (Summer 1975), 20–21.

23. Much has been written about the flamboyant Macfadden. Probably the most accessible is Robert Ernst, *Weakness Is a Crime: The Life of Bernarr Macfadden* (Syracuse, N.Y.: Syracuse University Press, 1990). Another good source is Ben Yagoda's "The True Story of Bernarr Macfadden," *American Heritage* 33.1 (Dec. 1981), 22. But also see Jan Todd, "Bernarr Macfadden: Reformer of Feminine Form," *Journal of Sport History* (Spring 1987), 61.

24. "My New Scheme," *Sandow's Magazine* 2 (1899), 27.

25. "My Scheme," *Sandow's Magazine* 2 (1899), 301.

26. "Sandow Curative Treatment by *Truth's* Investigator," 5.

27. Both quoted in Haley, *Healthy Body and Victorian Culture,* 123–24.

28. Ibid., 136.

29. Untitled anecdote, *Sandow's Magazine* 17 (1906), 801.

30. Thomas Hughes, *Tom Brown at Oxford* (London: Macmillan, 1880), 99.

31. Thomas Hughes, *Tom Brown's School Days,* part 2, chap. 5 (New York: Sears, 1920), 180–81.

32. Benjamin Rader, *American Sports* (Englewood Cliffs, N.J.: Prentice-Hall, 1983), 151.

33. G. P. Horne, "Muscular Christianity," *Sandow's Magazine* 2 (1899), 172.

34. H. X. Yoxhall, "Has Christianity Anything to Do with Sports?" *Health & Strength* 4.6 (June 1902), 304.

35. For further information on muscular Christianity and its effects on sport, see Guy Lewis, "The Muscular Christianity Movement," *Journal of Health, Physical Education and Recreation* 37.5 (May 1966), 27ff. Mark Girouard's *The Return to Camelot: Chivalry and the English Gentleman* (New Haven: Yale University Press, 1981) has much useful information on Kingsley and Hughes. Walter Houghton's *The Victorian Frame of Mind* (New Haven: Yale University Press, 1957) is indispensable in its discussion of force.

36. R. L. Bellamy, *Hints from Sandow* (London: Church Army, 1899), 42.

37. Adam, *Sandow's System of Physical Training*, 235.

38. David Webster, *Strength Lore and Strands* (Irvine, Scotland: by the author, 1978), 6.

39. *A Few Notes on the Sandow's System of Physical Culture* (n.p. [New York?], n.d. [c. 1900]), 6.

40. Undated Peck & Snyder catalog description, c. 1870.

41. For further information on home exercise, see Harvey Green, *Fit for America: Health, Fitness, Sport, and American Society* (New York: Pantheon, 1986), 195–201. Also see W. A. Pullum, "What the Home Exerciser Owes to Eugen Sandow," *Health & Strength* 63.15 (Aug. 2, 1941), 5.

42. Sandow, *Strength and How to Obtain It*, 2d ed., 16.

43. Ad in *Sandow's Magazine* (Sept. 1901), inside back cover.

44. Edmond Desbonnet, "Comment Sandow charma et conquit l'âme artiste des Parisiens: Où l'émotion artistique l'emporte sur la force brutale," *La Culture Physique* 33.471 (July 1929), 200–204. Desbonnet lists the two other principal members of the conspiracy against Sandow as being Joseph Bonelli and Noel le Gaulois. Like Apollon, these were weightlifters with beefy physiques, not more gracefully formed bodybuilders like Sandow.

45. *Graphic*, June 16, 1900, clipping in Victoria and Albert Museum collection.

46. Shaw Desmond, *London Nights in the Gay Nineties* (New York: McBride, 1928), 141.

47. Holograph letter from Milo Brinn to Attila in Todd-McLean Collection, University of Texas.

48. Stewart Dunbar, "Sandow's Endurance Tested: How the Cast Was Made for the British Museum," *Sandow's Magazine* 7 (1901), 357.

49. "Sandow in Plaster of Paris: A Unique Cast," *The Strand Magazine* 22.130 (Oct. 1901), 461.

50. W. E. St. John Turner, "The Sandow Cast," unpublished typescript dated 1951 based on the account in *The Strand Magazine* and an interview with Paul Ryan, manager of Messrs. Brucciani Ltd., in the author's collection.

51. Visual evidence from original, unretouched photographs taken by Arthur Weston, currently in Public Record Office. These were filed with the PRO in order to copyright them.

52. "Sandow in Plaster of Paris," 468.

53. Ibid., 468.

54. Terry Todd, "The Day Sargent Examined Sandow," *Strength & Health*, June 1965, 54.

55. "Sandow in Plaster of Paris," 462.

56. Ibid.

57. Currently, there are three copies of the British Museum cast that have been made through the years. The original is currently in storage in London. A duplicate was made at Sandow's request and was presented to his friend, Dr. Dudley Sargent, at Harvard University by Sandow himself. This copy has apparently been lost. Repeated attempts to find it by the staff at Harvard have been unsuccessful. The only other cast is in the Weightlifting Hall of Fame in York, Pennsylvania. This version was made for publisher Bob Hoffman by taking impressions from the original cast in London.

58. *Cincinnati Enquirer,* Jan. 15, 1908, clipping in the Billy Rose Theatre Collection, New York Public Library.

59. S. Lefe, *The Health of the People* (London: Gollancz, 1950), 77–78.

60. Howard D. Kramer, "Beginnings of the Public Health Movement in the United States," *Bulletin of the History of Medicine* (May-June 1947), 358.

61. Ibid., 355–56.

62. *Historical Statistics of the United States: Colonial Times to 1970* (Washington, D.C.: Bureau of Census, 1975), 15.

63. Kramer, "Beginnings of the Public Health Movement," 366.

64. James Morris, *Pax Britannica: The Climax of an Empire* (New York: Harcourt Brace Jovanovich, 1980), 218.

65. See Roberta J. Park, "Healthy, Moral, and Strong: Educational Views of Exercise and Athletics in Nineteenth-Century America," in *Fitness in American Culture: Images of Health, Sport, and the Body, 1830–1940,* ed. Kathryn Grover (Amherst: University of Massachusetts Press, 1989), 123–68.

66. Kramer, "Beginnings of the Public Health Movement," 366.

67. Quoted in Dudley A. Sargent, "The Physical State of the American People," in *The United States of America: A Study of the American Commonwealth* (New York: Appleton, 1894), 454.

68. J. A. Harris, *The Measurement of Man* (Minneapolis: University of Minnesota Press, 1930), 84.

69. Kramer, "Beginnings of the Public Health Movement," 367.

70. Haley, *Healthy Body and Victorian Culture,* 136.

71. "National Physical Education," *Sandow's Magazine* 6 (1901), 324.

72. McIntosh's *Physical Education in England since 1800* contains the best account of the history of physical education. There is also much valuable information in Emmett Rice, *A Brief History of Physical Education* ([New York: Barnes and Co., 1930], 118–23). I was also helped by a letter from Thelma Harrison, British expert on children's development (Harrison to author, June 26, 1982). American physical educators were similarly perplexed about the various, conflicting systems of organized exercise. For a fuller explanation of this "battle of the systems" in the United States, see Park, "Healthy, Moral, and Strong."

73. "National Physical Education," 325.

74. Sandow, *Life Is Movement,* 69.

Chapter 7: Triumphs and Travels, 1901–7

1. "The Great Competition," *Sandow's Magazine* 1 (1898), 79.

2. "La Statuette de l'Athlète Sandow," *La Santé par les Sports* 27.97 (Nov. 1923), 315–16.

3. Dardenne, *Historique de la Culture Physique,* 36.

4. "The Great Competition," *Sandow's Magazine* 2 (1899), 77.

5. "The Great Competition," *Sandow's Magazine* 5 (1900), 398.

6. "The Great Competition," *Sandow's Magazine* 7 (1901), 207.

7. Ibid., 286.

8. Josef Szalay, "The Sandow Competition," *Health & Strength* 3.5 (Nov. 1901), 245.

9. *Sandow's Magazine* 7 (1901), 286.

10. Ibid., 291.

11. *Times* (London), Sept. 16, 1901, 7, col. 3. Are bodybuilding contests really male beauty shows in disguise? Many have thought so both in Sandow's and our own times. Brian Pronger calls physique competitions "homoerotic burlesque," contending that unlike straight burlesque shows, where the erotic message is upfront, "body building exploits gay irony by passing its eroticism off as 'athletic' " (*The Arena of Masculinity: Sports, Homosexuality, and the Meaning of Sex* [New York: St. Martin's Press, 1990], 170).

This is, however, a specious argument. Although girlie shows might appeal to lesbians, that is certainly not their principal audience. The same might be said for bodybuilding contests. Like participants in every other sport, physique athletes can be both gay and straight, and so can the audience.

It must be admitted, however, that male bodybuilders are obviously obsessed with the male body—both their own and their competitors. Does this mean that they are either closet homosexuals or narcissists? Since there has never been any scientific study, this question must be begged for the moment. Until we know for sure what goes on in the secret recesses of a person's mind, it is as fascinating as it is fruitless to speculate.

12. Undated article from *Health & Strength* in the Ottley Coulter scrapbook at the Todd-McLean Collection, University of Texas.

13. For more information on William Murray, see Webster, *Barbells and Beefcake,* 38.

14. Szalay, "Sandow Competition," 245.

15. Webster, *Barbells and Beefcake:* 36–7, 41–2.

16. *New York Dramatic Mirror* 46.1, 191 (Oct. 19, 1901), 18.

17. Ibid.

18. Both quotes from ibid. 47.1, 211 (Mar. 8, 1902), 18.

19. Quoted in Paschal, "Behind the Scenes," 19.

20. Quoted in Webster, *Barbells and Beefcake,* 33.

21. *New York Dramatic Mirror* 47.1, 211 (Mar. 8, 1902), 18.

22. Arthur H. Saxon, *The Life and Art of Andrew Ducrow and the Romantic Age of the English Circus* (Hamden, Conn.: Archon, 1978), 149–51.

23. Jacques Garnier, *Forains d'Hier et d'Aujourd'hui* (Orleans: by the author, 1968), 219–20.

24. Webster, *Barbells and Beefcake,* 56.

25. Charles Smith in a letter to the author (Apr. 14, 1989).

26. Dudley Sargent, letter to the editor, *New York Herald,* undated clipping in New York Public Library, c. 1902

27. Ledyard W. Sargent, ed., *Dudley Allen Sargent: An Autobiography* (Philadelphia: privately published, 1927), 202.

28. Sandow, *Body-Building,* 129.

29. Ibid., 130.

30. Ibid., 132.

31. Quoted in "Mrs. Sandow Interviewed," *Sandow's Magazine* 10 (1903), 419.

32. Sandow, *Body-Building,* 134.

33. Ibid., 135.

34. Quoted in "Sandow on His World's Tour," *Sandow's Magazine* 10 (1903), 185.

35. Sandow, *Body-Building,* 137.

36. Ibid., 138.

37. Ibid., 149.

38. "Mrs. Sandow Interviewed," 420.

39. Sandow, *Body-Building,* 149–50.

40. Ibid., 142.

41. Ibid., 149.

42. Ibid., 144.

43. Ibid., 147.

44. Ibid., 134.

45. Ibid., 150.

46. John Rice, "Perseverance Wins," *Strength & Health,* Apr. 1946, 40.

47. J. M. Hendry, *Body-Building* (Sydney: by the author, n.d. [c. 1930]), 15.

48. Gaudreau, *Anvils, Horseshoes, and Cannons,* 2:42, 79.

49. "Notes of the Month," *Sandow's Magazine* 5 (1900), 369.

50. Webster, *Barbells and Beefcake,* 129.

51. *Sandow's College of Physical Culture* (Boston: Ellis, 1902). This is a lavish, forty-page prospectus for the new school.

52. "Introduction," *Sandow's Magazine* (American ed.) 1 (1903), 5.

53. For further information on the phenomenon of the dime novel, see Walter Evans, "The All American Boys: A Study of Boys' Sport Fiction," *Journal of Popular Culture* (Summer 1972), 104–21.

54. For further information, see Michael Oriard, "Jack London: The Father of American Sports Fiction," *Jack London Newsletter* 11.1 (Jan.-Apr. 1978), 1–11.

55. Green, *Fit for America,* 236–37.

56. "Our Ladies' Page," *Sandow's Magazine* n.s. 14 (1905), 75.

57. "Physical Pars," *Sandow's Magazine* 11 (1903), 14.

58. Quoted in *Sandow's Magazine* 13 (1904), 205.

59. "Sandow in South Africa," *Sandow's Magazine* 13 (1904), 237.

60. Ibid., 238.

61. *New York Clipper,* Mar. 7, 1908, clipping in the Billy Rose Theatre Collection, New York Public Library.

62. Souvenir menu in the author's collection.

63. Tromp van Diggelen, "My Memoirs," *Muscle Power* 15.5 (May 1953), 34.

64. David Willoughby, *The Super-Athletes* (South Brunswick: Barnes, 1970), 172.

65. Edgar Mueller, *Goerner the Mighty* (Leeds: Vulcan, 1951), 34.

66. E. H. Lawrence, "C. G. Pillay—South Africa's Superman," *Superman* 9.3 (Dec. 1938), 71–72. Also see Ray Van Cleef, "Strongmen the World Over" *Strength & Health,* Aug. 1949, 16.

67. "Sandow Returns to England," *Sandow's Magazine* 14 (1905), 335.

68. Ibid., 338.

69. "Eugen Sandow in India," *Sandow's Magazine* 15 (1905), 37.

70. "Sandow in the Indian Press," quoted in *Sandow's Magazine* 15 (1905), 185.

71. Undated reference from *London Standard,* quoted in *Sandow's Magazine* 15 (1905), 57.

72. Bill Hillgardner, "India's Wrestling Supermen," *Strength & Health,* June 1941, 21.

73. S. Muzumdar, "The Great Gama," *Your Physique* 10.4 (Jan. 1949), 8.

74. Robert L. Jones "Wrestling in India," *Strength* 13.7 (Sept. 1928), 29–30. Also see Walter Steinhilber "End of an Epic," *Strength & Health,* Mar. 1961, 29. I have not been able to find any references to the "Gamun Baliwala" in Sandow's account. Perhaps it is a simple misspelling of another name. "Baliwala" seems to be a corrupted form of *pahlwan,* so perhaps the other name is also misinterpreted. Perhaps it refers to the great Gama's elder brother since he also possessed the name "Gama." One thing alone seems clear: since the great Gama was only fourteen when Sandow visited India, it is extremely unlikely that he was the native wrestler mentioned in the strongman's story.

75. Valerie Pakenham, *Out in the Noonday Sun: Edwardians in the Tropics* (New York: Random House, 1985), 169.

76. Sandow, "My Reminiscences," 172.

77. "Sandow Returns to England," *Sandow's Magazine* 14 (1905), 338.

78. "Eugen Sandow in India," 362.

79. Webster, *Barbells and Beefcake,* 122.

80. R. S. Balsekar, "Presenting Professor K. V. Iyer," *Superman* (Apr. 1939), 186. See also David Chapman, "Gallery of Ironmen: Professor K. V. Iyer," *Ironman* 50.3 (Mar. 1991), 68.

81. "Sandow Returns to England," 343.

82. "Eugen Sandow," *Sandow's Magazine* (American ed.) (Jan. 1903), 13.

83. Ibid.

84. Sandow explained the closure this way in *Strength and How to Obtain It,* 4th ed., rev. (1911), 73: "The various schools which I founded in different parts

of the country I decided some time ago to discontinue, because I found it impossible to give to each and all of them that direct personal attention and supervision which I felt was necessary to carry out my propaganda on the lines I had laid down."

85. *Sandow's Magazine* changed from monthly to weekly in January 1905.

86. *Sandow's Magazine* 16.11 (Mar. 22, 1906); 16.12 (Mar. 29, 1906); 17.6 (Aug. 9, 1906).

87. *Sandow's Magazine* 18.7 (Feb. 21, 1907).

88. *Sandow's Magazine* 18.12 (Apr. 25, 1907), 535.

Chapter 8: The Final Years, 1908–25

1. Ernest E. Coffin, "Sandow: The Physical Marvel of the Universe," *Muscle Power* 4.5 (Feb. 1948), 8.

2. Robert J. Devenney, "Stars of the Big Top: Katie Sandwina," *Muscle Power* 3.2 (July 1947), 16.

3. Ray Van Cleef, "Strongmen the World Over," *Strength & Health*, May 1952, 23. Also letter dated June 14, 1989, to the author from Charles Smith, who knew Sandwina and her tavern well. For further information, see David Chapman, "Sisterhood of Strength," *Muscle & Fitness* 45.10 (Oct. 1984), 60, and Chapman, "Gallery of Ironmen: Kate Sandwina" *Ironman* 49.6 (June 1990), 90.

For a good general discussion of strongwomen including Kate Sandwina, see Lothar Groth, *Die Starken Männer: Eine Geschichte der Kraftakrobatik* (East Berlin: Henschelverlag, 1987), 71–82.

4. Sandow, *Strength and How to Obtain It*, 47.

5. "The Ladies' Pages," *Sandow's Magazine* 4 (1900), 490.

6. George Gordon, Lord Byron, "Childe Harold's Pilgrimage" in *Works of Byron*, ed. Ernest Hartley Coleridge, 12 vols. (London: Murray, 1904), 2:59.

7. Quoted in Fraser Harrison, *The Dark Angel: Aspects of Victorian Sexuality* (New York: Universe, 1978), 30.

8. Quoted in Banner, *American Beauty*, 140.

9. Sandow, *Strength and How to Obtain It*, 43.

10. Ibid., 57.

11. Ibid., 55.

12. Ibid.

13. Stephen Kern, *Anatomy and Destiny: A Cultural History of the Human Body* (Indianapolis: Bobbs-Merrill, 1975), 14.

14. Quoted in Rudofsky, *Unfashionable Human Body*, 182.

15. Sandow, *Strength and How to Obtain It*, 51.

16. "The Symmetrion," *Sandow's Magazine* 14 (1905), 63. According to W. A. Long, the symmetrion was ultimately unsuccessful because it required the clipping on of a belt and was therefore too much trouble; "The Sandow Story," *British Amateur Weightlifter and Bodybuilder* (June 1951), 22.

17. W. S. Gilbert, *Patience*, Act II.

18. David Webster, "A Chronology of Significant Events in the Life of Eugen Sandow," *Iron Game History* 2.4 (Nov. 1992), 18.

19. W. Buchanan-Taylor, *Shake It Again* (London: Heath Cranton, 1947), 181–82.

20. Van Diggelen, "My Memoirs," 34.

21. Quoted in an anonymous review of *Ideal Physical Culture* in *Health & Strength* 2.4 (June 1900), 5. Bankier (Apollo) further explains his opinion of Sandow by ridiculing his rival's reluctance to answer challenges. "[Sandow] has been challenged dozens of times by different athletes, including the writer. He tries to make the public believe that he treats all these challenges with contempt, but the real truth is he is afraid of falling off his pedestal. . . . His self-admiration is truly sublime. Sandow, when on stage, is seen at his best, as he works with his shoulders humped up most of the time, giving the impression that he is massive across the chest. But seen at a close view in his natural state, with the muscles relaxed, he is very disappointing, and not at all the ideal figure he makes himself out to be."

22. Cyclops [Apollo?], "A Criticism of Eugen Sandow," *Apollo's Magazine* 1.11 (May 1904), 398.

23. Webster, *Iron Game*, 22.

24. *Times* (London), July 4, 1908, 15.

25. Green, *Fit for America*, 199.

26. John E. Ruebsam, "Home Gymnasium: A New Invention for the Cure of Chronic Diseases," advertising brochure, 1885.

27. D. L. Dowd, *Physical Culture for Home and School* (New York: Fowler & Wells, 1895) (for further information see David Chapman, "Professor David L. Dowd," *Ironman* 52.5 [May 1993], 143); Anthony Barker, *Physical Culture Simplified* (New York: by the author, 1902); Russell Trall, quoted in Green, *Fit for America*, 183.

28. Lionel Strongfort, *Promotion & Conservation of Health, Strength, & Mental Energy*, advertising booklet, c. 1919.

29. Yagoda, "True Story of Bernarr Macfadden," 24.

30. "Sandow Curative Treatment by *Truth*'s Investigator."

31. Eugen Sandow, "How I Conduct Curative Physical Culture by Correspondence," advertising booklet published by Sandow's Institute of Physical Culture c. 1900.

32. *Toledo Blade*, Apr. 4, 1911, clipping in New York Public Library collection.

33. *Times* (London), July 24, 1909, 12.

34. Untitled clipping from *Police Gazette*, Nov. 31, 1925, in Todd-McLean collection, University of Texas.

35. Unidentified clipping from Ottley Coulter scrapbooks in Todd-McLean Collection, University of Texas.

36. Sandow, *Life Is Movement*, 15.

37. Ibid., 48.

38. Sandow's obituary in *Times* (London), Oct. 15, 1925, 14.

39. Sandow, *Life Is Movement*, 10.

40. Ibid., 52.

41. Ibid., 158, 262, 116.

42. Ibid., 410, 384, 386.

43. "Sandow Curative Treatment by *Truth*'s Investigator," 29.

44. Sandow, *Strength and How to Obtain It* (11th ed.), 25.

45. *Cincinnati Star,* May 20, 1913, clipping from New York Public Library Collection.

46. Sandow, *Life Is Movement,* caption to photo opposite p. 400.

47. "Sandow Curative Treatment by *Truth*'s Investigator," 29.

48. Earle Liederman, "Sandow: My Impressions When First We Met," *Muscle Power* 1.3 (Apr.-May 1945), 26–31.

49. Ad for Liederman's course in *Strength* 9.11 (Jan. 1925), 66.

50. Liederman, "Sandow: My Impressions," 31.

51. Ibid.

52. Earle Liederman, "More about Sandow," *Muscle Power* 7.4 (Mar. 1949), 38–39.

53. Obituaries in *Times* (London), *New York Times,* and *Springfield Union;* all from Oct. 15, 1925.

54. Desbonnet, "Eugène Sandow, le Sans-Pareil," 355.

55. Interview of Joe Assirati conducted by author in London, Aug. 29, 1987.

56. As indicated on death certificate, General Register Office, Somerset House, London.

57. W. A. Pullum, "The Editor Discourses," *Strong Man* 3.10 (Oct. 1925), 183.

58. Liederman, "More about Sandow," 38.

59. Ziegfeld, *Ziegfelds' Girl: Confessions of an Abnormally Happy Childhood,* 174.

60. Holograph note from Helen Sandow Strong to an unnamed correspondent, in the author's collection.

61. *Times* (London), Oct. 16, 1925.

62. Interview with Joe Assirati, Aug. 29, 1987. Mr. Assirati admits he may have been mistaken about seeing Launceston Elliot. There is a distant possiblity that the former Olympic lifter was at the services, but since he emigrated to Australia in 1923, the chances are not good.

63. H. W. Couzens, letter to the editor, *Health & Strength* 51.20 (Nov. 12, 1932), 580.

64. Gaudreau, *Anvils, Horseshoes, and Cannons,* 2:66.

65. *Times* (London), Dec. 31, 1925.

66. I am indebted to Mr. Christopher Davies of Sheffield, England, Eugen Sandow's great-grandson, for the information about his grandmother, Lorraine. To the best of my knowledge, all immediate members of the Sandow family are deceased.

67. David D. Gilmore, *Manhood in the Making: Cultural Concepts of Masculinity* (New Haven: Yale University Press, 1990), 222–23.

68. Ibid., 229.

69. Donald J. Mrozek, *Sport and American Mentality, 1880–1910* (Knoxville: University of Tennessee Press, 1983), 222.

70. Edwin A. Goewey, "How Good Were the Old-Time Strong Men?" *Muscle Builder* 5.1 (Mar. 1926), 25.

71. J. H. Nurse, "The Truth about Sandow," *Health & Strength* 50.39 (Mar. 5, 1932), 261.

72. Bob Hoffman, "How Good Was Sandow?" *Strength & Health,* June 1960, 28.

73. Sandow's obituary in *New York World,* quoted in *Literary Digest* 87.5 (Oct. 31, 1925), 47.

Afterword

1. According to the directors of Putney Vale Cemetery, the stone was arranged and paid for through the generosity of Thomas Manly, author of the novel *For the Love of Eugen.* See the bibliography for a complete citation.

2. Anonymous article in *Le Biceps: Journal mensuel s'occupant de tous les sports athlétiques: lutte, boxe, etc,* 1/1, (January 1900), 3. Apparently, the publication lasted for only a year before it folded. *L'union fait la force* is Belgium's motto since the nation combines two distinct linguistic groups, the Flemish and the French.

3. Edmond Desbonnet, "Sandow, comblé de gloire, d'honneur et d'argent, partit en pélerinage aux lieux qui furent témoins de sa jeunesse difficile où il fut abondonné, désemparé et malheureux," *La Culture Physique* 51/645 (October 1947), 6–8.

4. "Sandow Speaks" *The Sporting Life* (London), undated, unpaginated clipping in the Louis Cyr scrapbook in the collection at l'Université du Québec à Montréal. Since the article later indicates that Cyr was performing at the South London Music Hall, the article must have appeared around January 1892.

5. A. Zucca, *Acrobatica e atletica* (1902), as quoted in Livio Toschi, *Cento anni di storia 1902–2002* (Rome: FIJLKAM) 157. Bartoletti is also described as "Of medium stature, he appeared however to have a thick massive structure, although he was also agile and dexterous. He also performed in balancing acts. To whom did he owe his education, to whom the rudiments of wrestling? A mystery! He was, in all probability, a child of natural talents who grew up in a family of acrobats and gymnasts." G. Mantovani, *Così si diventa campioni* (1934), quoted in *Cento anni di storia,* 11.

6. Unnamed article in the publication *Il Littoriale* (June 10, 1929), quoted in *Cento anni di storia,* 12. Bartoletti's words are recorded in Roman dialect rather than standard Italian, probably to show that he was an unsophisticated person.

7. "Sandow at the Tivoli," *The Daily Graphic* (London), September 30, 1891, unpaginated photocopy from the collection of David Horne. Although his name is not given, the pianist that is mentioned was perhaps Sandow's good friend, Martinus Sieveking.

8. Edmond Desbonnet, "L'athlète Sandow et le tailleur" in *La Culture Physique,* 8/152 (May 1, 1911), 296–98.

9. "Anatomy and Art, A Lecture on Sandow," *The Daily Graphic* (London) December 17, 1891, 9.

10. Unnamed article from *The Music Hall and Theatre Review*, February 20, 1892.

11. "Sandow Speaks," *The Sporting Life* (London), undated, unpaginated clipping in the Louis Cyr scrapbook in the collection at l'Université du Québec à Montréal. Mrs. Sandow is also mentioned in a report in *The Sporting Life* of January 26, 1891 where she attended Britain's first major weightlifting competition held at the Café Monaco, Piccadilly. She is described as wearing "ear-rings of enormous size, a brooch equally large and finger rings in lustrous diamonds, but above all a superb diamond half moon which she wore in the front of her terra cotta dress." Her gaudy figure must have attracted as much attention as her "husband's." Quoted in David Webster, *The Iron Game: An illustrated history of weight-lifting* (Irvine, Scotland: private) 1976, 14. When I first wrote about this event in the main text of Sandow's biography, I assumed that the writer of the article must have made a mistake, but now I realize that "Mrs. Sandow" must have been familiar to sporting men in London in the early 1890s.

12. MACROBUTTON HtmlResAnchor http://www.ellisislandrecords.org/ There are several significant errors on the passenger record. Sandow's ethnicity is given as "England" and his place of residence is supposedly Bremen. His age is recorded as thirty-four (not his real age of twenty-six years). The record for his return trip from Liverpool on December 2, 1893 is more accurate, but it lists neither a place of residence nor a marital status.

13. "The 'Strong Man' Appears," *The New York Times*, June 12, 1893.

14. "Summer Theatre Bills," *The New York Times*, June 13, 1893.

15. Hjalmar Lundin, *On the Mat and Off: Memoirs of a Wrestler* (New York: Albert Bonnier) 1937, 13. The powerful Swede later became a successful wrestler.

16. "Cyr is the Champion," *New York Herald*, April 11, 1894. Clipping in the Louis Cyr scrapbook in the collection at l'Université du Québec à Montréal.

17. Richard and Paulette Ziegfeld, *The Ziegfeld Touch: The Life and Times of Florenz Ziegfeld, Jr.* (New York: Abrams) 1993, 26.

18. "La Famille Sandow," *La Culture Physique* 6/103 (April 15, 1909), 272. Desbonnet erroneously dates the episode as happening "about ten years ago," but it must have occurred (if it happened at all) closer to fifteen years earlier.

According to Chris Davies, the real story of his grandparents' meeting was much more prosaic. Sandow saw a photograph of his future wife in the shop window of the family's photography studio, and determined to make her acquaintance. The strongman's courtship was much more conventional than in the story he fed to Desbonnet many years later.

The issue of LCP is dedicated to the Anglo-German athlete. Sandow, his wife, and two children all adorn the cover of this issue; the cover photos are titled "La Famille idéale." Desbonnet says Mrs. Sandow recognizes the need for physical exercise and that Helen Sandow "looks surprisingly like her father." The entire family exercises daily, and the children each have little exercises and spring-dumbbells engraved with their names on them.

19. In a letter to the sporting editor of the *State Journal*, Lincoln, Nebraska, Sieveking discusses his dedication to physical fitness. He invites McIntyre, a boxer, to train with him and announces the impending visit of Eugen Sandow to Lincoln for exhibitions and a lecture at the university. In letters to Will Owen Jones, editor of the *Lincoln State Journal*, Sieveking emphasizes the importance of practice, notes his memorization of sixty pieces, discusses his physical training regimen, and mentions a planned cycling tour of Holland. The letter is not precisely dated, but it must be from 1895. Martinus Sieveking Letters in the Clifton Waller Barrett Library, Albert H. and Shirley Small Special Collections Library, University of Virginia, Charlottesville, Virginia.

20. MACROBUTTON HtmlResAnchor http://www.sandowmuseum.com/page18.html According to Hans Brofeldt in his site *Piano Music for the Left Hand Alone*, "Unfortunately Harold C. Schoenberg (in his otherwise marvellous book: *The Great Pianists*) contributes to the rumor that one Martinus Sieveking—(The Flying Dutchman) had the stupendous reach of two octaves, but in Sieveking's own words this was not true. It was in fact *only* an octave and a half." MACROBUTTON HtmlResAnchor http://hjem.get2net.dk/Brofeldt/ The "Dead Weight" principle is discussed in *Piano Mastery*, (New York: Frederick A. Stokes), 1917 second series.

I am grateful to Mr. Norman Stavely of Hull, England for alerting me to the reference to Sieveking in Hilton's novel *Lost Horizon*.

Paul Sieveking writes in *History of the Sievekings: A Memoir* (London: Fortean Times, 1986) that Martinus was only distantly related to a more successful branch of the Dutch family that had emigrated to Britain. For example, Sir Edward Sieveking had become physician in ordinary to Queen Victoria and was very prominent in English society. Martinus was the son of a poor Dutch music master, and when he first arrived in London in 1891, he passed himself off variously as Sir Edward's cousin or nephew in order to get an entrée into polite society. They young man was eventually found out and banished from playing in the city's important salons. One snobbish (or perhaps honest) member of the family dismissed Martinus as "socially lacking but a good accompanyist."

After returning to Europe from his tour with Sandow, Martinus's career gathered some needed momentum. He began to play regularly at the posh Grosvenor Gallery Club in Bond Street and other venues in the British capital. In later years, the young man toured and concertized all over Europe and reportedly had many admirers. On June 17, 1899 he eloped with one of these, a young lady that he had met in Vienna. They were married in Holland and honeymooned in England. I am grateful to Chris Davies for supplying photocopies from Paul Sieveking's book.

Passenger manifests at the Ellis Island website indicate that Sieveking arrived in New York in January of 1916 from Rotterdam.

Because Sieveking moved to Pasadena around 1920, there is a good chance that he did so for health reasons since the region's mild winters and dry climate were thought to help those suffering from consumption and other ailments.

21. See John D'Emilio and Estelle B. Freedman, *Intimate Matters: A History of Sexuality in America* (New York: Harper), 1988, 121–30. Also see *Walt Whitman's America: A Cultural Biography* (New York: Knopf) 1995, 391–403 for the lengths which some homosexuals (like Whitman) would go to cover up or gloss over their true feelings.

On the sexuality of modern bodybuilders (who have to deal with many of the same issues as their predecessors), see Alan M. Klein's groundbreaking work *Little Big Men: Bodybuilding Subculture and Gender Construction* (Albany: State University of NY Press) 1993.

22. "Leon W. Washburn's All New Enormous Railroad Shows" herald in the collection of the Circus World Museum, Baraboo, Wisconsin.

23. "Sandow Would Rather Pose" as reported in *The New York Herald,* April 11, 1894. Clipping in the Louis Cyr scrapbook in the collection at l'Université du Québec à Montréal. Historian Leo Gaureau discusses the question of whether Sandow was in the U.S. prior to 1893 in his book *Anvils, Horseshoes and Cannons,* II/50–52, but he concludes that this could not have been the case. A second well known strongman, Adolph Nordquest who was another of Attila's protetégés, billed himself as "Young Sandow" and performed under this name 1910–15.

Another athlete who appropriated the strongman's name was the German wrestler Paul Petra Sandow whose only claim to fame today is that he was featured in a primitive film. Max and Emil Sklandowsky recorded a very brief match between "Greiner and Sandow" in his early compilation, *Wintergarten-Programm* of 1895. Listed in Dr. Barrett Hodsdon, *The Dawn of Cinema 1894–1914* (Sydney: Museum of Contemporary Art) 1996, 27.

24. W. K. L. Dickson and Antonia Dickson, *History of the Kinetograph, Kinetoscope and Kinetophonograph* (New York: privately printed) 1895, 33–37. According to Richard and Paulette Ziegfeld in *The Ziegfeld Touch,* "Given [Florenz Ziegfeld's] later public statements decrying the film industry's influence, it is ironic that Ziegfeld was one of the first theatrical producers to become involved with the film medium," 27.

25. Lucius Beebe, *Boston and the Boston Legend* (NY: D. Appleton Century) 1935, 176. Mrs. Gardner's mansion near the Fens is today a wonderful art gallery. She was such an interesting, vivacious person, one wants to believe the story despite the evidence against it.

26. *The Daily News* (Chicago), January 19, 1895.

27. "Sandow the Strong," *The Baltimore American and Commercial Advertiser,* April 21, 1895.

28. "Sandow's Secret of Great Strength," *Leslie's Weekly* (New York), XCVIII, 2523, January 14, 1904, 34.

29. "King of Strong Men," *The Baltimore Sun,* October 22, 1894, 10. One part of the strongman's advice rang just as true then as now: "Many will say that they have no time for systematic exercise. This is rarely true. The truth

of the matter is that they cannot take time from their many pleasures and pastimes to think about it."

30. "Muscle of Women," *The Baltimore Sun*, October 26, 1894, 8.

31. "Gilmore's Auditorium," *The Philadelphia Evening Item* (Sunday Item), February 17, 1895.

32. "King of Strong Men," *The Baltimore Sun*, October 22, 1894, 10. According to Chris Davies, Blanche never did any housework even when she had a house. She was raised to be a wealthy society lady and would never have thought of doing any physical labor around the home. Blanche became incapacitated after Eugen's death and eventually had to be hospitalized for mental instability; her psychological state was such that she could not or would not even bring herself to sign important financial documents after her husband's death. Perhaps it was for this reason (rather than some animus for Eugen's philandering) that accounts for the lack of a monument on her husband's grave. Her death certificate states that Blanche Brookes Sandow died of cardiovascular degeneration and arteriosclerosis on August 7, 1959 at Redhill House, a nursing home in north London.

33. "A Chat with Sandow," *The Baltimore American and Commercial Advertiser*, October 22, 1894, 3.

34. "King of Strong Men," *The Baltimore Sun*, October 22, 1894, 10. Eustace Miles was understandably outraged by Sandow's comments about cigars and the necessity of cold baths after heavy exercise. Such advice is "ignorant and misleading; such verdicts should always be given as personal experiences. Directly a man begins to dictate to the world on such matters, we must at once condemn him; his data are insufficient." *Cassell's Physical Educator*, 283.

35. "Sandow and the Trocadero Vaudevilles," *The Philadelphia Press*, February 17, 1895, 12.

36. Quoted in "Gilmore's Auditorium," *Philadelphia Evening Item*, October 7, 1894.

37. Caroline Thomas de la Peña, *The Body Electric: How Strange Machines Built the Modern American* (New York: NY University Press) 2003, 68.

38. *The Ziegfeld Touch*, 28. This date was nearly three months prior to the normal end of the season.

39. T. H. L., *The Sketch* (London), December 2, 1896, 244. The report states that Eugen and Blanche were married by the Venerable Archdeacon Sinclair and that the child (erroneously reported as a boy) was four weeks old. Helen Eugenie Sandow was born October 6, 1896 and Fanny Lorraine Sandow was born June 11, 1903.

40. "Sandow Lectures Australians," *Sunday Times* (Melbourne) July 9, 1902, 5.

41. "Erste Athletenschule in Deutschland," *Kraft und Gewandtheit* (Munich) 10/20, 1901, 2.

42. "Vorwort zur vierten Auflage," *Sandow-Heft, Sonder-Heft der Zeitschrift*, Kraft und Schönheit (Berlin), no date (circa 1906), 1.

43. "Eugen Sandow," *Sandow-Heft*, 4.

44. *Kraft und wie man sie erlangt* was first published by Kraft und Schönheit

press (the same company that produced the *Sandow-Heft*. Later the book was produced by Gustav Möckel. Sandow's book received some good reviews in Germany, but they were not universally enthusiastic. J. Marcuse in *Zeitschrift für diätetische und physakalische Therapie* [Journal of Diatetic and Physical Therapy] (October 1905) remarks "Although he lacks precise scientific information and his frequent digressions interrupt the text, the little book is exceptionally readable; moreover, it reveals to energetic readers systematic methodology so that they might turn themselves into Greek gods."

45. *Verzeichnis der jenigen Herren, welche sich am Sandow-Kursus beteiligen* (1906), Nachlass Carl Diem, Sporthochschule Köln, Mappe 751. This remarkable manuscript document was brought to my attention by Dr. Bernd Wedemeyer who found it in the collection of Carl Diem, German Olympic organizer and founder of the Sporthochschule in Cologne.

46. The attacks on Sandow came from predictable sources such as the strongman's shifty nemesis Charles A. Sampson in *Strength: A Treatise on the Development and Use of Muscle* (Chicago: Rand, McNally) 1895. William Bankier, *Ideal Physical Culture and The Truth About the Strong Man* (London: Greening) 1900, was another of Sandow's former rivals who tried to show the superiority of his own system by taking shots at the Anglo-German strongman.

47. Eustace Miles, *Cassell's Physical Educator* (London: Cassell) 1904, 280–89. The best and most thorough biography of Eustace Miles is Geoffrey Palmer's *Eustace Miles and E.F. Benson: A Friendship* (Harleston: Hermitage) 1992.

48. "Chez les hommes forts," *La Presse*, November 6, 1901, 6. I am indebted to Gilles Janson, special collections librarian at the Université du Québec à Montréal, for locating and sending these references to me.

49. "Les hommes forts," *La Presse*, November 5, 1901, 3.

50. "Chez les hommes forts," *La Presse*, November 6, 1901, 6. Apparently, all was forgotten and forgiven a few years later, for on August 6, 1907 *La Presse* published on page 3 a long, complimentary article about Sandow and his discovery twenty years before of the German giant, Goliath. The author of the piece was Léon Seé, a French sports journalist who often worked for Desbonnet. The piece was apparently lifted from a French newspaper.

51. *The Bulletin* (Melbourne), September 9, 1902. Quoted in "Sandow Looking," Bob Petersen, unpublished lecture, June, 1998. Petersen describes *The Bulletin* as "the bushman's macho bible" and as its audience as "larrikins," i.e. rowdies or rednecks. For this publication to report favorably about Sandow was praise, indeed.

52. "Sandow Lectures Australians," *Sunday Times* (Melbourne), September 7, 1902, 5.

53. *The Gospel of Strength* (Melbourne: T. Shaw Fitchett) 1902, 6.

54. *The Gospel of Strength*, 8. The different connotations of the word "race" are also of utmost importance here. When Howard speaks of the "Australian race," he uses the word in a particularly Edwardian sense.

55. Caroline Daley, *Leisure & Pleasure: Reshaping & Revealing the New Zealand Body 1900–1960* (Auckland: Auckland Univ. Press) 2003.

56. *New York Dramatic Mirror*, April 4, 1903, 20.

57. *New York Dramatic Mirror,* April 18, 1903, 7.

58. *New York Dramatic Mirror,* May 16, 1903, 9.

59. Clippings from a Philadelphia newspaper, only the year (1903) is visible. Items are from the author's collection.

60. *The Scotsman* (Edinburgh), December 22, 1903. Photocopied clipping.

61. *The Theatre Magazine* (London), 2/1, 1906, 54.

62. "John Culme's Footlight Notes—Postcard of the week" MACROBUTTON HtmlResAnchor *www.gabrielleray.150m.com/ArchiveTextM/CarrieMoore. html*

63. "Miss Carrie Moore, The Sandow Girl," *Photo Bits* (London) July 14, 1906, 28–29. The reporter was apparently a little confused about the word "Symmetrion" since he misspells it (*symmentrian*), and obviously doesn't have a clue what it means. Another briefer report of the performance is given in "La culture physique au théâtre," *La Culture Physique* (Paris) 11/216, January 1, 1914, 19.

Although the chronology is a bit unclear, it appears that Carrie Moore created such a sensation that another woman, Miss Maude Odell began appearing at a rival theater in a similarly tight-fitting costume. This can be deduced from the caption on four postcards in the author's collection: "Miss Maude Odell (the Original Sandow Girl). Now appearing at the Palace Theatre, London as 'Galatea' (La Statue Humaine), a type of beauty attained by the use of the 'Sandow Symmetrion.'" circa 1910.

64. A tongue-in-cheek article in *La Culture Physique* celebrates Sandow's appointment as physical culture instructor to the King. Supposedly, the King suffered from fatigue and no one could help him until he began to work out with Sandow's exercisers. The royal gymnast is so happy that he sends a wireless message to French President Fallières who then contacts Desbonnet to work the same sort of wonders on him. Jack Cross "L'entraînement de S.M. George V et de M. Le Président Fallières", 8/154, 359–61.

65. "Doctors and the Sandow Institute—Charge of 'Infamous Conduct' found Proved," *Times of London,* May 27, 1911, 8.

66. "The Medical Council and the Sandow Institute," *Times of London,* December 1, 1911, 6.

67. "Failure of Actress's Libel Action—The Sandow Corset Case," *Times of London,* June 30, 1914, 4. Dover Street Studio was apparently a favorite of show people. This is the same studio that recorded Carrie Moore as a Sandow Girl in 1906.

68. The stuatue created by Frederick Pomeroy in 1891 has become perhaps the most familiar image of Sandow thanks to its presentation as the trophy at the Mr. Olympia bodybuilding competition. The fate of the original trophies at the Great Competition of 1901 are not so clear. According to historian David Webster, the first-place, gold statue was destroyed in the Blitz in the early years of World War II. The second-place, silver statue surfaced a few years ago when it was auctioned by Christie's of Melbourne, Australia. It was expected to bring A$3,000 to 4,000. *Weekend Australian* (Sydney), July 19, 1997, 68. The

bronze, third-place award was supposedly presented to Steve Reeves when he won the Mr. Universe contest in 1950. It is impossible to determine if this was actually the same prize given in 1901, but it was commonly believed to be so.

69. The standing statue and the bronzed copper bust are both in the author's collection. The marble version of the bust is in private hands. The information about the artist was found in *Dictionary of British Artists 1880–1940*, (Woodridge: Baron), reprinted 1980. The bust was found at an auction house in England by Joe Weider who purchased it in 1998 and presented it to the author. The original owner's grandfather had acquired the piece because he was interested in physical culture, but the grandson did not know how or when the bust came into the family's possession.

70. "New Premises for Sandow," *Times of London*, September 27, 1911, 9.

71. "Trade Mark Infringement against Sandow's Health and Strength Cocoa," *Times of London*, May 7, 1913, 3 and May 9, 1913, 3.

72. "Report to stockholders by Sandow's Cocoa Company," *Times of London*, October 15, 19.

73. "Sandow's Cocoa: Trade Libel," *Times of London*, February 20, 1915, 3.

74. As late as mid-1913, preferred shares were selling for 15 shillings each. Stock certificate in the author's collection.

75. MACROBUTTON HtmlResAnchor *http://www.sandowplus.co.uk/S/Miscellany/misc.htm*

76. E. Sandow "Combined Toy and Physical Culture Apparatus," U.S. Patent 1,123,570. Patented Jan. 5, 1915 (application filed Oct. 28, 1913).

77. E. Sandow. "Physical Exerciser," U.S. Patent 1,194,884. Patented Aug. 15, 1916 (application filed July 1, 1915).

78. "Strength and Longevity," *New York Times*, October 16, 1925.

79. Thérèse Pagès, "La Culture Physique à Londres «L'âme s'étant envolée, le corps s'est dissous»: Sandow mort, sa méthode est disparue," *La Culture Physique* (Paris), February 1939, 43/586, 41–43. The author got her dates a bit confused; Sandow was 58 years old when he died, not 57.

Bibliography

Works by Sandow

Adam, G. Mercer, editor and compiler. *Sandow on Physical Training.* New York: J. Selwin Tait & Sons, 1894. The title on the spine reads *Sandow's System of Physical Training.* There were at least three editions of this book. The earliest is bound in gray boards with gilt lettering, a second in gray boards with silver lettering, and another edition bound in orange boards. At least one other smaller and cheaper edition was produced.

Body-Building, or Man in the Making. London: Gale & Polden, n.d. [1904]. Editions of this work also appeared c. 1905 and 1911.

The Construction and Reconstruction of the Human Body. London: John Bale, Sons & Co., 1907.

"How to Preserve Health and Attain Strength." *The Cosmopolitan,* June 1894.

Life Is Movement. London: National Health Press, n.d. [c. 1918]. Reprint, Hartford: Simson & Co., n.d. [1919].

"My Reminiscences." *The Strand Magazine,* Mar. 1910.

Strength and How to Obtain It. London: Gale & Polden, 1897. There were subsequent revised editions of this work in 1900, 1905, 1911 (with ladies' chart), and 1922. Since only the first edition was dated, the other dates are only approximate. It was also translated as: *Fuerza y Modo de Adquirirla.* Santiago de Chile: Impr. Moderna, 1900. *La Force et Comment L'Obtenir.* Paris: Richonnier, n.d. [1912]. *Kraft und wie man sie erlangt.* Berlin: Kraft und Schönheit, n.d. [c. 1912].

Advertising Brochures Published by Sandow's Institute

Curative Physical Culture. London, n.d. [c. 1900].

A Few Notes on the Sandow's System of Physical Culture. New York, n.d. [c. 1905].

Health and Physical Fitness by Post. London, n.d. [c. 1919].

Health from Physical Culture. New York, n.d. [c. 1908].

How I Conduct Curative Physical Culture by Correspondence. London, n.d. [c. 1907]. Revised, [c. 1912].

Physical Development and Figure Culture. London, n.d. [c. 1920], 32 pp. Revised, London: Sandow's Curative Inst., n.d. [c. 1926].

A Remarkable Record. London, n.d. [c. 1917].

Reports of Cases Treated by Correspondence. London, n.d. [c. 1920].

The Sandow Body-Building Way to Physical Fitness & Great Strength. London: Sandow Society, n.d. [c. 1928].

The Sandow Curative Treatment by Correspondence. London, n.d. [c. 1908].

Sandow's College of Physical Culture. Boston: Ellis, 1902.

Sandow's Illustrated Health Library. London, n.d. [c. 1915]. There were 24 booklets in this series.

The World-Acknowledged Sandow Nature-Curative Treatment. London: Sandow Society, n.d. [c. 1928].

Frequently Consulted Works

Banner, Lois W. *American Beauty.* New York: Knopf, 1983.

Betts, John Rickards. *America's Sporting Heritage: 1850–1950.* Reading, Mass.: Addison-Wesley, 1974.

Dardenne, Georges. *Historique de la Culture Physique.* Ayeneux, Belgium: published by the author, 1986.

Desbonnet, Edmond. *Les Rois de la Force.* Paris: Berger-Levrault, 1911.

Gaudreau, Leo. *Anvils, Horseshoes, and Cannons: The History of Strongmen.* 2 vols. Alliance, Kans.: Iron Man, [1978].

Green, Harvey. *Fit for America: Health, Fitness, Sport and American Society.* New York: Pantheon, 1986.

Groth, Lothar. *Die starken Männer: Eine Geschichte der Kraftakrobatik.* Revised ed. East Berlin: Henschelverlag, 1987.

Haley, Bruce. *The Healthy Body and Victorian Culture.* Cambridge, Mass.: Harvard University Press, 1978.

Higham, Charles. *Ziegfeld.* Chicago: Regnery, 1972.

Levy, E. Lawrence. *The Autobiography of an Athlete.* Birmingham: Hammond, 1913.

Rader, Benjamin G. *American Sports: From the Age of Folk Games to the Age of Spectators.* Englewood Cliffs, N.J.: Prentice-Hall, 1983.

Rice, Emmett A. *A Brief History of Physical Education.* New York: Barnes, 1926.

Rudovsky, Bernard. *The Unfashionable Human Body.* New York: Prentice-Hall, 1986.

Webster, David. *Barbells and Beefcake: An Illustrated History of Bodybuilding.* Irvine, Scotland: published by the author, 1979.

———. *The Iron Game: An Illustrated History of Weightlifting.* Irvine, Scotland: published by the author, 1976.

Magazines and Newspapers

Apollo's Magazine (1903–11)
La Culture Physique (1904–50)
Health & Strength (1900–1984)
Muscle Builder (1924–26)
New York Times (1893–1925)
Sandow's Magazine (1898–1907)
La Santé par les Sports (1911–20)
Strength (1914–35)
Strength & Health (1932–86)
Times (London) (1901–25)
Your Physique (1940–52)

For a thorough listing of physical culture magazines, see Jan Todd, Joe Roark, and Terry Todd, "A Briefly Annotated Bibliography of English Language Serial Publications in the Field of Physical Culture," *Iron Game History* 1.4 and 5 (Mar. 1991), 25–40.

Updated Bibliography

Andrieu, Gilbert. *Force et beauté: Histoire de l'esthétique en éducation physique aux XIX et XX siècles*. Bordeaux: Presses Universitaires Bordeaux, 1992.
Andrieu, Gilbert. *L'homme et la force: Des marchands de la force au culte de la forme* (XIX et XX siècles). Joinville-le-Pont: Actio, 1988.
Bancel, Nicolas and Jean-Marc Gayman. *Du guerrier à l'athlète: Éléments d'histoire des pratiques corporelles*. Paris: Presses Universitaires de France, 2002.
Bertieri, Claudio. "Dal mito degli Alcidi al cinema verità," in *Cooroginnica: Saggi sulla ginnastica, lo sport e la cultura del corpo 1861–1991*. Adolfo Notto and Lauro Rossi (eds.). Rome: La Meridiana, 1992.
Buchholz, Kai, Rita Latocha, Hilke Peckmann, Klaus Wolbert (eds). *Die Lebensreform: Entwürfe zur Neugestaltung von Leben und Kunst um 1900*. Darmstadt: Institut Mathildenhöhe, 2001, 2 vols.
Buck, Joshua. *The Development of the Performances of Strongmen in American Vaudeville between 1881 and 1932*. Masters thesis: University of Maryland, 1999.
Budd, Michael Anton. *The Sculpture Machine: Physical Culture and Body Politics in the Age of Empire*. New York: New York Univ. Press, 1997.
Cooper, Emmanuel. *Fully Exposed: The Male Nude in Photography*. London: Routledge, 2004.
Daley, Caroline. *Leisure & Pleasure: Reshaping & Revealing the New Zealand Body 1900–1960*. Auckland: Auckland Univ. Press, 2003.
Dantec, Ronan. *Il y a un siècle . . . Le Sport*. Rennes: Éditions Ouest-France, 2003.
Defrance, Jacques. *L'Excellence corporelle: la formation des activités physiques et sportives modernes 1770–1914*. Rennes: Presses Universitaires Rennes, 1987.
Desbonnet, Richard (ed.). *Accord à Corps: Edmond Desbonnet et la Culture Physique*. Paris: Créaphis, 1993.
Dutton, Kenneth. *The Perfectible Body: The Western Ideal of Physical Development*. London: Cassell, 1995.

Fair, John D. *Muscletown USA: Bob Hoffman and the Manly Culture of York Barbell.* University Park: Pennsylvania State University Press, 1999.

Guttman, Allen. *The Erotic in Sports.* New York: Columbia Univ. Press, 1996.

Highwater, Jamake. *The Mythology of Transgression: Homosexuality as Metaphor.* New York: Oxford, 1997.

Kasson, John F. Houdini. *Tarzan and the Perfect Man: The White Male Body and the Challenge of Modernity in America.* New York: Hill and Wang, 2001.

Kimmel, Michael. *Manhood in America: A Cultural History.* New York: Free Press, 1996.

Klein, Alan M. *Little Big Men: Bodybuilding Subculture and Gender Construction.* Albany: State University of NY Press, 1993.

Kühnst, Peter. *Physique: Classic Photographs of Naked Athletes.* London: Thames & Hudson, 2004.

Luciano, Lynne. *Looking Good: Male Body Image in Modern America.* New York: Hill and Wang, 2001.

Manly, Thomas. *For the Love of Eugen.* London: Minerva Press, 2002.

Ohl, Paul. *Louis Cyr: Une épopée légendaire.* Outremont, Quebec: Libre Expression, 2004.

Petersen, Bob. "Sandow Looking" lecture given in June 1998.

Pultz, John and Anne de Mondenard. *Le corps photographié.* Paris: Flammarion, 1995.

Rotundo, E. Anthony. *American Manhood: Transformations in Masculinity from the Revolution to the Modern Era.* New York: Basic Books, 1993.

Segel, Harold B. *Body Ascendant: Modernism and the Physical Imperative.* Baltimore: Johns Hopkins Univ. Press, 1998.

Thomas de la Peña, Carolyn. *The Body Electric: How Strange Machines Built the Modern American.* New York: New York Univ. Press, 2003.

Toschi, Livio. *The Myth of Strength: Story of Weightlifting from the antiquity to the nineteenth century [il Mito della Forza: storia della pesistica dall'antichità all'ottocento].* San Marino: International Weightlifting Federation/European Weightlifting Federation, 2001.

Toschi, Livio. *Cento anni di storia 1902–2002.* Rome: Federazione italiana judo lotta karate e arti marziali and Federazione italiana pesistica e cultura fisica, 2002.

Waugh, Thomas. *Hard to Imagine: Gay Male Eroticism in Photography and Film from their Beginnings to Stonewall.* New York: Columbia Univ. Press, 1996.

Wedemeyer, Bernd. *Starke Männer starke Frauen: Eine Kulturgeschichte des Bodybuildings.* Munich: Beck, 1996.

Wedemeyer, Bernd. *Der Athletenvater: Theodor Siebert (1866–1961): Eine Biographie zwischen Körperkultur, Lebensreform und Esoterik.* Göttingen: Klatt, 1999.

Wedemeyer-Kolwe, Bernd. *«Der neue Mensch»: Körperkultur im Kaiserreich und in der Weimarer Republik.* Würzburg: Verlag Königshausen & Neumann, 2004.

Websites

MACROBUTTON HtmlResAnchor *http://www.sandowmuseum.com/index.html*
MACROBUTTON HtmlResAnchor *http://www.sandowplus.co.uk/*

Index

DAVID L. CHAPMAN is a writer and teacher from Seattle, Washington. Several years ago he acquired a cigar box label from 1894 that featured the image of a blond, muscled and earnest-looking man; the single word "Sandow" was embossed above the portrait. This item intrigued Chapman, and he became determined to find out more about Eugen Sandow's life. Unfortunately, he was soon frustrated by the scanty and unreliable information that was then available. The only solution was to delve into the subject more deeply. Along the way he managed to acquire a sizable collection of books, magazines, photographs, and other materials related to the history of weight training.

David Chapman writes about bodybuilding history for both popular and academic magazines, and he is also the author of half a dozen books on the history of physique photography. When he is not trying to accumulate more materials for his collection, Chapman enjoys the odd squeeze on a Sandow's Patented Grip Dumbbell.